THE MISSION

ALSO BY TIM WEINER

Blank Check: The Pentagon's Black Budget

Betrayal: The Story of Aldrich Ames, an American Spy

Legacy of Ashes: The History of the CIA

Enemies: A History of the FBI

One Man Against the World: The Tragedy of Richard Nixon

The Folly and the Glory: America, Russia, and Political Warfare 1945–2020

THE MISSION

THE CIA
IN THE
21st CENTURY

Tim Weiner

MARINER BOOKS
New York   Boston

Without limiting the exclusive rights of any author, contributor or the publisher of this publication, any unauthorized use of this publication to train generative artificial intelligence (AI) technologies is expressly prohibited. HarperCollins also exercise their rights under Article 4(3) of the Digital Single Market Directive 2019/790 and expressly reserve this publication from the text and data mining exception.

THE MISSION. Copyright © 2025 by Tim Weiner. All rights reserved. Printed in the United States of America. No part of this book may be used or reproduced in any manner whatsoever without written permission except in the case of brief quotations embodied in critical articles and reviews. For information, address HarperCollins Publishers, 195 Broadway, New York, NY 10007. In Europe, HarperCollins Publishers, Macken House, 39/40 Mayor Street Upper, Dublin 1, D01 C9W8, Ireland.

HarperCollins books may be purchased for educational, business, or sales promotional use. For information, please email the Special Markets Department at SPsales@harpercollins.com.

hc.com

The Mariner flag design is a registered trademark of HarperCollins Publishers LLC.

FIRST EDITION

Designed by Chloe Foster

Library of Congress Cataloging-in-Publication Data has been applied for.

ISBN 978-0-06-327018-3

25 26 27 28 29 LBC 5 4 3 2 1

For Kate, Emma, and Ruby

We must have the greatest immorality,
and we must have the greatest morality.

—HUGH CUNNINGHAM, director of training, Central Intelligence Agency

CONTENTS

PROLOGUE: The Spy and the Scribe — 1

CHAPTER ONE: The Dark Horizon — 7

CHAPTER TWO: Denial and Deception — 15

CHAPTER THREE: "It Was All Sadly Absurd" — 25

CHAPTER FOUR: The Bay of Goats — 32

CHAPTER FIVE: The New World — 41

CHAPTER SIX: "We Were All Making It Up as We Went Along" — 56

CHAPTER SEVEN: Unprecedented Trouble — 72

CHAPTER EIGHT: What You Do When You Do Not Know — 92

CHAPTER NINE: Sufi Mystics and Walking Zombies — 105

CHAPTER TEN: A Beautiful Operation — 119

CHAPTER ELEVEN: The Butcher's Bill — 131

CHAPTER TWELVE: Guerrilla Warfare — 140

CHAPTER THIRTEEN: The Black Cloud — 160

CHAPTER FOURTEEN: "How Far Were We Prepared to Go?" — 177

CHAPTER FIFTEEN: The God's-Eye View	189
CHAPTER SIXTEEN: No Middle Ground	200
CHAPTER SEVENTEEN: The Keys to the Castle	213
CHAPTER EIGHTEEN: The Right Side of History	228
CHAPTER NINETEEN: "Someone Is Always Watching"	238
CHAPTER TWENTY: Lethal and Legal	251
CHAPTER TWENTY-ONE: Face-Eating Baboons	265
CHAPTER TWENTY-TWO: The Useful Idiot	280
CHAPTER TWENTY-THREE: Ring-Kissing and Kneecapping	298
CHAPTER TWENTY-FOUR: The Enemy of Intelligence	310
CHAPTER TWENTY-FIVE: "We Are on the Way to a Right-Wing Coup"	326
CHAPTER TWENTY-SIX: The Glory Gate	343
CHAPTER TWENTY-SEVEN: Human Intelligence	358
CHAPTER TWENTY-EIGHT: The Morality of Espionage	371
EPILOGUE: Autocracy in America	388
ACKNOWLEDGMENTS	397
NOTES	399
INDEX	441

PROLOGUE: THE SPY AND THE SCRIBE

I first set foot inside the Central Intelligence Agency in 1988, a young newspaperman back from a long trip to Afghanistan. I had gone there to report on the CIA's multibillion-dollar arms shipments to the Afghan guerrillas, whose jihad against the Soviet invaders was the last great battle of the cold war. Before leaving, I had called up the CIA's spokesman to ask for a briefing, a request flatly denied. Off I went to Afghanistan. I hadn't been back at my desk in Washington for more than a day when the phone rang. How would I like to come in for that briefing now? I had no idea that I was about to discover my life's calling.

I made the seven-mile drive out to the woodlands of Langley, Virginia, and walked into the lobby of the CIA's headquarters. To my left, engraved in the wall, was the Gospel of John: *And ye shall know the truth, and the truth will make you free.* A thought struck me. Was it possible to know the truth about the CIA? Could I cover it as I had once covered the cops and the courts as a cub reporter? The only way to begin was to talk to its veterans, to listen, and to try to learn how a secret intelligence service operates in an open democratic society.

A few months later, I called up Richard Helms, the CIA's director for seven years under Presidents Johnson and Nixon, who had fired him for refusing to cover up the Watergate break-in on a spurious claim of national security. A charter member of the CIA at its creation, the chief of its clandestine service during the Cuban missile crisis and the early days of the Vietnam War, Helms was elegant as a British banker, an eloquent raconteur, and a man who enjoyed a beer at lunch. Over the course of many an hour, he gave me a master class in the history of the CIA. The mission at the outset in 1947 was to know the enemy. Spies would divine the secrets of the Kremlin, scholarly analysts would assay them, and directors would report to the president of the United States. "In the beginning, we knew nothing," Helms told me. "Our knowledge of what the other side was up to, their intentions, their capabilities, was nil, or next to it. If you came up with a telephone book, or a map of an airfield, that was pretty hot stuff. We were in the dark about a lot of the world." The chances for enlightenment were vanishingly small. Within a year, the mission changed. The Soviets had taken over more than half of Europe. The Pentagon and the State Department ordered the CIA to fight fire with fire and roll back the forces of communism. Knowing the world through espionage took a back seat to changing the world through covert action. Helms saw this as a tragic mistake. By 1950, the CIA had raised a paramilitary army, and it tried for four years to penetrate Russia, Poland, Ukraine, China, and North Korea with recruited foreign agents parachuting behind enemy lines. These were suicide missions, their plans purloined by communist spies. They stayed secret for many years, as did the violent right-wing coups and assassination plots against foreign leaders. Helms had kept those secrets. His successors, to the CIA's sorrow, had not.

He wanted me to understand that the agency hadn't dreamed up the idea of overthrowing Iran or killing Fidel Castro. Every president since Truman had commanded the CIA to intervene with guns and money to control the fate of nations when sending in the Marines was not an option. Its officers did what they were ordered to do. They were executing the foreign policy of the United States. They drew their power directly from the commander in chief. And the CIA's directors and spies and analysts depended on his faith in the intelligence they delivered; if they were not believed, they had no purpose. They learned it was perilous to tell him what he did not want to hear.

By the time I began covering the CIA for the *New York Times* in 1993, the cold war was over, the agency was in constant turmoil, and the old code of secrecy was breaking down. An astonishing number of senior officers and analysts at headquarters spoke openly with me, as did many members of the old guard, now retired after twenty or thirty years and shedding the cloak of clandestinity. The CIA slowly began to open up some of its files on cold-war covert actions in Europe and Asia and Latin America. A clearer picture of its past started to emerge. Espionage and covert action were not the glamorous and romantic adventure that the movies made it out to be. "It's not fun and games," Helms said. "It's dirty and dangerous." The reality was far more interesting than the fiction.

I began to grasp not only what the CIA did, but what it was like to work for it. Journalists and spies were not all that different. I could land in Khartoum or Havana and say, in so many words: "Take me to your leader." Soon thereafter I would meet the dictator of Sudan or Castro himself. CIA officers had that kind of entrée all over the world, both to the ruling class and the rebels seeking to overthrow it, if they played their cards right. Recruiting agents overseas was not unlike developing sources at the CIA, though reporters didn't pay for information and spies did, handsomely. The spy and the scribe both depended on establishing trust. They were driven by a thirst for a hidden truth. And they knew it could take years before the secrets they learned gave them a deep understanding of the way things really worked. The difference was that the journalist wanted to know the world and the CIA had the power to change it.

By the turn of the century, I had compiled a critical mass of declassified documents and conducted more than two hundred interviews. I thought it might be possible to write a history of the first sixty years of the CIA. *Legacy of Ashes* was published in 2007, in the wake of the revelations of the CIA's secret prisons and the tortures that went on therein. The CIA had been ordered to become a secret army once again, and in the name of counterterrorism, its disciplines of espionage and analysis had been diminished. Its false reporting on Saddam Hussein's arsenals had led the United States to invade and occupy Iraq, the most disastrous foreign policy decision since the Vietnam War. In some ways, the book reflected the darkness of that time.

Looking back, there was so much I didn't know about what the CIA was doing at home and abroad after the September 11 attacks—and so much to be learned about its secret history in the decades thereafter. So I set out to write *The Mission* in the spring of 2022. The book you hold in your hands is the first chronicle of the twenty-first-century CIA, told in the words of those who lived it. Once again, as when I first started out on the CIA beat, I found an amazing number of people who agreed to speak to me. They had fought in Iraq, Afghanistan, Pakistan, Syria, and a dozen other nations. They had run espionage campaigns from the Mediterranean to the Pacific. They had faced criminal investigations for their lethal counterterrorism and counternarcotics operations. They had struggled to penetrate the Kremlin and succeeded. They had built lifelines for the soldiers and spies of Ukraine. Among them was the man who created the CIA's secret prison system, the woman who helped take down the world's biggest nuclear-weapons technology smuggling ring, a deep-cover spy who had put presidents on his payroll, station chiefs who served on four continents, and the sitting chief of the CIA's clandestine service—a man who had been undercover for thirty-three years and had never talked to a journalist in his life. Thanks to their candor, and their trust, this book was written on the record, without anonymous sources or blind quotes.

The Mission is being published in a time of great peril. The United States is governed by a man who admires dictators and despots, aspires to rule as an autocrat, despises civil liberties, and threatens to imprison his opponents. Now that the Supreme Court has ruled that presidents cannot be prosecuted for crimes committed in office, they can abuse their power freely. They can instruct the CIA to spy on Americans, to subvert their domestic enemies, to conduct political assassinations with impunity, to start a war in secret.

The CIA has been twice transformed since the dawn of the twenty-first century. In the beginning, it knew next to nothing about al Qaeda, and failed to prevent a disaster more devastating than Pearl Harbor. Then its false reporting on existential threats terrified the White House and lit the fuse for the disastrous war in Iraq. These calamities were the consequence of a lack of good intelligence. Over the past decade, with the diminution of the war on terror, the CIA has slowly returned to its original purpose of espionage. Its spies are now called upon again to understand the intentions and capabilities of America's enemies in Moscow and Beijing, Tehran and Pyongyang. A new cold war is slowly escalating toward existential danger. Only good intelligence can prevent a surprise attack, a fatal miscalculation, a futile war. But even the best intelligence will not sway a leader who will not heed it. Among the CIA's greatest challenges in the days to come will be the man in the White House, an authoritarian leader who presents the clearest danger to the national security of the United States since this century began.

Chapter One

THE DARK HORIZON

On the morning of April 20, 2001, George Tenet gazed out the glass wall of his seventh-floor suite at the Central Intelligence Agency, looking upon a vision of serenity, tall green trees reaching as far as the eye could see. He knew something terrible was out there on the horizon. He had tried and failed to convince the president of the United States that the nation faced a cataclysmic attack. And he feared that a great gap lay between what the CIA was capable of doing and what it would be called upon to do after the catastrophe struck.

Tenet had taken charge of the CIA in July 1997, its fifth director in six tumultuous years. The agency had marked its fiftieth anniversary that summer, and the celebration had been muted. Many of its cold war leaders were in mourning at how far American intelligence had fallen. "The only remaining superpower doesn't have enough interest in what's going on in the world to organize and run an espionage service," said Richard Helms. "We've drifted away from that as a country."

The end of the cold war had devastated the world's most famous secret intelligence agency. How could it be great without a great enemy? The fall of the Soviet Union had hit the CIA like "the meteor strikes on the dinosaurs. Nothing was the same afterwards," wrote Richard Kerr, its deputy director from 1989 to 1992. "It was easy, once upon a time, for CIA to be unique and mystical," said the last chief of the Soviet division of the clandestine service, Milt Bearden. "It was not an institution. It was a mission. And the mission was a crusade. Then you took the Soviet Union away from us and there wasn't anything else. We don't have a history. We don't have a hero. Even our medals are secret. And now the mission is over. *Fini.*"

The CIA did have a history, although the American people knew little of it. Its classified annals were filled with short-term triumphs and some long-running successes in the struggle against the Soviet empire, the individual triumphs of brave spies and brilliant analysts. But the public record was a litany of institutional failures, replete with flawed covert operations mandated by the foreign policies of every president since World War Two.

President Harry Truman had created the CIA in 1947 to prevent the next Pearl Harbor, not to fight the cold war. "The idea was that we've got to get an organization where analysts could look at everything from overseas, no matter how secret," Helms said. "The agency was created to analyze intelligence, not for covert action." Only "an accident of history" had compelled the CIA to change the world. President Dwight Eisenhower had commanded the agency to overthrow the freely elected governments of Iran and Guatemala in secrecy, but the coups were anything but silent. The CIA's officers had made a great deal of noise in executing his orders. "They attracted a lot of attention," Helms said, and "with the attention, the CIA was identified with covert action," a force freely wielded by imperial presidents in perilous times.

President John F. Kennedy's faith in the CIA had been shattered after he ordered it to invade Cuba and crush Fidel Castro in 1961; the Bay of Pigs had become an indelible emblem of disaster. The CIA had helped to avert a nuclear war during the Cuban missile crisis in 1962, but thereafter rarely divined the intentions and capabilities of the Kremlin through espionage. The agency's best analysts frequently briefed Gerald R. Ford, the House minority leader and a top overseer of military spending, in the late 1960s and early 1970s. "They had charts on the walls, they had figures," President Ford had recalled in retirement. "And their conclusion was that in ten years, the United States would be behind the Soviet Union in military capability, in economic growth, in the strength of our economy. It was a scary presentation," Ford said, but "they were 180 degrees wrong. These were the best people we had, the CIA's so-called experts."

In the spring of 1975, as Saigon fell, the CIA's ramparts were breached by Senate investigators. They would expose the agency's history of failed assassination plots against foreign leaders and its fraught connections with right-wing governments, generals, and goon squads. The investigations "set back our liaison relationships around the world," President George H. W. Bush, who was then the agency's director, said in 1997. "They caused many people abroad to pull away from cooperating with the CIA, and they devastated the morale" of its spies, whom Bush had called "perhaps the finest group of dedicated public servants this country has." In 1985, President Ronald Reagan's CIA director, William J. Casey, had enmeshed those spies in a harebrained and highly illegal scheme to sell weapons to Iran, skim the profits, and slip them to the contras fighting a covert war in Central America. The stratagem had led to criminal charges against senior CIA officers, all of whom President Bush had pardoned days before he left the White House in December 1992. Among them was Duane "Dewey" Clarridge, the founding father of the CIA's counterterrorism center. In retirement, he argued that the CIA was at the point of failure. The agency was "finished as a really effective intelligence service," Clarridge had written in 1997, and it would only be reinvented "after some appalling catastrophe befalls us."

"A burning platform"

Soon after arriving in the director's suite that summer, Tenet had a nightmare vision of the future. He saw himself standing on "a burning platform," the captain of a rusting ship in a rough sea fighting a fire in the engine room. If he didn't extinguish the blaze, "the organization and all of us in it would sink into the sea."

Tenet had vowed to rebuild the CIA for the twenty-first century, and like the Soviet Politburo, he had a five-year plan. But as time passed, his goals always remained five years away. Yet officers were running some remarkable operations at the dawn of the new millennium. They were rounding up war criminals in the Balkans and shipping them to the International Criminal Court in the Hague, capturing Islamic terrorists and sending them to prison cells in Cairo, plotting to take down smuggling rings run by a Pakistani scientist selling nuclear-weapons technology to North Korea and Libya, and trying to capture Osama bin Laden in Afghanistan. The CIA still had spies capable of skillful espionage and analysts with deep expertise. It still had some foreign palaces and parliaments wired; more than a few presidents and prime ministers still couldn't sneeze without the CIA overhearing. It had built new spy services in nations where the Soviets once reigned, from Poland to Uzbekistan. It maintained lavishly financed liaisons with foreign spymasters who traded intelligence for cash.

But the CIA was no longer a global intelligence agency. Many countries once deemed crucial now went uncovered. More than thirty overseas stations and bases had been shuttered in the 1990s, and many that remained were a third of the size they had been a decade before. Essential intelligence wasn't being collected, and what was collected wasn't being thought through. At the dawn of the information age, the CIA's officers and analysts worked with outmoded technology, struggling to distinguish the clear signals of significant facts from the cacophony of background noise. Hank Crumpton, the deputy chief of the counterterrorism center, described the state of affairs in its basement offices: "We had stacks of paper spread out over the floor. We had accumulated cartons of raw intelligence, with people toiling through reams of paper, page by page." This was no way to run a twenty-first-century spy service.

Americans might once have imagined the CIA as an all-powerful force, with crystal balls foreseeing the future and silver bullets that could change the world through covert action. But Tenet had warned the White House and his overseers in Congress that the agency was half-broken, starved for money, bleeding talent and expertise. The CIA's secret budget that year was roughly $3 billion—adjusted for inflation, less than at the close of the Korean War. The Clinton administration had cut it by more than $600 million, a peace dividend never reinvested. A quarter of the CIA's personnel, nearly five thousand people, many with decades of experience, had walked out the door in the 1990s, leaving the ranks desperately depleted. The clandestine service, the heart and soul of the CIA—the spies, station chiefs, case officers, and deep-cover cadres whose missions included running covert operations, recruiting foreign agents, penetrating hostile intelligence services, dismantling terrorist networks—was barely a thousand strong. As Tenet kept telling anyone who would listen, there were more FBI agents in New York than CIA officers abroad. The brain drain among the intelligence analysts was especially dispiriting, and the despair among the talented tenth who remained was deepened by the rudderless drift of American foreign policy in the post–cold war world. They longed for "a sense of direction, a sense of what the mission is," said their director, John Gannon.

Precious little new blood had infused the agency. Recruitment had dwindled to the vanishing point. When Tenet arrived, precisely six people had passed the CIA's latest six-month training course at the Farm, its boot camp for new officers outside Williamsburg, Virginia. What would motivate a talented graduate student to sign up for the difficult, often dangerous, sometimes dirty business of espionage when they could make a fortune on Wall Street or explore the frontiers of the newborn World Wide Web at Silicon Valley startups like Google? The world of information looked more promising than the world of secrets.

In the face of fierce criticism from Congress, scathing newspaper stories about blown operations and bungled reporting, and internal studies suggesting that he was realigning deck chairs on the *Titanic*, Tenet ferociously defended the CIA in public and private, rallying his troops when their morale flagged. A charming man, affable in the extreme, a backslapper in a city of backstabbers, Tenet radiated cheer as he chatted with the worker bees in the CIA's cafeteria, barged into their cubicles unannounced to ask what was up, dribbled a basketball down the agency's pastel corridors, and enlivened seventh-floor conferences by belting out the anthems of his youth. (Aretha Franklin's "Respect" was a favorite.) Unlike some of his predecessors, Tenet was a self-made man, a son of war refugees from Greece and Albania who had settled in Queens and run a greasy spoon called the 20th Century Diner. He looked like a New York City homicide detective: corpulent, compulsively chewing damp cigars, his suits rumpled, his skin sallow, his eyes red-rimmed.

"I spent plenty of sleepless nights wondering, given the monumental task before me, if I was up to the job," Tenet wrote in his memoir. "No previous experience had prepared me."*

Things kept going wrong on Tenet's watch. The CIA had botched a major covert operation to undermine Saddam Hussein; scores of its recruited Iraqi agents had been captured, tortured, and killed. Its analysts had failed to warn of India's clear intentions to test a nuclear weapon, an event that altered the world's balance of power. A former station chief in Bucharest serving as an instructor at the Farm was convicted of spying for Moscow; he had handed over the identities of three years' worth of newly minted spies. He was one among four CIA and FBI turncoats of the era who had given the Kremlin a lasting power to defeat American intelligence operations, manipulate the CIA's reporting, mislead the White House, and mystify the Pentagon. None of this was a secret. Nearly every one of the CIA's travails were front-page news in the *New York Times* and the *Washington Post*, a recurring nightmare for its leaders and a suppurating wound to its public image and political standing.

The awful truth was that the CIA faced a dizzying disparity between its diminished capacities and its immense responsibilities. "The system is sufficiently dysfunctional that intelligence failure is guaranteed," warned Russ Travers, a career analyst who later became a top counterterrorism official, in a 1997 article published by the CIA's in-house journal. By 2001, he predicted, America might be "completely surprised" by a terrorist attack. Tenet and his peers reached an identical conclusion in a highly classified report: Unless they made "substantial and sweeping changes in the way the nation collects, analyzes, and produces intelligence," the United States soon would suffer a "catastrophic systemic intelligence failure." The date of that warning was September 11, 1998.

---

* Before Tenet became the deputy director of central intelligence in July 1995, at the age of forty-two, he had led the staff at the Senate intelligence committee and served as intelligence director at the National Security Council. Tenet was acting director from December 1996 until his formal appointment as director in July 1997.

A month before, al Qaeda had blown up truck bombs at two American embassies in East Africa at once, killing twelve Americans, eleven Tanzanians, and 224 Kenyans. Bin Laden's ability to hit two targets at the same time, three thousand miles from his base in Afghanistan, revealed a level of strategic planning and sophisticated execution that was something new in the world—a terrorist network with the ability to strike anywhere on earth. The CIA saw for the first time that bin Laden was capable of carrying out his declaration of war against the United States. As the CIA pursued the bombing suspects across Africa, the Middle East, and the Balkans, a growing number of spies in the field and analysts at headquarters grappled with the question of how to stop the next al Qaeda attack.

Tenet saw this as the CIA's new mission. A war on terrorism might become a semblance of what the war on communism had been.

For fifty years, the CIA had served as the pointed end of the spear of American foreign policy. Every president had used it as a secret weapon. At Tenet's impassioned request, on December 24, 1998, Bill Clinton authorized the CIA to mount a manhunt in the wilds of Afghanistan and kill bin Laden with the aid of recruited Afghan warlords.*

Congress had passed and Clinton had signed a law authorizing "all necessary means, including covert action and military force, to disrupt, dismantle and destroy international infrastructures used by international terrorists." The CIA's lawyers, skilled at nuance, interpreted *infrastructures* meant anything and everything that supported a terrorist—including the terrorists themselves. But the CIA lacked the money and the manpower and, above all, the intelligence to make war against al Qaeda. It took nine

---

* Clinton and Tenet both developed an impenetrable amnesia surrounding the delicate matter of assassination. "You have this kill order for bin Laden that President Clinton signed on, literally, Christmas Eve of 1998," said Philip Zelikow, who served as executive director of the 9/11 Commission. But "Tenet claimed he had no memory" of the order. Then, in February 1999, the CIA wanted to use a new group of Afghan warlords to carry out the mission, so it needed an updated authorization. "They go back to the President saying, 'Would you please sign this again?'" Zelikow said. "It's the same thing he had signed in 1998. He crosses out the key kill language and writes in his own hand; he basically turns it into capture.... I put this in front of Clinton and said, 'Why did you do this?' He said, 'I have no memory of it. I don't know.'" (Zelikow oral history, Miller Center, University of Virginia.)

months and a change in leadership at the counterterrorism center before the CIA came up with a plan that had a slim chance of succeeding. In the meantime, Clinton had lost confidence in its abilities and revoked its license to kill. A fatal mistake had diminished Tenet's standing at the White House.

The Pentagon had invited the CIA to pick a target during NATO's air war in Serbia, which aimed to oust the genocidal leader Slobodan Milošević. After the target was hit, on May 7, 1999, Gen. Wes Clarke, the commander of American forces in the Balkans, had called headquarters in a rage. "Why did the CIA tell me to bomb the Chinese embassy in Belgrade?" he demanded. He'd been informed that the building was a Serb military warehouse. His smart bombs had killed three people at the embassy and wounded twenty more. The Chinese ambassador, understandably, called it a barbaric act. Tenet was in London when he got a call from Clinton's national security adviser, Sandy Berger. "You better get back here right away," he said. "I'm trying to save your job." It took a lot of doing, but Tenet stayed on.

He was sure he would be fired when he met President-elect George W. Bush nine days before his inauguration on January 20, 2001. Tenet was a Clinton man, and no CIA director had survived a transition of presidential power from one party to another since Richard Helms in 1969. He had braced himself for the ax, but it didn't fall. "'Why don't we just let things go along for a while and we'll see how things work out?'" Bush said. "I was neither on the team nor off it," Tenet recounted. "I was on probation."

So long as he didn't preside over a catastrophe, he would remain the director of central intelligence. Three months later, on April 20, 2001, came a calamity unlike any in the history of the CIA.

Chapter Two

DENIAL AND DECEPTION

Tenet remembered the day as his worst at the CIA, up to that point.

That morning, the station chief in Lima, a tall young officer with a sandy moustache named Steph Milliken, had walked into the office of Roberta Jacobson, the deputy chief of mission at the American embassy in Peru. He was a happy man. "We got one!" he said. "It's a great one." The CIA had scored another kill in America's war on drugs, shooting a small plane out of the clear blue sky over the Amazon jungle.

"An hour later he came back, white as a sheet," Jacobsen remembered. When Hugh Turner, the number two man in the clandestine service, saw the flash cable from Lima, he rushed down the hallway on the seventh floor to see John McLaughlin, the deputy director of central intelligence. *There's been a disaster down in Peru*, he said. McLaughlin's executive assistant, Luis Rueda, a veteran of the CIA's wars in Latin America, gazed at Turner with a gimlet eye.

"What did you do?" Rueda said. "Shoot down a planeload of nuns?"

An airborne covert operation had shot down a family of American missionaries. The CIA's officers had no intelligence that their plane was carrying drugs. They made no attempt to identify the aircraft before they gave the orders to attack it. Veronica Bowers and her infant daughter, Charity, had been riddled with .30-caliber machine-gun bullets and killed instantly. The pilot, Kevin Donaldson, was shot in the leg, and he screamed,

"They're killing us!" before crash-landing. He had somehow survived his grave wounds, as had Veronica's husband and son.

Tenet and his top aides spent a few frantic hours that night trying to find out exactly what had happened. Over the weekend, they told Vice President Dick Cheney, national security adviser Condi Rice, the State Department, Congress, the press, and the American people that the deaths were a unique aberration in an otherwise perfectly managed and professionally executed mission run by the CIA's Latin American division. This was a lie.

"A remarkable lack of judgment"

The CIA and its Peruvian allies had shot down fifteen planes and killed some of their crews in the Airbridge Denial Program between 1995 and 2001. Every one of those shootdowns had violated explicit rules of engagement set by the president of the United States. The rules had been painstakingly crafted to protect CIA officers from a charge of murder under American law. The CIA always had told Congress and the National Security Council that the highly classified program had operated under strict procedures to prevent killing innocent people. But the rules had been broken in every shootdown, and CIA officers had covered up that fact from the Amazon jungle to the seventh floor.

The cover story hid the history of the Airbridge program, which had been the CIA's only long-running lethal mission under Tenet, shielding the agency from responsibility and protecting the officers who ran the drug-interdiction program from investigation and prosecution. One, in particular, evaded the judgment of outsiders: Jose Rodriguez, who had been in charge of the program in its heyday as chief of the Latin American division. In a year, Tenet would make him the CIA's counterterrorism chief, in charge of hunting, imprisoning, interrogating, and killing America's enemies. And after thirty brutal months in that post, he became the chief of the clandestine service, the most powerful spy in the world at the height of the war on terror.

He was "a damn-the-torpedoes leader, willing to take risks on covert actions despite the likelihood that his judgments would be reviewed, and sometimes harshly critiqued," wrote Philip Mudd, who served for twenty months as his deputy at the counterterrorism center. "He had a well-founded reputation as a quick decision-maker who didn't mind dirty choices and high stakes. 'Fuck it,' he might say in the midst of a tough decision, 'what else are we going to do?'"

Rodriguez was a handsome man, in the manner of a movie villain, with thick black hair and a macho handlebar moustache. Born in Mayagüez, Puerto Rico, he had been partly raised in Bolivia, where as a boy he took riding lessons from an army captain named Luis García Meza, later the nation's murderous right-wing dictator. As a young CIA officer, in the 1980s, his missions included supporting El Salvador's dirty war against the left; in those days, he always carried a 9 mm Browning pistol and kept a sawed-off shotgun in his truck. He had been the station chief in Panama and then the deputy chief of the CIA's new Crime and Narcotics Center before his promotion to chief of the Latin American division, overseeing operations from the Texas border south to Tierra del Fuego, in October 1995. He had lost that job two years later after an inspector general's report said he had shown "a remarkable lack of judgment"—not in his conduct of the Airbridge program, but in his personal interventions on behalf of an old friend facing cocaine charges in the Dominican Republic. The rebuke had done little to change his image as a hard-charging officer who protected his people, chafed against higher authority, and let the ends justify the means.

The CIA had been a reluctant conscript in the war on drugs, seeing it as a losing battle. But after the cold war, new missions were a necessity. Peru was the source of 60 percent of the world's cocaine in the mid-1990s; crack had been devastating American cities for a decade. President Clinton had declared that the CIA's role in the drug war was a matter of national security, and Congress committed tens of millions of dollars to the mission, creating a CIA Crime and Narcotics Center flush with people, money, and power. Clinton's orders were clear: "Beat the crap out of the cartels," said Jack Devine, who had joined the CIA in 1967 and served as chief of the Latin American division from 1992 to 1994. The Airbridge Denial Program was the result.

The Latin American division would take command of the mission, and the Crime and Narcotics Center would supply money and intelligence.* The CIA's paramilitaries and contractors would provide pilots and crews for a light Citation aircraft, with a video recorder and a Peruvian communicator. They would fly alongside a Peruvian Air Force Cessna A-37, a small fighter plane first designed for counterinsurgency warfare in Vietnam. The CIA officers would give the orders and the Peruvians would shoot. After each mission, senior CIA officers would review the videotapes to ensure the rules had been followed.

But a seemingly unsurmountable problem had arisen in 1994. The Justice Department's Office of Legal Counsel said that CIA officers who aided or abetted a lethal shootdown of a civilian plane could be charged with murder under American law. "The question then was: Is there a legal way around this?" said Rand Beers, who had run the National Security Council's counterterrorism and counternarcotics directorates and succeeded Tenet as the NSC's intelligence director in 1995.

There was. John Rizzo, a charming and cunning lawyer who had been the clandestine service's in-house counsel since 1979, helped to draft a presidential order for Clinton's signature. Its strict rules were crafted to keep the CIA out of legal jeopardy. First, identify the suspect plane as a narcotrafficker and reach its pilot via radio. Second, use internationally recognized warning signs: the Peruvian interceptor had to wag its wings, flash its navigational lights, lower its landing gear. Third, fire warning

---

* The Airbridge program was run in partnership with Peru's intelligence czar, Vladimiro Montesinos, who had power over the military. He was arrested in June 2001 and later convicted of murder, drug trafficking, bribery, and embezzlement, among other crimes. The CIA station in Lima had paid him $1 million a year during the 1990s, one of many such secret liaisons with foreign leaders and intelligence chiefs. It had to keep paying him if it wanted to operate the Airbridge program with a free hand. The chief of the CIA's Crime and Narcotics Center overseeing the Airbridge program in 2001 told the author she was both unaware of the payments to Montesinos and unfamiliar with exactly who he was. This strongly suggested, among other things, that the CIA did not know its own history. Montesinos had been recruited as an agent in the 1970s, served a year in prison in Peru for espionage, and remained on the CIA's payroll thereafter.

shots. Finally, if all else failed, seek approval from Peruvian commanders on the ground—and then go ahead and shoot. Following these procedures to the letter would indemnify CIA officers from indictment. The directive further commanded CIA chieftains to "regularly monitor compliance with agreed procedures and immediately report irregularities through their chain of command."

These orders did not prevent an awful premonition among the few who knew both the iron-clad rules and the rule-breaking reputation of the Latin American division. "We all used to say the worst possible outcome is if we were to shoot down a plane full of nuns," Beers remembered. "That was the exact phrase we used to use."

The Latin American division long had harbored a contingent of cowboys, officers who undertook risky or reckless operations.* Its leaders had prosecuted President Reagan's secret wars in Central America, arming the anticommunist contras even after Congress had cut off funds for their guerrilla campaign, slipping them millions in off-the-books money skimmed from illegal arms sales to Iran. The Iran-contra investigation brought indictments raining down on the division, whose standard-bearer was Dewey Clarridge, its leader from 1981 to 1984 and the first chief of the CIA's counterterrorism center. He was a buccaneer and proud of it. Some of the division's top officers in the 1990s were his acolytes—among them Jose Rodriguez, who had risen through the ranks under Clarridge's command.

"There was a pattern of not following the rules," said Devine, who became acting director of the clandestine service in May 1995. "And this was the residue of Dewey, the ghost of Dewey. He created a cult."

That cult had been the subject of a scathing headquarters report in September 1995 rebuking the Latin American division for a pervasive "lack of candor"—lying by commission or omission—that took place "between the chief of station and the Ambassador, between the station and

---

* Rodriguez disputed this reputation. He told the author that he and his fellow Latin American division officers were not rule-breakers or renegades, but professional intelligence officers who were "comfortable working with issues that are neither black or white but rather shades of grey."

the directorate of operations' Latin America division, between the directorate of operations' Latin America division and the deputy director for operations, and between the CIA and the Congress." In an attempt to root out this malfeasance, headquarters had taken the rare step of dismissing, demoting, or disciplining a handful of top Latin American division officers. Tenet then chose a new division chief: Jose Rodriguez, who later said the punishments imposed by his superiors had taught him "valuable lessons, which I used in the years following 9/11 to try to protect the people who worked for me."

The Airbridge program was remarkable for its rule-breaking. CIA officers in Peru consistently defied the president's edicts. They often carried out random intercepts of planes that looked like righteous targets. They once ordered the strafing of a downed plane and its passengers, a war crime under international law. In ten of the fifteen shootdowns, no more than two minutes elapsed between the moment CIA officers saw a suspect plane and the moment it was attacked. The documented history of one shootdown that took place under Rodriguez showed that CIA officers had no intelligence on the plane. They never identified it by tail number. They never made radio contact. They never made visual contact. They never fired warning shots. They never had authorization to shoot to kill from the Peruvian commander on the ground. The videotape of the shootdown revealed all this—and then the videotape disappeared.

"The mission became more important than the rules"

The cover-up began a few hours after the missionary shootdown. Early on Saturday, April 21, senior CIA officers from the Latin American division, the special activities division, and the Crime and Narcotics Center sketched a report for Vice President Cheney. The CIA's chief of public affairs, Bill Harlow, used their work to brief reporters on background. Tenet used the briefing as his prepared text when he testified to the congressional intelligence committees on April 23.

"Tenet provided misleading testimony to Congress," the CIA's inspector general, John Helgerson, later wrote in a scathing 289-page report on the program. "He did not provide a full, factual, and accurate accounting." That report eventually led the Justice Department and the FBI to open a criminal investigation of the program and its leaders, including Rodriguez.*

Helgerson's words carried great weight in the American intelligence community. No ordinary inspector general, he had served as the CIA's director of intelligence analysis, director of congressional affairs, and chairman of the National Intelligence Council, overseeing the CIA's deepest reporting. He was appointed by President Bush and confirmed by the Senate. Only the president could fire him. But the seventh floor could restrain him. Three CIA directors successfully suppressed the gist of the report from the public until 2010.

Jack Devine read it twelve years later. "In the aggregate," he said, "you have a crime"—specifically, lying to Congress. CIA officers overseas have to lie about who they are and what they do. Espionage is illegal everywhere, deception is its essence, and lies are its bodyguard. Lying to your fellow Americans was another matter. If you were caught, tradition held, your career was over. But if you were absolutely determined to run the risk—whether to protect the agency, the secrets you were sworn to keep, or yourself—you had best lie by omission.

The officers of the Airbridge program had been devoted to the mission of shooting down drug planes and their passengers. The credo of the CIA demanded it. "The mission had to come first," Tenet would write in his memoir. "Country, mission, CIA, family, and self."

Devine saw it differently. "The mission became more important than the rules," he concluded. "And that is a dangerous thing."

---

* Rodriguez called his dealings with the inspector general one of the lowest points in his long career. "I rarely ever read an IG report that I believed was fair and completely impartial, to include an investigation against me when I was chief of the Latin America division," he told the author. As for the Airbridge report, "I was appalled by how flawed it was," he said. "The officers involved in the matter spent years in limbo waiting for resolution of the case. For most it meant the end of their careers, dipping into their savings to pay for lawyers and dealing with the agony and uncertainty of not knowing what was going to happen to you." The FBI dropped its investigation without bringing charges in 2005.

"I felt betrayed"

On April 24, Tenet formed a Peru Task Force to conduct an internal investigation. He instructed A. B. "Buzzy" Krongard, the newly appointed executive director of the CIA, and his deputy, John Brennan, a future CIA director, to "provide guidance and support to the Peru Task Force as well as to ensure that the Agency's corporate interests are addressed in the actions we take." In this instance, the CIA's interests and the truth were not one and the same.

The task force found that the presidential rules of engagement had been violated from the start. Many of the CIA's officers in Peru had no grasp of the rules. CIA station chiefs in Lima and base chiefs in the jungle town of Pucallpa had either failed to convey them or failed to enforce them. A senior officer who commanded the Pucallpa air base told the inspector general that he'd had plenty of misgivings about the conduct of the program, but "there are always tradeoffs between saluting the flag and personal beliefs, and he had saluted and carried on." The CIA's officers in Peru had sworn that they'd followed the rules. Their reporting went up the chain of command to their superiors at headquarters, who repeated those falsehoods to Congress and the White House. No one at the CIA ever came clean with Cheney or with the congressional intelligence committees, whose members and staffs were told a dozen times that the program had always followed the rules.

This put Tenet in a tightening noose. He had a legal duty to correct the record and his testimony. But if he did, he would reveal the CIA's lack of candor. The facts, if disclosed in full, could have exposed senior officers to prosecution for making false statements to the executive and legislative branches of government. His counsel, John Rizzo, protected those officers by making sure the task force report was buried. He had it stamped DRAFT—and a draft report was not subject to discovery, in both the legal and literal sense. ("The mere mention of the word 'discovery' sends shivers through intelligence officers," noted Fred F. Manget, a former CIA deputy general counsel.) Rizzo advised all concerned that "we need to be careful about what is committed to paper." He instructed that all internal reporting on the program should be delivered in oral briefings, not written ones.

All this ensured that no outsiders saw the work of the task force—or knew that it existed. Not the members of the Senate intelligence committee, which wrote an anodyne report hewing to the cover story. Not the Justice Department and the FBI as they opened their fruitless criminal investigation. And not the White House, where the national security adviser, Condi Rice, asked Rand Beers, now the assistant secretary of state for international narcotics and law enforcement, to lead an independent outside review of what had happened in Peru.

Beers had overseen America's international counternarcotics programs since the 1980s. He had counted Tenet as a friend from their days at the National Security Council. He was deeply familiar with how the CIA worked from his years running intelligence policy at the NSC. He knew some of the key players, including Rodriguez, who had impressed Beers as a rule-breaker when they met while he served as chief of station in Panama. He asked the right questions. He just didn't get truthful answers. His fact-gathering largely depended on the cooperation of Rizzo and the clandestine service officer assigned as his liaison, Regis Matlock, who had been desk-bound at headquarters since helping to oversee blown operations to undermine Saddam Hussein in 1996. They hewed to the cover story. They never told Beers that the Peru Task Force existed. They never told him that the presidential rules and reporting requirements had been ignored. They never told him there were any problems whatsoever with any shoot-downs other than the missionary plane, and they shifted the blame for that tragedy onto the Peruvians.

Beers learned only that the CIA had abridged the rules for reasons of air safety in 1999, rather than broken all of them from the beginning. But this alone was enough to infuriate Rice after Beers briefed her. She immediately fired off a furious email asking Tenet to tell her precisely "who gave the approval for CIA to 'change the procedures' that were so clearly required by the President" and who oversaw the program at headquarters and in the field. Rice kept asking, but neither Tenet nor anyone else ever answered her questions. This defiance had no real precedent in the recent history of the CIA. The agency was usually exquisitely sensitive to inquiries from the White House. Stonewalling the national security adviser was a dangerous risk for Tenet to take. So was deceiving his friend and colleague Rand Beers. Twenty-one years later, Beers first saw the inspector general's report, detailing the subterfuges that had shielded the CIA. "How bitter it was to read this," he said. "I felt betrayed."

Tenet never corrected the record or held anyone to account. He had his reasons. Neither he nor the CIA could easily withstand another blow to their credibility. He was still on probation with the president. He didn't need the White House, Congress, or the FBI peering over his shoulder. He urgently wanted to look ahead, not back. He had a far bigger crisis than two dead Americans on his hands.

Chapter Three

"IT WAS ALL SADLY ABSURD"

The threat from terrorism is real, it is immediate, and it is evolving," Tenet had told the Senate Armed Services Committee on March 7, 2001. That same week, he had drafted a finding—a presidential covert-action order—for the National Security Council. Rizzo had crafted it to be "as direct and unambiguous as I could make it: We would be given authority to either capture or kill bin Laden, period. In other words, dead or alive."

Rice told Tenet to take it off her desk. She was unwilling to consider it, much less show it to the president. She didn't see the urgency. Nor did Defense Secretary Donald Rumsfeld, who had been Bush's first choice to replace Tenet before he and his advisers thought better of it. Rumsfeld spoke for many in the Bush administration when he told the Joint Chiefs of Staff a few days later: "For the first time in decades, the country faces no strategic challenge.... We don't have to wake up every morning thinking something terrible is going to happen."

Tenet had failed to convince Bush, Cheney, Rumsfeld, and Rice that something terrible *was* going to happen. They refused to help him take action against al Qaeda. And the man Tenet had named chief of the clandestine service wasn't leading the charge.

Jim Pavitt was an espiocrat, an elegant man with sky-blue eyes, a thousand-dollar suit, a silk pocket square, a full head of well-coiffed white hair, and a mastery of office politics, polished by three years at the White House as the National Security Council's intelligence director under the first President Bush, preceding Tenet in that post. Pavitt had worked to rebuild the clandestine service, now more agile if not much larger than it had been three years before, and he had founded the CIA's counterproliferation division, whose mission was to disrupt the nuclear-weapons programs of rogue nations. He had little rough-and-tumble experience in dangerous places, though he'd once been arrested and expelled from East Germany. During his quarter century at the CIA, his only stint as chief of station had been in a small, rich, strategically insignificant European country; behind his back, some officers referred to him not by name but as "COS Luxembourg." His seventh-floor office featured opera posters from Europe and stylish Art Deco furniture. Some days he would check his watch after the director's five o'clock all-hands conference and go home to mix a martini and put a steak on the fire, while his underlings labored deep into the night.

The rap against him among some of the CIA's operations officers was his reluctance to approve daring covert action. He had cancelled two missions aimed at capturing bin Laden, to the great frustration of the CIA's counterterrorism chieftains, and he wanted to cut back on paramilitary training, seeing little need for it on the horizon. This outraged the growing number of gung-ho operators who fervently wanted to bring the fight to al Qaeda in Afghanistan. Their leader was the counterterrorism division chief, Cofer Black, whom Tenet had charged with developing a plan of attack against bin Laden.

Black was a big, bull-headed man whose officers had nicknamed the Hulk. Born and raised in the wealthy and lily-white town of Ridgefield, Connecticut, he had cut his teeth in the Reagan years, backing anticommunist guerillas in Angola supported by apartheid South Africa. He had been station chief in Sudan from 1993 to 1995, when America deemed it a terrorist state. Bin Laden had lived there, too, in those years, and the CIA had placed him under surveillance; by Black's account, bin Laden once had tried to kill him.*

---

* The CIA station and the American embassy in Sudan shut down shortly after Black's departure on the basis of threat reporting he had sent to Washington. The CIA was compelled to withdraw those reports in 1996 after concluding that the source was a fabricator who had been crying wolf in exchange for cash.

Three years had passed since the Saudi terrorist had proclaimed it a religious duty to murder Americans anywhere on earth. Everyone on the seventh floor sensed the clock was ticking.

"This country needs to go on a war footing right away"

Black's new strategy against al Qaeda had no code name. He simply called it The Plan. He had sent Gary Schroen, deputy chief of the Near East division of the clandestine service, to Afghanistan to rally the warlords whom the CIA had armed with billions of dollars of weapons in their jihad against the Soviets during the 1980s. After the Red Army withdrew in 1989, President Bush the elder had washed America's hands of Afghanistan. Seven years of chaos followed as the warlords battled for power, until the Taliban rose up to impose their cruel regime of medieval law and order in 1996.

"I initially had a positive view of the Taliban, personally," said Zalmay Khalilzad, the only Afghan in the American national-security establishment, and the key negotiator for an American surrender to them under President Donald Trump. "I felt bad about the anarchy and civil war in Afghanistan after the Soviets had left. The Taliban, at least, had stabilized most of the country. However, once in power, they became tyrannical and allied themselves with al-Qaeda." Their Islamic republic had created a safe haven for bin Laden, who moved from Sudan to Afghanistan in 1996, paying the mullahs and commanders of the Taliban handsome sums to protect him. The core group of al Qaeda who had sworn allegiance to bin Laden in Afghanistan wasn't huge, but the men and women of the CIA's counterterrorism center—a smaller group, roughly two hundred strong—estimated that al Qaeda had thousands of adherents in some sixty nations.

Gary Schroen had delivered money and encouragement to the Northern Alliance, a loose-knit confederation commanded by Ahmed Shah Masood, and supported by Iran, Russia, and India. From 1992 to 1996, Masood and a rival commander whom the CIA had supported went to war and leveled much of Kabul with surface-to-surface missiles, many supplied by the CIA during the Soviet jihad. Their indiscriminate shelling killed tens of thousands of men, women, and children. Their forces had committed murders, kidnappings, and rapes. The CIA thought Massoud incorruptible. It knew his lieutenants were not. But they were among America's few friends in Afghanistan. Schroen had worked with them to create a network of spies who could track bin Laden as he moved furtively among his training camps and safe houses. The well-paid Afghan agents had built a base of operations on a farm with a working vineyard, but they never got close to bin Laden. The few outsiders whom the CIA had briefed on The Plan had grown deeply frustrated, among them the American ambassador in Pakistan, Bill Milam. "What are they waiting for—the wine to ferment?" he asked the station chief, Robert Grenier.

Black saw that the bounty-hunting operation would never come to fruition. He revised The Plan, and now called for a contingent of senior CIA officers to lead the warlords' forces, with support from the Pentagon's Joint Special Operations Command. The CIA's deputy counterterrorism chief, Hank Crumpton, envisioned creating a base next to Masood's redoubt in the Panjshir Valley, north of Kabul, so that his officers could carry out the hunt for bin Laden themselves. He saw it as a calculated risk with a great reward.

Pavitt had rejected the idea—too dangerous.* Crumpton then asked Rich Blee, the son of a prominent Soviet division officer and the chief of

---

* Later, in August 2000, Black, Crumpton, Rich Blee, and Greg Vogle, a paramilitary chief, had organized an armed eight-man team to travel overland to Masood's headquarters on a route traversed by aid groups like Doctors Without Borders. Crumpton and Vogle would lead the mission. Once again, at the last minute, Pavitt scrubbed it. As Crumpton wrote: "Cofer, Rich, Greg, and I wondered how unarmed aid workers grew bigger balls than the CIA." Seven weeks later, Crumpton led a CIA team investigating the October 12, 2000, suicide attack by al Qaeda on the USS *Cole*, which killed seventeen sailors as the guided missile destroyer refueled in the harbor of Aden in Yemen. He wrote directly to Pavitt from Aden, urging him to plan an attack against al Qaeda in Afghanistan: "This time would be different, I thought. The United States would counterattack. . . . It was war. The government had no choice but to pursue the enemy." But, he lamented, "I could not have been more wrong." Henry A. Crumpton, *The Art of Intelligence: Lessons from a Life in the CIA's Clandestine Service* (New York: Penguin, 2012), pp. 163–66.

the headquarters cell devoted to tracking bin Laden, to work on using a Predator drone to seek out their prey. The Predator's field of vision was a soda straw; it would require a fusion of human intelligence, signals intelligence, technical expertise, and blind luck to find bin Laden. Tenet and Pavitt had been reluctant to use it, but after a bloody internal battle, they agreed to a trial run. The drones had flown over Afghanistan sixteen times in the fall of 2000. And then the Predator had looked down upon a tall Saudi in white robes walking into an al Qaeda compound called Tarnak Farms, outside Kandahar, and transmitted the video feed to CIA headquarters. A flash message went to the White House and the Pentagon—we found him. And the response was: do you know for a fact that he will be there for six more hours? That was how long it would take for Navy ships in the Indian Ocean to arm, aim, and fire cruise missiles against him.

"We had Bin Laden in our electrical-optical sights, but we had no realistic policy, no clear authority, and no meaningful resources to engage the target with lethal speed and precision," Crumpton lamented. "It was all sadly absurd." He and Black were half-crazy with frustration; they felt they were staked to the ground like junkyard dogs. They had pushed as hard as they could for the inauguration of drone warfare in Afghanistan— arming the Predator with Hellfire missiles, turning it from a tool of espionage into a killing machine. Pavitt had been adamantly opposed, but he lost that argument. The question of who would pull the trigger remained unresolved. No one foresaw that drones would transform the art of war.

The CIA's threat reporting on al Qaeda had escalated throughout the spring of 2001. Though the most ominous intelligence was often maddeningly vague, the CIA and its foreign partners had detected and disrupted al Qaeda plots to blow up the American embassies in Paris and Sana'a, the capital of Yemen, among other targets. By the start of the summer, the threat had become all-consuming. On July 10, Tenet heard Cofer Black lay out seven specific pieces of intelligence, all gathered within the past twenty-four hours, predicting a spectacular al Qaeda attack against American targets abroad.

"The briefing he gave me literally made my hair stand on end," Tenet remembered. "When he was through, I picked up the big white secure phone on the left side of my desk—the one with a direct line to Condi Rice—and I told her I needed to see her immediately." Tenet, Black, and Rich Blee were in the national security adviser's office within the hour. Blee said the attack would come within a few weeks or months. Bin Laden's ultimate goal, he said, was the destruction of the United States.

What should we do? Rice said plaintively.

Black responded with great force: "This country needs to go on a war footing right away."

How? Rice asked.

"He didn't know why he was President"

Tenet wanted the president's approval to let his officers kill Osama bin Laden *now*. The National Security Council had to have a full-dress meeting *now*, so Bush could sign the finding *now*. Rice did not make that happen. She put the issue on the National Security Council's agenda for September 4.

Rice did not have much faith in Tenet. She still didn't grasp his sense of emergency, and he couldn't make her see it. She wouldn't act on his request because the president didn't have a policy on al Qaeda, and she wasn't prepared to consider one for his approval. Bush didn't have a policy on al Qaeda because he didn't have a policy on Afghanistan. He didn't have a policy on Afghanistan because he didn't have a policy on Pakistan, whose military dictator pretended to support America, whose army possessed nuclear weapons, and whose all-powerful intelligence service backed the Taliban to the hilt. Rice's job was to make the president focus on all these issues, which would soon be matters of life and death. But she could not forge consensus among the National Security Council's principals: the president, the vice president, Secretary of Defense Rumsfeld, and Secretary of State Colin Powell. The result was a state of strategic incoherence at the White House. America had no plan to defend itself against al Qaeda except The Plan.

Bush remained unfocused on his role as the leader of the free world.

"He didn't know why he was President" until America was attacked, as his deputy secretary of state, Richard Armitage, put it bluntly. Rumsfeld disdained Powell and Powell distrusted Rumsfeld, whose neoconservative deputies were sharpening their knives for him, a four-star general they deemed a closet liberal. "This marriage was not made in heaven," Powell reflected. "The State Department is always the enemy for these people—and CIA. They don't like CIA either."

Tenet's star had been fading in the national security firmament all summer. "There was no way Cheney wanted Tenet to continue," his deputy executive director, John Brennan, had been hearing. "They would even talk of Rumsfeld running the agency for a while." Both men harbored a deep skepticism about the CIA's capabilities. Their mistrust stretched back for thirty years. They had risen to power under President Nixon, who had savaged the work of the CIA, seeing it as a cabal of closet liberals dead-set on subverting him.

They thought the al Qaeda threat might be a grand deception designed to mislead the White House and the Pentagon, to distract them from more urgent matters. They had another battle plan on their minds.

Chapter Four

THE BAY OF GOATS

On August 4, 2001, Luis Rueda began creating a detailed plan of covert action to help overthrow Saddam Hussein.

He had gotten a glimpse of the big picture of the Bush administration's thinking by reading summaries of National Security Council staff meetings in his role as right-hand man to the CIA's deputy director, John McLaughlin. He had been struck by the fact that "Gulf Affairs" had been on the agenda two or three times a week since Bush's inauguration. The president himself had chaired two NSC meetings devoted to the topic. What's that about? he asked his boss. Oh, McLaughlin said, that's Iraq. They're talking about regime change.* This riveted Rueda, whose job gave him the ability to choose his next assignment. He became the new chief of the CIA's Iraq Operations Group.

The Bay of Pigs had made him an American. He was born in Havana and named after his father, who had worked to overthrow Fidel Castro until the CIA's invasion of Cuba ended in catastrophe. Rueda's mother brought him to the United States, where he decided to take up the battle his father had lost. He had joined the CIA's Latin American division early in the Reagan administration's war on communism. He ran paramil-

---

* "What we really want to think about is going after Saddam," Rumsfeld had told the NSC on February 1, 2001, Bush's eleventh day in office. "It would change everything in the region and beyond it. It would demonstrate what U.S. policy is all about."

itary and propaganda operations in Central America, heard Reagan give a speech at headquarters praising the agency as "the tripwire of democracy" that could take down totalitarians, watched as his superiors were indicted in the Iran-contra debacle, rose to serve as a chief of station, righted a number of ships that had run aground, and emerged with a stellar reputation. He had a wicked sense of humor, a finely tuned bullshit detector, and a facility for imposing order on chaos. These qualities would stand him in good stead.

And a bold plan to topple Saddam was just what Tenet needed to make the White House happy.

Rueda went to work in his new sixth-floor office. He called for the in-house clandestine service histories of the CIA's missions in Iraq, to review the hard lessons learned. They could not be found and no one knew where to find them. Nonetheless, he knew full well that they had failed spectacularly, undermined by bad tradecraft and wishful thinking. After the 1991 Gulf War led by General Powell and Defense Secretary Cheney ended with swift victory but left Saddam in power, President Bush had openly encouraged the people of Iraq to rise up, and he ordered the CIA to support them. Saddam had slaughtered them by the thousands. In the years that followed, the CIA had backed Kurdish dissidents in the north of Iraq, Shiites in the south, Iraqi exiles in London, and military defectors in Jordan, all with the intent of building enough internal opposition to the regime to mount a coup. These efforts added up to roughly $100 million worth of blown operations. The CIA had established a base in Kurdish territory, trying to build a resistance force and recruit members of Saddam's inner circle. Saddam overran the base and wiped out the CIA's allies in July 1996. Over the next two years, prominent Iraqi exiles had sweet-talked CIA officers into half-baked attempts at espionage; Saddam's secret police had penetrated their ranks and arrested, tortured, and killed their recruited agents. The essential elements of these deadly fiascoes had been published by the handful of newspaper reporters on the intelligence beat in Washington.

Regime change in Iraq had been the official foreign policy of the United States ever since Congress had passed and Clinton had signed a highly unusual law proclaiming that goal in October 1998. This act of political theater had not spurred the Iraq Operations Group to new heights. It had conducted no new covert action since then. Rueda's predecessor told him that his mission was to make sure that the words *CIA*, *Iraq*, and *debacle* did not appear together on the front page of the *Washington Post*. The Iraq Operations Group consisted of eighteen people in the summer of 2001, two of whom were experienced case officers. One of them was about to retire, and the other one was Rueda. No system at the CIA beyond a quick training course served to indoctrinate new officers in the intricate realities of covert action, political warfare, propaganda, and paramilitary missions. On-the-job training was the only training they had.

"We left the job undone last time. I'm going to finish it."

The first man Rueda consulted was one of the only people still in the agency who actually had helped change a regime—Frank Archibald, a bespectacled bear of a man who would become the chief of the clandestine service a decade later.

Archibald had enlisted in the Marines upon graduating from a small-town South Carolina high school and joined the CIA's special activities division as a paramilitary officer in 1983. He was forty-seven but looked older, with a fringe of white hair and a medicine-ball belly. He had just returned from running the CIA's operations in the Balkans, leading a cadre of officers working with the Pentagon's special forces and British commandos, hunting down war criminals, and undermining the murderous president, Slobodan Milošević. Their targets had committed countless atrocities after Yugoslavia imploded into warring factions of Serbs, Bosnians, and Croatians at the end of the cold war. Among the Serbs charged by the International Criminal Court with slaughtering thousands of Bosnian Muslims was President Milošević, who in 1999 had become the first sitting head of state ever indicted for war crimes. The United States and NATO had gone to war to topple him. When that failed, Archibald oversaw a well-financed covert propaganda campaign, in concert with an overt

State Department political effort, backing a patriotic and profoundly democratic get-out-the-vote operation that defeated Milošević in a September 2000 election. Milošević would die in a prison cell in the Hague. A case where the interests of the CIA and human rights were one and the same.

Archibald was a master of the intricate mechanics of espionage. His manhunts flowed from an alchemical fusion of intelligence, covert operations, and military force. CIA officers recruited Serb agents, including Milošević's spy chief, paid them for legally actionable intelligence, and worked with the Pentagon's Joint Special Operations Command to capture their targets. "This was the only war we had at the time, and the CIA's intel was driving it," said Gen. David Petraeus, who made his name as a one-star commander working with Archibald in the Balkans and became a star-crossed CIA director ten years thereafter. Armed with sealed indictments, guided by the National Security Agency's electronic eavesdroppers and Predator surveillance drones, the joint force of Archibald's spies, Petraeus's soldiers, and British commandos knocked down doors, grabbed the war criminals, bound their wrists and ankles, stuffed them into vans, unloaded them into helicopters, and shipped them to the Hague. And as they hunted, they discovered that the Balkans had become a hub for Islamic jihadists—among them, Afghan veterans of the CIA-backed jihad against the Soviets who had turned against America and sided with al Qaeda. The CIA kidnapped a dozen of these men, stole their documents and hard drives, drugged and hog-tied them, and flew them to prisons in Cairo or Amman. The Balkans, Petraeus said, was "a really interesting training ground" for the manhunts he would lead in Iraq five years later.

Archibald had some wisdom to impart to Rueda. He knew what had gone wrong for the CIA in Iraq, and he thought he knew why. "If you can, work with patriots," he told Rueda. "Don't work with guys who want money. Don't work with guys who are in it for the power. They'll fuck you over every single time. They'll let you down. They'll betray you." Armed with that counsel, Rueda went to the White House to brief the vice president.

Cheney got right to the point. What could the CIA do to topple

Saddam? "You're not going to get a coup," Rueda said. "He has killed all the opposition inside the country," murdered their families, burned their villages, and the few who survived had been exiles for decades. For covert action to succeed, Rueda told Cheney, there had to be the political foundation of an Iraqi opposition upon which to build American power. None existed.

America's last good look inside the regime had ended in December 1998. United Nations inspectors had been searching fruitlessly for weapons of mass destruction, and they had given CIA officers cover to monitor the communications of Saddam's military and intelligence officers. When Saddam had expelled the team, the CIA's eyes and ears went with them. The CIA had not gathered intelligence on Saddam's arsenal since then. It had not recruited an agent in his inner circle. Its efforts had been limited to trying to collect the telephone numbers of Iraqi military leaders so the CIA could contact them in the improbable event they decided to mount a coup. "We had nothing," Rueda said twenty years later. "And you cannot conduct a covert action program without intelligence"— much less start a war.

If the White House saw fit, he told Cheney, he would draft a finding aimed at getting the CIA back in business in northern Iraq: recruiting spies, building a resistance, penetrating Saddam's regime, and paving the way for a military invasion. Cheney liked the idea. And he said so in an indelible way. "We left the job undone last time," he told Rueda. "I'm going to finish it."

"And what will we have? A Bay of Goats."

Rueda went to the Pentagon to brief Paul Wolfowitz, the deputy secretary of defense, and a man impervious to facts that failed to fit his preconceptions. He believed, without evidence, that Saddam was responsible for the 1993 World Trade Center attack and maintained secret links to al Qaeda; he had constantly pressed the CIA to provide the nonexistent proof. He saw Saddam as the root of all evil in the Middle East, and he thought that if the tyrant were toppled, Iraq would become a democracy, dictatorships throughout the region would fall like dominoes, the Palestinians would make peace with the Israelis, and America would have dominion in the Arab world. In time, the president of the United States would embrace this vision.

Bob Gates, the CIA director under the first President Bush and the last man to succeed at the job, had caught wind of Wolfowitz's appointment before it was announced. He called Condi Rice and raised hell. "I just have one piece of advice for you," he said. "Whatever you do, don't give Paul Wolfowitz an operational role, because he can't manage his way out of a paper bag. So, of course, they gave him the biggest managerial role in the government"—deputy secretary of defense. It could have been worse, Gates said: "He was being rumored to head CIA, which I thought would be a *really* big catastrophe."

Wolfowitz had requested the briefing from Rueda, but he showed little interest in his plans. He quickly turned the conversation to the one man he thought could transform Iraq: the unctuous and duplicitous Ahmed Chalabi, a convicted embezzler who led an exile group in London called the Iraqi National Congress. Chalabi claimed to wield great influence in his native country, despite the fact that he hadn't been in Baghdad since 1958. The CIA had worked with Chalabi from 1991 to 1996, to its enduring sorrow. "I could not believe we were giving him money to try to overthrow Saddam Hussein," wrote Kenneth Pollock, a leading CIA analyst on Iraq in those years. "I could not believe anyone would buy what he was trying to sell." Both the CIA and the State Department had him pegged as a liar and a thief; the clandestine service had issued a rare "burn notice" banning officers from working with Chalabi and barring analysts from believing a word he said. "That guy is a weasel," Armitage said to anyone who asked. "And he will only lead us into trouble."

Wolfowitz knew of these strongly held views, but he dismissed them. For years, Chalabi had been wooing powerful American politicians and influential journalists, retired intelligence chieftains like Dewey Clarridge and the former CIA director James Woolsey, and conservative power brokers like Cheney and Wolfowitz. Now he was claiming to have riveting intelligence on Saddam. And he was pushing a plan to liberate Iraq, which had the direct imprimatur of Clarridge.

Wolfowitz now tried selling that scheme to Rueda. A squadron of F-18s would fly off an aircraft carrier and bomb the hell out of southern Iraq. Then American commandos would insert a battalion of Chalabi's men, all of whom had lived for years in the United States or Europe. This army of civilians, trained and financed and armed by its American allies, would march north, liberate the capital, and install Chalabi as the new leader of a democratic, free-market, secular Iraq. This visionary plan had the full support of Rumsfeld's top deputies. It did not impress the retired four-star general Anthony Zinni, who had commanded American forces in the Persian Gulf. He summarized it pithily: "Some silk-suited, Rolex-wearing guys in London gin up an expedition. We'll equip a thousand fighters and arm them with $97 million worth of AK-47s and insert them into Iraq. And what will we have? A Bay of Goats."*

The Bay of Goats was not what Rueda had in mind. He drove back to headquarters and drafted a finding for the president's signature. He proposed to requisition three hundred people and spend $200 million a year to execute his plan. Its essential elements were espionage, penetration, recruitment, disinformation, sabotage, and direct action—that is, killing people. Rueda proposed to send two teams of CIA officers and special-forces soldiers into northern Iraq to reestablish relations with the leaders of the Kurds, the stateless tribesmen who had fought Saddam, and often one another, since the 1970s. The United States had seduced and betrayed the Kurds throughout those years, and they were justly skeptical

---

* Rueda also met with Zalmay Khalilzad, newly installed as the NSC's point man for the Islamic world, who was about to receive orders from Bush to prepare for an Iraq without Saddam. Khalilzad later served as Bush's ambassador to Iraq, Afghanistan, and the United Nations, and ultimately as the diplomatic architect of America's disastrous withdrawal from Kabul in 2021. He impressed Rueda as a man who was in thrall to Chalabi, profoundly disorganized, and potentially a danger to himself and others. For his part, Khalilzad evidently wasn't listening to what Rueda was saying. "I think the question of a coup was a possibility. The CIA folks thought that this could be a way to address war as an issue," he said. That was the exact opposite of Rueda's briefing. (Khalilzad oral history, Miller Center.)

of America's resolve. Winning their trust with money and weapons was crucial: their guerrillas had long experience fighting Saddam's army in the mountains, and their small intelligence service, created with the CIA's support in the 1990s, was capable of conducting espionage in the cities of Iraq. Rueda would use their contacts to build networks of informants, spy on the regime, and recruit Iraqi agents to penetrate and subvert Saddam's military and security services. He would supply the Kurds with enough firepower to make them a fighting force capable of pinning down Iraqi divisions in the north, killing them in battle while sabotaging army depots and bases.

A crucial component of Rueda's plan was carefully crafted propaganda. An Iraq Operations Group unit based in Jordan—the station chief was Charlie Seidel, regarded as the most skilled Arabist in the CIA—would create channels of disinformation designed to deceive Saddam. The idea was to make him believe there really was an internal opposition in Baghdad where none existed, that members of his inner circle were plotting against him, compelling him to kill his loyalists in order to quash a coup that wasn't coming. All this would serve to pave the way for a military invasion; Rueda knew Saddam was unlikely to be overthrown unless and until "the 82nd Airborne landed in Baghdad and started killing everybody." He swiftly completed his covert-action plan and code-named it ANABASIS, after the annals of a Greek mercenary army led by Cyrus the Younger to seize the throne of Persia from his brother in 401 BC.*

By the end of August, his plan was ready for consideration by the White House and the Pentagon. All that remained was a cause to go to war. But first the National Security Council had another covert action on its agenda.

---

* The president gave Rumsfeld a formal order to prepare for war against Iraq on November 21, 2001. Ten days later, Rumsfeld told Gen. Tommy Franks, the leader of Central Command, to draw up battle plans to remove Saddam from power. Franks briefed Bush, Cheney, Powell, Rice, and Tenet on his plans, which incorporated Rueda's, on December 28. Bush signed the covert-action finding launching ANABASIS on February 16, 2002. The choice of the code name had overlooked the fact that Cyrus had been killed and his forces routed twenty-five centuries before.

"There was so much we did not know"

On September 4, 2001, the NSC finally considered a presidential directive on al Qaeda. Cheney, Rumsfeld, Powell, Rice, and Tenet were among those gathered in the White House Situation Room. But the lethal finding Tenet had sought in July, authorizing his officers to kill bin Laden, was not on the table. The far more modest proposal before them focused on increasing money and support for the Northern Alliance warlords in Afghanistan, with the goal of taking down bin Laden and his jihadists over the course of three to five years. Tenet agreed to arm the Predator drones with Hellfire missiles, but the issue of who would pull the trigger remained a stumbling block. Nothing was resolved beyond a collective agreement to forge ahead in the not-too-distant future, pending the president's approval. No one at the table expressed a sense of dread about the threat.

The CIA's reporting that an attack by al Qaeda was imminent, which had been escalating since April, had inexplicably diminished in early August, a few days before a soon-to-be-infamous warning Bush had received at his Texas ranch. The President's Daily Brief for August 6, headlined "Bin Laden Determined to Strike in US," was the thirty-sixth alert the CIA had delivered to Bush about al Qaeda. It included unique intelligence from the FBI, reporting "suspicious activity in this country consistent with hijackings." But Bush had shrugged it off. He thought he had heard it all before. The president and his aides would protest, after the fact, that they'd had no warning at all. In truth, the CIA's leaders had sounded the loudest and longest-lasting alarm in its history, but that was not enough. They had to make sure Bush and his brain trust heard it, and they hadn't.

Anticipating a surprise attack from afar was the highest mission of the CIA. For a want of intelligence, the plot it could not forestall would succeed in a way it could not imagine. "We were at the very low end of our knowledge about al Qaeda," Tenet wrote twelve years later. "There was so much we did not know."

Chapter Five

THE NEW WORLD

Just after eight o'clock on the morning of September 11, Mike Morell walked into a suite at the Colony Beach & Tennis Resort in Sarasota, Florida. Morell looked like an exceedingly bright and eager graduate student, though he was forty-two. The son of an autoworker and a homemaker from Cuyahoga Falls, Ohio, he had been an intelligence analyst for twenty years. In a dozen more he'd be running the CIA. He had been up since three thirty a.m., preparing to deliver the daily intelligence brief to the president. "There was nothing in the briefing about terrorism," he remembered. "It was very routine."

The first plane hit the World Trade Center at 8:46 a.m. Bush had gone to a classroom at the Emma Booker Elementary School for a photo op to publicize his No Child Left Behind legislation. He was reading aloud from a children's book when the White House chief of staff, Andy Card, whispered into his ear: *A second plane hit the second tower. America is under attack.*

The third plane hit the Pentagon at 9:37 a.m. "The building shook and the tables jumped," Rumsfeld recalled. "I assumed it was a bomb." Air Force One took off like a rocket, its destination uncertain. After they were aloft, Bush asked Morell: "Who did this?" as if he hadn't been warned.

Tenet ordered CIA headquarters evacuated. John McLaughlin went home and wrote: *Nothing will ever be the same.* He remembered: "I could already sense that we'd crossed into a new world." John Rizzo remained at his desk. He began drafting a new covert-action order, scribbling *lethal, capture, detain,* and *interrogate* on a legal pad. "I let my imagination run wild," he remembered. "I was totally winging it." At about eleven a.m., Tenet called Gen. Michael V. Hayden, the director of the National Security Agency, America's electronic eavesdroppers, at his headquarters in Fort Meade, Maryland.

"What do you have?" Tenet asked.

"It's al-Qaeda," Hayden said.

"Do you have proof?"

"Well, we're hearing the celebratory gunfire on the network."

This fact did not affect Bush, Rice, and Rumsfeld. Down in the White House bunker that afternoon, Rice remembered, "We all asked ourselves: *Could Iraq somehow have been involved?*" She called the British ambassador, Christopher Meyer, and said: "We are just looking to see whether there could possibly be a connection with Saddam Hussein." Rumsfeld remained at the burning Pentagon for hours. At 2:40 p.m. he instructed a top aide to see if the intelligence was good enough to hit Saddam right away. "We've got to do Iraq," he said that evening in the bunker. In the morning, the president and his inner circle, shocked and frightened, gathered at the White House. In the afternoon, hours after Tenet told him face-to-face that bin Laden was without question behind the attacks, Bush grabbed the White House counterterrorism coordinator Richard Clarke by the arm and said: "See if Saddam did this," as if he hadn't understood a word Tenet had said.

On the evening of September 12, the CIA held a supper on the seventh floor. Four tables were set in a square and laid with white linen in a charmless conference room, where white-jacketed waiters silently served drinks. Sir Richard Dearlove, chief of MI6, Britain's foreign intelligence service, and Eliza Manningham-Buller, deputy chief of MI5, Britain's FBI, had arrived in a private jet from London. The British spymasters had come to embrace Tenet, express solidarity with the CIA, and pledge support for its counterterrorism efforts. They were joined by David Manning, a principal foreign-policy adviser to Prime Minister Tony Blair, and a coterie of the CIA's barons, including Jim Pavitt, his deputy Hugh Turner, and Cofer Black.

Manning had heard the war drums pounding. "I hope we can all agree," Manning said, "that we should concentrate on Afghanistan and not be tempted to launch any attacks on Iraq." Absolutely right, Tenet replied: "None of us wants to go that route."

Everyone thought bin Laden could strike again any day. No one knew where. The CIA had no idea of his intentions and capabilities. But it did have a plan to destroy al Qaeda, and it was the only institution of the American government that did. In the days ahead, Tenet would take on the role of a combatant commander and his civilian intelligence agency would become a clandestine army mounting a desperate struggle to stop the next attack. The officers and analysts who regrouped at CIA headquarters were seething with anger, tempered by guilt and sorrow and the fear that they might be crucified for failing to prevent the catastrophe. And as they began to sharpen their swords to go to war against al Qaeda, they sensed that one day they might be crucified for that as well.

"We're fucked," Cofer Black told his deputy Hank Crumpton a few days later. "It's just like the Soviet Union in World War Two. The political commissars executed the generals who lost. They executed the generals who won. The political commissars are always waiting with guns loaded."

"Either way," Black said, "we get it in the head." This proved prophetic.

"If war comes, it will be a disaster for everyone"

On Thursday, September 13, the National Security Council met in the White House Situation Room. Black, red-faced and growling, gave a firebreathing speech, vowing revenge: the CIA would unify the fighters led by its Afghan allies, prepare the battlefield for an attack, direct devastating American air strikes against Taliban strongholds, and hunt down the terrorists who had murdered more than three thousand Americans. He had brought storyboards with photos of bin Laden and his top lieutenant, Ayman al-Zawahiri. "Bin Laden, dead," he said, tossing the pictures over his shoulder and against the wood-paneled wall. "Zawahiri, dead." How long would it take to destroy al Qaeda? the president asked. When the

CIA was through with them—in a matter of weeks, Black said—"They will have flies walking across their eyeballs." Morell was aghast. He thought: *He cannot deliver on that promise. We don't have that kind of intelligence. We don't have the capability to do that.* But Bush liked Black's bloodlust. In the afternoon, he told the press that he wanted bin Laden dead or alive.

At sunrise on Saturday, September 15, the war council reconvened at Camp David, the rustic presidential retreat in the Catoctin Mountains of Maryland, sixty-two miles north by northwest of the White House. Tenet laid out a global strategy: the CIA would mount operations in ninety-two nations, pay vast sums to mobilize friendly foreign intelligence services, and attack terrorist networks around the world. As a first step, he said, his officers would take up arms in Afghanistan in a matter of days, and they would destroy al Qaeda in battle with the warlords of the Northern Alliance.* Rumsfeld protested that the United States had to attack Iraq too. "If it's a global war of terror," he said, "you need to show it's global." Wolfowitz argued that Saddam surely had a hand in 9/11, that he was the head of the snake of international terrorism. Black shot Tenet an incredulous glance and insisted with great force that Saddam had nothing to do with the attacks.

Okay, Bush said, we'll leave Iraq for later. But not for long. "I think it really had been decided that first weekend after 9/11," Colin Powell said sixteen years later.

After breakfast, Bush stepped outside to chat with Black and Morell. Powell walked over and strongly suggested that America's first response to the attack should be diplomatic, using persuasion and coercion to convince the Taliban to turn over bin Laden. It was a short conversation. When the secretary of state was out of earshot, Bush said: "Fuck diplomacy. We are going to war."

But diplomacy could serve the cause of war as well. That weekend,

---

* The leader of the Northern Alliance, Ahmed Shah Masood, the CIA's strongest confederate in Afghanistan, had been killed by bin Laden's assassins on September 9. By murdering Masood, bin Laden was preparing the battlefield for the American counterstrike he knew would be coming. His intent was to draw the United States into a long war, knowing that Afghanistan was where empires went to die.

ambassadors and station chiefs alike set out on a worldwide search for allies, telling foreign leaders and their spymasters that they must side with America against al Qaeda or face its wrath. In Islamabad, Ambassador Wendy Chamberlin and CIA station chief Robert Grenier gave an ultimatum to Pakistan's military ruler, Gen. Pervez Musharraf, and Gen. Mahmud Ahmed, who led Pakistan's all-powerful Inter-Services Intelligence directorate, the ISI. They had to meet America's demands: arrest al Qaeda members fleeing into Pakistan, intercept Taliban arms shipments flowing into Afghanistan, and end all support for bin Laden. This was a fantasy. The ISI's ranks included committed al Qaeda sympathizers. It had helped to create the Taliban, to some degree controlled it, and continued to supply it with weapons, ammunition, transportation, fuel, and vital intelligence. Mahmud soon thereafter told the Taliban's ambassador in Islamabad: "You will not be alone in this jihad against America. We will be with you." Musharraf bobbed and weaved before agreeing to work with the United States against al Qaeda. But he was a two-faced ally who would play a double game for years to come.

Grenier then went to Quetta, on Pakistan's border with Afghanistan, to meet the Taliban's deputy foreign minister and its military commander for southern Afghanistan. His message was blunt: tell the Taliban's emir, Mullah Omar, to turn over al Qaeda's leaders to the United States or prepare for battle.

"If war comes," Grenier warned, with sharp foresight, "it will be a disaster for everyone, victor and vanquished alike."

William J. Burns, the assistant secretary of state for the Middle East—and twenty years later the CIA director—sent his deputy Ryan Crocker to Geneva on a highly sensitive mission to enlist Iran's support. Burns knew the Iranians hated al Qaeda and the Taliban and thought they would happily help the CIA fight them. For years, their spies and their Revolutionary Guards had infiltrated Iran's 580-mile border with Afghanistan, sending guns, money, intelligence, and military advisers to the CIA-backed Northern Alliance. Crocker met a delegation led by Mohammad Ebrahim Taherian-Fard, Iran's envoy to Tajikistan. The Iranians owed the United States a favor: the CIA had helped them arm the Bosnian Muslims as they battled the Serbs in the Balkans during the 1990s. "They brought in maps and said, 'Okay, here's our info on Taliban strong points. . . . Here's what our agents believe they think you're going to do,'" Crocker recounted. He then proposed to "hook up our CIA guys in northern Afghanistan with the Iranian Revolutionary Guards in northern Afghanistan." That proved too much for the Iranians, though the CIA was game. But for the moment, on the timeless principle that the enemy of my enemy is my friend, America and Iran were partners in the war on terror.*

Bush and Tenet sent a high-level team to Moscow—including Rich Armitage, Cofer Black, and Jose Rodriguez—to enlist their Russian counterparts in the battle against al Qaeda. The mission was the first of many such efforts. Putin pledged $10 million of Russian weapons, provided America paid for them; predictably, his spies kept trying to double-cross the United States. The former Soviet republics of central Asia were America's gateway to Afghanistan. But the CIA station chief in Dushanbe, four hundred miles north of Kabul, reported that Russian intelligence officers in the Tajik capital were pressuring the government and its neighbors to close their air space and military bases to American forces. Farther north, in Tashkent, the Uzbek capital, the American ambassador and the CIA outmaneuvered the Russians, locking down basing rights for Predator flights in a deal with the country's authoritarian ruler, a man who tortured and murdered his opponents but was pleased to help the Americans for the right price.

Since 1997, the CIA had paid and trained Uzbek officers as a strike force. Now, as it prepared to deploy them in the hunt for al Qaeda, the agency set up one of the first among its many international counterterrorist intelligence centers in Tashkent. (The very first had been established to hunt war criminals in the Balkans.) Tenet soon flew to Yemen and Indonesia and beyond to open more intelligence hubs fusing the work of the CIA and foreign spies. The CIA would supply money, weapons, helicopters,

---

* The Iranians kept aiding the American war on terror in Afghanistan until Bush placed them in the "axis of evil" with Iraq and North Korea during his January 2002 State of the Union address. That killed the cooperation Crocker had skillfully elicited.

cars, night-vision goggles, and eavesdropping technology; the host service would kick down doors and capture or kill terrorist suspects.

Money always had been the most effective weapon the CIA possessed, buying intelligence and renting allegiances from recruited agents and recalcitrant nations alike. Now Tenet needed an unlimited supply of cash. At the Camp David meeting, he had sought and received the president's promise for an immediate supplement of $3 billion, instantly doubling the CIA's budget. A billion went straight to the counterterrorism center. Black soon requisitioned a battalion of case officers from all over the clandestine service, hired squadrons of CIA retirees and military veterans as contractors, and created a new Office of Terrorism Analysis, staffed with some three hundred people from across the agency, not all of whom had great expertise on the subject. Huge sums soon flowed to foreign intelligence services across the world; for years to come, a station chief could express his thanks to his counterpart with a briefcase stuffed with a million dollars.

On Monday morning, September 17, Tenet brought the covert-action finding Rizzo had drafted to the White House for Bush's signature. The president granted the CIA powers previously unimaginable: to take up arms and fight the war on terror, destroy al Qaeda, kill bin Laden, and capture everyone responsible for 9/11. In the past, findings had almost always received months of intensive scrutiny by the National Security Council, the State Department, and the Justice Department. This one, by far the most aggressive order in the CIA's history, had been vetted for no more than four days. The dozen counterterrorism programs covered by the finding carried the code word GREYSTONE. Each one incorporated a multitude of secret operations. Thousands of covert actions would be carried out under its aegis, far more than the number undertaken against the Soviet Union and its allies during the cold war. How to execute the president's command was up to Tenet. He still had barely more than a thousand officers in the clandestine service. He would have to double and redouble that number. He would have to expand the counterterrorism center tenfold. He would have to supercharge the CIA's analytic powers to anticipate surprise attacks, warn Bush every morning about a multitude of threats, and stop any one that might materialize. And he had to overthrow the Taliban.

That evening, at the British embassy, Black briefed his counterpart, the MI6 counterterrorism chief Mark Allen, on the CIA's plans. Allen, an Arabist of long experience, was a bit taken aback. Then what? he asked. What are we going to do once we've hammered the mercury in Afghanistan and al Qaeda's cadres spread all over the Islamic world? Black had no answer.

"We didn't know jack shit about al Qaeda"

A great fear gripped Washington as the mass graves smoldered, reeking of jet fuel and burned flesh, a dreadful foreboding that the worst was yet to come. Every day was "a living hell," Tenet remembered. "It was inconceivable to us that bin Laden had not already positioned people to conduct second and a possibly third and fourth waves of attacks inside the United States." So began a search for intelligence at any cost and by any means necessary.

"The reality is that on 9/11 we didn't know jack shit about al Qaeda," said Bob Gates, the former director of central intelligence and future secretary of defense. "That's the reason a lot of this stuff happened, the interrogations and everything else, because we didn't know anything. If we'd had a great database and knew exactly what al Qaeda was all about, what their capabilities were and stuff like that, some of these measures wouldn't have been necessary. But the fact is that we'd just been attacked by a group we didn't know anything about."

When Bush asked where al Qaeda might strike next, Tenet produced the worst-case scenarios of analysts he had assigned to imagine a holocaust; when those analysts ran out of ideas, the CIA hired Hollywood screenwriters to dream up new ones. The target lists Tenet brought to the Situation Room included the Washington Monument, the Statue of Liberty, Mount Rushmore, military bases, airports, harbors, bridges, sports stadiums, Wall Street, Disneyland, and the White House itself. Tenet sent word to every allied spy service in the world to warn the CIA about any and all potential threats. Many of these reports were rank speculation, and others were the fabrications of bad actors screaming "Fire!" in a crowded theater.

"Every single threat report that we got, no matter how apparently farfetched, would be chased to ground," said Winston Wiley, the CIA's most senior analyst on 9/11. "Many, many, many, many, many of these were probably without basis, but we had no ability to be confident of that." The CIA brought this torrent to Tenet's morning briefing in the Oval Office. "*All* of the intelligence about threats was coming into the White House with no filters," Gates said. "Every day, reports of imminent attacks with nuclear weapons on Washington, New York, LA, and Chicago. Those were just flooding into the White House. They were just buried in threats."

Every day at eight a.m., Tenet and his aides delivered a terrifying fusillade of bullet points to the president and the vice president. Their barrage was "a God-awful idea," Morell reflected. Tenet knew most of the warnings were false alarms. He just didn't know which ones. He said "you could drive yourself crazy believing all or even half" of what the CIA was reporting—but he could not tell the president which half to believe. "The fear was such that you were running down and reporting everything, because you could not afford not to," said Linda Weissgold, who led the CIA's efforts to divine al Qaeda's plans and intentions, briefed Bush for two years, and later became the CIA's chief of intelligence analysis. "Every day was September 12"—and the fear escalated every night.

The tension at headquarters was unbearable. Cindy Storer, a top terrorism analyst, picked up her phone and heard Jennifer Matthews, a founding member of the bin Laden station, screaming with rage. "You did this, this is your fault," she shouted at Storer, whose desk was only a few yards away. "And I screamed back at her and slammed the phone down," Storer recalled. "I actually really never spoke to her again. . . . I think it was just a manifestation of her passion and her sense—her own sense of guilt. I mean, everybody felt it."

On September 18, and for two months thereafter, letters containing anthrax arrived at the offices of broadcast networks, newspapers, and two United States senators. The biotoxin killed five people and infected seventeen more. Bush feared that this was the leading edge of the new wave of al Qaeda attacks, a fear amplified by the daily bombardment of raw intelligence. "The biggest question during the anthrax attack was where it was coming from," Bush wrote in his memoir. "A CIA briefing on the threat of terrorists spraying anthrax over a city from a small plane was fresh in my mind" when he gave his first press conference after 9/11. He gave a long and unprompted discourse on how a crop duster could kill the citizens of the United States. The FBI took seven years to name an American scientist at the government's biodefense laboratory as the anthrax attacker. Bush immediately suspected Saddam Hussein. And Saddam was very much on his mind at that press conference.

"There's no question that the leader of Iraq is an evil man," he said. "We know he's been developing weapons of mass destruction." That knowledge came to him from the CIA. Bush needed no convincing when Tenet and Morell told him in no uncertain terms that Saddam had WMD—specifically, a chemical weapons program and a biological weapons production capability—and was working on acquiring a nuclear weapon. What they didn't tell him was that most of the intelligence dated back to before the 1991 Gulf War.

Now a new war lay ahead. A war that would be fought on every front, Bush pledged, against all terrorists anywhere on earth, and against all governments supporting or sheltering them. Afghanistan was just the beginning. "Our war on terror begins with al Qaeda, but it does not end there," the president told the American people on September 20. "It will not end until every terrorist group of global reach has been found, stopped, and defeated." The war had no strategy beyond that soaring vow.

The CIA took charge of the attack in Afghanistan, for Rumsfeld had no plan and Bush had no vision but vengeance.

"Our strategy is to create chaos"

The towering ambitions of the war on terror far eclipsed the capacities of the clandestine service. The CIA could undermine the Taliban through its Afghan allies and pursue al Qaeda to the ends of the earth. But it could not make war. Nor could it shape a strategic vision for the United States.

Only the president and the Pentagon could do that. "Our strategy," Bush told the National Security Council on September 26, "is to create chaos, to create a vacuum" in Afghanistan, knocking out the Taliban in order to flush bin Laden from hiding and kill him before he struck again. Creating chaos did not constitute a strategy.

The White House was in bedlam: false alarms ringing ceaselessly, every chirping cell phone a harbinger of doom, life-and-death decisions being made in a dark state of dread, everyone trying to keep their heads above the tidal wave of threats, rarely able to see past the edges of their desks, and all too often at one another's throats.* The secretary of defense was a constant source of friction. Rumsfeld was furious that America's spies would have boots on the ground in Afghanistan well before his soldiers, and he took perverse pleasure throwing sand in the CIA's gears. In the Situation Room one morning, "they were talking about who is in charge in Afghanistan—Tenet and Rumsfeld, back and forth. I'm looking at it like I'm watching a tennis match," Armitage remembered. Bush asked him: "What do you think?" Armitage was not one to mince words. "Mr. President," he replied, "It's FUBAR"—fucked up beyond all recognition. "In the chaos of the times," McLaughlin remembered, clear thinking was rare and wisdom fleeting at the White House.

Remaking the CIA as a global paramilitary force while mounting a worldwide scramble for intelligence was akin to repairing a fighter jet in midair while on a combat mission. Tenet and Black started by reconfiguring the cockpit. Black recalled Hank Crumpton from Australia, where he

---

* Gallows humor often was the only relief. Cheney was at a white-tie dinner in New York and Bush was at a global conference in Singapore during a secure White House video conference call on October 18 when the vice president suddenly said: "I've got terrible news, Mr. President." He reported that the deadly biotoxin ricin had been detected in the White House. Tenet went home from the Situation Room. His son John, a high school freshman, asked if he could stay up late and watch the Yankees in the baseball playoffs. Tenet thought: "Well, I've just been told I'm going to die and here my only son wants to stay up with his dad. . . ." Of course, he replied, and then he said: "Don't tell your mom, but before you sit down, you see that bottle of scotch? Go get the big glass and bring me that big bottle." He lived to laugh about it the following morning. (Colin Powell and Richard Armitage oral history, Miller Center, University of Virginia.)

was newly installed as station chief, and ordered him to lead the Afghan battle as the head of the counterterrorism center's new special operations division, with the promise of hundreds of officers at his command, the power to requisition hundreds more and throw them into battle, and operational control of the armed Predator drone, which was being rushed toward readiness. Neither man ever had set foot in Afghanistan. But they were clear-eyed about the mission.

"I will give you whatever you want, or whatever we have," Black told Crumpton. "You focus on the enemy. You kill as many as you can."

Then Black called upon Jose Rodriguez, whom he'd known since they were classmates at the Farm in 1976. Rodriguez had been in limbo at headquarters, without an onward assignment, the specter of pending investigations by the Justice Department and the inspector general hanging over his head. "We'll find something for you to do," Pavitt had told him, somewhat unconvincingly. Black found something big. He didn't have time to manage the counterterrorism center; he was spending days on end at the White House and the Pentagon and abroad, flying around the world in a CIA Gulfstream jet to forge alliances with foreign intelligence services. Out of necessity, without much forethought, he ceded a great measure of control over the daily operations, explosive growth, and global sprawl of counterterrorism to Rodriguez, despite the record of an official reprimand for his poor judgment.

"I was no expert in counterterrorism," Rodriguez wrote. "I did not know enough about al Qaeda, just what little I had read in the press. It was not my specialty." Black gave him no guidance—"No clear job, no office, and no title"—and so "I created them for myself." He chose to call himself chief operating officer, effectively third in command of counterterrorism. On Black's authority, he began grabbing people from across the agency's divisions and disciplines, special-operations cadres from the Pentagon, eavesdroppers from the National Security Agency, and newly graduated trainees from the Farm. "We were very much flying by the seat of our pants," he recalled. Bereft of knowledge, gripped by urgency, he and his troops struggled to make sense of it all.

"We are going to make some mistakes," a top terrorism analyst warned

Tenet at the daily five o'clock conference in the director's suite. "We can't afford mistakes," Tenet said. "Mistakes will kill us."

Black gave dominion over the rest of the world's terrorist organizations to Enrique Prado. A martial man, a black belt, and a skilled knife-fighter, Prado regarded his mission as a sacred duty. His family had fled Castro's Cuba for Florida, and he had joined the Latin American division as a paramilitary officer in 1981, fighting in the jungles of Honduras with the contras. He had run operations against jihadists in the Philippines and narco-guerrillas in the Andes, used cash and coercion trying to recruit North Koreans, and, like Black, he had served as chief of station in Khartoum, a city at the edge of the civilized world. He had been among the first to lead the hunt for al Qaeda back in 1996, as deputy of the headquarters unit known as the bin Laden station. Now, at the pinnacle of his career, he had the power to pick his targets and the means by which to eliminate them.

Prado wanted to create "an intel collection program with teeth"—sharp teeth. He went to work forming a platoon of spies and paramilitary officers to subvert and destroy terrorists anywhere in the world. "We need to make book on two or three assholes from every terrorist group in the world," he told Tenet and Black, "and, in extremis, take them out, like we should have done with bin Laden." Taking out a terrorist could mean many things, from compromising and blackmailing up to kidnapping and killing. As Prado put it delicately: "If he happens to fall off a balcony, too bad." He was proposing to create an assassination squad, a force the CIA had never possessed.

A certain logic lay behind this. The 9/11 plot had been hatched by an al Qaeda cell in Hamburg, Germany. What if another terrorist cell with an imminent plot were uncovered in the heart of Europe? You couldn't send an armed Predator to London or Madrid. So why not assassinate them? He went to the White House with Tenet, where "we briefed the vice president and Rice, and we got the nod of approval," he said. Cheney was especially enthusiastic. Prado began to train his handpicked hit team. But many months passed before he won the seventh floor's approval to take action. His mission was stalled by "a lack of political will," Prado said. In the end, once again, Pavitt got cold feet. "I should have seen it coming,"

Prado reflected. "You know what he said? 'We need to gauge the political ramifications.'" A certain logic lay behind that too.

Black chose the principal author of The Plan, Gary Schroen, to blaze the trail into Afghanistan. A roughneck from the half-ruined Rust Belt town of East St. Louis, Illinois, Schroen was seven weeks away from his mandatory retirement at the age of sixty. He had joined the CIA in 1969, overseen the CIA's $700 million-a-year weapons pipeline to the Afghan holy warriors fighting the Soviet occupation from 1986 to 1989, and worked hand in hand with the Northern Alliance on the hunt for al Qaeda. His mission was to lead the CIA's eight-man teams gearing up to land in Afghanistan, lash them together with the Northern Alliance and American special forces, topple the Taliban, and kill Osama bin Laden. Black specifically told him: "I want bin Laden's head shipped back in a box filled with dry ice."

"The consequences of victory"

On September 26, Gary Schroen and his team landed in Afghanistan.* He served six weeks as the CIA's field marshal, working with the commanders of some eight thousand Northern Alliance fighters as they gathered intelligence on Taliban strongholds, laying the groundwork for strikes by American gunships, fighter-bombers, and missiles. He began the battle, but didn't finish it before he turned sixty and his time ran out. Crumpton selected his successor, Gary Berntsen, who had spent years working with the Northern Alliance and stalking al Qaeda and Hezbollah. He recalled Berntsen's reaction: "His jaw clenched. His thick neck bulged. His head thrust forward. He then barked in his Long Island accent: 'Thank you for the opportunity to serve under your command. And sir, we will destroy those motherfuckers.'"

The two Garys, as headquarters called them, bought the Northern Alli-

---

* On that same day, Rumsfeld wrote in his day planner that Bush had told him: "I want you to develop a plan to invade Iraq. Do it outside the normal channels."

ance warlords' loyalties with tens of millions in cash and tons of weapons. They kept them from one another's throats, and they skillfully led the CIA officers under their command. They organized the alliance into assaults on enemy strongholds and coordinated special-operations soldiers whose laser guidance would direct American air strikes aimed at killing thousands of Taliban, seizing their cities, and toppling them from power, once the Pentagon finally was roused into the fight. They did a masterly job, despite the fact that the White House and the Pentagon provided no strategy to guide them. Crumpton was the one who laid out a ten-part war plan for them on the eve of the first American bombing raids in Afghanistan on October 7. It included the targeted killings of Taliban and al Qaeda leaders—the first coordinated assassinations in the CIA's history—and preparations for the interrogation of prisoners. He wrote it in a controlled rage, burning for retribution.

The bombing was devastating once it began. "The morale of the Taliban just plummeted," Rumsfeld said. "The effect of being able to call in a precision strike and have it hit the Taliban leadership with laser-guided weapons, suddenly it was a whole new game. They got discouraged. They ran." But air power alone would not win the war. On November 7, as the CIA's officers fought their way across northern Afghanistan, Crumpton sat silently, his back to the wall in the Situation Room, as Bush listened to Cheney, Rumsfeld, Rice, and others arguing about how to wage the battle. They gave no thought of what might happen after the bombs stopped falling. "There was no mention of the consequences of victory," he reflected, "no thought of how to win the peace." Gen. Richard Myers, who became chairman of the Joint Chiefs of Staff on October 1, remembered: "The tasking going into Afghanistan is, 'We're going to go in, we're going to go after al Qaeda, and we're out.' . . . The president said, I remember specifically, 'We're not going to do nation-building.'"

The fate of the nation now lay in the hands of a rough-hewn CIA paramilitary officer and the princely Afghan under his protection.

Chapter Six

"WE WERE ALL MAKING IT UP AS WE WENT ALONG"

The CIA had been at the heart of almost every American attempt to overthrow foreign governments for more than fifty years, supporting uprisings, subverting rulers, stealing elections. But rarely had its officers conducted covert operations that catapulted the leader of a nation to power. In the cold war, the station chief in the Congo had installed the tyrant Gen. Joseph Mobutu, a coup in Iran had put the imperious Shah on the Peacock Throne, counterinsurgency in the Philippines kept the kleptocrat Ferdinand Marcos secure. These three had reigned for decades, backed by American intelligence, diplomacy, and weapons. The United States supported their brutal and corrupt regimes as bulwarks of anticommunism and American power in Africa and the Middle East and Asia. They brought stability, until they fell.

Hamid Karzai was America's man in Afghanistan and he ruled for almost thirteen years. He was not a dictator or a despot, but a tragic hero corrupted by power. Though the CIA's guns and money were not the only factors in his rise to the presidency and his resilience in his palace, they were the essential ones. Karzai owed his life and his political survival to the CIA, and in particular to a whip-smart, crazy-brave paramilitary officer who looked like a motorcycle outlaw. He was Greg Vogle, a star of the CIA's special activities division. Karzai came to call him "my best friend." Their fates were linked from the day they met.

Karzai was a Pashtun princeling, the forty-three-year-old elder of a small tribe of the Durranis, whose leaders had been kings of Afghanistan from 1747 to 1973. He was elegant and eloquent, and he spoke good English. Karzai was no warrior, but a diplomat and politician in the Afghan style, in which allegiances can change with the prevailing winds. He was willing to work with anyone, but he had a hard time choosing sides. He had raised money for the CIA-backed Afghan resistance from the safety of Pakistan in the 1980s, then joined the post-Soviet government in 1992, serving as deputy foreign minister until Mohammed Fahim, the intelligence chief of the Northern Alliance, arrested and jailed him on a charge of espionage.* As Karzai told the story, he escaped prison when an errant rocket fired in the murderous power struggles wrecking Kabul knocked a hole in the prison that held him. After fleeing for his life, he had joined the Taliban government not long after it seized Afghanistan in 1996, but two years later he resigned and returned to exile in Pakistan. And then, after the Taliban murdered his father in 1999, he had thrown in with the one force that could provide him with the firepower and the cash to take revenge. He became a regular visitor to the American embassy and the CIA station in Islamabad, offering what little intelligence on al Qaeda he could glean from his tribal network, and urging the Americans to take up arms against the Taliban; the Americans in turn asked him to use his high-level contacts among the Taliban to convince them to hand over bin Laden to the United States.

Early in the summer of 2001, he had met Greg Vogle, newly arrived to run the CIA base in Peshawar, the chaotic Pashtun city that lay thirty miles from the Khyber Pass, the ancient gateway of Afghanistan. Vogle was a country boy from Alabama who had joined the Marines in 1981 after graduating as a cadet from the Citadel, the military college in South Carolina founded in 1842. Over the next five years, he learned

---

* Fahim became Karzai's first defense minister and then his vice president after the fall of the Taliban government in December 2001. The following year, the CIA suspected he was plotting Karzai's assassination. Dismissed in 2004, he returned as vice president after Karzai's fraudulent reelection in 2009. Such were the vicissitudes of political life in Afghanistan.

the black arts of marine reconnaissance—running long-range clandestine patrols, calling in close air support, providing security for VIPs—all skills he would put to good use in Afghanistan. His first taste of counterterrorism had come in October 1983, when his company flew into Beirut after the newborn group Hezbollah blew up a barracks housing American troops sent by President Reagan on a peacekeeping mission in Lebanon. In the deadliest day for American forces since the 1968 Tet Offensive turned the tide in Vietnam, 220 Marines, eighteen sailors, and three soldiers had died. Three years after that deployment, Vogle joined the CIA's special activities division, the most secretive branch of the government of the United States, and he had hunted terrorists in Saudi Arabia and jihadists in Bosnia during the 1990s. He unwound with a brutal exercise regimen that would try the soul of a hardened triathlete.

"On the surface, they made a very odd pair," reflected Robert Grenier, the CIA's station chief in Pakistan, who had brought them together. "As smooth and polished as Hamid was, Greg was blunt and profane. A tough, wiry paramilitary specialist with an outrageous Fu Manchu moustache and an even more outrageously ironic sense of humor, he did his best to hide an incisive intelligence beneath multiple layers of self-deprecation. Also hidden beneath that flinty exterior, though, was a rather thin skin, and a sensitive soul." Grenier, the elegant Ivy Leaguer, and Vogle, the rough-and-tumble leatherneck, had bonded while bending elbows at the Khyber Club, one of the only places in Peshawar where you could get a drink despite Pakistan's prohibition on alcohol. The station chief's admiration, already high, soared when Vogle learned a modicum of Pashtu, a tongue so difficult that the nineteenth-century British officers who tried and failed to occupy Afghanistan called it "the language that would be spoken in hell."

As Grenier and his officers conceived a strategy to use Karzai in their mission to overthrow the Taliban, "our thinking was very much influenced by Greg," he recounted. "But the truth was we were all making it up as we went along."

"How in the world could this be happening?"

Grenier fought a constant rearguard battle with headquarters. When the officers of the clandestine service fought together, they were a powerful force; when they fought one another, they were like mafiosi gone to the mattresses. Hank Crumpton, who was spending many hours briefing Bush in the White House, kept micromanaging the station chief, questioning his judgment, twisting and turning him with a seven-thousand-mile screwdriver. Grenier found Crumpton supercilious and cocksure and unversed in the intricacies of Afghan politics.

Crumpton and the counterterrorism center had put all their money on the Northern Alliance. President Bush and General Franks had followed their lead. They didn't understand that before the rise of the Taliban in 1996, the Tajiks and Uzbeks of the Northern Alliance had fought a bloody four-year battle for Kabul with the leaders of the Pashtuns, who had ruled in the capital for centuries. If the Northern Alliance seized Kabul now, it would be an American-led power grab by Afghanistan's lesser tribes, and an incitement to a brutal power struggle.* Grenier and Vogle fought night and day to make the seventh floor see that Hamid Karzai was the future of Afghanistan.

By the morning of November 13, American bombs and missiles were killing thousands of Taliban foot soldiers, their trajectories guided by the CIA's officers and their special-forces comrades. The agency's warriors, led by Berntsen, and the Alliance's warlords, led by Mohammed Fahim, once Karzai's jailer, had seized key cities in the north and were speeding south toward Kabul. The White House had no plan for what would happen

---

* Pashtuns traditionally ruled in Kabul because they represented close to half of Afghanistan's population, Tajiks a quarter, and Uzbeks a tenth. In Pakistan, home to millions of Pashtuns, General Musharraf and the ISI saw the Northern Alliance—backed by his nation's bitter enemy, India, and India's allies, Iran and Russia—as barbarians at the gates of the Khyber Pass. So did hundreds of high-ranking Pashtun officers who led Pakistan's military in the tribal areas bordering Afghanistan.

when they got there or who might rule in Kabul after it fell. Bush led the National Security Council in a dangerously unfocused meeting that day. He insisted that an international peacekeeping effort backed by the United Nations would secure the country until the rival factions created a government. But no such force existed. The newly appointed United Nations special representative for Afghanistan, Lahkdar Brahimi, had sought guidance from the State Department's director for policy planning, Richard Haass. What did America want to happen after the Taliban fell?

"I can assure you," Haass replied, "we have no idea what to do or what needs to be done."

No strategy was in place. No one was responsible for making it. "There was just no process to do post-war mission planning," the deputy national security adviser Stephen Hadley later lamented. Bush was eight days away from ordering Rumsfeld to draw up war plans for Iraq, and they both wanted American forces out of Afghanistan as soon as possible. A month earlier, they had agreed in writing that America would not "commit to any post-Taliban military involvement since the U.S. will be heavily engaged in the anti-terrorism effort worldwide." The president said only one task was left for America in Afghanistan: obliterating al Qaeda and its weapons of mass destruction. (Bin Laden had just proclaimed: "If America used chemical or nuclear weapons against us, then we may retort with chemical and nuclear weapons. We have the weapons as a deterrent." He didn't. He was bluffing.) Rumsfeld pointed out that the highest priority for American forces was sealing the border with Pakistan so bin Laden could not escape. Bush retorted: "If he moves elsewhere, we're just going to get him there."

The president's preoccupation with Iraq, his fixation on chimerical weapons of mass destruction, and his failure to order a military dragnet for the man he said he wanted dead or alive would haunt American spies and soldiers for many years. So would Cheney's response to a call from General Musharraf. The Pakistani leader said a contingent of his ISI officers assigned to monitor the Taliban was trapped in the city of Kunduz, two hundred miles north of Kabul, surrounded by Northern Alliance forces. He wanted to evacuate them, in the name of his nation's dignity. He got the go-ahead. A grievous mistake: the ISI secretly flew several hundred

Taliban and al Qaeda fighters out of the battle and into Pakistan, where they disappeared.

"The most irresponsible and foolish act of the war," Berntsen said years later. "The height of stupidity. . . . I thought to myself how in the world could this be happening? How could they have been so snookered as to do this?"

"Our greatest weapon in the war"

On the evening of November 13, Kabul fell, to the surprise and consternation of the Situation Room and the seventh floor. Bush had repeatedly assured General Musharraf that, in return for his agreement to support the war, the Northern Alliance would not be allowed to capture the capital. "When we went into the city, Pavitt was panicked," Berntsen recounted. "The White House assumed that the Northern Alliance would stop five miles outside the city. None of us believed that." Now the last stronghold of the Taliban lay in and around Kandahar, three hundred miles southwest of Kabul. Between the two cities lay a no-man's-land where death could come at the hands of al Qaeda's Arab, Chechen, and Pakistani fighters as well as the Taliban's soldiers. The war would not be won until the city was taken.

That same night, in a video conference with headquarters, Grenier convinced Tenet to put his faith in Hamid Karzai, the only Pashtun leader whom the CIA could trust to take Kandahar and to rule in Kabul when the battle was over. Vogle and a team of veteran CIA officers who knew Afghanistan assembled a plan of attack at a safe house in Pakistan, basing their strategy on Karzai's understanding of tribal politics in and around Kandahar, where he was born and raised. They knew not to bring American air power into the battle until Karzai had assembled a battalion of his Afghan tribesmen to hold a swath of territory and secure a landing zone for an assault.

Karzai aimed to gather hundreds of his people and seize the town of Tarin Kowt, one hundred miles north of the city, the birthplace and the beating heart of the Taliban movement; Mullah Muhammad Omar and most of the other Taliban leaders came from that area, and their extended families still lived there. Karzai said the taking of Tarin Kowt would deliver a stunning psychological blow and turn thousands of Pashtun villagers to Karzai's side. Armed with that understanding, Vogle and Capt. Jason Amerine made plans to seize the surrounding mountain passes, lay siege to the town, and draw the Taliban into battle, where they would be slaughtered by overwhelming air power. Then they would head south, and as they did, Karzai predicted, every village along the way would strike the Taliban's white flag and raise the red, green, and black banner of Afghanistan. Then Kandahar would fall, the Taliban government would surrender, and the war would be won.

The following evening, on a moonless night marking the start of Ramadan, Team Echo went to war—six CIA officers commanded by Vogle, a twelve-man Green Beret A-team led by Captain Amerine, and a three-man Joint Special Operations Command unit. On the road to Kandahar, Karzai was running two campaigns in sync with the CIA, one military, one political. He was in constant contact with his international allies, his enemies in the Taliban, his rivals in the Northern Alliance, and, crucially, prominent American and British journalists. "The satellite telephone was his greatest weapon," Captain Amerine said. "Arguably, it was our greatest weapon in the war." Millions of people following the news from Afghanistan had been hearing about him, sometimes in his own firsthand reports. He had been featured in stories broadcast by the BBC in both English and Pashtu; he had long known and trusted the BBC's Lyse Doucet, later in life the network's chief international correspondent, who had reported from Afghanistan since the last days of the Soviet occupation in 1988.* A profile in the *New York Times* noted that if Karzai survived, "he could emerge as the hero

---

* Doucet was the most important independent international voice from Afghanistan, and not only for Western audiences. At the time of the American invasion, the BBC's shortwave news broadcasts in Pashtu, Dari, and English had been the most vital source of independent information for millions of Afghans for twenty years. Nearly every village of any significant size had at least one shortwave radio, and every Afghan tribal elder knew by mid-November 2001 that the Taliban had all but lost the war. They shifted their loyalties accordingly.

of the resistance to the Taliban and as the ruler of considerable swaths of liberated Afghan territory. If he does not, he will be remembered as a brave man who took incredible risks for his tribe and country."

For the moment it looked like he might live. As Karzai had predicted, the taking of Tarin Kowt panicked the Taliban's leaders. They sent a thousand men in a hundred trucks to counterattack. At dawn on November 17, from a mountain ridge overlooking the rutted roads, the Americans directed flights of Air Force and Navy jets to destroy the convoy, killing hundreds of fighters. Over the next week, despite constant danger, Karzai and Team Echo slowly advanced southward.

On November 20, Ambassador James Dobbins was in a CIA turboprop headed for the newly liberated Bagram air base north of Kabul. Dobbins was the State Department's crisis manager, handling conflicts in Somalia, Haiti, Bosnia, and Kosovo, always in coordination with the CIA. He was the first American diplomat to set foot in Afghanistan since 1989, and he was planning an international conference on the nation's future. Dobbins asked his seatmate, the Northern Alliance's foreign minister, for some advice. "Abdullah Abdullah was the first Afghan to suggest Hamid Karzai should become president of Afghanistan," he remembered. Abdullah's remarkable concession was the result of some serious arm-twisting from the other two passengers on the plane: Gary Berntsen and Philip Mudd, a senior CIA terrorism analyst. Dobbins and Mudd worked side by side, and they had discovered during a whirlwind five-nation tour that Karzai already had won over diplomats and spies in Pakistan, Uzbekistan, Tajikistan, Turkey, and Iran, all of whom seemed to be well aware he had the CIA's backing. "Everywhere we went, people talked about the same man," Mudd remembered. "The consensus emerged so clearly that there seemed to be no other path."

"The U.S. didn't want peace. We wanted the war on terror."

On November 25, Greg Vogle set up the first of three secure calls between Karzai and Dobbins. Karzai told the ambassador that he was negotiating via sat phone with senior Taliban officials in Kandahar, offering his protection if they surrendered peacefully within forty-eight hours. If they put down their weapons and handed over al Qaeda fighters under their protection, their leaders could receive amnesty from the Americans, and the war would be over. "Karzai was clearly making things up as he went along, as we all were," Grenier recounted. "There was no one close to him, the redoubtable Greg notwithstanding, to whom he could turn for a definitive readout on American policy, as indeed no clear policy existed." The strategic void at the White House was being filled by a CIA case officer and his Afghan agent in a mud hut, out on a combat mission in enemy territory.

That same day, the present author, then a foreign correspondent for the *New York Times*, sent the following dispatch from Jalalabad, Afghanistan:

> Osama bin Laden was seen this week at a large and well-fortified encampment 35 miles southwest of this city, a minister of the self-proclaimed government here said tonight.
>
> The official, Hazrat Ali, the law and order minister for the Eastern Shura, which claims dominion over three major provinces in eastern Afghanistan, said trusted informants had told him that Mr. bin Laden was spotted near Tora Bora, a village where two valleys meet in deep mountains in Nangarhar Province.
>
> "We have some people who told us that three or four days ago, Osama bin Laden was in Tora Bora," Mr. Ali said. "I trust them like my mother or father."
>
> "He is moving at night on horseback," he said, citing his informants. "At night he sleeps in caves."

I thought I had a scoop. What I didn't know was that Hazrat Ali was Gary Berntsen's recruited agent, that Berntsen already had relayed this electrifying news to General Franks, and that Franks did not believe a word of it.

"On the day that someone first told me, 'Tora Bora is the deal, Franks. He's in Tora Bora'—literally on that same day I had an intelligence report that bin Laden had been seen yesterday at a recreational lake northwest of Kandahar and that bin Laden had been positively identified someplace in the ungoverned western areas of Pakistan," Franks said in an oral history interview. "If he was in Tora Bora, obviously we missed him."

"To this day you're not convinced that he was even there?" his interviewer asked. "Absolutely not," Franks said.

Bin Laden was definitely there. In the general's defense, he was distracted. He had just begun to contemplate the intricacies of an assault on the eleven-thousand-foot heights of Tora Bora when, on November 27, he had to turn his attention fourteen hundred miles westward to Baghdad: Rumsfeld ordered him to create a plan to go to war against Iraq.

As Karzai haggled with the Taliban, Dobbins and Lahkdar Brahimi convened the Bonn Conference on the future of Afghanistan at the regal Hotel Petersberg, which had served as the seat of the Allied High Commission that shaped the fate of Germany after World War Two. The UN's Brahimi, an Algerian diplomat, oversaw the Afghan delegations, who were housed in a separate wing in rooms bugged by the CIA. They met by night, after breaking the Ramadan fast. The Northern Alliance's leaders knew Karzai was the CIA's chosen one. They saw that the Bonn agreement would concentrate immense power in the new Afghan leader, and in exchange for backing him, they demanded control of all the key ministries: defense, national security, foreign affairs, and more. Over the next week, Dobbins consolidated support for Karzai among the Afghan, Pakistani, Indian, Iranian, Russian, and Turkish delegations. And after one last all-night session, on December 5, the next ruler of Afghanistan was proclaimed in a castle four thousand miles from Kabul.

At nine o'clock that morning, Karzai, Vogle, Amerine, and their men were drinking tea in a shambles of a government outpost twenty miles north of Kandahar. Karzai, awaiting a delegation led by the Taliban's defense minister to discuss terms of surrender, sat talking with tribal chieftains and local leaders as Vogle listened in. Amerine had fresh intelligence that Taliban fighters were preparing to attack from a hideout over the next ridgeline. His air support officer made a careless and catastrophic error when he sent the coordinates to a B-52H Stratofortress bomber ready to attack. He had called in an air strike on his own position.

A two-thousand-pound smart bomb came screaming across the sky and struck Team Echo. "The doors and windows flew out," Karzai recounted six months later to a reporter. "I got injured on my face and my head, and I saw this very good fellow, a very nice man, Greg, jump out of his place and just throw himself on me. It was very remarkable, very remarkable. And the tribal chiefs followed; they all covered me from all around." Dirt and rocks and flesh and bones rained down. Explosions shook the earth, and the stunned and shellshocked Afghans thought that the town was under attack by bin Laden's Arab fighters. But it wasn't al Qaeda; it was Team Echo's arsenal of rocket-propelled grenades cooking off. Dazed and bleeding, Karzai saw scores of dead and wounded outside the compound. He slowly realized that "it was not a rocket attack on our room or an RPG attack on our room. It was something else." It was the worst friendly-fire attack by American forces in the decade since the 1991 Gulf War against Iraq. Three American special-forces officers were killed and twenty soldiers and spies were wounded. At least fifty Afghans died.

Fifteen minutes after the bomb exploded, Karzai's satellite phone rang. The BBC's Lyse Doucet was calling from Bonn. "She said, 'You have been selected to lead the government.'" Karzai recounted. "Nine twenty, the call about Bonn. Ten o'clock, ten fifteen, the Taliban came to surrender. One hour." Karzai accepted their surrender thirty minutes after American helicopters flew the dead and wounded away. Seventeen days later, he was sworn in as the new leader of Afghanistan.

Karzai offered a peace deal to the Taliban. It could have spared years of bloodshed had it held. "There would be a complete amnesty," said Barnett Rubin, among America's most respected Afghan experts and the newly appointed senior adviser to the UN special representative for Afghanistan. "There was no power-sharing with the Taliban." But Rumsfeld vetoed the decision shortly after Karzai struck it.

"The U.S. didn't want peace," Rubin said. "We wanted the war on terror."

"Karzai had nothing"

On January 4, 2002, the CIA's Mike Morell delivered his last briefing to President Bush. It was his unhappy duty to report that bin Laden had escaped from Tora Bora, likely into the wilderness of Pakistan's tribal lands. "The president shot the messenger," Morell recounted. "How the hell did you lose him? How could he possibly have eluded you?" Bush shouted in fury. The honest answer was that Bush, Rumsfeld, and Franks had allowed bin Laden to live to fight another day. The Taliban melted back into the mountains and waited. The CIA pursued the leaders and foot soldiers of al Qaeda for the next twenty years. As the American occupation of Afghanistan began, so did the CIA's longest war since its officers first arrived in South Vietnam in 1954. No one could have imagined that one day American soldiers and spies would flee Kabul as it fell, just as their forerunners had taken flight from Saigon long ago.

At the start of the new year, Ryan Crocker flew in to Kabul as the interim American ambassador. The embassy's chief political officer was Michael Metrinko, who had been one of the fifty-two Americans held hostage in Tehran for 444 days during the 1979 Iranian revolution. The station chief was the counterterrorism center's Rich Blee. Hamid Karzai began his thirteen-year reign in the presidential palace, where in time he became an exemplar of the axiom that power corrupts.

Karzai was "a man with a mission impossible," Ambassador Crocker said. "The devastation in Afghanistan at the end of '01, beginning of '02, was almost absolute. Just driving in from Bagram to Kabul, not a building standing, bridges out, we had to ford a river, whole city blocks of Kabul were gone. It looked like pictures of Berlin in 1945. This was not because of us. It wasn't because of the Taliban. It was a result of the Afghan civil war in the 1990s" between the Northern Alliance and their Pushtun rivals. The city had had no electricity or oil or gas for years. People burned wood and manure to stay warm, and a thick miasma of smoke, dust, and grit hung in the cold gray air. After a quarter-century of war and conflict and a five-year drought, Afghanistan was the most godforsaken country on earth.

"Karzai had nothing," Ambassador Crocker said, "no real authority and nothing to work with, no military, no police, no civil service, no functioning society." But what he did have from the start were bags of cash delivered to his presidential offices by the CIA—many tens of millions of dollars over the years. He used it to grease the wheels of his government, and to cement his power and authority. "We called it 'ghost money,'" said Khalil Roman, Karzai's deputy chief of staff from 2002 until 2005. "It came in secret, and it left in secret." Much of it went to purchase the loyalties of Afghanistan's warlords and power brokers, some of whom had been recipients of the CIA's largesse since the Soviet occupation. They all knew Karzai was the one person with "the ability to represent Afghanistan to the foreigners who give the money that keeps Afghanistan running," said Mike Metrinko, the rare American official who knew the language, the history, and the culture of the country. "He is in power because he can do that. He's the ultimate fixer." Among the ten thousand things Karzai had to do was choose ministers and provincial governors. "He would ask me, 'Who should be governor of Ghazni?' Like I had a clue," Ambassador Crocker said. "And he made some really bad choices." Karzai gave Afghanistan's most powerful warlords almost all the top positions in the central government and twenty of thirty-two provincial governorships, and he made sure they received their cut of the ghost money.

The CIA had dominion in Kabul. "There wasn't a great deal of high-level interest anywhere in Washington as to what happened next in Afghanistan," Ambassador Crocker said. "The CIA . . . carried an awful lot of the effort there, including support for Karzai." Vogle all but took up residence in the presidential palace. He was as influential as the ambassador, sometimes more so. Rich Blee took over the Ariana Hotel, about a quarter mile from the barely functional American embassy building and far better equipped; the new CIA station soon featured an invitation-only watering hole called the Tali-Bar. Scores of newly minted officers arrived in Kabul on their first tour that winter. Some had been rushed through training and handed a carbine without much schooling in the arts of espionage and intelligence gathering. "They were very good about passing out big bags of money, new SUVs, and wonderful little satellite radios to people,"

Metrinko said. "But as far as any real knowledge of what was happening, where they were, what they were trying to get done, the past, the present, the future.... Zero."

The CIA's executive director, Buzzy Krongard, flew out to survey the situation. His strongest impression was that hiring Afghans as security guards to protect the CIA station was a terrible idea. Returning to headquarters, he quickly struck a $5 million deal with an immensely wealthy former Navy SEAL named Erik Prince, the first of some $600 million in classified contracts the CIA awarded to his private army, Blackwater, over the next five years. First scores and then hundreds of Prince's men, many of them recently recruited military veterans, arrived in Afghanistan, and they formed cadres not only to secure the CIA station but to join in the hunt for terrorists. The CIA's paramilitary officers and the contractors walked around Kabul "in this sort of weird military getup with lots of leather and extra holsters and bandoleros, and places to put guns and knives, and bandanas, and neck scarves, weird shirts," Metrinko said. "They looked like they had come out of a Rambo movie." They were the face of America to the Afghans.

"They were quite prepared to let the country go to hell"

Afghanistan was a CIA country now, like Iran in the 1970s, when the former director of central intelligence, Richard Helms, had served as the American ambassador. The CIA's money created a modicum of security for the new government, and that sense of stability was essential for the CIA to carry out its mission of hunting al Qaeda. The money was equally essential to Karzai's presidency. His ministers and governors depended on it. Few of them were invested in the future of Afghanistan.

"These were people interested in their own power, lining their own pockets, and they were quite prepared to let the country go to hell if it meant that they could become richer," Metrinko said. "The CIA would work with any criminal and every corrupt whore they could find." Chief among them was Ahmed Wali Karzai, a valued CIA asset like his brother

Hamid. A gangster who spoke perfect English with a Chicago accent, he became the strongman of Kandahar province, building an empire by gaining control over security forces, commerce, and contracting. He extracted huge fees from drug traffickers to protect their immense poppy fields and their opium and heroin shipments. He owned the real estate surrounding the rapidly expanding American military headquarters in Kandahar—thanks in large part to a United States government loan quickly arranged in 2004 by the newly arrived American ambassador, Zalmay Khalilzad—and he collected rent as the landlord of the adjacent CIA base, the former compound of Mullah Omar. The next ambassador, Ronald Neumann, sent an urgently worded cable in 2005 headlined "Confronting Afghanistan's Corruption Crisis." He cited Karzai's penchant for tolerating political thievery and pointed out his brother's involvement in the heroin trade. He concluded that "President Karzai . . . needs to remove and possibly prosecute some of his government's most notoriously corrupt officials." He singled out four provincial governors, three of whom were on the CIA's payroll, along with Ahmed Wali Karzai.

All this fell on deaf ears in the Oval Office. President Bush chose to ignore "the cronyism, the closed character, the impunity" enveloping the presidential palace after Karzai took power, said Stephen Hadley, his national security adviser in his second term. He was blind to the fact that the failures of the American-backed government would become the biggest recruiting tool for the Taliban. With his eyes now firmly fixed on Baghdad, Bush wanted as little as possible to do with Kabul—not peacekeeping, not security, and certainly not nation-building. Soon enough, "the situation in Afghanistan goes south," Hadley said. "And the problem is . . . we started it."

The problem was corruption, and at its core was the way the CIA did business in Afghanistan, with stacks of shrink-wrapped hundred-dollar bills. "Given the interest that defined the mission, concerns about corruption did not trump those of covert action," Barnett Rubin said. And when the American occupation of Afghanistan started to crumble in the coming years, the Taliban were not the cause. "The ultimate point of failure for our efforts wasn't an insurgency," Ambassador Crocker said. "It was the weight of endemic corruption."

Greg Vogle received the CIA's highest honor, the Distinguished Intelligence Cross, for saving Hamid Karzai's life.* The citation recognizes "extraordinary heroism involving the acceptance of existing dangers with conspicuous fortitude and exemplary courage." He would serve two tours as chief of station in Kabul. His salutation to each and every newly arriving officer was always the same: *Your mission is to kill al Qaeda. Any questions?* His devotion to that mission drove him all the way up the ranks. Vogle became the chief of the CIA's clandestine service four months after Karzai fell from power.

He had left Afghanistan for the first time in the spring of 2002, thinking that America was winning the war on terror. But the order of battle was changing, and not for the better. As Roger Pardo-Maurer, a deputy assistant secretary of defense deployed to Kandahar as a reserve Special Forces commander, reported: "The situation we're in now is that al Qaeda have licked their wounds and are regrouping in the southeast, with the connivance of a few disgruntled junior warlords and the double-dealing Pakistanis. The shooting match is still very much on. Along the border provinces you can't kick a stone over without Bad Guys swarming out like ants and snakes and scorpions. It's amazing how many are foreigners."

---

* As of this writing, only thirty-nine people have received the Distinguished Intelligence Cross in the history of the CIA. Many of these awards were posthumous and almost all remain classified.

Chapter Seven

UNPRECEDENTED TROUBLE

Al Qaeda had struck again on March 11, 2002, six months to the day after the fall of the World Trade Center. The target was Africa's oldest synagogue, on the Tunisian island of Djerba. A truck bomb exploded outside the ancient house of worship, killing fourteen German tourists, five Tunisians, and two French citizens. The linchpin for the attack was "Ibrahim the German," a psychopath named Christian Ganczarski. He took orders from Khalid Sheikh Mohammed, 9/11's mastermind. An al Qaeda video recorded in Afghanistan fourteen months before showed him sitting in the first row among hundreds of armed fighters, listening to bin Laden speak.

The CIA found a way to remove him from the battlefield: a subtle espionage sting, run by Margaret Henoch, the chief of operations for the European division and one of the few high-ranking women in the clandestine service. In liaison with French intelligence, she lured Ibrahim the German onto an Air France flight from Riyadh bound for Bonn, and a CIA officer seized him when the flight stopped in Paris. He has spent the rest of his life in a French prison and at this writing remains under indictment in the United States for conspiring to kill Americans.

That was one way to render a terrorist unto justice, but it was the old-fashioned way.

Four years earlier, George Tenet had struck a deal with Omar Suleiman, the Egyptian intelligence chief, to imprison Islamic militants abducted by the CIA. Fourteen of these presidentially authorized "extraordinary renditions" had taken place before 9/11, including the capture of al Qaeda's branch chief in Albania, hunted down by CIA officers in the Balkans in 1998. The White House, the State Department, and the CIA knew very well that Suleiman tortured his prisoners for information. That wasn't an issue. The goal was taking bad guys off the street. If they talked, so much the better. But before 9/11, interrogations were not the CIA's concern.

After 9/11, among the first men the CIA had sent to a Cairo prison was Ibn al-Sheikh al-Libi, whose name was in a set of some forty terrorism dossiers that the Libyan intelligence chief Musa Kusa had handed over to the CIA in October 2001. Al-Libi had tried to overthrow Muhammar Qaddafi and fled to Afghanistan to fight the Soviets with the CIA's weapons. He then became an ally to bin Laden, and he was captured fleeing the battlefield in November. Six weeks later, the CIA rendered al-Libi to Cairo. Under torture, answering questions posed to Suleiman by CIA analysts, the prisoner said Iraqis had trained al Qaeda in chemical and biological warfare. "It turned out he lied about it," said Kristin Wood, then chief of the Iraq branch at the Office of Terrorism Analysis. Once returned to the CIA's custody, he immediately recanted, insisting he had invented his answers to stop the pain. Yet his lies were what Tenet had reported to the president in the morning briefings, and they were highlights of the speeches Bush and Cheney gave as they contemplated war against Saddam Hussein.

Tenet felt a need "to run immediately to the White House" with breaking news, said Tyler Drumheller, chief of the European division of the clandestine service from 2001 to 2005, "and once you tell the President something, especially President Bush, it's very hard to go back and say 'you know, we hadn't quite checked it out enough.'" The CIA was "wrong and misguided to send people to places like Egypt, thinking you're going to get a great truth," he said. "No military commander would ever go into combat based on this, because they know they can't verify it."*

---

* After the invasion of Iraq, the CIA withdrew al-Libi's torture-driven testimony. Then it disappeared him into its network of black sites for three years before sending him back to a prison cell in Libya, where he died in 2009.

"What are we going to do with these guys?"

By the spring of 2002, the CIA began to realize that extraordinary rendition was not the answer. Some two thousand Arab, Afghan, Pakistani, Chechen, Turkmen, and Chinese Uigur fighters had been captured in Afghanistan, along with al Qaeda suspects arrested by the ISI in Pakistan. The new military prison at Guantanamo Bay in Cuba had received three hundred inmates. Many hundreds more, including a handful labeled as "high-value detainees," had been shipped to Camp Rhino, the Marine base southwest outside Kandahar commanded by Brig. Gen. James Mattis, later President Trump's secretary of defense. Mattis wanted nothing to do with them. They were the CIA's problem.

"What are we going to do with these guys when we get them?'" Buzzy Krongard had wondered aloud. "We've never run a prison. We don't have the languages. We don't have the interrogators."

On the night of March 27, 2002, the prisoner dilemma became a matter of great urgency. Pakistani officers had shot, grievously wounded, and captured Zayn al-Abidin Muhammad Husayn, aka Abu Zubayda. CIA case officers at the Islamabad station, guided by the analysts at headquarters, had traced him to a safe house in the city of Faisalabad. Tenet immediately told Bush that Abu Zubayda was al Qaeda's third-in-command, deeply involved in its biggest attacks, and Bush promptly told the world. "He's one of the top operatives plotting and planning death and destruction on the United States," he proclaimed at a Republican fundraiser. Zubayda was nothing of the sort. He was not a sworn member of al Qaeda, and if bin Laden had meted out military ranks, he would not have been a general, nor a lieutenant, but a sergeant major. But he was nonetheless an important figure: a logistician and a gatekeeper who knew whom to call and when to call them. He knew the names and aliases of many members of al Qaeda's hierarchy. He knew who had come and gone from its training camps in Afghanistan. He was the first prisoner of consequence in the CIA's control.

"We needed to take responsibility for high-level terrorists ourselves,"

Jose Rodriguez said. The CIA still knew very little about al Qaeda. It was still warning the White House of an imminent attack on the United States. It thought each prisoner could be a ticking time bomb. It hoped that interrogating them might stop a catastrophic plot in the nick of time.

Rodriguez set out to create a plan for CIA officers to imprison and interrogate al Qaeda captives. He called upon the Office of Technical Service for help.* OTS was where the clandestine service went for spy gear—sophisticated bugs, surveillance cameras, covert communications systems, fake passports, undetectable disguises. The office also had a team of psychologists with a vault of institutional knowledge on how to break people without killing them. Their cold war predecessors had run the mind-control experiments known by the code name MKUltra. Among other sins, they had drugged unsuspecting human subjects—for example, dosing federal prisoners with LSD every day for eleven weeks on end—all in the name of a new way to interrogate the enemy.

When the CIA director Allen Dulles had created the office in 1951, at the height of the Korean War, he urgently wanted to know if a truth serum existed. His officers already were grilling a handful of suspected Soviet double agents in secret prisons on American military bases in Germany and Panama, precursors to Guantanamo. His initiative led directly to MKUltra, its pharmacopeia of magic pills, and its two-decade search for ways to loosen tongues, which ended in 1973. Over the years, the CIA's psychologists wrote case studies of American prisoners brainwashed by Chinese soldiers during the Korean War and German captives sealed in standing coffins by Soviet officers during World War Two. They created a class for spies and U-2 pilots called "Enduring Enemy Detention,"

---

* The origins of the office lay in the Research and Development Branch of the Office of Strategic Services, the CIA's predecessor, which devised "dirty tricks and deadly weapons in a subversive war against Hitler and Emperor Hirohito," as a CIA historian had written on the occasion of OTS's fiftieth-anniversary celebration at headquarters in August 2001. Over the years, OTS had invented remarkable spy gadgetry, perfected the art of invisible writing, and investigated paranormal phenomena. Its finest hour in the twentieth century was the remarkable forensic work that eventually helped convict a Libyan perpetrator of the 1988 bombing of Pan Am 103 over Lockerbie, Scotland, which had killed 270 people, among them the CIA's deputy station chief in Beirut.

eschewing physical abuse of its trainees but depriving them of sleep and locking them in cramped spaces; the course continued until it was eliminated, like so much else at the CIA, after the end of the cold war.

The military had a tougher regimen called SERE—Survival, Evasion, Resistance, Escape—developed in part by scientific studies secretly funded through MKUltra. It taught people how to resist brutal interrogation by brutally interrogating them. SERE's instructors incorporated the experiences of POWs held by the German, Japanese, North Korean, Chinese, and North Vietnamese military between 1942 and 1972. Its methods included prolonged isolation, forced nudity, sleep deprivation, extreme heat and cold, and confinement in cramped boxes. Each military service adapted the training based on its veterans' experiences. The Air Force SERE program at the turn of the twenty-first century was largely based on the testimony of downed American airmen tortured by the North Vietnamese—who, significantly, had sought to extract false confessions for propaganda, not to gain intelligence for battle. The waterboard, a technique dating to the Spanish Inquisition, was used only in the Navy's SERE resistance course. Deputy secretary of state Rich Armitage remembered being strapped to it before he was deployed to Vietnam in 1968. Was it torture? "Absolutely," he said forty years later. "No question."

The psychologists at the Office of Technical Service had helped write the CIA's first guidelines on interrogation during the Vietnam War. In 1983, those rules were revised in the Human Resource Exploitation Manual. CIA officers and a contingent of Green Berets used the manual to advise their allies in Central America. It recommended stripping prisoners naked and using sleep deprivation, prolonged isolation, and raw fear to destroy their will to resist.

The following year, the CIA reprimanded a clandestine service officer named Charlie Wise for misconduct in training the contras how to torture their captives. Their human rights abuses were so severe that the CIA shut down the training program in 1985. After newspaper reporters exposed the abuses, John Helgerson, Tenet's inspector general, then serving as the CIA's chief of congressional affairs, had told the Senate intelligence committee that "inhumane physical or psychological techniques are counter-productive because they do not produce intelligence and will probably result in false answers." Richard Stolz, then the chief of the clandestine service, had testified that "physical abuse or other degrading treatment was rejected not only because it is wrong, but because it has historically proven to be ineffective."

This history was not uppermost in the minds of the CIA's leaders in 2002. When Jose Rodriguez went looking for a chief interrogator, he chose Charlie Wise, the only serving officer he could find with hands-on experience breaking prisoners. And when he chose techniques to break them, he relied on two longtime Air Force SERE psychologists, James Mitchell and Bruce Jessen, who had been hired as counterterrorism consultants to the Office of Technical Service. In the first week of April 2002, he presented a dozen of their proposals to George Tenet and John Rizzo. The list incorporated waterboarding and the rest of the harshest SERE methods. Rodriguez added some enhancements—stuffing the prisoner in a tiny coffin with a large insect, burying him alive, keeping him awake for eleven days on end—and he wanted to use them all on Abu Zubayda immediately.

"The gloves are off"

These techniques struck Rizzo as "sadistic and appalling." The waterboard, in particular, shocked his conscience. Rizzo had been legal counsel to the clandestine service for twenty-seven years, long enough to have "a gut instinct about what could get the Agency—and its people—into trouble down the road. And this had huge, unprecedented trouble written all over it." Rizzo took a long walk around the CIA's campus, strolling amid the blooming flowers and smoking a cigar, "trying to process what I just heard and to figure out what the hell to do next." If and when this program leaked, CIA officers could be indicted, forever tarnished as torturers. But as he weighed these consequences, he also considered "the ultimate nightmare scenario: Another attack happens, and Zubayda gleefully tells his CIA handlers he knew all about it and boasts that we never got him to tell us about it in time." Americans would die and the CIA would be destroyed for failing to save them. As he recalled: "I fully realized that either way, someday, somehow, we would be screwed."

Filled with foreboding, Rizzo sat down with Tenet and Rodriguez in the director's office, looking out the wide windows at the greening trees sloping gently down to the Potomac. He confessed that as their lawyer, he couldn't say whether these techniques were torture or not. But if they were, he said, they could not be justified, even if intended to prevent the next attack. A long and uncomfortable silence ensued. Rodriguez broke it.

"Our people won't do anything that involves torture," he vowed. But that wasn't good enough for Rizzo, who had some experience regarding Rodriguez and his respect for rules. Mindful of the laws on torture, which carried a twenty-year prison sentence, Rizzo said that Tenet needed a ruling from the White House and the Justice Department. The CIA would wait for nearly four months, until August, to hear back from the lawyers, each day fearing the clock was ticking toward a cataclysm. Rodriguez wasn't willing to wait. He wanted the president's imprimatur now. Torture could not be un-American if Bush blessed it, and if he blessed it, it could not be torture.

"I approved the use of the interrogation techniques," including the waterboard, after Tenet briefed him, Bush wrote in his memoir. Rodriguez had the president's backing a fortnight after Abu Zubayda was taken prisoner. But by then he had told the Americans almost everything he knew.

At a jungle base near Chiang Mai, Thailand, an FBI agent, Ali Soufan, a Shia Muslim fluent in Arabic and deeply versed in the workings of al Qaeda, had won the captive's cooperation. Abu Zubayda had identified Khalid Sheikh Mohammed as the mastermind of 9/11 and revealed his code name—"Mukhtar," the brain, a revelation that would lead to his capture eleven months later. This was a huge breakthrough: the CIA had known he was a dangerous terrorist, but not that he was bin Laden's right hand. Abu Zubayda had named a host of other al Qaeda operatives in the Middle East and Europe, freely described his work in smuggling money and people on bin Laden's behalf, and described plots that had been conceived before the attacks.

In retrospect, some of these ideas seemed delusional. One was a plan to destroy the Brooklyn Bridge by secretly cutting its cables with blowtorches and plunging it into the East River. "We were watching *Godzilla* one day," the prisoner told Soufan. "We saw what happened when Godzilla stepped onto the bridge, and we imagined the devastation we could cause." Another was the brainchild of a Brooklyn-born gangbanger and al Qaeda wannabe named Jose Padilla, who proposed to build a "dirty bomb" and detonate it in the United States. The plan, it turned out, was to obtain a shovelful of uranium, put it in a pail, tie a rope to the handle, and swing it around to separate the isotopes.*

Tenet was both stunned by these confessions and furious that his people had let the FBI get to the prisoner first. His anger spurred Rodriguez onward. He convened a meeting of forty people in the counterterrorism center's main conference room and said the CIA had "credible intelligence that a nuclear attack . . . on one or more U.S. city was imminent"—which made the harshest interrogations imperative. Rodriguez intended to send Mitchell to Thailand along with two other officers—Marty Martin, until recently station chief in Jordan, and Albert El Gamil, his deputy, who had recently been reprimanded for misconduct—and two top bin Laden station analysts, Jennifer Matthews and Alfreda Bikowsky, whose devotion to the mission was suffused with a religious intensity. All five fervently supported the harshest techniques. "The gloves are off," Rodriguez told them. Mitchell and Matthews immediately flew to Chiang Mai on a

---

* A mentally unstable Pakistani living in Ohio—a double agent working as an FBI informant while reporting to al Qaeda—had researched the likelihood of bringing down the Brooklyn Bridge but deemed the plot unlikely to succeed. He was convicted of terrorism charges in 2003. The "dirty bomber" got his plans from a satirical website post that began: "Making and owning an H-bomb is the kind of challenge real Americans seek." In a memo titled "Don't Put All Your Uranium in One Bucket," the chief of the Counterterrorism Center's Chemical, Biological, Radiological and Nuclear Group later noted: "Padilla admitted that the only reason he came up with a so-called 'dirty bomb' was that he wanted to get out of Afghanistan and figured that if he came up with something spectacular, they'd finance him." Padilla was arrested with great fanfare after flying to Chicago in May 2002. Attorney General John Ashcroft called him part of "an unfolding terrorist plot" to unleash a nuclear device. He was held as an enemy combatant and convicted on entirely unrelated charges in 2007. Without fanfare, the CIA later took Padilla off the list of its successes in the war on terror.

Gulfstream jet and arrived at the improvised black site, which the CIA had secured hastily after it had grabbed Abu Zubayda, seized his diaries and hard drives, treated his near-fatal gunshot wounds in Pakistan, and flown him twenty-four hundred miles away.

The psychologists delivered a message from the analysts. The prisoner was withholding critical threat information. The president had told Tenet to find out what he knew about the second wave of attacks. Time to get tough. The CIA interrogators stripped him naked, chained him hand and foot to the floor, and blasted death metal music in his ears. They kept him awake for seventy-six hours until the medics at the site intervened. The interrogators told Soufan these techniques had been approved at the highest levels. But they didn't work: Abu Zubayda stopped talking when the abuse started.

Then they built a coffin to confine him. Ali Soufan took one look at the casket and asked a CIA officer to let him check it out. "I lay down inside and he closed it," Soufan wrote. "It was pitch black in there. It was just possible to move my head and arms a little. After a few seconds I asked him to open the cover . . . and I quickly climbed out. 'This is insane,' I told him."

"There were no illusions"

At this crucial juncture, the CIA dismissed its commander in the war on terror. Cofer Black had become the most influential leader in the CIA short of the director. He reported directly to the president and Tenet, bypassing Pavitt in the chain of command. The counterterrorism center had become more powerful than the clandestine service. Black controlled more money and more people than Pavitt. His budget was approaching $3 billion, roughly equal to the CIA's spending in 1998. A quarter of the people on the agency's payroll now belonged to him. His lieutenants stalked the corridors of the CIA, buttonholing promising officers and analysts and telling them they now were working for Black. He had gone to Pavitt directly and demanded the services of hundreds more officers assigned to Europe and Latin America. He strongly believed that he would replace Pavitt as chief of the clandestine service. One afternoon, Ric Prado was waiting to see Pavitt in his seventh-floor suite. Black stormed out, steaming. Pavitt was red-faced. "Your boss just told me how to run my directorate!" he snarled at Prado.

The power struggle between them had been raging for months. In May, their confrontation exploded. Pavitt told Black he was out. He offered him a new job running the CIA's National Resources division, which debriefed international businessmen and recruited foreign nationals traveling abroad. The division had long been a stepchild, by reputation a rest home for burnouts. The backhanded slap resounded through the ranks of counterterrorism officers loyal to Black. Some felt it was as if Eisenhower had removed Gen. George Patton during the Battle of the Bulge and made him the Postmaster General. Black declined the offer. He soon left the CIA, served two years as the State Department's counterterrorism coordinator, and then became the highly paid vice chairman at Blackwater. He never had the chance to keep his promise to the president to kill bin Laden and destroy al Qaeda.

The new chief of counterterrorism at the Central Intelligence Agency was Jose Rodriguez. His supporters, and there were many, loved him for his fierce devotion to the mission, his unswerving dedication to the officers below him, and his cool disregard for bureaucrats and regulations. His detractors thought his career should have ended in the Latin American division, that he had been promoted far beyond his capabilities, and that his appointment betrayed a remarkable lack of judgment on the part of his superiors.

In June, Rodriguez chose Michael D'Andrea to succeed him as chief of operations at the counterterrorism center. D'Andrea was a second-generation CIA officer who worked one hundred hours a week, his face pale for want of sunlight, his mind burning with an eternal flame of zealous intensity. He was both a vegetarian and a chain-smoker. He had converted from Catholicism to Shia Islam when he married his wife, a wealthy businesswoman from Mauritius, an island nation off the coast of east Africa. He had been chief in Dar es Salaam, Tanzania, when bin Laden tried to blow up the American embassy and the CIA station there in August 1998, and he had been among the leaders of the global manhunt for al Qaeda ever since. D'Andrea would later succeed Rodriguez, serving as chief of counterterrorism for a decade. He became by any measure the most lethal officer in the history of the CIA. He immediately took charge of the CIA's drone strikes; the first one outside Afghanistan came in November 2002, killing six suspected members of al Qaeda, including an American citizen, in Yemen. These were the deadliest secret missions the CIA had undertaken since Vietnam. Few thought they'd stay secret forever.

"We all knew Americans would find out at some point about everything we were up to," Phil Mudd, who served as Rodriguez's deputy, said a decade later. "There were no illusions."

Rodriguez next turned to Jim Cotsana, chief of the Operational Readiness Group at the Office of Technical Service. One among the CIA's brotherhood of ex-Marines, Cotsana was a calm and collected Vietnam veteran who had been pursuing a PhD in philosophy, with a focus on epistemology, the theory of how we know what we know—a good background for an intelligence officer—when a CIA recruiter had cold-called him in 1980. He had worked around the world on espionage and counterintelligence operations targeting Russians, Iranians, and terrorists. He commanded all the bases providing tech support for CIA stations and operations around the world. He was also the man to see for extraordinary renditions. He ran them worldwide, with a core group of ten officers. Rodriguez named Cotsana as his chief of special missions. (At the CIA, as in the military, the word *special* denotes operations of extraordinary secrecy and sensitivity.) The biggest of his missions was creating and running a new rendition, detention, and interrogation group to handle the al Qaeda prisoners thought to have crucial intelligence about the next attack.

"We really had no experience with interrogating or housing high-value detainees," Cotsana said. "We were pretty much starting from scratch." He needed to create a network of black sites. He had to find interrogators and linguists, debriefers and doctors, security and support officers, and analysts who knew what they were talking about when it came to al Qaeda. "The shortage of personnel able and willing to participate in the program was a huge challenge," the CIA noted in a 2013 review of the program. "Language-capable officers were in particularly short supply." Nonetheless, Cotsana's operation soon grew to twelve hundred officers, bigger than the entire clandestine service before 9/11, and it spent well over a quarter of a billion dollars before it began to unravel. Over the years, the CIA's black sites would hold 119 prisoners. Fourteen "high-value detainees" were subjected to the harshest interrogations. "Only three detainees were ever waterboarded," Rodriguez said. "Three killers that had American blood on their hands were waterboarded by us. Give me a break."*

Looking back on what the CIA had learned from the prisoners twenty-one summers later, Cotsana said: "We figured out how they were moving money. The money laundering, we had some really sharp people with banking experience to figure that out. We were able to disrupt that. We figured out how they were getting passports, how they were getting people from point A to point B. We were able to disrupt that. And we figured out that there was a courier"—a man named Abu Ahmad al-Kuwaiti, whom bin Laden used to communicate with the outside world. His number had been found in Abu Zubayda's phone book when he was captured. Prisoners held by two of the CIA's Arab allies had identified the courier in the summer of 2002. Under questioning by the FBI, Abu Zubayda had given up an al Qaeda operative named Hassan Ghul, who called al-Kuwaiti bin Laden's most important aide. But that breakthrough was achieved before the CIA began to use the waterboard and the rest of its brutal methods.

Could the rendition, detention, and interrogation group have carried out its mission without torture? "Highly unlikely," Cotsana said. "We had to protect this country. And what we did, what we thought was best, was to get as much actionable intelligence as we could, because we all thought a second attack was coming. If people thought we did something illegal, something immoral, we'll live with it. I'll live with it."

---

* "Waterboarding as practiced by the Chinese, the Nazis, the Spanish Inquisition is torture and has always been torture. But the waterboarding that was applied [by the CIA] was different. It's different because it doesn't use as much water. They don't drown anybody," Rodriguez argued in a 2015 television documentary, *The Spymasters*.

Cotsana's search for real estate to serve as secret prisons was a mad scramble. The counterterrorism center considered and rejected some far-flung sites, including an island in the world's largest reservoir, Lake Kariba, on the border between Zambia and Zimbabwe. Money was no object. Nor was protocol. Station chiefs sought help from interior ministers and spymasters around the world, sometimes without telling the American ambassador. In Poland, Lithuania, and Romania, they were met with open arms by the leaders of ex-communist intelligence services trained and supported by the CIA after the fall of the Berlin Wall. The CIA and the Poles had been intimate partners for twenty years; the agency's crucial covert support to the Solidarity movement had helped its leaders strike a heavy blow against the Soviet empire.

Tenet enlisted the president of the United States to seal the deal with Poland. On July 17, Bush buttonholed its president, Aleksander Kwaśniewski, before a state dinner in his honor. "We were absolutely alone in the Oval Office," Kwaśniewski recalled. "Bush took me aside and whispered. He told me it was important." The Warsaw station delivered $30 million in two cardboard boxes to the Polish intelligence service for the free use of a two-story villa in Stare Keijkuty, a training base hidden deep in Poland's northern woods, not far from the Russian exclave of Kaliningrad. It dated back to World War Two, when it had served as an outpost for Nazi intelligence officers.

Cotsana's task of finding experienced interrogators was even harder. Beyond Charlie Wise, the bench was exceedingly thin. The mild-mannered deputy director John McLaughlin had interrogated prisoners as an intelligence officer in Vietnam, but you couldn't very well send him to Poland to strap a man to a waterboard. In addition to his other responsibilities, Cotsana's special missions included creating a network of new mini-stations overseas where counterterrorism officers and analysts could work with their foreign partners, forming a team charged with seizing and exploiting documents and hard drives taken from al Qaeda captives, and overseeing another branch devoted to conducting surveillance operations against terrorists worldwide—bugging their hideouts, wiretapping their phones, photographing them with long-range lenses. The group was nicknamed Snapshots.

Rodriguez was immediately impressed with the deputy chief of Snapshots. Her name was Gina Haspel, and she became the CIA's director in 2018. Like D'Andrea, she had made her name pursuing al Qaeda operatives immediately after the 1998 embassy bombings in Africa. Haspel had played a key role in breaking up a bin Laden ring planning an attack on the American embassy in Baku, Azerbaijan, while she served as station chief in September 1998. At least three jihadists were rendered to a Cairo prison after Haspel's operation; one had served as a right-hand man to Ayman al-Zawahri, the second-in-command of al Qaeda. She had spent the following two years as deputy chief of station in Turkey, where her targets included Russian spies. After 9/11, when Russian operations were no longer a priority, Haspel became a key officer in the counterterrorism mission at headquarters.

Rodriguez would make her his chief of staff. But first he told her to go to the black site in Thailand, code-named Cat's Eye, and prepare to lead the brutal interrogations the president had authorized. For on August 1, Tenet and Rodriguez had received the license they had long sought.

"The waterboard was not the silver bullet"

Torture was made an institution of the government of the United States on the word of a thirty-two-year-old lawyer named John Yoo at the Justice Department's Office of Legal Counsel, and the concurrence of Attorney General John Ashcroft. Yoo, who had clerked for Justice Clarence Thomas, had an expansive view of the president's powers: Bush could abrogate laws and constitutional constraints, order the military to massacre a village, or authorize cruel and inhuman interrogation. It wasn't torture as long as the prisoners weren't killed or severely injured in mind or body. And if it wasn't torture, it was what the CIA said it was, a refined set of "enhanced interrogation techniques." The CIA had never told the

White House or the Justice Department how it intended to apply those techniques—for example, that its interrogators would chain a detainee from the ceiling and deprive him of sleep for a week or more. Bush wrote in his memoir that Tenet had assured him that "all interrogations would be performed by experienced intelligence professionals who had undergone extensive training." If so, that was an empty promise.

At 6:15 p.m. on August 4, Mitchell and Jessen wheeled the waterboard into Abu Zubayda's interrogation cell in Thailand. The two men had never used the device. They had no experience of interrogating foreigners and no background in intelligence operations. They had been hired by the counterterrorism center as consultants, not inquisitors. The seventh floor did not see the difference between the rigidly controlled SERE resistance training and what was about to happen in the black site. Abu Zubadya didn't understand what was about to happen either. The prisoner, who had spent the past seven weeks in solitary confinement, thought the waterboard was a hospital gurney for treating his open gunshot wound.

The interrogators pulled the straps down tight over the wound, tilted him back, and began pouring water down his throat and up his nose for forty seconds at a time. He choked, gagged, vomited, howled, and writhed. The waterboarding went on until 8:54 p.m. Then they locked him in a box the size of a small dog kennel, 21 inches by 30 inches by 30 inches, and kept him there all night. They repeated the waterboarding for four days, demanding that he tell them about the second wave of attacks. "I have nothing more," the prisoner said. "I give you everything." Then they waterboarded him again and again and again. "It seems the collective opinion that we should not go much further," the interrogators told headquarters on August 8. Two days later they reported that it was highly unlikely that their prisoner knew anything about future plots. The interrogators kept going at the urging of the counterterrorism center, their officers at the black site, and the bin Laden analysts, though the Bangkok chief of station, Mike Winograd, observed that those calling the shots were "not knowledgeable of the target," and the CIA officers in Thailand insisted that he hadn't told them anything he hadn't already told the FBI. Mitchell and Jessen "pushed back hard and threatened to quit," Mitchell remembered. "We were told, quote, 'He's turning you. You are not turning him.' The officers we were dealing with, midlevel CTC officials, really pissed us off by saying, 'You've lost your spines.' They insisted that if we didn't keep waterboarding Abu Zubaydah and another attack happened in the United States, it would be 'your fault.'"

On August 15, Abu Zubayda nearly died on the waterboard, and in days to come, trying to stop the torture, he told his tormentors whatever they wanted to hear, inventing fantastical future plots. These false confessions pleased headquarters. They allowed the interrogators to ease up on the waterboard after the eighty-fourth session.

All of this was videotaped. The tapes were there, in part, to make sure that the CIA's interrogators followed the rules. But they didn't. They used the waterboard far more often and in a completely different way than the CIA had told the Justice Department in seeking its approval. Instead of placing a damp cloth over the prisoner's mouth and pouring pints of water on it, they poured quarts directly down the prisoner's windpipe over and over again. The intensity and frequency of the waterboarding raised immediate and grave concerns among the Agency's medical staff at the black site. Some CIA officers who witnessed the interrogations firsthand were sickened by their ferocity and "profoundly affected . . . some to the point of tears" by the orders to go on.* So was at least one of their superiors at headquarters. The chief of the CIA's Office of Medical Services, Terry DeMay, later called the interrogations "little more than an amateurish experiment, with no reason at the outset to believe it would either be safe or effective." He concluded that "there was no evidence that the waterboard produced time-perishable information which otherwise would be unobtainable."

Cotsana confirmed this. "The waterboard was not the silver bullet," he said. "Sleep deprivation was."

---

* The difference between "knowing the facts of what happened at those sites and seeing, firsthand, how the prisoners were treated" could be devastating, the deputy counterterrorism chief Phil Mudd recounted. "One senior Agency officer visiting a site wept on seeing a shackled, hooded prisoner. This was not an unheard-of response." Philip Mudd, *Black Site: The CIA in the Post 9/11 World* (New York: Liveright, 2019), p. 157.

Less than a year after 9/11, the search for intelligence had led the United States to adopt the methods of its worst enemies. The waterboard would become an indelible symbol of secret government gone haywire.

"There's a new sheriff in town"

On November 12, chief interrogator Charlie Wise began running his first eight trainees through a one-week course. The day after it ended, an undisciplined first-tour CIA officer, Matt Zirbel, let a prisoner named Gul Rehman freeze to death while chained naked from the waist down to the concrete floor of a fetid hellhole codenamed the Salt Pit, at Bagram Air Base north of Kabul. Before Zirbel was sent to Afghanistan, his superiors had questioned the assignment and his character, citing his "lack of honesty, judgment, and maturity." He was living proof that the CIA had no business running prisons.

He strung men up in chains from the ceiling for up to seventeen days at the Salt Pit, and presided over mock executions and beatings by black-clad masked guards, whose headlamps were the only illumination in the dark site. Wise himself participated in the cruelty by putting a prisoner in an ice bath, which was decidedly not an approved technique. He later told the CIA's inspector general that the Salt Pit "is good for interrogations because it is the closest thing he has seen to a dungeon."

The prison was overseen, if that was the word, by two successive Kabul station chiefs who paid little attention to it, as they were focused on hunting al Qaeda fugitives. Though the Afghan cells held nearly half of the CIA's 119 detainees over the course of two years, they were outside Cotsana's jurisdiction. Headquarters took no direct responsibility for them, and Tenet later claimed to be only dimly aware of their existence. A few days after Gul Rehman was buried in an unmarked grave, soldiers of the Army's 519th Military Intelligence Battalion beat two Afghan detainees to death in a prison adjacent to the Salt Pit. Their commanding officer later received a promotion and took the battalion to Iraq, where it ran interrogations at Abu Ghraib. The tortures at Bagram were transported directly to Baghdad.

Mitchell and Jessen had arrived at the Salt Pit the week before Gul Rehman died. Jessen had seen the prisoner abused and he had filed a report to headquarters and the station chief about the "unsupervised brutality" he had witnessed. The two had gone to Afghanistan to pick up a new high-value detainee, Abd al-Rahim al-Nashiri, a Saudi who had led al Qaeda's deadly 2000 attack on the USS *Cole* in Yemen and, under verbal interrogation in Dubai after his arrest, had confessed to drawing up aborted plots to attack an American warship in that city's immense harbor, Port Rashid, and to sink civilian oil tankers in the Strait of Hormuz.

They took al-Nashiri to the black site in Thailand on November 14. The new chief of base was Gina Haspel.

"Day one of the aggressive interrogation . . . began at 0415 hours" on November 15, Haspel reported to headquarters. "Interrogators told subject . . . they wanted information to stop ongoing operations against the United States. Subject was warned not to lie, and if he lied, he would suffer the consequences, and his life would become infinitely worse. . . . They wanted to know who, what, when, where, and how ongoing operations would take place, and would stop at nothing to get it."

When the prisoner simply repeated his earlier confessions, Mitchell and Jessen, along with the guards, pummeled him, threw him to the floor, ripped off his clothes, shaved his head, and locked him in the coffin box for twelve hours. More violence, sleep deprivation, and shackling followed, to no avail. "We began switching to noncoercive social influence techniques," Mitchell recounted, "at which point al-Nashiri started to open up." He revealed plans to attack the diplomatic quarter in Riyadh, which al Qaeda would carry out the following year, killing fifty-six people and wounding 282 after the Saudis disregarded the CIA's warnings. But when the prisoner said that was all he had, the bin Laden analysts asked Rodriguez for permission to roll out the waterboard. Permission granted. The prisoner was subjected to three simulated drownings, to no effect. Mitchell reported that al-Nashiri was cooperative, truthful, not withholding important threat information. Nonsense, the bin Laden analysts insisted: "It is inconceivable to us that al-Nashiri cannot provide us concrete leads. . . . When we are able to capture other terrorists based on his leads and to thwart future plots based on his reporting, we will have much more confidence that he is, indeed, genuinely cooperative on some level."

At the end of November, Rodriguez sent an urgent message to Haspel. The *New York Times* was asking questions about the black site. She had ninety-six hours to shut it down and erase the evidence of its existence. The CIA flew Mitchell and the prisoners to Poland, where the second black site, secured with an assist from the president of the United States, was ready to receive them. Charlie Wise was waiting there on December 5. The first thing the chief interrogator said to Mitchell was: "There's a new sheriff in town. I'm calling the shots now." He announced that he was applying the techniques he had used on his captives in Central America.

"There were rules," Cotsana said. "The first thing Charlie did was to go out and break them." The mission was more important.

Wise and his newly minted acolytes used a medieval technique called the strappado, binding al-Nashiri's elbows behind his back with a leather strap until they touched, then chaining his arms high above his head, nearly dislocating his shoulders. They bent the prisoner backward with his shoulder blades on the floor and a broom handle behind the crook of his knees, nearly dislocating them as well. They ripped off his clothes, soaked him with freezing water, and used a stiff-bristled brush to scour his scrotum. The counterterrorism center sent the former Amman station officer Albert El Gamil to handle the interrogation while Wise took a Christmas holiday. El Gamil, never trained as an interrogator, spent the last three days of 2002 with al-Nashiri. He bound his wrists, chained him to the ceiling, blindfolded him, and held a cocked gun and a whirring power drill to his head in a mock execution.

By the start of the new year, the CIA's inspector general had been alerted to the death at the Salt Pit and the abuses in Poland. Helgerson began to take a deep look at the program; in time, it would lead to a criminal investigation of Jose Rodriguez. Cotsana took a first step to bring things under control: henceforth, each black site would be run by a senior intelligence officer. After Mitchell blew the whistle on Wise, the chief interrogator was recalled to headquarters and handed his walking papers. He died of a heart attack three days later, at the age of fifty-three. After his death, Mitchell and Jessen formed a corporate consultancy to oversee the interrogation program; the CIA paid their company $81 million over the course of five years.

Once the inspector general began his work, Tenet was newly alert to the potential for a disastrous exposure of the CIA's deepest secret. Determined to defend and expand the program, Tenet issued formal guidelines on "enhanced interrogation techniques" hewing to the rules for the first time, nearly six months after the waterboarding began, on January 28, 2003.

That same day, Tenet faced a matter of life and death. The president had ordered Colin Powell to make the case for going to war against Saddam Hussein. Powell wanted Tenet to help him make it. He was coming to CIA headquarters to review the evidence that Saddam possessed weapons of mass destruction. He needed Tenet to make sure the indictment was ironclad before America went to war. The charge was a crushing burden to bear.

On that night, Tenet skipped President Bush's State of the Union speech and went to sleep.

Chapter Eight

WHAT YOU DO WHEN YOU DO NOT KNOW

I was exhausted from fifteen months of nonstop work and worry since the tragedy of 9/11," Tenet wrote in his memoir. The day before the State of the Union, he had been handed a copy of Bush's speech in the Situation Room. His job was to review it line by line and ensure the veracity of its accusations against Saddam Hussein. "I remember going back to headquarters and giving the draft to one of my special assistants, unread," he recalled. "I gave it no further thought."

The vetting had fallen to Alan Foley, the chief of WINPAC, the CIA's Weapons Intelligence, Non-Proliferation, and Arms Control Center. Foley presided over "a culture of enforced consensus" at WINPAC, in the words of an authoritative presidential commission; he had told his senior analysts a few weeks before the State of the Union: "If the president wants to go to war, our job is to find the intelligence to allow him to do so." And as the director later discovered to his great dismay, Foley had focused solely on making sure the speech did not reveal the CIA's sources and methods. "In other words," Tenet wrote, "as long as the language didn't give away any secrets about how the intelligence was collected, they didn't worry about whether we believed the assessments were accurate. That was a terrible mistake." *Mistakes will kill us*, he had said.

Tenet had known for at least six months that the president wanted to go to war and needed the intelligence to justify it. In July, he had so informed the British spy chief Sir Richard Dearlove, who had told Prime

Minister Tony Blair that the invasion of Iraq "was now seen as inevitable. Bush wanted to remove Saddam, through military action, justified by the conjunction of terrorism and WMD. But the intelligence and facts were being fixed around the policy."

"Where did this piece of garbage come from?"

At the State of the Union, Bush stood before Congress and millions of Americans, delivering dreadful warnings about Iraq's weapons of mass destruction, its networks of mobile germ-warfare labs, its uranium-smuggling rings, its stockpiles of lethal toxins, and its links to al Qaeda's terrorists. Some of these alarms of a looming Armageddon had come from Tenet and his analysts, some from Cheney and his acolytes. "Before September the eleventh, many in the world believed that Saddam Hussein could be contained," Bush said. "But imagine those nineteen hijackers with other weapons and other plans, this time armed by Saddam Hussein. It would take just one vial, one canister, one crate slipped into this country to bring a day of horror like none we have ever known."

Bush had vowed to "rid the world of evil-doers," and he had called that cause a crusade. He wanted to project American power in the name of Western civilization and Christendom, and thus transform the Middle East. He was ready to wage America's first preemptive war since 1898, when President William McKinley made the nation an imperial power by seizing the Philippines, Puerto Rico, and Guam from the Spanish empire, annexing Hawaii, occupying Cuba, and establishing a permanent naval base at Guantanamo Bay. But a preemptive attack launched without international support and the approval of the United Nations would be seen as a war of aggression. The United Nations Security Council could be convinced it would be a just war by seeing indisputable intelligence that Iraq posed a clear and present danger to the world. Bush needed to sell the war. And he knew his word alone would not suffice. He needed a salesman.

"I need you to go make the case to the world," Bush told Colin Powell after the State of the Union. "You have the most credibility of the whole team. Frankly, the only credibility." Powell said, "Yes, sir."

The secretary of state was the most popular American general since Eisenhower, a man who could have been president had he summoned the will to run. He had warned Bush in August that if he hit Iraq, it would break "like a crystal glass. It's going to shatter. There will be no government. There will be civil disorder." An American invasion of Iraq could destabilize the Middle East, he said, and an American occupation would inflame the Muslim world. But he now stifled his grave doubts. He went to see Condi Rice, and asked her for the speech the president wanted him to deliver before the Security Council. His copy came bound with a cover depicting a mushroom cloud. He handed it to his chief aide, Col. Lawrence Wilkerson, who read it and asked his boss: "Where did this piece of garbage come from?"

It had come from the dark side of the White House. Cheney had constructed his own shadow National Security Council. "We had two. One that belonged to Condi Rice and the other one belonged to the Vice President," Powell said. "He inserted himself totally into the information flow as if he were the chief of staff, and into the foreign policy flow. That caused a great deal of confusion. The President tolerated this." As Armitage put it: "There was never any policy process" in Bush's first term. "There never was one from the start. Bush didn't want one."

Cheney's subterfuges created momentous presidential decisions and documents that appeared without discussion or debate, no visible fingerprints upon them. They shaped the foreign policy of the United States.*

---

* "John Rizzo calls me up and says: 'What the hell are you all doing down there?'" remembered John Bellinger III, Rice's legal counsel at the NSC. "I said, 'John, what are you talking about?' He said, 'Military Order No. 1.' I said, 'What Military Order No. 1?' He said, 'It's just come across the screens.' Sure enough, the President has just signed Military Order No. 1"—the indefinite detention of terrorist suspects by military tribunals at Guantanamo, promulgated in November 2001. Bellinger went to Alberto Gonzales, the president's lawyer and future attorney general, and asked: "How can this have been done when the national security advisor and the director of central intelligence don't even know anything about it?" Gonzales mumbled something about the need for speed in a time of crisis. "I frankly think this is one of the top two or three greatest national security legal mistakes of the Bush administration." Bellinger said.

The speech Powell had received was an indictment charging Saddam with maintaining secret ties to al Qaeda and possessing an illegal arsenal of lethal weapons posing an imminent danger to the United States. Cheney had told Bush that it was intended as a legal brief, written as if "you're defending an ax murderer," as Powell remembered. "So Scooter Libby, at the Vice President's suggestion, the President's decision, he was given the mission to write it." Libby was a lawyer who served as Cheney's chief of staff and national security adviser. He was so devoted to the cause of war that he vengefully outed an undercover CIA officer whose husband, a former ambassador, had undermined the argument that Saddam was building a nuclear bomb. Then he lied to a federal grand jury about what he'd done.

The speech was based largely on unsubstantiated and unverifiable reports ginned up by Doug Feith, a neocon ideologue who served as the undersecretary of defense for policy. Feith wielded power at the White House because he sometimes served as Rumsfeld's trusted interlocutor with the president. He ran a bucket shop at the Pentagon called the Office of Special Plans, which he saw as the intellectual engine room for the ship of state. Its vague name masked its true purpose: producing policy papers based on propaganda masquerading as intelligence. His leading source on Iraq was Ahmed Chalabi, the scoundrel who had secured a sinecure in the Pentagon and promises of great power once Saddam fell. Feith was a bright man but a blinkered fool. He saw himself as a philosopher king; the sharp-tongued General Franks described him as either "the fucking stupidest guy on the face of the earth" or "the stupidest motherfucker in the government," depending on the slightly divergent memories of two CIA officers who heard the general's rant at Central Command headquarters in Tampa. Feith was smart enough to turn his opinions into presidential pronouncements and, on occasion, into policy. He contended with great passion that the secular Saddam and the religious fanatic bin Laden were coconspirators—after all, hadn't Hitler and Stalin made a secret pact in 1939?—and he raged at the CIA when it doubted his word.

"We will suffer from it for the next forty years." (John Bellinger oral history, Miller Center, University of Virginia.)

"Much of the fight about prewar intelligence had to do with that issue," Feith said. "The CIA's work was not professional, it wasn't properly skeptical, it was overly ideological," a case of the pot calling the kettle black if ever there were one. Feith had stated his views on Iraq succinctly in September: "War is not optional," he wrote to Tenet. "At stake is the survival of the United States."

Powell's address to the UN was one week away. His own small but superb State Department intelligence bureau called the speech he had been handed a grab-bag of rumors, hearsay, and innuendo, unfit for public consumption. But he kept his composure. "I'm still not panicking," he recounted. "Because I do have the NIE."

A National Intelligence Estimate was by tradition the most authoritative and deeply considered distillation of what American intelligence analysts thought about the great issues of the day, drawing from the work of the CIA's spies, the National Security Agency's electronic eavesdropping, the Pentagon's photoreconnaissance satellites, and the State Department's best minds. This NIE was different.

Senate Democrats had demanded it in a written request, which had arrived, by fax, at CIA headquarters on a Sunday afternoon, September 8, 2002. A watch officer wearing a hijab had handed it to Mark Lowenthal, the assistant director of central intelligence for analysis and production. "It said: We want a technical update of the 1998 estimate on Iraq WMD. You have three weeks," he recalled. (The earlier work dated from the withdrawal of United Nations weapons inspectors and undercover CIA officers from Iraq.) The demand for a rush job was absurd; estimates typically took a minimum of four to six months to prepare. Even then, the best of them still had an element of guesswork. Some of the most consequential estimates in the history of the CIA—on the power of the Soviet nuclear arsenal and the strength of the army of North Vietnam—hadn't settled the issues but set off furious arguments that went on for years. Sherman Kent, a founding father of the CIA's Office of National Estimates and the namesake of the training school for analysts it had established in May 2000, once observed that "estimating is what you do when you do not know." And what the CIA didn't know about Iraq's weapons far exceeded what it did.

The intelligence estimate, entitled "Iraq's Continuing Programs of Weapons of Mass Destruction," cobbled together the work of WINPAC, fragments of intelligence from the agency's Iraq files, frightening paragraphs from the President's Daily Brief, and alarming CIA reports already sent to the White House, such as "Iraq: Expanding WMD Capabilities Pose Growing Threat." It came to four conclusions and stated them with "high confidence" in its first pages: Saddam had huge stockpiles of chemical and biological weapons, and he was building both nuclear bombs and ballistic missiles. "We were wrong on the chemical weapons judgment, we were wrong on the biological weapons judgment, and we were wrong on the nuclear weapons judgment," Andy Makridis, a nuclear-weapons expert who delivered the President's Daily Brief to Bush from 2002 to 2004, said two decades later. "Saddam no longer had these programs. He had stopped them. He had disarmed."

How did the CIA get it wrong? First and foremost, the analysts had next to no intelligence to work with. "There was a 10,000-piece puzzle to be solved to create the whole big picture," said Kristin Wood, chief of the Iraq branch in the Office of Terrorism Analysis. "We had a hundred pieces, but they weren't all necessarily for the same puzzle." The CIA had been ordered by Congress to overthrow Saddam through covert action in 1998, not to conduct espionage against his regime, and it had collected precious little intelligence since then. Iraqi scientists who had worked on Saddam's weapons programs in the 1980s, when Iraq was at war with Iran, were almost never allowed to leave the country. It was exceedingly difficult for American spies to contact them in the decade after the American embassy and the CIA station in Baghdad closed on the eve of the first Gulf War in 1991. And as the Iraq Operations Group chief Luis Rueda put it: "There were few incentives we could offer these people that compared to Saddam's disincentive of having your entire family tortured and killed."

Crucially, the CIA didn't understand until years later that Saddam wanted to deceive the Americans and his archenemy, the Iranians, into thinking his deadly arsenal from the 1980s still existed. He had hoped that imaginary weapons could deter a real attack. And, as Makridis explained twenty years later, "he thought the CIA was so good that it would see through that secret and know that the weapons were gone; that once this happened, the U.S. would lift the sanctions against Iraq that were strangling his economy; and that once sanctions were lifted, Saddam would be free to re-arm. We know this because Saddam told us this during his captivity." The CIA's "high confidence" was a mirage. "The analysts did not really think about that statement before making it," Mike Morell said years later. "It was a reflection of their gut view."

"WE HAVE TO SAY IRAQ HAS WMD"

For decades, the CIA's analysts had believed, not without reason, that they were the smartest people in the government of the United States, running the world's greatest think tank. But at the turn of the twenty-first century, after the post–cold war brain drain, the average analyst had only a few years' experience and a few months' training, if that. As Mark Lowenthal observed, they needed to have time to think, and "to spend some time on thinking about *how* you think. Very few analysts come by it naturally and almost none are taught to do it. Crisis-driven as they are, they don't have a lot of time to step back and say: 'Have I missed something? Is this the right way of thinking?'" And now, after 9/11, there was far less time to think. The best of the analysts had deep expertise and first-rate minds. The worst were arrogant and ambitious and amateurish; they didn't know how much they didn't know. Alan Foley, WINPAC's leader, was convinced that clandestine service officers were too ignorant to grasp the technical details of weaponry, and he demanded and won the power to send his analysts to meet and debrief recruited foreign agents overseas. But those analysts weren't spies, they had never handled an agent, and they often lacked the skills to assess whether the sources were telling them the truth. Inevitably, they clashed with case officers who knew from bitter experience that agents could be, and often were, manipulative and deceptive.

"WINPAC was a nightmare," said Margaret Henoch, the clandestine service's chief of operations for Europe, who had knocked heads with its senior analysts while spying on the International Atomic Energy Agency in Vienna before 9/11. Henoch was now mounting a battle to stop WINPAC from using thirdhand reports that the Pentagon's Defense Intelligence Agency had obtained through the German intelligence service from an Iraqi émigré code-named Curveball. He had claimed that Saddam had built a fleet of mobile labs designed to evade detection while producing tons of deadly toxins. CIA case officers had never met him, the head of Germany's spy service would not vouch for him, and the analysts had no idea if he were telling the truth. Yet he was the pillar of WINPAC's biological-warfare estimate—and, as it developed, a very slender reed indeed. Henoch had fought over Curveball with a top WINPAC analyst named Beth Kinney, who claimed that the Iraqi's depiction of the mobile bioweapons labs was technically exquisite. We corroborated what he said on the internet, she argued. "Gee, how do you know that's not where he found it?" Henoch remembered telling her. "And nobody could answer me." Henoch argued a salient point, to no avail: no one at the CIA knew who Curveball was, and knowing that was far more important than knowing what he said.

Tenet had created WINPAC in April 2001 with a clear mission: "Enable policymakers and warfighters to prevent surprise and protect the United States" by predicting threats from weapons of mass destruction. But the CIA's powers of prediction were stretched to the breaking point. Since the weapons center had little intelligence on Iraq's arsenal, its analysts looked for any fragments which might confirm their convictions that Saddam had the weapons, discarding everything that didn't fit their preconceptions. Chalabi and his Iraqi National Congress pumped their falsehoods into the stream of reporting through the Pentagon, and the analysts swallowed some of those lies. Foley and his superiors empowered them to make the intelligence fit the president's policy, using inference and intuition instead of hard facts. Their assumptions morphed into judgments.

The CIA's director of intelligence analysis, Jami Miscik, flyspecked their work for caveats and uncertainties, words like *probably* and *maybe*. "Jami read all the source information and reviewed virtually everything that went to senior policymakers, and she wasn't shy about making changes," said the chief Iraq analyst, Jane Green. "She knew what George wanted.

George wanted to please the First Customer. And the First Customer wasn't pleased by the use of caveats."

The National Security Agency had collected reams of evidence on Iraq's arsenal, said Gen. Michael V. Hayden, its leader from 1999 to 2005, and the CIA's director from 2006 to 2009. "We had tons of it, but it was circumstantial," Hayden said. "It wasn't like, 'Ah, there it is, that's got to be it,' click, all the tumblers move, and the safe door opens. Instead, it was: 'Why are they doing this?' Probably because they need that for a nuclear weapons program. 'Why are they buying that material?' Well, it's dual use, but I think it's for a nuclear weapons program, that sort of thing. I think the error in logic for everyone was we began with a hypothesis, they're doing this, and then we just looked for the evidence that supported the hypothesis. And if you do that, you can really build up a pretty good body of stuff. I actually said that to Condi privately *before* we went to war. I said, "Condi, I've got a roomful of stuff on this, but it's all circumstantial.""

In the aftermath, some of the CIA's leaders blamed the White House for leaning on the analysts. After all, Cheney had declared in a speech to the Veterans of Foreign Wars in August that there was "no doubt that Saddam Hussein now has weapons of mass destruction," and he came to headquarters every week in search of evidence to support that claim. "It was clear that the Bush administration would frown on or ignore analysis that called into question a decision to go to war and welcome analysis that supported such a decision," wrote Paul Pillar, the national intelligence officer for the Middle East from 2000 to 2005, a highly respected terrorism expert who had a hand in overseeing the NIE. "Intelligence analysts—for whom attention, especially favorable attention, from policymakers is a measure of success—felt a strong wind consistently blowing in one direction. The desire to bend with such a wind is natural and strong, even if unconscious."

But Bush and Cheney didn't skew the CIA's intelligence. The CIA skewed itself.

"Some analysts got the clue that the White House wanted to hear certain things. And shamefully, they would only supply info slanted in that area," said Jim Lawler, a leader of the CIA's counterproliferation division, who was cleared for the highest levels of weapons intelligence but never saw any to support the charge against Saddam. Tenet never asked the analysts how they knew what they said they knew. He was consumed with the work of the counterterrorism center and convinced, with good reason, that America was going to war in Iraq no matter what he said. He never admitted to Bush, or to himself, how little the CIA really knew.

Tenet restated the highly confident conclusions of the Iraq NIE for Bush in the Oval Office four days before Christmas, accompanied by John McLaughlin and Andy Makridis. But their presentation left the president cold, in part because the daily briefings he had heard for the past six months had been more scary. On Christmas Eve, Jami Miscik went to Camp David in Tenet's stead to deliver the daily briefing for the president and his father. Bush the elder told her that he'd heard the WMD discussion at the White House had gone poorly. The CIA had to do better, said his son.

Miscik vowed to review the case again. She woke up before sunrise on Christmas Day with a terrible premonition. What if the weapons weren't there?

Bush harbored no such doubts. But he asked "if we didn't have better information," Tenet recounted, "and I said I was sure we did." He said the CIA could pull together more highly classified intelligence—intercepted Iraqi conversations, spy-satellite photos, defectors' statements. He reassured the president that strengthening the case to put before for the American people would be a "slam-dunk." McLaughlin instructed Bob Walpole, the national intelligence officer who had overseen the production of the NIE, to corral the top analysts and sharpen the argument with the new evidence, even though Walpole hadn't seen all of it, as he lacked the security clearances. When the two men met with Condi Rice on December 28, Walpole started dutifully reciting the NIE's conclusions. And as he did, a sense of dread began to dawn on the national security adviser. Was the CIA sure? Or was it just guessing? You've gotten the president way out on a limb here, Rice said. Angry and embarrassed,

McLaughlin returned to headquarters and calmly encouraged the analysts to refine a crystal-clear presentation of the case. Walpole frantically emailed them: "WE HAVE TO SAY IRAQ HAS WMD."

What if they hadn't said that? "Do we invade Iraq? Probably not," Rice mused eight years later. Rueda, the Iraq operations chief, wasn't so sure. "These guys would have gone to war if Saddam had a rubber band and a paper clip that could put your eye out," he said.

"They swore by everything"

Powell arrived at CIA headquarters on Saturday, February 1, for a very long weekend of work. In one hand, he had Libby's fifty-nine-page speech, which he was ready to throw out. In the other, he had the ninety-two-page NIE. Thus armed, he commandeered Tenet's seventh-floor conference room and convened the director and his most trusted analysts. For three days and three nights, the secretary of state and the director of central intelligence fashioned the case for war. "I sat there every night with George Tenet and his people, beating up on them," Powell said. "'You've got sources for this? If it ain't multiple-sourced, it ain't going in.' They swore by everything."

They went over the presentation together line by line. When Libby and his colleagues from the dark NSC arrived, trying to relitigate the case for a link between Saddam and al Qaeda, they fended them off as best they could. When Powell questioned a statement or its source, Tenet called in his experts to corroborate them. On Sunday, they convinced him that Iraq had lethal biological-weapons agents, including anthrax, which it could quickly weaponize with bombs, missiles, and aerial sprayers. The case for mobile biological weapons labs rested on satellite reconnaissance photos of suspicious-looking trucks and the stellar secret source in Germany. "The really strong stuff was Curveball," said a senior Iraq analyst, Bill McLaughlin, who had been a chart-flipper at the "slam-dunk" meeting with the president. "It was the centerpiece of the discussion." It was also unverified intelligence from an unvetted and unquestioned source. Without Curveball, the bioweapons case would crumble. Then what? Mike

Morell thought Powell and Tenet surely would have wondered: What else is wrong with this picture?

Morell was wracked by doubt that weekend. He was regarded as one of the CIA's smartest and most skillful analysts, and he saw what was happening with clarity. "Point by point Powell would ask for backup information on the assertions, and as we dug into them, many seemed to fall apart before my eyes," he wrote in a memoir published after he had served as deputy director and acting director of the CIA. "And the material falling apart was not the White House assertions. My team had already removed those. No, what was collapsing was some of the facts used in the NIE to support the judgments there." He shared his doubts with no one. His silence was a dereliction of duty, and he knew it, and to his shame he kept it.*

Tenet never questioned the case. The spies who loved him for his devotion to their cause came to believe that the analysts had betrayed him, betrayed them all, by pandering to the president. A few thought that if the CIA were a military organization, they would have been court-martialed.

Powell had swallowed his own doubts and chosen to serve as the president's loyal warrior. On February 5, the secretary of state told the United Nations and the world that the case against Saddam was overwhelming. "Every statement I make today is backed up by sources, solid sources," he said. "What we're giving you are facts and conclusions based on solid intelligence." But there were no smoking guns, only smoke, and the solid intelligence soon evanesced into thin air. "There were some people in the intelligence community who knew at that time that some of these sources were not good, and shouldn't be relied upon, and they didn't speak up," Powell said three years later. "That devastated me." Four years before

---

* "Mike Morell . . . wrote this book and he made a point of sending me this one paragraph in the book where he is talking about how it got all screwed up," Powell said in 2017. "He closes the paragraph by saying, 'I apologize to Secretary Powell for what we did.' I just let it be known he doesn't owe an apology just to me; the apology should go to the President, should go to the country, should go to the international community. Don't give me this 'I apologize to Secretary Powell.' I've had to live with this." (Colin Powell and Richard Armitage oral history, Miller Center, University of Virginia.)

he died, he prophesied that the speech, with its falsehoods and fatal consequences, would be in the first paragraph of his obituary. It was.

Tenet had been sitting right behind him, silently bearing false witness. His face was gray, his eyes hollow. He had been up past three a.m. staring blindly at the speech. It was one thing to be too tired to think. He was so deprived of sleep that he had lost the ability to speak, or the vision to see that the CIA had deceived itself.

Once Powell had spoken, the war was on. The CIA was its pointed spear. It had been on the ground in Iraq for seven months. Two hundred miles northeast of Baghdad, a brilliant officer named Tom Sylvester was on a mission to subvert and destroy Saddam Hussein.

Chapter Nine

SUFI MYSTICS AND WALKING ZOMBIES

Hunkered down at a freezing mountain outpost on a wind-blasted ridge in northeastern Iraq, Tom Sylvester had recruited a Sufi sheikh and his tribe of flesh-piercing mystics to help America spy on Saddam. For once, at long last, the CIA had religious fanatics on its side.

Sylvester led a ten-man Northern Iraq Liaison Element—six CIA officers, three Ground Branch paramilitaries from the special activities division, and a communicator, along with three commandos from the Tenth Special Forces Group out of Fort Carson, Colorado, whose motto was *De oppresso liber*, "to free the oppressed." His team included Mick Mulroy from the CIA's paramilitary Ground Branch, later the deputy assistant secretary of defense for the Middle East; Marc Polymeropoulos, later deputy chief of the CIA's Europe and Eurasia operations, focused on Russia; and Andrew Warren, later station chief in Algiers. (Warren went to prison for date-raping women while station chief. Apart from him, officers who served under Sylvester tended to go on to greater things.)

Sylvester, who in twenty years' time would be the chief of the clandestine service, had the lean look of a long-distance runner and the dry wit of a foreign correspondent trying to make sense of a world gone mad. He had spent six years with SEAL Team Two, whose specialty was arctic warfare, before joining the CIA in 1991, starting out in the Cairo station and spending a decade as an Arabic-speaking counterterrorism officer before 9/11.* He now had linked up with the Kurdish fighters of Iraq—the *peshmerga*, or "those who face death"—who had a long and bitter history of being seduced and abandoned by the United States. His mission was to work with them to penetrate Saddam's military and spy networks, recruit agents from within the regime, and gather intelligence to support the coming American invasion, executing the essential elements of Luis Rueda's ambitious covert-action plan for the Iraq Operations Group.

Sylvester delivered millions of dollars to Jalal Talabani, the longtime leader of the Patriotic Union of Kurdistan, who ruled in the mountains of northern Iraq under the protection of the Northern Watch, a fleet of American planes patrolling a no-fly zone since the 1991 Gulf War. Talabani was fully on board, seeing an opportunity to gain political power in Iraq by being allied with the United States, which in time he did. Talabani had significant and long-standing support from Iran and an uneasy alliance with the rival Kurdish Democratic Party; a second Northern Iraq Liaison Element worked with the KDP. The CIA had bought the allegiance of the Kurds for many years. It had left them to face Saddam's wrath twice before—once in 1975, selling them out on orders from Secretary of State Henry Kissinger, and again in 1996, following its fatally compromised operation to subvert the Iraqi dictator. Tenet twice met face-to-face with the Kurdish leaders in 2002 to urge them to unite, to pledge his support, and to promise them that the third time would be a charm.

Talabani's fighters had turned Sylvester on to a man who possessed a remarkable power. Among the Sufis, the mystics of Islam, Sheikh Muhammad Abdul Karim al-Kasnazani and his sons stood out for the intensity of

---

* Sylvester came from a long line of admirals and diplomats. His father, trained as a Navy pilot, joined the Foreign Service and served at the Saigon embassy during the Vietnam War, then served as political counsel at the Beijing mission from 1976 to 1979 and as the consul general in Shanghai from 1987 to 1989. His grandfather was a Navy vice admiral, his great-grandfather commanded the Navy in the Pacific before World War Two, and his great-great-grandfather helped rescue Beijing's foreign legations during the Boxer Rebellion of 1900. Like both Presidents Bush, he was a product of Andover, the elite prep school founded in 1778, where he had been cocaptain of the wrestling team, and at his graduation from the United States Naval Academy in 1985, he had shaken President Reagan's hand.

their worship and the influence they secretly wielded in Saddam's regime. The Kasnazani flock was led by ecstatic Sufis; the most devoted of the sheikh's followers were dervishes who pierced their faces with long skewers, stabbed their bodies with sharp knives, and ate broken glass to prove the sheikh's *baraka*, his divine blessing and spiritual strength. "With God's and the sheikh's permission, nothing happens to us, and the wounds heal right away," in the words of one acolyte, Calipha Abdul al-Rahman. This metaphysical power had won the sheikh a multitude of devotees among Saddam's military, intelligence, and security officers. Over the course of twenty years, hundreds of them had come to worship and witness the rites of ritual mortification at his mosque in Baghdad. They believed the sheikh was a descendant of the Prophet Muhammad and that God spoke to them through him. They thus heeded his orders.

Tell them. Answer the questions. Speak!

Sylvester had been slightly incredulous about the Sufi mystics until he put their powers to the test. He paid the sheikh and his two sons $1 million a month, and in return, they produced a handful of Saddam's generals along with scores of senior officers, military pilots, army base commanders, and members of the SSO, Saddam's Special Security Organization, which was responsible for guarding his life against spies and traitors.

Saddam had made the mistake of persecuting the sheikh and his circle in Baghdad—despite the fact that they had a strong following among his intelligence and military establishment, men who were willing to work with the CIA if the sheikh so commanded. A parade of spies and soldiers came to Talabani's safe house, a pistachio-colored building in the village of Qalah Chulan, or to outposts near the Green Line. They had been smuggled out of Baghdad, not knowing where they were going, and when they saw Sylvester their eyes blazed with hatred. Then the sheikh would command: *You're cooperating. Tell them. Answer the questions. Speak!* And they spilled the secrets of Saddam's plans to fight the Americans.

To the south of Sylvester's position, Saddam's forces included 150,000 conscripts, two divisions of the elite Republican Guard, and sophisticated air defense bases along the Green Line, a hundred-mile line of control protecting Iraqi troops based in the cities of Mosul, Kirkuk, and Tikrit, Saddam's birthplace. The American war plan called for a strategic deception: feigning a full-scale attack in the north to distract Saddam's forces from the actual invasion in the south. The feint would pin down six Iraqi divisions and keep them from moving toward Baghdad once the war began. A key element of the plan called for the Air Force to insert one thousand Special Forces soldiers from a base in Romania into northern Iraq by flying a circuitous 590-mile route at five hundred feet above ground, skirting Syria and Turkey and dodging Iraqi antiaircraft defenses, then linking up with the *peshmerga*—the longest low-level combat infiltration since World War Two. The special-ops commanders called it Operation Ugly Baby. Sylvester found a way to swaddle it.

One of the first officers he recruited through the sheikh was part of Saddam's air defense corps. He had access to a mobile surface-to-air missile system controlled by the Republican Guards; its shoot-and-scoot capability made it a difficult target. Sylvester instructed Saddam's man to turn on the system's radar at a set time so a Northern Watch plane could locate it, lock a missile onto it, and take it out before the war began. In short order, it was destroyed. Many more such missile systems would meet the same fate.

Sylvester provided his Iraqi agents with Thurayas, satellite phones the size of a shoe, linked by a satellite hovering over the holiest site in Islam. (The phones were infallible once you pointed their antennas toward Mecca, and everybody in the Middle East knew which way Mecca was.) They could now report to the CIA without making the risky trip north of the Green Line. Sylvester then organized the *peshmerga* into teams gathering intelligence on Saddam's forces south of the Green Line, running from the mountains into the streets of Baghdad and back.

One night, Sylvester received a CD-ROM with the personnel files of Saddam's top military and security officers, along with the order of battle of the Republican Guard. A year before, almost no American spies or agents had been operating in Iraq. Now more than one hundred had infiltrated Saddam's regime. By February 2003, operating from his dismal mountain outpost, Sylvester had achieved the deepest penetration of Saddam's Iraq—or of any nation in America's military crosshairs—in the history of the CIA.

Sylvester's team provided daily updates to Central Command's sprawling forward headquarters in the suburbs of Doha, Qatar, set among sand dunes seven hundred miles southeast of Baghdad, and led by General Franks. In Doha, the CIA's Charlie Seidel was juggling three herculean tasks: keeping the irascible general happy, never an easy matter; coordinating the work of his fellow spies inside Iraq, Jordan, Kuwait, and throughout the Middle East; and harmonizing their work with American and British special-operations commanders.

"How do I know you guys aren't going to create another KGB?"

Seidel had been station chief in Baghdad when the 1991 Gulf War began, and he would be station chief again once Baghdad fell. His father had been a CIA officer who served all over the Arab world, and he had been a hippie kid who had come to a fork in the road, followed his father's footsteps, and joined the CIA in 1980, rising to serve as station chief in Egypt, Jordan, and Saudi Arabia. "I'd known Charlie for years and loved working with him," said Bill Burns, the American ambassador in Jordan and later the assistant secretary of state for the Near East from 1998 to 2005. "He had the trust of lots of Arab leaders across the spectrum from those who were close partners to those who definitely weren't." He had not only mastered Arabic but the dialects and aphorisms of the nations where he had lived. A bon vivant who savored Scotch whisky and Cuban cigars, "Charlie was on a first-name basis with kings, prime ministers, tribal sheikhs, street sweepers, and shopkeepers," the CIA's Marc Polymeropoulos wrote. "Mentioning Charlie within the halls of power and palaces in Iraq, Jordan, Egypt, or Saudi Arabia would gain you instant access to officials who mattered." Seidel reported to the chief of the Near East division, Rob Richer, but he had a direct line to Tenet too.*

Among the CIA officers Seidel oversaw in Iraq was Tomas Rakusan. He had spied on Russia since before the end of the cold war, operating throughout Central and Eastern Europe, and he spoke several Slavic languages well enough to pose as a native citizen. He went into Baghdad under diplomatic cover as a member of a Czech interior ministry team drawing up security and evacuation plans for their country's embassy in early 2003. His mission was to collect ground truth for the invasion. Moving around the city at night, he located air defense systems, discovered troop concentrations, and assessed the load-bearing capacity of bridges, filing reports to Seidel and U.S. Central Command in Doha every day. He was awarded the Distinguished Intelligence Cross for his work in Iraq. Rasukan would serve four stints as a station chief before he became the leader of the Near East division and, in 2017, the chief of the CIA's clandestine service.

The only other officer who received the CIA's highest honor for operations in Iraq was Jim Marsh, who worked in concert with the Kurds and the former Iraqi general Mohammed al-Shawani, a CIA asset of long standing, to create a force called the Scorpions, formed by exiled Iraqi veterans loyal to the general and living in the United States, Europe, and the Middle East. The original idea under Rueda's covert-action plan was to use the Scorpions for sabotage inside Iraq, to create the illusion of a coup, distracting Saddam from the real threat of war. Rumsfeld and Cheney hated the idea. They wanted Chalabi to lead his own exile group, the Free Iraqi Forces, to present the illusion of Iraqis liberating themselves. Marsh weaved his way through these and other obstacles and mobilized the Scorpions, who received training from British commandos in Jordan and worked for American special forces in western Iraq as scouts and interpreters. The Scorpions also had their own military unit, which ambushed an Iraqi motorized column and killed an Iraqi general in the

---

* Seidel twice was awarded the Intelligence Star for bravery. He retired in bitterness in 2006, at the age of fifty, and died suddenly while on a business trip to Riyadh in 2019.

first days of the war. They later served the CIA as spies and paramilitaries, and conducted brutal interrogations of their prisoners.

After the invasion, General Shawani would become the first director of the new Iraqi National Intelligence Service created by the CIA, serving alongside five station chiefs in Baghdad over the following six years. Tenet would face fierce resistance about his appointment from Condi Rice, whose faith in the CIA had by then evaporated. Tenet had tried to explain: Iraqi officers spoke the language, knew their own history and culture, and could far more easily recruit and handle sources than a white guy from Wichita. Rice remained dubious. "How do I know you guys aren't going to create another KGB?" she asked. Such was the depth of her trust in Tenet.

"They're not cheering"

Of all the spies in the clandestine service, Sylvester produced the most startling intelligence on Iraq. As always, the best came from agents in place. He had penetrated Saddam's Special Security Organization to the extent that he received up-to-the-minute reports of the dictator's comings and goings. Three days before the war was set to start, he sent an electrifying prediction to headquarters: Saddam would arrive at one of his hideouts, Dora Farms, a rural retreat southwest of Baghdad, on the following night: March 19, 2003.

Alerted by his flash message late that afternoon, Tenet and Rueda rushed to see Rumsfeld at the Pentagon. The three of them went to the Oval Office to confer with Bush, Powell, and Rice. Sylvester, exhilarated, was feeding real-time intelligence back to Tenet in the White House. American spy satellites looking down at Dora Farms had seen "a large number of regime vehicles hidden under palm trees," and one of Sylvester's Sufi agents was reporting directly from the hideout, Rueda said: "Tom's NILE team kept sending updated intelligence throughout the day and evening. They expected Saddam to arrive shortly after midnight, Iraqi time, and depart no later than 3 a.m." But Bush already had sent an ultimatum for Saddam to surrender power. Iraq had until seven a.m., their time, to remove Saddam. Bush had insisted that he could not strike before the deadline.

"Tenet briefed the president," Rumsfeld remembered. "Then Tenet would periodically go into the National Security Advisor's private office off to the side and talk to the CIA folks on the ground. The president went around the room. 'What do you think?' Everyone said, 'Let's do it.' It was before the deadline, which was a little uncomfortable, but if you could decapitate and regime change that way, given where you were at that point—you were very close to going in and committing a lot of U.S. lives. It was a three-minute decision."

A barrage of cruise missiles and smart bombs rained down on Dora Farms. The devastating attack killed Sylvester's Sufi agent and scores of Iraqis at Dora Farms. "They reported that they saw a stretcher come out with Saddam in it," Rumsfeld said. "They still believed they'd gotten him. It turned out the intelligence was all wrong." To this day, Sylvester believes that Saddam had been there. If so, he was gone before the attack.

It took two weeks and thousands more American bombs and missiles before the troops of the Third Infantry Division rolled into downtown Baghdad. On April 2, their leader, Lt. Gen. William Wallace, called Maj. Gen. James D. Thurman in Doha. "Okay, Bubba, we're here," Wallace said. "Now what?" The answer was up to Rumsfeld. His strategy was deceptively simple. The Americans would be showered with candy and flowers. The Iraqis would welcome them as liberators. The United States would turn over power to an Iraqi government headed by Chalabi and leave in a matter of weeks.

On April 5, Tenet was shocked to learn that, on orders from Wolfowitz, the Pentagon had airlifted the talented fabricator Chalabi and hundreds of his Free Iraqi Forces into the city of Nasiriya, 230 miles south of Baghdad. Once on the ground, Chalabi's men, trained in Iran, commandeered houses, cars, and wealth in the name of his Iraqi National Congress. Chalabi fully intended for the Americans to proclaim him Saddam's successor at the cessation of hostilities.

On April 7, Charlie Seidel and a contingent of CIA officers entered Baghdad, and the next day, Saddam's government was all but gone. At the

White House, Bush and Powell watched a live television shot of American soldiers streaming into the Iraqi capital. "He watched the people in the street and the troops moving," Powell remembered. "He turned to me and said, 'They're not cheering.'" No, sir, Powell said. They aren't.

On April 16, General Franks emailed Rumsfeld: time to declare victory and pull out. The general would retire, abruptly, five weeks later. He recommended that Jay Garner, a retired three-star general selected by the secretary of defense, should begin overseeing the reconstruction of the conquered nation.

"You'll have 50,000 enemies in this city before the sun goes down"

Garner arrived on April 21 and immediately got to know the new chief of station. "Seidel was a natural leader," Garner said. "He had a hard side. But he never said no to a mission unless it was impossible." Garner, Seidel, and Lt. Gen. David McKiernan, the commander of American ground forces, agreed that the highest priority was to begin reconstituting elements of the Iraqi military, police, and civil service to secure the capital. They aimed to lock down the army's guns and mortars, repair the damage from the invasion, and put the country back on its feet. Garner's plan, approved by the National Security Council, called for retaining five divisions of the Iraqi army, about fifty thousand soldiers, and putting them to work.

On May 12, Paul "Jerry" Bremer arrived in Baghdad to lead the newly proclaimed Coalition Provisional Authority. He would preside from Saddam's palace as the American viceroy of Iraq. Bremer, an old friend of Scooter Libby's, reported only to Bush and Rumsfeld, and only when he pleased. He was a protégé of Henry Kissinger's, whom he'd served for fifteen years, as a chief of staff during the Nixon administration and as managing director of the former secretary of state's lucrative consultancy. Like his mentor, he was supernally haughty and incurably secretive. Kissinger himself called Bremer "a control freak"; it took one to know one.

Upon taking power, Bremer immediately declared that no member of the Ba'ath Party—the organizing force of Iraqi society—could play a role in the nation's future. Party membership had been essential for almost every government job, from the army to the police to the civil service to the schools. His next pronouncement dissolved all branches of the Iraqi military, including the Ministry of Defense, the Iraqi Intelligence Service, the Special Security Organization, and the paramilitary forces. It cut off their pay and prohibited thousands of high-ranking officers from public employment. With two strokes of a pen, Bremer had set Iraq on fire.*

At 6:15 a.m. on May 13, Garner saw a draft of CPA Order 1. He was horrified. He rushed to see Seidel, who was equally appalled. They went to see Bremer. "I said, 'Charlie, tell him what's going to happen if you do this,'" Garner remembered. "And Charlie said—in a cowboy way, but with some elegance—'You'll have 50,000 enemies in this city before the sun goes down.'" They begged him to change his mind. Bremer waved them away. He then announced his plans to the White House via videoconference. It came as a rude shock.

"No one else around the table—excluding Don Rumsfeld and Doug Feith and possibly the vice president—knew what was going on," said Frank Miller, the NSC's senior director for defense policy. "This was presented to the war cabinet as, 'This is what we're going to do.'" Even the president seemed taken aback. After ten or so seconds of silence, Bush said to Bremer, "Jerry, you're the guy on the ground"—meaning *It's up to you, not me*. The strategic incoherence of the White House now reached a high-water mark from which it would not recede for three years. The

---

* Bremer's edicts had come from the fertile minds of Feith and Chalabi. Feith had presented his "de-Ba'athification" proposal to the National Security Council on March 10. But not all of it: he was cut short by Rumsfeld because the plan was inchoate. The NSC had agreed that the top-ranking Ba'athists had to be banned—1 percent of the party's two million members—but it had never approved the idea that that all party members had to be purged. Bremer delegated the implementation of de-Ba'athification to none other but Chalabi. His orders were based on "the World War Two model of de-Nazification," said Gen. John Abizaid, who succeed Franks as CENTCOM commander in July 2003. "Saddam is Hitler, the Republican Guards the SS, and the Ba'ath Party the Nazi Party. This notion of this great crusade against evil had no bearing in reality to what was on the ground and the historical context of Middle Eastern politics and Iraq politics in particular."

president had no answer for General Wallace's question—*Now what?* Only Charlie Seidel had offered a highly educated guess. Bush's man in Baghdad had paid no heed. And in that moment, the American occupation of Iraq was foredoomed, its end predestined by its beginning.

The imperial orders Bremer issued were met with a searing and insatiable rage. "The disbandment of the army probably is the origin of the insurgency," Condi Rice said five years after Bush left the White House.

No one at the top of the Bush administration would acknowledge this. Rumsfeld simply refused to believe that an insurgency existed. As a direct consequence, the United States would have no strategy for counterinsurgency in Iraq until 2007, when David Petraeus, now a four-star general, took command of the war. "You really should have a deep understanding of a country and all aspects of it before you invade it," Petraeus said in retirement. "The truth is, we really didn't have that kind of understanding. And I think our actions betrayed that."

A week after the viceroy handed down his edicts, insurgents began to pay young men $100 to kill a U.S. soldier and $500 to disable a Bradley fighting vehicle or an Abrams tank. On June 3, Seidel reported to Bremer and CIA headquarters that the attacks were aimed at military checkpoints "and, increasingly, to higher profile targets such as helicopters and tactical-level military headquarters." Over the following three months, the insurgents attacked with small arms, mortars, rocket grenades, improvised explosive devices, car bombs, and a cement mixer loaded with dynamite, all looted from Saddam's unguarded stockpiles. First by hundreds, then by thousands, cashiered troops and their commanders went to war against the Americans and their allies.

Some CIA officers fought back. Seidel's deputy chief of station was Greg Vogle, newly decorated for saving the life of Hamid Karzai. Upon his arrival in Baghdad, Vogle attached himself to a Special Forces unit, grabbed a weapon, and went hunting for the enemy; he wasn't one to hang around the office having meetings. Vogle served six scalding months risking death in combat and counterterrorist operations, for which he was secretly awarded the Intelligence Star, the CIA's equivalent of the military's Silver Star for valor.

"We didn't know who we were fighting"

As summer began, Seidel worked and slept in the hideous grandeur of the presidential palace, a setting "reminiscent of the bar scene in *Star Wars*," swarming with Americans "armed and unarmed, veterans of post-conflict situations and young Republican neophytes, the hardworking and committed and certifiably clueless," as Bill Burns described it. In the palace, American diplomats, generals, and intelligence officers slept twenty to a stifling room, without electricity, running water, or air-conditioning. The heat was agony, 120 degrees by day and 95 at night. Signs warned against sweating into laptops lest they short-circuit. In this brain-fogging setting, Seidel had to create a CIA station, hunt for weapons of mass destruction, and figure out who the insurgents were.

He saw that America's occupation of Iraqi was igniting the fires of jihad throughout the Middle East. The Iraqi insurgents soon were joined by Jordanians, Syrians, Iranians, Saudis, Sudanese, and Yemeni fighters flowing in from Syria to spark a violent uprising against the occupiers. For months, "we didn't know who we were fighting," said Bremer's deputy, the retired American ambassador Clayton McManaway. "Bremer and I would often talk at night, and I'd tell him that we didn't even know who was killing us." Seidel actually had a pretty good idea who was doing the killing, and why. But neither he nor anyone else knew who was commanding and controlling the insurgency. At the start, there was no central command; many groups went by many names throughout the summer and fall. Bremer and the military wanted the CIA to give them the insurgents' order of battle, an organizational chart with boxes and lines; they could not face the idea of a shape-shifting, many-headed hydra, much less fight it. Seidel tried his best. He met first thing every morning at CPA headquarters with Bremer and Ricardo Sanchez, the three-star commander of American ground forces, accompanied by the CIA's chief Iraq analyst, Jane Green, who served as the Baghdad station's briefer in chief.

All summer long, "we saw looting of factories and other heavy industry, not just the taking of parts and equipment, but the dismantling of the facilities themselves, which was the equivalent of dismantling the Iraqi economy," Green said. "Soon we saw that weapons and ammunition storage depots were being emptied" by cashiered Sunni military officers. "We saw the rise of Shia militias with support from Iran. In some cases, the goal of some of these militias was to take revenge on the Sunnis and to make sure they never had the ability to subjugate the Shia populace again." The Iraq army's enlisted men were largely Shia, as was two-thirds of the nation; the officer corps was overwhelmingly Sunni, as was Saddam. All they had in common was a hatred for the American occupiers.

Seidel filed grim assessments detailing the chaos and anarchy. "In the current environment of confusion, uncertainty, and dissatisfaction," he reported to headquarters on July 8, "the risk exists for violence to quickly become acceptable and justified in the minds of broader sectors of the population." Bush and Rumsfeld and Wolfowitz tossed the CIA's intelligence aside and pushed back. They thought the Iraqis "were supposed to be rejoicing that Saddam's regime was gone," Green said. "And it took them a long time to accept our judgment that the Iraqi people were devolving into civil war."

Rumsfeld rejected the station's reporting outright. Wolfowitz, on a quick trip to Baghdad, had the audacity to tell Seidel: "You don't understand the policy of the U.S. government, and if you don't understand the policy, you are hardly in a position to collect the intelligence to help that policy succeed."

"We knew a shit storm was coming"

Seidel's overriding orders from Tenet were to find the missing weapons of mass destruction. The station chief oversaw the Iraq Survey Group, an intelligence organization of fourteen hundred civilians and soldiers created in June by Tenet and led by a former UN weapons inspector, David Kay. They both were sure the secret caches were out there somewhere in the blazing desert. Nothing turned up that month, or the next one, or the next.

In early August, Bremer called Tenet, who was taking a desperately needed vacation on the New Jersey shore. "I had to get him off a beach to a secure phone," Bremer recounted. He demanded more CIA officers and analysts to attack the insurgents. That month alone, they had blown up the United Nations headquarters and the Jordanian embassy and the holiest Shia mosque in Baghdad, killing hundreds. Tenet said he would try his best, but the CIA was focused on finding WMD. "The imbalance was staggering," said McManaway, "between the intelligence analysts working on weapons of mass destruction and those working on the insurgency." And yet day after day, Kay reported no results, and as the search went on, the insurgency spread like a whirlwind. "The liberation of Iraq has sparked a revolution among the Shia," Seidel warned. The American occupation faced a future of "violence and instability."

After six months under the gun, Seidel returned to his post in Amman in late summer, scathed by his experiences and sapped by his unfailing efforts to support his embattled officers and analysts. The CIA was having a hard time selecting his successor; every senior officer in the Near East division knew the Baghdad station was overwhelmed. "Everyone at the leadership level seemed exhausted, almost like walking zombies," said Luis Rueda, who visited the station as Seidel was leaving. Everyone knew the CIA was in bad odor at the White House, which was willfully blind to Baghdad's reporting on the insurgency and seething with rage that the weapons still were nowhere to be found.

Late one August afternoon, Tenet came down to the Near East division chief Rob Richer's sixth-floor office to talk things over with Richer and Rueda. He was, as ever, chewing on a dead cigar. Deeply downhearted, exhausted after six years at the helm, he was thinking hard about quitting. He saw waves of reality slowly eroding the CIA's sand castle of conjectures about the weapons of mass destruction. He had a fair idea of what it would mean if he were proved wrong. One of the CIA's missions was to take the hit for the president when things went bad, he said. "He was looking really down when he said that, as if he knew *he* would take the hit over WMD," Rueda remembered. "At that point, we knew a shit storm was coming."

Chapter Ten

A BEAUTIFUL OPERATION

For every great debacle, there was a beautiful espionage operation. As the political firestorm over the phantom weapons intensified, a handful of CIA officers foiled a global nuclear threat and forced one of the twentieth century's foremost terrorist leaders to give up his arsenal without firing a shot.

A beautiful op requires creativity, cunning, luck, time—spying is waiting, as John le Carré wrote—and a few great spies. Three highly experienced CIA officers—Robert Gorelick, Paula Doyle, and Jim Lawler—helped bring down the world's biggest nuclear smuggling ring at the end of a nine-year covert action, culminating in a naval interception on the high seas of the Mediterranean on October 4, 2003. The operation, Jim Pavitt said, entailed "million-dollar recruitment pitches, covert entries, ballet-like sophistication, and a level of patience we are often accused of not possessing."

Robert Gorelick was chief of station in Rome that autumn. He resembled the tenured professor he had once aspired to be, albeit a well-tailored and worldly one.* He spoke four languages fluently, and he could sell you a rug in a few more. In the last decade of the cold war, he had been a rare breed of case officer, working under nonofficial cover, without the protection of a

---

* Gorelick had obtained research materials for his 1982 PhD thesis at the University of Geneva by smuggling copies of documents out of the Arab League's offices in Cairo and Tunis. The CIA's job interviewers were duly impressed.

diplomatic passport or a desk at an American embassy. His cover included many different names and disguises as he recruited foreign envoys and promising politicians around the world, two of whom later became their nation's presidents. After twice serving as a chief of station, Gorelick had returned to CIA headquarters to lead the counterproliferation division of the clandestine service at the end of 2000. For more than two years, he had led a team of ten officers so secret that few within the CIA knew it existed: the division's Special Activities Unit. Its roots lay in a 1994 presidential covert-action finding aimed at keeping weapons of mass destruction out of the hands of tyrants and terrorists. Its highest goal was penetrating the global network run by a Pakistani metallurgist named Abdul Qadeer Khan.

A. Q. Khan had been secretly gathering the tools for building a nuclear bomb ever since 1974. His research center near Pakistan's capital employed thousands of people, with its own apartments and schools, a hospital, and a cricket team. His work had enabled his country to carry out a successful test of its nuclear weapons in 1998, making him a national hero—the father of the Islamic Bomb. And then Khan secretly flipped the switch, reversing his role from importer to exporter, selling almost everything a nation needed to build nuclear weapons. He would work with anyone among the renegades of the world. Though he had been on the radar of the CIA and several European intelligence services for a quarter of a century, no one had done anything to stop him until Jim Lawler and Paula Doyle set their sights on his invisible empire.

Lawler and Doyle had first met while running counterproliferation operations in Europe in 1994. They proved to be great partners and became lifelong friends. A fiercely intelligent woman from a tiny South Dakota town, Doyle had worked on nonproliferation programs at the State Department before joining the CIA. She came to see nonproliferation—diplomacy at stopping the spread of nuclear weapons—as essential but ineffective. *Counter*proliferation, backed by aggressive covert operations, was the new order of the day. She had joined up with Lawler, the man who became chief of the unit, a slim, intense, bearded Texan who was an adept recruiter of foreign agents, the most highly valued skill in the clandestine service. His nickname was, somewhat incongruously, Mad Dog, the result of an encounter with a rabid German shepherd in Paris. Sly Fox might have been a better handle.

If the Bolsheviks could do this, why can't we?

The A. Q. Khan takedown first took shape after Lawler had a brainstorm. He had heard the FBI's David Major, at the end of a stellar career chasing Russian spies, give a lecture at CIA headquarters about The Trust, the first international operation ever run by Soviet intelligence. The Trust was, in essence, a sting. In the early 1920s, the Soviet spy service, the Cheka, sought to exterminate exiles who opposed the Bolshevik Revolution. They created a front operation—a fake resistance movement—to attract and entrap Russian counterrevolutionaries and foreign spies. Their enemies came like moths to the flame to be captured and killed. Lawler thought: *If the Bolsheviks could do this, why can't we? I have to become a proliferator!*

"So, Paula and I set up some entities," he said. He was the chief; she was his deputy. They went into business running front companies, dealing in the nuclear black market, stalking their prey across Europe and the Middle East. Among their operatives were a Cuban exile who had served in three air forces—under Fidel Castro, at the CIA's invasion at the Bay of Pigs, and rescuing downed pilots off the coast of Vietnam. Another was a cerebral woman who pioneered the CIA's cyber operations. By Lawler's account, she engineered and executed daring feats of cyberespionage and risky breaking-and-entering operations around the globe. The team also included a manager of the front companies, a finance officer who devised impenetrable labyrinths of bank accounts and shipping networks so that no outsider could follow the money, an in-house nuclear-weapons expert, and a deep-cover spy who infiltrated Khan's international network. In his communications with the British intelligence officers who became part of the A. Q. Khan operation, Lawler gave the members of his team code names from the legend of King Arthur and his pursuit of the Holy Grail. The computer wizard was the Lady of the Lake, the front-company overlord Galahad, the Cuban spy Sir Lancelot. And he dubbed the op Excalibur.

"We were good," Doyle remembered with a smile. She spent the better part of six years undercover overseas, building the infrastructure and wiring for the fronts, gathering intelligence on A. Q. Khan's operations, and working with the cyberwarriors of the CIA's Information Operations Center to ransack his computers. A decade later, she would become one of the highest-ranking women in the history of the clandestine service, overseeing espionage in air, land, sea, and cyber missions as an assistant deputy director of operations. But in her years abroad, very few people at headquarters knew about her involvement in the Special Activities Unit, whose nerve center was an unmarked vault, sealed off from the rest of the CIA. Its mission was so secret and so tightly compartmented that it reported only to the division chief, the seventh floor, and the president of the United States. "We had colleagues and other folks whose lives were on the line," Lawler said, "so we had to be extremely careful about who was briefed."

Earlier in his career, Lawler had spied on dealers in weapons of mass destruction technologies in Germany, Switzerland, and Austria whose customers came from Iran, Libya, and Syria, so he knew "who was who in the zoo" of proliferators. "After a while, we attracted the right people. And that's how we became aware of what A. Q. Khan was," Lawler said. "The intelligence community had never thought that somebody could take proliferation private, and just simply equip countries with a full-scale, turn-key nuclear-weapons program."

By the time Gorelick arrived at headquarters to lead the counterproliferation division in December 2000, Lawler had set up shop in Dubai, the Persian Gulf emirate that drew shippers and smugglers from around the world, its free-trade zone devoid of rules and regulations, home to A. Q. Khan's main warehouse, a Walmart for nuclear-weapons components called Gulf Technical Industries. The unit had uncovered the work of a Swiss family named Tinner—the father, Friedrich, and his sons, Urs and Marco—who had supplied Khan for decades.* The CIA wiretapped the Tinners, stole their files, penetrated Swiss banks to uncover their finances. Then, at the

---

* The involvement of the Tinners in the A. Q. Khan network is a matter of public record in Swiss court documents. Lawler and Doyle did not discuss the identities of any of their sources in our interviews.

right moment, Lawler recruited them, paying $1 million under a business-services contract with a CIA front called Big Black River Technologies.

When Khan and the Tinners set up a sprawling nuclear-components factory in Kuala Lumpur, the capital of Malaysia, a CIA officer who spoke Malay opened a business next door. The Special Activities Unit built a three-dimensional computer replica of the factory, wired the building for audio and video, and watched skilled machinists building centrifuges to enrich uranium and other bomb-building components. They had Khan's Pakistan laboratory and its computers under electronic surveillance. They were inside his offices, inside his warehouses, inside his house.

"We could make CIA its own nuclear state"

President Bush had come to tour CIA headquarters two months after taking office, and Tenet had put on a good show for him. Among the highlights was a meeting with Lawler in the director's seventh-floor suite. The two Texans hit it off. "We briefed Bush on the treachery of what A. Q. Khan was doing, and how dangerous this was to the world," Lawler said. Tenet told Bush he was a threat equal to or greater than Osama bin Laden. But they were on to him, Lawler confided. His front companies were now a trusted component of the Khan network. He had stolen Khan's blueprints and technologies for enriching uranium and designing nuclear weapons.

"Mr. President," he said with a flourish, "we could make CIA its own nuclear state."

By the start of 2001, A. Q. Khan had become a one-man axis of evil. Lawler and Doyle knew he had worked with Iran.* They strongly suspected

---

* Doyle later played a leading role in cutting-edge cyberoperations aimed at disrupting Iran's well-established nuclear-weapons program, which included some of A. Q. Khan's technologies, between 2004 and 2007. The CIA's highly sophisticated cyberattack against Iran, the first of its kind, also involved the Israeli, Dutch, German, and French intelligence services in varying roles. By 2007, the operation had planted a virus in Iran's weapons lab, damaging one-fifth of its five thousand centrifuges and setting the program back by years. At this writing, Iran has not tested a nuclear weapon after five decades of research and development.

he was dealing with North Korea. But without question his best customer was Muhammar Qaddafi, the dictator of Libya since 1969 and the sponsor of a dozen major terrorist attacks during the twentieth century. The question of what to do about him gained the highest priority after 9/11. "Can you imagine the shit that was going on when the seventh floor learned that Libya, a state sponsor of terrorism, was gaining a nuclear weapon and, suddenly, my God, terrorists are attacking the United States?" Lawler said. "Could Qaddafi give a nuclear weapon to a terrorist group?" An even more urgent question: was Osama bin Laden working with Khan to have the wherewithal to build a bomb? He had invited a prominent Pakistani nuclear engineer to Kandahar three weeks before 9/11, where he had expressed his interest in obtaining a nuclear weapon.

"This was the nightmare scenario that we had to resolve," remembered Rolf Mowatt-Larssen, a former Moscow station chief newly appointed to lead the counterterrorism center's weapons of mass destruction division. "We correctly believed that senior people in al Qaeda were aware that A. Q. Khan had been shopping his wares. We had no more information than that, nothing burning holes in our pockets. But we couldn't rule it out." In time the question would drive the CIA to torture prisoners who might know the answer.

Tenet and Gorelick met Bush and Cheney once a week from October 2001 onward to decide what to do about the threat. ("Bush once asked me, 'Bob, why does A. Q. Khan hate America?'" Gorelick remembered. "I changed the subject. I was shocked.") In the militant mindset after 9/11, one school of thought was to kidnap Khan, render him, disappear him. But then, as Gorelick said, he would become a legend, "the Jimmy Hoffa of Pakistan." Another idea was to destroy his factory in Malaysia. The CIA gave Bush that option by shipping a satchel of C-4 plastic explosive to the American embassy in Kuala Lumpur and training a paramilitary team to plant it. Bush and Rice were unable to make a decision, so the CIA did it by default. Cooler heads prevailed. Better to wait. Best to keep spying than to blow up a building, and with it, an exquisite espionage operation.

"I made an appeal to the seventh floor," Lawler said. "My point was that this would be like turning the lights on in the kitchen and watching roaches run for cover, because we had already penetrated the organization from multiple directions. And if we stopped it kinetically in one isolated point, we would have destroyed, I don't know, maybe a couple of million dollars' worth of equipment. But this wouldn't have stopped A. Q. Khan." Cheney heard that argument and took the plan to blow the factory up off the table. But the sense of urgency remained. As Lawler and his team deepened their espionage into Khan's operations and his Libyan connections, their nuclear-weapons expert came to see him. "She came into my office, shut the door, and stood next to me as I was gleefully reviewing the latest intelligence we had obtained," he recounted. "She said: 'I know you're enjoying this immensely. But you realize you have to stop this before they have a nuclear weapon.'"

Gorelick went after North Korea, the hardest target on earth. The CIA suspected, with good reason but without solid evidence, that the regime was violating a 1994 agreement to freeze weapons development, a deal struck by former president Jimmy Carter. There wasn't any evidence because North Korea was a black hole, "the longest-running intelligence failure in the history of the CIA," in the words of Don Gregg, who'd served both as station chief and ambassador in South Korea. The CIA could not conduct espionage inside the country; it was impossible to send outsiders into the hermit kingdom. The CIA's gung-ho operator Ric Prado had spent two years at the turn of the century trying to recruit North Koreans overseas, cornering them at international conferences, flashing briefcases full of cash in hotel rooms. If a prominent North Korean was flying from, say, New York to London, he'd likely find a CIA officer seated next to him on the plane. But nothing had succeeded yet.

First Gorelick set up more clandestine business fronts posing as international merchants of death, seeking to entrap the North Koreans. Then he flew to Beijing to ask the Chinese Ministry of State Security to help the CIA spy on Pyongyang. "The Chinese were horrified to learn that North Korea was getting nuclear weapons," he said. "But they didn't help." And then, at last, a breakthrough: a Pakistani agent provided documents showing that Khan's network had shipped centrifuges to North Korea.

Gorelick and the counterproliferation division provided the first proof of the progress of the North Korean nuclear program. It led the CIA to report to Congress in October 2002: "We did not obtain clear evidence indicating the North had begun constructing a centrifuge facility until recently. We assess that North Korea embarked on the effort to develop a centrifuge-based uranium enrichment program about two years ago." The report continued: "We recently learned that the North is constructing a plant that could produce enough weapons-grade uranium for two or more nuclear weapons per year when fully operational—which could be as soon as mid-decade." (The prediction was precise: North Korea conducted its first nuclear test on October 9, 2006.) As it developed, the North Koreans had shipped missiles to Pakistan in exchange for Khan's technology, weapons designs, and test data. And they had sent 1.6 tons of uranium hexafluoride to Libya for use in Khan's centrifuges, a crucial step on the path to placing a nuclear bomb in Qaddafi's hands.

"Very serious business"

The invasion of Iraq had riveted the Libyan dictator. He was well aware that the case for war had been based on the Americans' assertions that Saddam had weapons of mass destruction. He had seen the bombs falling on Baghdad. He feared he might be the next target.

As the war began, Libya's spymaster, Musa Kusa, sent word through Mark Allen, the counterterrorism chief of Britain's MI6, that Qaddafi wanted to talk with the Americans about his own arsenal. This wasn't the first such opportunity for the Libyans. Six weeks after 9/11, the State Department's Bill Burns and the counterterrorism center's top analyst, Ben Bonk, had gone to London to meet Kusa. He was a suave man with a diplomat's polish—and a prime suspect in the 1988 bombing of Pan Am 103 over Lockerbie, Scotland. The attack had killed 270 people, among them Matt Gannon, the CIA's deputy station chief in Beirut, who was a close friend to Burns. Kusa had said that Qaddafi wanted to renounce terrorism; he had given Bonk and Burns secret intelligence which helped prevent an al Qaeda plot to destroy the American embassy in Yemen. In the course of a long discussion, Bonk had asked point-blank if Libya had a nuclear weapon in the works. Kusa had flatly denied it.

Allen flew to Washington as the invasion of Iraq began on March 20, 2003. He told Tenet that Qaddafi was thinking about giving up his weapons programs if, in exchange, the West would lift the long-standing economic sanctions imposed for his thirty years of supporting terrorism. Tenet assigned the deputy director of the clandestine service, Steve Kappes, to work with Allen to negotiate that surrender. They seemed an odd couple. Allen was a vanishing breed in the ranks of Anglo-American intelligence, a brilliant eccentric, a bit foppish; he had written a book on falconry and sported pink elephant cufflinks. Kappes, a former Moscow station chief, was a balding, bearded, ex-Marine with a drill-sergeant demeanor, steely eyes, a rigid jaw, and a ramrod posture, respected but unloved by his underlings. They had more than a few things in common despite their outward differences. Both were pious Catholics. Both were highly ambitious men who aspired to run their respective services. And both wanted to bring Qaddafi to heel, if they could.

"Steve was selected to be the face of the operation because of his impeccable persuasion skills and senior rank, which were absolutely crucial," Paula Doyle said. "Musa needed to face down someone on the American side that he *feared*, not just listened to. Our job was to get Libya to admit their WMD programs and renounce them or risk war. Very serious business." Bush's instructions to Kappes were clear: no concessions unless Americans could see with their own eyes that Qaddafi had clean hands. Over the next six months, Kappes and Allen met repeatedly with Musa Kusa. In September, Bill Burns joined them for a meeting in Tripoli with Qaddafi. The half-mad dictator now maintained that he had no weapons of mass destruction programs to reveal. Throughout it all, Kappes said, "We just kept showing up like we knew what we were doing, exerting steady pressure." But they could not seal the deal.

The Special Activities Unit did. It found a way to confront Qaddafi with irrefutable proof. The impeccable intelligence came from Lawler's recruited agent, Urs Tinner, in Malaysia. A German ship called the *BBC China* had left Dubai. In its hold were five shipping containers with thousands of uranium-enrichment centrifuge components falsely labeled as used machine parts. The ship was transiting the Suez Canal and entering the Mediterranean Sea, bound for Tripoli.

"The card that is so high and wild"

On Friday evening, October 3, Robert Gorelick, now the chief of station in Rome, called his counterpart, Alberto Manenti, the Italian intelligence service's longtime counterproliferation chief and later its director. Their mission was to stop the ship on the high seas and force it to dock at the port of Taranto, next to a NATO base on the southern shores of Italy, without revealing the nature of the cargo to customs inspectors, dockworkers, or anyone else. "Our challenge," Manenti said twenty years later, "was to do all this and keep it secret." They also had no legal authority to do it. But breaking the laws of other nations is the CIA's stock in trade.

A very long weekend began with a sleepless night. They wanted to send a message to the ship's owners in Bremen through a senior officer from the BND, the German intelligence service. But they discovered, to their dismay, that Germany's spies were out of the office for a three-day weekend, a national holiday marking the 1990 reunification of East and West Germany, the beginning of the end of the cold war. When they finally raised someone in high authority, they at first met Teutonic resistance. "Very legalistic, the BND," Manenti said dryly. "The Germans said, 'Where is the evidence?'" Meanwhile, he had mobilized an Italian Navy destroyer with a five-inch cannon to meet the German ship broadside in the Mediterranean. "The *BBC China*'s captain was really upset," Manenti remembered. He refused to comply with an order to change course, arguing that he was in international waters, not a court of law. He would only obey the word of his corporate masters in Bremen. Gorelick and Manenti put their heads together with their counterparts in Germany and Great Britain, and they conceived an audacious ultimatum for the shipowner.

"The U.S. would have closed the company's access to U.S. ports," Manenti said. "Eighty percent of their routes had American destinations and customers." The shipowner bowed to the logic of force, and the Italian destroyer escorted the ship and its nuclear contraband to harbor.

Doyle was on the seventh floor briefing the CIA's leaders. It was a busy Saturday. "Iraq was on fire, Afghanistan was about to have its first free elections, and a suicide bomber blew herself up along a Haifa beach," she said. "I just remember running all day, waiting for good news from Jim's end." And as soon as the news came, Lawler flew to Rome and onward to Taranto.

"I recall dancing a happy jig in front of those five containers and smiling at the sweet result of that almost decade-long effort," he said. "Our negotiators in Libya," namely Kappes and Allen, "were then armed with that information, and that was ultimately the precious hole card they played with their Libyan counterparts, who until then had been stonewalling on the question of whether Libya had a nuclear weapons program. They rapidly folded and conceded that there was indeed a nuclear weapons program in Libya. Everything was removed from Libya as quickly as was practical."

Lawler remembered a verse from Leonard Cohen's "The Stranger Song" floating into his head:

> *Like any dealer he was watching*
> *For the card that is so high and wild*
> *He'll never need to deal another.*

"We found that card," he said.

Bill Burns described the denouement as "an adventure full of strange meetings in the middle of the night in the middle of the desert with Qaddafi, to this day the strangest leader I've ever met." It took two months before Qaddafi agreed to demands from President Bush and Prime Minister Tony Blair for a public statement revealing his nuclear weapons program—for which he'd paid Khan somewhere in the neighborhood of $100 million—along with his formidable stockpiles of missiles and chemical agents. In the end, on December 18, 2003, Qaddafi caved. He was doubtless mindful of the fate of Saddam Hussein, who five days earlier had been captured hiding in a spider hole near Tikrit, and would in time face the hangman's noose.

There remained the question of A. Q. Khan's future. First Tenet confronted President Musharraf of Pakistan face-to-face and demanded an end to the proliferation and the proliferator. Musharraf pleaded ignorance but professed to be outraged. He told Tenet: "I'll kill the son of a bitch." He did nothing of the sort. Then Armitage flew to Islamabad and threatened to suspend American aid to Pakistan unless Khan was indicted. Faced with the loss of $3 billion, Musharraf announced that the father of the Islamic bomb would indeed be criminally prosecuted. Then he pardoned him five days later. On February 5, 2004, Khan submitted to house arrest, and with that, his global nuclear-arms network collapsed.

The CIA's operation had proved that intelligence, and intelligence alone, could destroy an existential threat and disarm a dictator. It was the high point of George Tenet's seven years in power. From that day forward, the CIA began a descent that brought it to the brink of ruin.

Chapter Eleven

THE BUTCHER'S BILL

Tenet hadn't spoken in public since the Iraq war began. He wouldn't admit that the CIA had erred grievously on the question of Saddam's arsenal. He didn't see what had gone wrong, or why. But he couldn't stand mute any longer. On February 5, 2004, he broke his silence in an address at his alma mater, Georgetown University. He defended the CIA to the last.

He only wavered once. "Now, I'm sure you're all asking, 'Why haven't we found the weapons?'" he told his audience. But he had no answer. The speech did not go down well in Washington. Nor did Colin Powell appreciate a series of calls from Tenet telling him that the pillars of his UN speech were crumbling, one by one. The director's relationship with the president was increasingly strained; he had heard rumors that he might be fired. He had offered to resign; Bush wouldn't let him. He wanted no defections in an election year.

But now a butcher's bill was coming due. The inspector general John Helgerson was completing a searing 109-page report on the deaths of three CIA prisoners and the abuses interrogators had inflicted on others in Afghanistan, Thailand, and Poland. He would conclude that CIA officers and contractors under the command of counterterrorism chief Jose Rodriguez might be held liable for inflicting cruel and inhuman punishment on prisoners, and for violating the rules laid down in the Justice Department's torture memos. Those officers, he noted, rightly feared the inevitable revelation of the program; their reputations, and the CIA's, could be ruined. The gist of the highly classified report appeared in the *New York Times* almost immediately after its completion.*

Helgerson hadn't yet finished that work when he was compelled to investigate a homicide at the Abu Ghraib prison in Iraq. Nineteen years passed before the facts came out. His report, declassified with redactions in May 2023, reviewed "the events surrounding the death of Manadal al-Jamaidi, an Iraqi detainee who died on 4 November 2003 during interrogation by CIA." When the horrors of Abu Ghraib became public six months later, pictures of two happy-go-lucky, thumbs-up young American soldiers posing over al-Jamaidi's corpse, packed in ice, appeared around the world. The Ice Man became an indelible symbol of the American occupation of Iraq and a recruitment ad for America's enemies. But the CIA interrogators pinned his death on the SEALs who had captured him.

"That was their way of keeping their hands clean"

Before departing as Baghdad station chief, Charlie Seidel had discovered that a handful of his officers and a group of the SEALs were brutalizing prisoners at Camp Nama, on the edge of the Baghdad International Airport. Seidel had blown the whistle in a cable to CIA headquarters, which responded by forbidding its officers in Iraq from participating in the brutality. The rules for al Qaeda prisoners in the black sites were one thing. The rules for Iraqis held in military prisons were another: the Geneva Conventions were in force. John Rizzo had sent written orders for the

---

* The accounting, entitled "Counterterrorism Detention and Interrogation Activities (September 2001 to October 2003)," was dated May 7, 2004. On May 13, the *Times* reported: "The Central Intelligence Agency has used coercive interrogation methods against a select group of high-level leaders and operatives of Al Qaeda that have produced growing concerns inside the agency about abuses, according to current and former counterterrorism officials." The article was the first to mention waterboarding as an interrogation technique. The story was published immediately after the Army's abuses at Abu Ghraib were revealed, and its impact was diminished as a result.

Baghdad station: "Don't hold prisoners yourself. Defer to the military on questioning. Only participate when invited to do so. Don't try to force yourself into these interrogations. Obviously, no enhanced interrogation techniques." The station received a cable every month thereafter reenforcing those rules.

Seidel's successor violated them. Gerry Meyer had taken command of the Baghdad station at the end of the summer of 2003. Pavitt had chosen him over objections from Steve Kappes, his deputy, and Rob Richer, the Near East division chief, who thought he wasn't qualified. Meyer held the civil service rank of GS-15, making him a colonel, not a general, in the CIA's hierarchy. He had spent barely a year as chief of station in Kuwait, where he had won over Pavitt by taking him rug shopping and treating him to a luxurious nighttime barbeque in the desert. When Meyer took a Christmas vacation, the deputy chief of the Near East division, Hendrik van der Meulen, filled in for him. He heard so many complaints about the station chief's conduct that he returned to lead an inspection tour six weeks later, in early February 2004. His report found that Meyer was out buying carpets when he should have been running the station, skipping country team meetings with American commanders and diplomats, paying too little attention to operations as the insurgency exploded, and leaving the hard work to his deputy, Gordon Prouty. There was worse. His officers had been beating and abusing Iraqi prisoners. Now they had the blood of the Ice Man on their hands, and Meyer was either oblivious to the fact or complicit by his silence.

A cadre from SEAL Team Seven and the CIA station had captured al-Jamaidi, who was suspected of a role in the bombing of the Red Cross headquarters in Baghdad, which had killed thirty-four people and wounded 224. They had taken him to the base at the airport, and bludgeoned him at the CIA officers' behest. This was standard practice. "That was their way of keeping their hands clean but getting our hands dirty," a SEAL named Dan Cerrillo told the journalist Seth Hettena, who first broke the details of the al-Jamaidi story. "They used us. They used our lack of understanding of wartime law against us." The SEALs had seen worse, including CIA officers making death threats backed up at gunpoint.

In an interrogation cell the SEALs called the Romper Room, a short, bearded, forty-four-year-old CIA officer named Mark Swanner, a lie-detector operator deployed as an interrogator, strapped al-Jamaidi's arms to the wall and threatened to break his hands with a wooden mallet. The prisoner wasn't talking. Steve Stormoen, the head of Baghdad station's Detainee Exploitation Cell, ordered Swanner and a SEAL to take al-Jamaidi to Abu Ghraib. Once inside its walls, he became a ghost.

Abu Ghraib, where Saddam had tortured and killed thousands of prisoners, signified the horrors of his regime to millions of Iraqis. After the invasion, Bremer had commanded the American military to take charge of it. It now held seven thousand inmates, some of whom were beaten, terrorized by snarling dogs, and subjected to sexual sadism by their American military jailers. Within its walls stood a CIA cellblock overseen by Stormoen, a middle-aged paramilitary officer recently returned from Afghanistan. He had struck a deal with Lt. Col. Stephen Jordan, who led the military's Joint Interrogation Debriefing Center. They would make the CIA's detainees disappear.

The ghost prisoners wouldn't see the light of day after they were logged into Abu Ghraib under a false name, then moved from cell to cell so that the Red Cross would never know they existed. The deceptions violated Army doctrine and the laws of war. Their pact also allowed CIA officers to interrogate prisoners without the presence of Army personnel, breaking the rules laid down by headquarters. An Army investigation later concluded that "CIA detention and interrogation practices led to a loss of accountability, abuse [of prisoners], and an unhealthy mystique that further poisoned the atmosphere at Abu Ghraib."

During the half-hour drive to the prison, the convoy stopped, and a SEAL yanked al-Jamaidi, hooded and naked from the waist down, out onto the road and beat him, breaking five of his ribs. The beating was standard practice too. "When an individual was apprehended, they would be taken to Abu Ghraib, but on the way the convoy would stop before arriving at the prison, and the prisoner taken out of the vehicle and worked over by military personnel," Iraq operations group chief Luis Rueda said.

"That was designed to soften the individual prior to commencing the interrogation. That was totally unauthorized. Prohibited. And the station was not telling headquarters. People in the detainee exploitation cell knew what they were doing was not sanctioned, but they were doing it anyway."

At about five a.m., Swanner and a CIA translator, accompanied by military police serving as jail guards, took the prisoner to the CIA's cellblock, his wrists handcuffed behind his back. They grabbed a leg iron, locked it onto the steel bars of a window, and chained his arms above the back of his head. Though the prisoner's arms were already "almost literally coming out of his sockets," as MP Walter Diaz later testified, Swanner called the guards back and told them to reshackle al-Jamaidi's hands even higher on the window frame. Half an hour later he spewed blood into his hood and died. The Army ruled the death a homicide. The guards placed him in a body bag and packed him in ice. Neither Meyer nor any senior member of the Baghdad station went to Abu Ghraib to investigate what had happened.

A few weeks before the depravities of Abu Ghraib shocked the world in April 2004, the CIA removed the station chief and his deputy from Baghdad. Meyer resigned rather than accept a demotion. Prouty spent a year in the penalty box at headquarters but went on to serve as chief of station in the United Arab Emirates. (The third-ranking officer at the Baghdad station, the chief of operations, also lost his post.) The inspector general referred Stormoen and Swanner to the Justice Department for criminal charges. Rizzo's skill at deflecting discovery and the dilatory work of a special prosecutor, John Durham, ensured that the cases were slow-rolled until after the statute of limitations expired. No one ever received more than a letter of reprimand for the death of the Ice Man.

"Everyone was over their heads"

Bob Kandra took over as Baghdad station chief in the spring of 2004. A beefy man with a trim beard starting to gray at the edges, Kandra had a great record in both espionage and counterterrorism. He had helped run the hunt for war criminals in the Balkans, and he would go on to lead the special activities division. He now commanded the largest CIA outpost since Vietnam.

The Baghdad station and its outlying bases had more than three hundred people, at least seventy-five of them case officers. Many were in their twenties, fresh off the Farm, on their first tour, innocent of espionage, counterterrorism, or recruiting and running agents. Some had volunteered out of the purest patriotism, some for the adventure, some for a paycheck; when you factored in the bonuses for serving in Baghdad, newly minted officers could make roughly $150,000 a year, about twice what they would have earned at home. They worked long days and slept uneasily in trailers without fortifications, while up to fifty mortars a day fell around them. The station was housed in a relatively modest Green Zone palace called "the Villa," with its own chow hall, its own swimming pool, and its own watering hole. The Babble-On Bar, a glorified trailer with a patio and a lounge, was the scene of serious drinking and furtive hookups among the station and the soldiers. The CIA's officers wore loaded Glocks at the bar, leading to the occasional drunken mishap. "The bar was a nightmare," Rueda said. "People got shit-faced every night and guns went off because there was a policy of being armed all the time in the event of an attack. Sex was rampant, and during Kandra's reign I believe every manager was having an affair with a subordinate."

The sex and the booze took the edge off the nightmare confronting the Baghdad station. The occupation was descending into chaos. Every action Bremer and his team took generated more enemies. The American commander in Baghdad, Lt. Gen. Ricardo Sanchez, wanted strategic intelligence, the big picture of the insurgency and its Shia supporters in Iran. Military officers wanted on-the-spot tactical intelligence to launch raids against the insurgents. Bremer wanted political intelligence on the Iraqi power brokers vying for power in a provisional government. The station did not have the wherewithal to do all that.

CIA officers and analysts worked as hard as they could, trying to run espionage and counterterrorism operations by recruiting Iraqi agents from inside the rapidly expanding insurgency. Plenty of analysts stood ready but they had little to analyze if case officers weren't collecting intelligence by running agents. That proved almost impossible. It typically takes at least a year of careful preparation and cautious vetting for a case officer to recruit any source, much less a terrorist. The military demanded rapid recruitments, usually after one or two meetings, before taking action on a source's report. As a consequence, the source often had a very short life span, and the case officer was back to square one.

Orders from headquarters made espionage even more difficult. The seventh floor was understandably terrified that CIA officers could be captured, tortured, and killed in the back alleys of Baghdad. It forbade them from traveling without a military convoy, usually three armored vehicles manned by six hulking soldiers. This was not conducive to conducting clandestine meetings with Iraqis. The station's sources had to come into the Green Zone among the crowds looking for work. Inside, the CIA had two safe houses to debrief them, one right next to the other. This was not good tradecraft.

"Often, we had to escort sources through the Green Zone's Qadisiyyah checkpoint," said Ilana Berry, a twenty-eight-year-old Farsi-speaking law school graduate with a military intelligence background, who had volunteered for the counterterrorism team on her first tour as a CIA officer. "I knew most of the Fourth Brigade Combat Team soldiers there, who allowed my sources instant access without questions. But this checkpoint was also a favorite target for vehicle-borne suicide bombers. My partner case officer and I would take turns escorting sources, figuring we cut our chances of dying in half." The car bombers eventually succeeded in attacking the post, killing a soldier she knew well.

None of this was good for morale, and the station's managers did little to improve it. "There was an unspoken code: nobody wanted to acknowledge how bad it was," said Berry, who would receive a CIA award for her counterterrorism work in Baghdad. "If you spoke up, you were slapped down. Everyone was over their heads. Everyone was afraid. None of us spoke Arabic. We just didn't know what we were doing. No one knew how miserably we would fail. We had little leadership, little direction. We felt gutted, lost."

"A fundamental breakdown in trust"

Tenet felt the same. He knew his days as the CIA's leader were drawing to an end. The 9/11 Commission had held its hearings and it was assembling its final report; he knew it would be searing. And, as he had feared, the White House had hung him out to dry when Saddam's arsenal turned out to be chimerical. He had told the commission on April 14 that it would require "another five years of work to have the kind of clandestine service our country needs." Several commissioners wondered aloud at this. Tenet had said the same in 1997.

Three days after he testified, he picked up the *Washington Post* and read a story that the White House had fed to Bob Woodward. It said the march to war in Iraq had begun with "Tenet's assurance to the President that it was a 'slam dunk' case that Iraq possessed weapons of mass destruction." Tenet always contended that *slam dunk* meant he could surely present a stronger case for public consumption, not that the case itself was iron-clad. But this nuance hardly mattered now. Woodward had ignited a bonfire "and I was the guy being burned at the stake." He called Andy Card, the president's chief of staff, and told him that what the White House had done to him was "about the most despicable thing I have even seen in my life." Card said nothing in response, and "in that silence, I understood that there had been a fundamental breakdown in trust between the White House and me. In short, it finally, absolutely was time to go." He announced that he would retire in July, on the seventh anniversary of the day he became director.

Not long thereafter, the White House called him out of the blue. The president's staff secretary, the future Supreme Court justice Brett Kavanaugh, told him that Bush wanted to award him the Medal of Freedom, the nation's highest civilian honor, alongside Jerry Bremer and Tommy

Franks. Tenet accepted, in the hope that the ceremony might be a fitting closure to his tenure at the CIA. But the ribbon on the medal would hang like a noose around his neck. The final nail in his coffin was hammered by Porter Goss, the patrician Republican chairman of the House intelligence committee throughout Tenet's seven years. He had signed a cruelly worded report written by his highly partisan staff, dated June 21, 2004. It said Tenet had made the clandestine service "nothing more than a stilted bureaucracy incapable of even the slightest bit of success," which was a falsehood, and that he had steered the CIA "down a road leading over a proverbial cliff," which had the unpleasant odor of truth.

"This is tragic," Goss concluded. "It should never happen again."

The president had two men in mind to succeed Tenet. One was Rich Armitage, who thought about working with Cheney and Rumsfeld for four more years, shuddered, and declined. Then Bush offered the job to James A. Baker III, who had served his father as secretary of state and masterminded the legal battles that secured victory for Bush in the disputed 2000 election. "Dick Cheney called me and said, 'The president wants to know if you'd be willing to come up here and replace George Tenet as the CIA director,'" Baker recalled. He came from a political tradition in which you said *yes, sir* to the president when he asked you to serve the country. "I said no. I didn't think I could do that."

Then Bush decided that Porter Goss was just the man to run the Central Intelligence Agency. "He knows the CIA inside and out," Bush said, standing alongside the congressman in the Rose Garden on August 10. "He's the right man to lead this important agency at this critical moment in our nation's history."

The only politician ever named to serve as director of central intelligence had been his own father. Bush the elder had been beloved at headquarters; he had protected and defended the CIA in a time of crisis. But Goss presided over the decapitation of his own office. His reign began with a political purge of the CIA's leaders and ended with the FBI festooning the seventh floor with yellow tape reading: CRIME SCENE DO NOT CROSS.

Chapter Twelve

GUERRILLA WARFARE

The CIA was wounded, and its enemies smelled blood. "We were being beaten like little baby seals on the beach," said John McLaughlin, who stayed on as deputy director under Porter Goss until he couldn't bear it any longer. A three-front war with the president, politicians, and the press raged outside the barbed wire surrounding headquarters. Inside the wire, every day brought fratricidal battles, as the new director and his right-hand men set off an uprising by the old guard.

The very survival of the agency was an open question in the summer and fall of 2004. The Republican chairman of the Senate intelligence committee proposed to dismantle the CIA root and branch. The WMD fiasco fueled calls for a radical reordering of espionage and analysis. The clandestine service faced attacks from "so-called human rights organizations, congressional overseers . . . and our own inspector general's staff," in the words of Jose Rodriguez. The 9/11 Commission's report, released on July 22, proposed an overhaul of American intelligence, and politicians from both parties endorsed the call.

The most immediate danger was a barrage of sniper fire coming from within the White House. As the American occupation of Iraq descended into anarchy, Bush bitterly blamed the CIA, seemingly blind to his own bending and twisting of intelligence, which his press secretary later called part of "a carefully orchestrated campaign to shape and manipulate" public opinion. The president's wrath had increased every time the CIA warned that Iraq faced a civil war led by a many-faceted insurgency whose rise was a direct consequence of the occupation.

Late in July, Bush read a new National Intelligence Estimate foreseeing chaos in Iraq. He erupted when its essence appeared in the *New York Times* on September 16. The CIA was "just guessing," Bush said five days later, during a photo opportunity with Iraq's new interim prime minister, Ayad Allawi, a well-financed CIA asset since 1991. *Just guessing* was an explicit vote of no confidence. His opponent in the presidential election, Senator John Kerry, shot back: "The CIA? They're not just guessing. They're giving the president of the United States their best judgment. . . . The president ought to read it and he ought to study it and he ought to respond to it." Bush tossed the estimate aside. He knew Iraq could cost him a second term; the November election would be a referendum on his conduct as commander in chief in his war on terror. He was sorely displeased that the CIA had contradicted his cheery rhetoric about how America had brought democracy and freedom to Iraq. But he was truly enraged that the estimate had leaked.

That wasn't the only secret seeping into the newspapers as the election approached. CIA analysts made it known that they had accurately predicted, before the war, that the occupation could spark both the insurgency now engulfing it and a firestorm of anti-American rage throughout the Muslim world, and they pointed out that the president's repeated claims that Saddam and bin Laden were coconspirators were falsehoods. "There were a lot of leaks coming out of the intelligence community to the *New York Times* that were designed to try to discredit the president and get him not reelected, no question about that," said Stephen Hadley, who would succeed Condi Rice as national security adviser after the election. "It had a real impact on the president's confidence in the intelligence community." Hadley cut the CIA out of the flow of intelligence from the National Security Council until after the election.

The bitterness of the battle between the White House and the CIA was unlike anything since President Nixon fired the director of central intelligence, Richard Helms, in November 1972, in part for refusing to help him cover up the Watergate scandal. Bush believed, as had Nixon, that the CIA was a leftist organization seeking to undermine him. His aides fed the ammunition for a fusillade of conservative editorials and opinion pieces calling the agency an enemy within. "If we lived in a primitive age, the ground at Langley would be laid waste and salted, and there would be heads on spikes," David Brooks wrote in the *New York Times*. The *Wall Street Journal* editorial board warned that Bush now had "two insurgencies to defeat: the one that the CIA is struggling to help put down in Iraq, and the other inside Langley against the Bush administration."

Porter Goss intended to crush the insurgency.

At first, he was greeted with open arms at headquarters when he arrived on September 24. A courtly multimillionaire with a five-hundred-acre farm in Virginia and a summer estate on Long Island Sound, Goss had been a gentleman spy in the 1960s, recruited out of Yale and serving as a case officer in the CIA's Latin American division, before buying a newspaper in Florida and parlaying that into a secure congressional seat representing a heavily Republican district. He had chaired the House intelligence committee since 1997, so hopes were high when he arrived, since he knew how the CIA worked and he seemed to have the president's ear. But it immediately became clear that his orders from Bush were to police the building, root out the unfaithful, and above all, stop the leaks.

To that end, he imported a half dozen members of his congressional staff as his closest aides, some of them CIA veterans whose careers had ended badly, all of them hell-bent on a hostile takeover, to do the dirty work for him. They were inevitably dubbed the Gosslings. They later earned another epithet—the Hitler Youth. They started driving out the CIA's top officers and analysts, deeming them disloyal to the president and the director, setting a vicious and vindictive tone that prevailed for a year and a half at headquarters. Goss himself was too well-bred to be a tyrant. He left the throat cutting, and much else, to his staff.

"Taken in by a con man"

The Goss era began in full in late October, after he selected Kyle Dustin "Dusty" Foggo to serve as his executive director—the number three man at the CIA. Goss gave him dominion over day-to-day operations, and the power to promote his favorites, keelhaul his enemies, and protect officers facing discipline by shielding them from accountability.*

Dusty Foggo had spent his career in the CIA's directorate of support, one of the four pillars of the agency's architecture, along with operations, science and technology, and analysis. His job was supplying CIA officers with their material needs, from cars to carbines. Foggo was a glib, glad-handing sycophant, always trying to ingratiate himself with his superiors, and usually succeeding. He showed visiting congressmen and staffers from the intelligence and armed services committees a good time when they traveled overseas to tour CIA stations at American embassies—excellent liquor, expensive cigars, and, if his guests desired, more exotic pleasures. Foggo enjoyed all three; he had been reprimanded for his undisclosed relationships with foreign women, a violation of security rules. He had first made his name running guns and money into Honduras during the contra wars of the 1980s, and when that battle was over, he went to Vienna to support the station chief, James Olson.

One day in 1989, the American ambassador to Austria, Henry Grunwald, the former editor of *Time* magazine, had summoned Olson into his offices. The ambassador was furious over a rare formal diplomatic protest from the Austrian government. Foggo had beaten a bicyclist with his fists in a road rage on the streets of Vienna and, when arrested for the assault, had flashed his phony State Department credentials to claim diplomatic immunity and fend off criminal charges. The fact that the ambassador knew about the arrest before the station chief did was awkward in the extreme. Called on the carpet, Foggo invented a tale about having been

---

* Goss first had appointed his intelligence committee staffer Mike Kostiw as the CIA's executive director. The news went out in an email sent to thousands of retired officers on October 2. The next day, citing four sources, the *Washington Post*'s veteran intelligence reporter, Walter Pincus, reported that Kostiw had been fired from the CIA for shoplifting a pound of bacon from a supermarket in 1981. Kostiw stepped aside. As Gen. Mike Hayden, Goss's successor, said half-jokingly: "The CIA guys, you know what they do for a living, right? When they decide to play hard, they play hard." (Michael Hayden oral history, Miller Center, University of Virginia.)

shaken down for a bribe by the police. He knew all about that kind of crooked conduct, he explained, having once been a cop in San Diego.

"I found Mr. Foggo's explanation entirely unrealistic and implausible," Olson said in a sworn deposition years later. "I told him that if he were lying to me, I would dismiss him from my station and send him back home." The station chief reported all this to the CIA's office of security, expecting them to follow up with a lie-detector test, knowing that Foggo could be rebuked or fired for—in Olson's words—his "lack of candor." The derogatory report was filed and forgotten. Even though "I considered Mr. Foggo to be morally suspect at that point," Olson said, "I recognized that Mr. Foggo was talented at his job as a chief of support, and I recommended him for continued employment." Once more, the mission overshadowed the rules.

The talented Mr. Foggo ascended ten years later to serve as the CIA chief of support in Frankfurt, working out of the immense United States Air Force base at Ramstein, running the international supply hub for intelligence operations throughout Europe, the Middle East, and Africa. After 9/11, he became the quartermaster for the war on terror, supplying the Northern Alliance warlords with horses and saddles, the Tali-Bar at the Kabul station with whiskey and gin, the first-tour officers in Baghdad with Glock pistols and Kevlar vests. He once airlifted an entire frozen pig into a remote base in Afghanistan for a morale-raising barbeque. On the eve of the American invasion of Iraq in March 2003, he received a new mission from Jose Rodriguez, the counterterrorism chief: his services were required to build three new black sites for interrogation in Romania, Lithuania, and Morocco. Foggo turned to his oldest friend, a crooked defense contractor named Brent Wilkes, to help with the nuts and bolts of building and equipping the secret prisons. They created a lucrative series of padded invoices and luxurious kickbacks, a grift so blatant that it would begin to unravel in two years' time.

Foggo's character was not a well-kept secret. His colleagues compared him to Milo Minderbinder, the maniacal mess officer turned war profiteer in *Catch-22*, though no one yet knew he was making money off the war on terror. "While he was good at being a 'fixer,' there was little in his record to suggest he was the right guy to become the third-ranking person at the CIA," Rodriguez recounted, save one fact: "The Goss crowd thought he would be loyal to them." Jim Olson, who had gone on to serve as the CIA's chief of counterintelligence during the 1990s, said he was "flabbergasted" when he heard that Foggo had been named executive director. "I found Director Goss's selection to be quite revealing, that Mr. Goss would be taken in by a con man" who was "seriously flawed, ethically and morally, who would cut corners to achieve his aims." His aims, as it developed, were to use his position at the CIA to get rich, curry favor on Capitol Hill, and amass the political clout to succeed his role model, a flagrantly corrupt San Diego congressman, Randy "Duke" Cunningham, who was Brent Wilkes's partner in crime.

"It was imperative to me," Goss said a few years later, that Foggo be "someone whose personal and professional conduct was beyond reproach. I asked him directly whether there was anything I needed to know about his candidacy that would reflect poorly upon the director's office or upon the CIA. He denied that there was anything." The old spy bought the bold lie.

For reasons no one really understood, least of all the CIA's counterintelligence chief, Mary Margaret Graham, Goss and his staff were hell-bent on Foggo's promotion. She had found the red flags in Foggo's personnel file, including his arrest for assault in Vienna and, as Rodriguez put it delicately, the fact that he had "associated with some people with less-than-sterling reputations." She learned that Foggo had told Jeanette Moore, who was his superior and the highest-ranking African American woman in the CIA, that he would have Moore's head once he became executive director; Moore, who had reprimanded him for an extramarital affair with another CIA officer, resigned days after Goss announced the appointment.

Goss's chief of staff, Pat Murray, told Graham in the crudest terms that if any of those facts leaked, she would be fired. Graham had steel nerves—she had been chief of station in New York on 9/11—but the threat alarmed her. She consulted her predecessor in the counterintelligence post, Mike Sulick, now second-in-command at the clandestine service under Steve Kappes. Sulick confronted Murray. A furious argument ensued. Murray told Goss to tell Kappes to fire Sulick. Kappes refused. News of this confrontation spread in a flash around headquarters, to CIA stations worldwide, among the closely knit circles of CIA veterans, and in very short order into the press.

Two days later, on Friday, November 12, McLaughlin announced his retirement as deputy director of the CIA. The following Monday, Kappes and Sulick quit in a rage; twenty more senior officers and analysts followed them out the door. Goss had been in office for seven weeks. He had created an upheaval without precedent in the history of the CIA.

"I don't do personnel"

On Monday afternoon, Foggo told Jose Rodriguez he would become the new chief of the clandestine service.

Rodriguez was burned out by thirty months of running the counterterrorism center, overseeing the black sites, and pursuing al Qaeda. He had been contemplating retirement after twenty-eight years at the CIA. But no one ever had turned down a promotion to that high rank. Then the inspector general reminded Goss of the matter of his demotion as head of the Latin American division, seven years before, for his noted lack of judgment. "For the next eight to ten hours it looked as if I was about to be told that I was not suitable for the position I had very reluctantly agreed to accept," Rodriguez recalled. But Goss made the appointment official late that evening. In the morning, Rodriguez ascended from his windowless bunker at the counterterrorism center to a suite on the seventh floor.

He saw the clandestine service as under siege by the reformers, swamped by the counterterrorism struggle, and fighting to fuse intelligence and covert operations in battle. He believed, correctly, that the CIA was badly in need of a new five-year plan to look beyond al Qaeda, Afghanistan, and Iraq, and to confront the threats posed by Iran, North Korea, Russia, and China. To that end, forty-eight hours after his appointment, Bush ordered the CIA to double the number of clandestine officers, intelligence analysts, and science and technology experts by 2009. Rodriguez would not last to see any of those missions accomplished. He remained under cover, his name unknown to all but a few Americans. But his past as chief of counterterrorism soon would return to haunt him, and unveil him with a searing light.

With Bush narrowly reelected and the CIA's ranking officers purged, Goss isolated himself in the director's suite, protected by his Praetorian Guard. He was aloof, detached, absent even when physically present. At the daily counterterrorism meeting, he sat nodding genially, saying little; his subordinates waited for his commands, and received none. He often kept to a congressman's schedule, leaving Washington on Thursday evening for a long weekend, returning on Monday morning, then complaining about how much work he had to do. After McLaughlin departed, Goss left the deputy director's position vacant for seven months. "I don't do personnel," he told his top officers.

By default, Dusty Foggo was running the CIA. He was a busy man: not only overseeing the agency's daily operations, but working to ensure that no one would be held responsible for the deaths and abuses inflicted on the CIA's prisoners.* On the side, he was juggling two CIA mistresses while promoting both to senior posts in the directorate of support and the general counsel's office, steering more classified contracts to Wilkes and reaping the kickbacks, and partying after hours in his office with the Gosslings. As they drank and caroused, they plotted on behalf of Goss to resist the overwhelming political consensus that American intelligence needed to be overhauled, beginning with the office of director of central intelligence.

Ever since 1947, the director had been both the chief executive officer of the CIA and the chairman of the board of all American intelligence

---

* Foggo stymied the inspector general when he found CIA officers responsible for grave misconduct and dismissed the findings of CIA accountability boards convened to impose discipline and punishment, however mild. In one case, he rejected a ten-day suspension for Matt Zirbel, who let a prisoner freeze to death while chained naked from the waist down at the Salt Pit outside Kabul. The inspector general had charged Zirbel with "reckless indifference" and falsifying his reports to headquarters. Zirbel went on to serve as a deputy chief of tribal operations in Pakistan.

agencies, now sixteen in number. The two hats had proved too many for any one mortal, much less one serving as the combatant commander of the war on terror. Bush had agreed with the 9/11 Commission's proposal to create a new superstructure with a new leader, the national intelligence director. Congress had created the position without writing provisions about making it work. Under the new law, Goss would be left with one job—CIA director. He had no intention of letting that happen. He had made it clear from the outset that he was also going to be the Oval Office briefer, the director of central intelligence, the national intelligence director, and the leader of a new National Counterterrorism Center. He would not wear one hat, or two, but five. This proved delusional.

Bush signed the Intelligence Reform Act into law on December 17 and went looking for someone to serve as director of national intelligence. The first offer went to Bob Gates, who had strongly opposed the new legislation. "Imagine, then, my astonishment when I got a call, in early January 2005, from Hadley, asking me if I'd be willing," Gates recounted. "It was clear that having passed the law and recognizing it was unworkable, they had decided among themselves there was only one person who could try to make the unworkable work." Gates put aside his misgivings and thought long and hard about it. Like James Baker and everyone else who had served the elder President Bush, he came from a world where you had to salute when the commander in chief asked you to serve. He said no. The job went begging as Bush began his second term.

"There was just no way of preventing it"

On January 20, 2005, in his second inaugural address, Bush proclaimed that his goal was "ending tyranny in our world." The war in Iraq was "in the great liberating tradition of this nation," freeing tens of millions of people from oppression. "We have lit a fire . . . in the minds of men. It warms those who feel its power. It burns those who fight its progress. And one day this untamed fire of freedom will reach the darkest corners of this world." A test of this proposition was at hand.

In ten days, an election was scheduled in Iraq to create a National Assembly charged with drafting a new constitution. The question was whether the vote should take place, in view of the untamed fires of violence and vengeance. Would it achieve a step toward democracy or simply draw voters into a killing zone for the insurgents? Would it unify the country or divide it into warring sects of Shia and Sunni and Kurds? From the Baghdad station, Bob Kandra, at the end of a yearlong tour, filed a grim report, noting that the insurgency still was gaining strength, launching a hundred attacks a day, up from sixty or seventy in December. But the American ambassador in Iraq, John Negroponte, who had arrived in June to run the largest diplomatic mission in American history, wasn't buying what the CIA was selling. Negroponte had a jaundiced view of the CIA's intelligence; as Bush's ambassador to the United Nations, he had sat alongside Tenet when Colin Powell delivered his disastrous indictment of Saddam Hussein and his arsenal. In Baghdad, his antipathy deepened.

"The CIA at that time was providing frightfully pessimistic information" about the course of the occupation, Negroponte said. "Actually, quite a bit of it was really quite bad, low quality, like they just decided they didn't like Iraq any more, and they do this sometimes. I know the CIA would do this; I've seen it before.* They had a couple of people who had a bee in their bonnet about how this place wasn't worth the effort anymore and they gave, in my opinion, unnecessary weight to defeatist views about the situation in Iraq, and they were feeding the President that stuff." Negroponte presented a far sunnier picture in secure videoconferences with

---

* "I had a lot of experience dealing with the Agency: Vietnam, Central America, the contras," Negroponte said. He had served as the American ambassador in Honduras during the contra wars; the contra command center, with Dusty Foggo as quartermaster, was in his embassy from 1981 to 1985. He had worked closely with the CIA director William J. Casey and helped to draft a top secret presidential finding authorizing support for the contras. He had served as the deputy national security adviser, under Colin Powell, as the Iran-contra scandal enveloped the White House and the CIA in 1987 and 1988. In that post, he was deeply involved with the CIA's failed efforts to overthrow the corrupt dictator Manuel Noriega of Panama, who had been on the agency's payroll for most of the prior twenty years.

the president. Bush liked that. He decided to make Negroponte the new intelligence czar.

Negroponte read the law establishing the post of DNI, the director of national intelligence, on the flight back to Washington. "I think the reason it got created was that the WMD fiasco just got everybody so mad that there was a reaction on the Hill that said don't just stand there, do something," he said. "I don't think President Bush wanted the DNI. I don't think he wanted the reform legislation." But the Curveball case—the CIA's embrace of an unvetted fabricator—had been the last straw. "It's because of Curveball that this all happened," he said. "If it had just been 9/11, I don't think we would have had intelligence reform. But then when it came out that that source, Curveball, had been a phony, and that came out in the summer of 2004, there was no stopping reform, there was just no way of preventing it. I think the President just decided he had no choice but to go along with it. Why would a man who is the son of a former CIA director voluntarily, willingly, strip that office of significant authority?"

Negroponte was a diplomat, not an espiocrat. ("I knew quite a bit about intelligence," he said. "I'd just never been an intelligence officer.") He did not have the time or the experience to renovate American intelligence without a blueprint. For that task, Bush chose Gen. Mike Hayden, director of the National Security Agency since 1999, as Negroponte's principal deputy, the number two man. In short order, Hayden became the most influential voice in American intelligence and remained so for the following four years.

Appointed along with Negroponte on April 21, 2005, and charged with creating the wiring diagrams for the new national intelligence superstructure, he went to work with Magic Markers and butcher paper taped to the wall in the Old Executive Office Building next to the White House. "The law was very unspecific as to what the structure should be," Hayden said. "How should we organize ourselves? How many deputy directors do we need? What should they be doing?" He was sketching out the most significant structural changes to American intelligence since 1947.

"We began with some big ideas . . . and made it up as we went along," said Thomas Fingar, the DNI's new chief of analysis. Fingar, who had run the State Department's small but superb intelligence branch, took measure of the CIA's demoralized analysts, and he determined that "nobody had any idea of who was doing what where." He commandeered the most talented among them, took charge of the President's Daily Brief, and imposed a new intellectual rigor on the preparation of National Intelligence Estimates. His mission was clear: never repeat the WMD fiasco, which had brought shame upon the American intelligence community and paved the path to war.

All these changes wrenched power away from the seventh floor. Negroponte thought he could handle Porter Goss: they had been fraternity brothers at Yale, graduating together in 1960, and they were both gentlemen from the same patrician Republican establishment. He regarded Goss as a friend, as did Hayden. But every time they tried to assert their new powers, Goss and Foggo pushed back vehemently. "The CIA to this day does not like what happened with the reform," Negroponte said. "I think they continue to value and want to uphold the premier position in the intelligence community, and where they felt they could resist some of these changes, they did." He defined his own job as delivering the daily brief at the White House, taking charge of intelligence analysis, and creating new centers for counterterrorism, counterintelligence, and counterproliferation, all requiring a combination of foreign and domestic intelligence, and each demanding CIA expertise. Early on, Negroponte requisitioned more than seventy CIA analysts for the new National Counterterrorism Center under his command, fusing the thinking of the CIA, the FBI, the Pentagon, and Homeland Security, among other agencies. Goss refused to send them, and a bitter confrontation ensued. "It became a serious point of contention," Negroponte said. "They chose to resist it. I think what they didn't expect was that I was going to enforce the authority that I had."

This fight was one among many cases of what General Hayden called "significant and actually self-destructive pushback" from the CIA. "It wasn't Porter, it was his deputy, Dusty Foggo, and Dusty waged guerrilla warfare," Hayden said. "Porter was such a hands-off manager and Dusty was just being so obstructionist, up to and including vehicles. 'No, you can't have vehicles.' *'What do you mean, I can't have vehicles?'* " At Hayden's suggestion, Negroponte sent a message to all the CIA's station chiefs, saying that in addition to their current duties, they would also be his representatives to allied foreign intelligence services. "And I'll be damned if Dusty doesn't send a message out saying, *Disregard first telegram until further notice*," Hayden said. "I actually went to CIA and had a meeting in George's conference room, now it's Porter's conference room, with senior leadership, saying, 'Guys, you know me; we're not trying to screw you.' It was just very difficult. It had an awful lot to do with the Agency's prestige in a very difficult period."

The difficulties multiplied throughout the fall of 2005. In October, Congress passed the Detainee Treatment Act, Senator John McCain's effort to ban cruel, inhuman, or degrading treatment of prisoners, including the CIA's terrorist suspects. "This isn't about who they are," McCain said. "This is about who we are. These are the values that distinguish us from our enemies, and we can never, never allow our enemies to take those values away." Goss went to the White House to urge the president to veto the bill, arguing that it did not adequately protect the CIA's officers from prosecution. When it became clear that Bush would sign it, Rodriguez convinced Goss to play tough. The director wrote to Hadley informing him that the CIA's still-secret interrogation program would have to be shut down if the bill became law. Bush thought he had a deal with the director to keep the program going, despite the risks. He would never put much faith in Goss again.

The program didn't stay secret. On November 2, Dana Priest of the *Washington Post* published a story that detailed with exacting precision the existence and the origins of the CIA's prisons. It began: "The CIA has been hiding and interrogating some of its most important al Qaeda captives at a Soviet-era compound in Eastern Europe." It continued: "The secret facility is part of a covert prison system set up by the CIA nearly four years ago ... referred to as 'black sites' in classified White House, CIA, Justice Department and congressional documents." For the first time, the

American people began to understand the scope of the CIA's program, and the role the White House had played in authorizing it. The Bush administration, led by Secretary of State Condi Rice, stonewalled and obfuscated about the secret prisons; Bush himself would not acknowledge they existed for ten months. In a follow-up article, Priest cited General Hayden's more forthright conversation with a delegation from Human Rights Watch, whose investigators had traced CIA flights from Afghanistan and the Middle East to the black sites in Poland and Romania.

"We're going to live on the edge" of the law, Hayden had said.

"A horrible, horrible spot"

Two days after the *Post* exposed the existence of the black sites, Rodriguez and his chief of staff, the future CIA director Gina Haspel, decided to destroy evidence of what had gone on within them. Back in December 2002, when she was the chief of base at the CIA's prison in Thailand and he was the new chief of counterterrorism, she had asked him what to do with the stack of ninety-six videotapes recording the brutal interrogations of Abu Zubayda and Abd al-Rahim al-Nashiri, the CIA's first high-value detainees, who had been stripped naked, chained, deprived of sleep for days on end, and waterboarded. The tapes had recorded CIA officers and analysts who had both inflicted the torture and been brought to tears by it. Rodriguez had been seized by an overwhelming impulse to destroy them. He had wisely checked with the CIA lawyer John Rizzo first, and he argued his case with great force.

Rizzo recoiled. "I thought that destroying the tapes was fraught with enormous risk for the Agency," he said. "I informed Jose that he was not to do anything with those tapes. Not then, and not until further notice." Rodriguez had no intention of obeying his counsel. This simmering dispute had started boiling over after the pictures of torture at Abu Ghraib had surfaced in April 2004. The tapes, Rodriguez feared, would destroy the clandestine service if they became public. The American people, he said, would not distinguish between the depravities of military police in Iraq leading prisoners on dog leashes and the CIA's wringing answers from its detainees with brutal force. "When we started to take prisoners, we just did not know what we were doing. We are not jailers. We don't have those skills. And abuses were made. But shit happens, you know," Rodriguez said a decade thereafter. "I knew that the tapes would play as if we were all psychopaths and that's something that we didn't want."

On November 4, at Rodriguez's direction, Haspel drafted a cable to the Bangkok station chief authorizing their destruction. On November 8, Rodriguez called up the directive on his computer and hit *send*. He deliberately did not copy CIA lawyers or anyone else in authority. The next day the station chief emailed headquarters saying he had tossed the tapes into an industrial shredder. A lawyer from the counterterrorism center forwarded that message to Rizzo. "Within seconds of reading it, I e-mailed my own one-word comment back to him: '"WHAT?!?!"'" Rizzo recounted. Rodriguez had chosen "to ignore and defy the White House, the director of national intelligence, and the director of the CIA. And, of course, me. In my thirty-four-year career at CIA, I never felt as upset and betrayed as I did that morning."

Dusty Foggo received a disturbing message from Goss's chief of staff on the evening of November 10:

> While I understand Jose's "decision" (and believe the tapes were bad news) I was just told by Rizzo that [the CIA's lawyers] DID NOT concur on the cable—it was never discussed with him (this is perhaps worse news, in that we may have "improperly" destroyed something).
>
> Cable was apparently drafted by [Haspel] and released by Jose; they are the only two names on it, so I am told by Rizzo. Either [Haspel] lied to Jose about "clearing" [the cable with CIA lawyers and the Inspector General] . . . or Jose misstated the facts. (It is not without relevance that [Haspel] figured prominently in the tapes, as [Haspel] was in charge of [the black site] at the time and clearly would want the tapes destroyed.)
>
> Rizzo is clearly upset, because he was on the hook to notify [White

> House counsel] Harriet Miers of the status of the tapes. . . . Rizzo called Harriet this afternoon and she was livid, which he said was actually unusual for her. Rizzo does not think this is likely to just go away.*

It did not go away.

Goss kept his head down and his mouth shut. But the director soon determined that he had to fire Rodriguez. He discreetly offered the job to several senior CIA officers whom he'd gotten to know as chairman of the House intelligence committee, dispatching his new deputy director, Vice Adm. Bert Callen, to make the pitch in person so there would be no written record. He found no takers. Then Goss gave up. He did nothing to discipline Rodriguez. But he never trusted him again.

"Jose knows how I feel about it," he said a decade later. "He left me in a horrible, horrible spot."

By the start of 2006, with trust broken, the secret prisons a public scandal, and investigations by the press and federal prosecutors flourishing, Goss had brought the upper echelons of the CIA to their lowest point since the Iran-contra debacle two decades before. The momentum in the war on terror had been "squandered by infighting" at the CIA, as Rodriguez himself admitted. The hunt for bin Laden and his followers had gone cold; al Qaeda in Iraq was flourishing. Their spectacular coordinated attacks had shocked the world—one in the London subway system, which killed fifty-two people, another on the luxury hotels of Amman, which killed fifty-seven. Rodriguez's deputy, Rob Richer, resigned after ten months on the job. He let it be known to his colleagues and to the Senate intelligence committee that he had lost confidence in the director. Not long thereafter, Rodriguez would fire Robert Grenier, the former Islamabad station chief, who had replaced him as the CIA's counterterrorism czar.

---

* This email, which the author has edited for clarity—relying on Rizzo's memoir and declassified documents to reverse the CIA's redactions—was reproduced in a judge's 2011 order in the American Civil Liberties Union's litigation with the CIA over the destruction of the tapes. It should be noted that Rodriguez, not Haspel, had "misstated the facts" about obtaining the approvals of higher authority.

Rodriguez had found Grenier lacking the requisite flies-walking-across-their-eyeballs militancy. The dismissal made the newspapers, another chapter in the saga of a CIA in turmoil. And now another departure, far stormier, was brewing.

Goss knew that Dusty Foggo was under investigation by the FBI, the IRS, and the inspectors general of the CIA and the Pentagon. The director did nothing about it. Foggo would resign four months later, after the FBI raided CIA headquarters and sealed his seventh-floor office. Indicted for fraud and money laundering, Foggo fought the law, and he fought dirty. Facing twenty years in prison, he claimed to be a hero in the war on terror. He used graymail—a tactic favored by turncoat spies—to foil his prosecutors. They warned the judge that he was vowing "to expose the cover of virtually every CIA employee with whom he interacted and to divulge to the world some of our country's most sensitive programs" if the case went forward. Foggo's threats forced the prosecutors to drop all but one charge. He eventually pleaded guilty and served thirty-seven months in prison.*

"No alliance could be as infuriating or as productive"

Far removed from the CIA's internal warfare, something new was taking shape in the battle for Iraq. Maj. Gen. Stanley McChrystal, the Joint Special Operations Command's leader, and Mike D'Andrea, the single-minded counterterrorist who had become Baghdad station chief in March, were assembling a formidable team to hunt for the man who had blown up the UN headquarters and the Jordanian embassy in the summer of 2003, and gone on to kill thousands of Iraqis and hundreds of American soldiers

---

* On the day Foggo was indicted, a federal judge sentenced a CIA contractor named David Passaro to eight years and four months for killing an innocent man, a farmer named Abdul Wali, at a CIA compound in Asadabad, Afghanistan, in 2002. Passaro beat him to death with his fists. The CIA had hired him despite the fact that he had been dismissed from the Hartford, Connecticut, police department for beating a man in a brawl.

ever since: the thuggish Jordanian terrorist Abu Musab al-Zarqawi, the self-appointed leader of al Qaeda in Iraq.

The CIA's Nada Bakos, branch chief of the unit targeting al-Zarqawi, memorably described him as "a fanatical, hypocritical, murderous dropout who was capable of masterminding a terror network that for years confounded the most powerful military and intelligence agencies in the history of creation yet who had the general maturity of a nineteen-year-old." His goal was to create chaos by attacking Shia leaders in Iraq, provoking Sunni retaliation, and igniting a religious war that would tear the nation apart. He was well on his way to a catastrophic success. He killed Muslims mercilessly while brandishing the banner of al Qaeda, and he broadcast images of slain Americans as a lure to attract foreign fighters from around the world. He had become the face of the insurgency.

McChrystal and D'Andrea were starting to create a counterforce against al Qaeda in Iraq: American and British special forces schooled in spy craft, paramilitary men from the ground and air branches of the CIA's special activities division, CIA officers and analysts, National Security Agency surveillance experts, FBI agents skilled in forensics, and overhead reconnaissance planes and satellites to map the battlefield. McChrystal's deputy, the SEAL commander William McRaven, who would go on to lead the CIA's mission to kill Osama bin Laden in 2011, had told him bluntly that the military needed all of them in the fight.

McChrystal created an open-plan war room in his headquarters at the Balad Air Base, forty miles north of Baghdad, to fuse intelligence and covert operations with military force. The union was a shotgun wedding following a fierce struggle among headstrong men. "No alliance could be as infuriating or as productive as my relationship with the CIA," General McChrystal wrote. "We worked more closely with it than any other agency, and the effort tried the patience of both sides. . . . At best, we were fighting parallel, fractured campaigns against al Qaeda; ours had to be a unified fight." As the task force began to coalesce, "we started closing in on Zarqawi," McRaven said. "I believe that is what really brought the CIA and the task force together. . . . Before long we were driving the train and the agency was very happy to be part of it."

But winter brought dark days for the CIA's counterterrorists, and the darkness descended in full after February 22, 2006, when al-Zarqawi blew up the golden dome of the al-Askari mosque in Samarra, sixty-five miles north of Baghdad, severely damaging one of the world's holiest Shia shrines. The country soon erupted in sectarian rage. The violence had been escalating for many months; the bombing was a barrel of gasoline dropped on a bonfire. Iraqi society was "dissolving at the point of a gun, at the blade of a knife," said David Satterfield, the number-two man at the American embassy in Baghdad under Ambassador Zalmay Khalilzad. "This was extremely distressing, because if it continued, a true civil war was actually possible." Al-Zarqawi wanted the government and civil society to collapse, and if that came to pass, he wanted America defeated by a guerrilla insurgency, much as it had lost the war in Vietnam. "We, as a nation, were being viewed exclusively through an Iraq success-or-failure prism," Satterfield said. "And we ourselves had cast that prism." If the American occupation failed, it would be the purest manna for the leaders of al Qaeda and their many multinational subsidiaries. Bin Laden could proclaim that Islamic holy warriors had knocked off one superpower by defeating the Soviet occupiers in Afghanistan, and knocked off another by repulsing the Americans in Iraq—a pronouncement that could inflame the minds of millions.

Bush was now "at the nadir of his sentiments about Iraq," Negroponte recounted. "He's totally depressed. . . . Bordering on despair." Yet the bombing of the mosque and the ensuing slaughter did not shock him into clarity. He still did not see that the civil war the CIA had long foretold was now an inferno, and the fire was spreading from Iraq throughout the nations of Islam and beyond. Bush continued to assure the public that America was winning. Ambassador Khalilzad's surrealistically sunny video briefings from the Green Zone had helped convince him that he was on the right track. The president kept saying his generals would provide him with a strategy for victory, and the generals, terrified of contradicting Rumsfeld's insistence on staying the course, kept telling him their plans were working, against all evidence to the contrary—including the CIA's now-relentless reporting from Baghdad.

"We'd gotten those terrible intelligence assessments that said this is lost, we're losing, the circumstances are terrible. And these continued, really, through 2006," Secretary of State Rice said ruefully nine years thereafter. "Not only was the strategy not working, but we couldn't explain to anybody what it was we were trying to do. . . . I don't think you can explain something that doesn't exist."

The strategic black hole at the White House was devouring tens of thousands of lives and hundreds of billions of dollars. The war in Iraq was breeding terrorists far faster than the CIA and American soldiers could capture or kill them. "The Iraq jihad is shaping a new generation of terrorist leaders and operatives," warned a new National Intelligence Estimate, the first in four years to analyze worldwide terrorism trends. "Perceived jihadist success there would inspire more fighters to continue the struggle elsewhere. The Iraq conflict has become the 'cause celebre' for jihadists, breeding a deep resentment of US involvement in the Muslim world and cultivating supporters for the global jihadist movement."

The CIA had helped to win the struggle against Soviet communism by practicing political warfare—conducting espionage, broadcasting propaganda, fixing elections, bankrolling presidents and prime ministers. But none of those weapons were working in the war on terror. By his conduct of the war, Bush had squandered the moral authority to project power in America's name. Absent a strategy, the CIA was a ship in irons, adrift, with no wind in its sails. Its officers on the front lines received no coherent direction from headquarters or the White House. Bereft of leadership, they soldiered on, fighting implacable enemies in Iraq, Afghanistan, Syria, and beyond.

Chapter Thirteen

THE BLACK CLOUD

Tom Sylvester, three years removed from the freezing slopes of Iraqi Kurdistan, now commanded a more perilous post: the CIA's station chief in Damascus. His mission was to penetrate the Syrian government and uncover the secret alliances of its dictator, Bashar al-Assad, who had made his nation a switchboard in the global network of jihad. Sylvester ran a black station, its existence kept secret from Assad's intelligence services, which required extraordinary precautions and excruciating discipline among his officers. Syria was a police state, and they were under unremitting physical and electronic surveillance by counterspies.

Damascus served as a regional headquarters for Hezbollah, the terrorist force led by Imad Mughniyeh, America's most wanted jihadist after bin Laden. The other sinister presence in the Syrian capital was Qasem Soleimani, commander of the Revolutionary Guards' Quds Force, created in 1979 to export the Iranian revolution across the nations of Islam and beyond. The Quds Force had given birth to Hezbollah in Lebanon in 1982, sponsored Mughniyeh's murderous attacks on Americans, and now contributed $100 million a year to its coffers. Soleimani, the most feared intelligence officer in the Middle East, oversaw spying and sabotage operations, bankrolled politicians and terrorist groups, and ran assassination squads from Beirut to Baghdad. He led what became known as the Axis of Resistance, uniting the Quds Force, Hezbollah, Hamas, Shia militants, and the Syrians against America and its allies. He aimed to make Iran the winner of the American war in Iraq.

On the day after the fifth anniversary of 9/11, the Damascus station was attacked by an al Qaeda death squad armed with a huge truck bomb, grenades, and AK-47s. They assaulted the American embassy, trying to breach its high walls and kill everyone inside. As the first shots rang out, Sylvester and his deputy, Marc Polymeropoulos, who had served under him in Iraq, donned body armor and grabbed their weapons. Sylvester sent a FLASH cable to headquarters and every station chief in the Middle East, warning against a coordinated regional attack. Syrian guards in the diplomatic compound killed the hit team. But for a faulty fuse on the truck bomb—a delivery van loaded with explosives strapped to propane gas canisters—dozens of Americans could have died in the biggest attack on an American embassy since the East Africa bombings of 1998. After the all clear was sounded, Polymeropoulos bagged a fragment of the severed head of one of the terrorists, popped it into the embassy's freezer for an FBI forensics team, and promptly forgot about it, to the eventual horror of his colleagues who discovered it.

"Who is the enemy?"

On March 6, 2006, Sylvester flew to Kuwait, joining a conclave of twenty-eight American spies, soldiers, and diplomats, led by General McChrystal, the special-forces commander, and Hank Crumpton, who had left the CIA to serve as the State Department's counterterrorism ambassador. The group included American ambassadors and charges d'affaires from Iraq, Syria, Saudi Arabia, Kuwait, Turkey, and Jordan, along with CIA station chiefs Peter Enzminger from Amman, Joe Forcier from Kuwait, and Thaddeus Troy from Ankara.

They met with a shared sense of emergency: America was losing in Iraq, American generals were out of ideas, American foreign policy was at a dead end, and al Qaeda was very much alive. A new generation of jihadists was rising, young men driven by anger over Abu Ghraib, Guantanamo, and the black sites. These abuses had sabotaged America's image in the world and the CIA's vital liaisons with intelligence services in Europe and the Middle East—"Undermining international confidence in the United States' ability to conduct an effective war on terrorism that remains true to American values," as the Kuwait group bluntly put it in a subsequent cable to Washington. The American military now held some twenty-five thousand Iraqi prisoners, largely Sunnis, in dismal conditions. They were creating new enemies by detaining innocent people, killing and brutalizing civilians, destroying homes, wielding blunt force against an insurgency that had been embedded in the citizenry.

But the American occupation was no longer the leading cause of the violence in Iraq. The country was being torn apart by thousands of foreign fighters. They were flying into Syria from afar, traveling across the open border into Iraq, strapping on suicide vests, detonating car bombs, and planting EFPs, explosively formed projectiles. These sophisticated roadside bombs with powerful shaped charges of molten copper pierced the most heavily armored vehicles, and "there was zero question where they were coming from," McChrystal said. "We knew where all the factories were in Iran." The EFPs killed hundreds of Americans, accounting for about a fifth of the combat deaths in 2006. Many of the Pentagon's generals and colonels in Baghdad had been staring at this lethal caravan of foreigners like a cow watching a train go by. They saw Iraq as if it were an island, without thinking of how it fit into the map of the world.

McChrystal and Mike D'Andrea—now the new chief of counterterrorism at headquarters—had developed a clearer picture of the enemy. Their goal was to find al-Zarqawi, kill him, capture his acolytes, seize their laptops and phones, and develop deeper intelligence on who the insurgents were, where their sources of support lay, and what they were planning in secret.*

---

* The joint task force did kill al-Zarqawi on June 7, 2006—a spectacular if fleeting success. "Zarqawi's death was an achievement, but it was only symbolic," a member of McChrystal's task force told the journalist Mark Bowden. "Zarqawi had hoped to incite a sectarian war . . . and he accomplished that. His strategy worked: Target the Shia so they will retaliate. When we killed Zarqawi, there were ten just like him to take his place." The insurgency in Iraq evolved into ISIS, the Islamic State. (Mark Bowden, "The Ploy," *The Atlantic*, May 2007.)

Al Qaeda in Iraq kept meticulous records, and as the joint task force gathered strength and confidence, the CIA and the commandos began mapping the human terrain of the insurgency. "In Iraq, when we first started, the question was, 'Where is the enemy?'" McChrystal said. "As we got smarter, we started to ask, 'Who is the enemy?' And we thought we were pretty clever. And then we realized that wasn't the right question, and we asked, 'What's the enemy doing or trying to do?' And it wasn't until we got further along that we said, 'Why are they the enemy?'" The answers required a deeper fusion of the CIA and the military than America had yet achieved.

The foreign fighters came from Saudi Arabia, Libya, Syria, Jordan, Lebanon, and across North Africa and Central Asia. Their supporters were in Riyadh, Amman, Tunis, Hamburg, and London. Their political and military leadership was in Damascus and Tehran. Their networks were linked through jihadist internet sites, encrypted communications, and covert supplies of money and weapons. After they arrived at Damascus International Airport, some carrying thousands of dollars in contributions for the insurgency, smugglers took them through a series of safe houses into Iraq, where their handlers sorted them out, assigning the smarter ones to make bombs and the less savvy to be suicide bombers.

Sylvester saw the network of foreign fighters as a threat that transcended Iraq; one day al Qaeda might marshal them to attack American allies and American outposts around the world. Jihadists were flourishing in Algeria, Azerbaijan, Bosnia, Chechnya, Dagestan, Eritrea, Indonesia, Kashmir, Kosovo, Palestine, the Philippines, Somalia, Tajikistan, Thailand, and the United Kingdom, where British intelligence had detected the deadliest plot since 9/11 taking shape, a conspiracy to blow commercial airliners out of the sky over the Atlantic.

The Kuwait conferees agreed that America's soldiers and spies couldn't kill their way out of this morass. But they had to begin by trying to staunch the flow of foreign fighters from Syria. Short of bombing the Damascus airport—an option being weighed in Washington—it would fall to Sylvester and his handful of officers to try to recruit and run agents in Syria's military and intelligence services, and use them to begin to penetrate the networks and sanctuaries of the foreign fighters.

It was hard enough to recruit a Syrian. It was harder to talk with him once he was recruited. To meet a recruited agent in a safe house was incredibly risky; such a meeting would last a minute or two at the most, at the end of a surveillance detection run that might last eight hours or more. The only other ways to communicate were old-fashioned tradecraft—a dead-drop message in a hollowed-out rock, a brush pass on a busy street—or arranging a meeting beyond Syria's borders.

And if that could be done—and, remarkably, it was—it was only one piece of the puzzle. The CIA's officers needed terrorists' cell phone numbers. They needed their fingerprints. They needed to trace their families and their finances. They needed a great deal of help from allied spy services in Jordan and Saudi Arabia. They needed new ways to fuse human intelligence, signals intelligence, airborne reconnaissance, and counterterrorism operations. They needed fresh intelligence as badly as the military needed fresh troops. They needed new talent: the ambassadors gathered in Kuwait acknowledged that no one person in any of their six embassies was in charge of counterterrorism. They needed the CIA's paramilitaries, case officers, and analysts to work ever closer with American special forces on the battlefield.

In short, the Kuwait conference reported, the war on Iraq and the war on terrorism required "a highly coordinated and flexible response at the whole-of-government level"—a plan of attack "that brings to bear all instruments of national power" against the growing threat. This would demand a revamping of American strategy at the highest levels. And that would require new thinking and new leaders in Washington.

"What the hell is going on here?"

On May 5, Bush fired Porter Goss. The president's father approved. The next day, Goss got on a plane to deliver the commencement address at Tiffin University, a small college ninety miles west of Cleveland, Ohio. He introduced himself as "a recovering politician" and he offered some bitter wisdom. "If this were a graduating class of CIA officers, my advice would be short and to the point," he said. "Admit nothing, deny everything, and make counteraccusations"—a fitting epitaph for his stint on the seventh floor.

Looking back, Mike Morell, the future deputy director, called that dismal nineteen-month tenure the worst stretch of his three decades in the CIA. Some at headquarters compared the reign of Goss to the Republican Palace under Bremer, with zealous apparatchiks carrying out imperial edicts. Others called to mind Cambodia under the dictator Pol Pot, who killed people who wore glasses because they could read. Goss had been the wrong man at the wrong time. He would be remembered as one of the worst directors in the history of the CIA.

Gen. Mike Hayden took over on May 30, the first professional intelligence officer to lead the CIA since Bob Gates left the building in 1993. The son of a welder and a homemaker, born in Pittsburgh, Pennsylvania, just before V-E Day in 1945, Hayden often displayed an unusually sunny disposition for a commander in the war on terror. He thought his first task was restoring order at headquarters. "From the outset," he said, "my approach was to settle these people down." He immediately fired the Gosslings and brought back the two best men they had driven out—first Steve Kappes to serve as his deputy, then Mike Morell as his executive director. He saw the CIA as deeply demoralized, bruised by continuous crisis since the end of the cold war, battered by its public image as brutal jailers. He began a battle to heal its self-inflicted wounds.

"I was told by people who were there, and really starkly by people who were no longer there, that this was about the existence and the future of the institution," Hayden remembered.

He saw the architecture of the CIA's secret prison system crumbling. The inspector general had ruled that its interrogation techniques likely violated the laws against torture. The black sites had been in limbo for six months, ever since Bush had reluctantly signed the congressional ban on brutalizing prisoners. On June 29, the Supreme Court ruled in *Hamdan v. Rumsfeld* that the Geneva Convention covered al Qaeda terrorists. The legal foundation for their indefinite detention—the military commissions set up by Cheney's shadow national-security network after 9/11—was unconstitutional. Bush and Cheney had violated the laws of war and the United States.* But the CIA had taken the rap.

"This black cloud," as Hayden called it, had to lift. And the only way to do that was to let a little sunlight in. A director determined to selectively declassify the CIA's secrets is in dangerous political terrain. It's like clearing land mines in a battlefield: the way forward is safer, unless one explodes beneath you.

Hayden gazed out from the seventh floor at the green horizon, turned to his computer, drafted a two-page memo, and took it to Stephen Hadley, the national security adviser. First of all, Hayden said, the CIA needed a way out of the dark labyrinth it had created. It had taken prisoners believing they would never see the light of day again. It now had squeezed almost all of the information possible out of those it held. It had no exit strategy for them, or for itself. Hayden wanted to empty the secret cells and send fourteen "high-value" prisoners to the ultimate black site—the CIA's Camp 7 at Guantanamo—but keep the prisons open and retain the legal authority to deprive detainees of sleep and solid food should the CIA ever capture a major terrorist suspect again. Then came two truly risky ideas. He wanted to brief the full membership of the congressional intelligence committees on the secret prison program, and he recommended that Bush come clean with the American people.

Hayden packed a set of Air Force dress blues with four stars on each shoulder and took off for Iraq in early August, the first stop on a tour that would include Pakistan and Afghanistan. He flew into Baghdad on a hulking C-17 cargo jet with a large contingent of officers led by Jose

---

* Colin Powell called the military commissions "one of the dumbest things we've ever done. There was no consultation. Rumsfeld was against it. Suddenly I'm away on a trip and the next thing I hear is that the Vice President with the help of his folks, his lawyer associates at the Justice Department, had come up with this order and had walked it into the President with no further deliberation, no further discussion, and had the President sign it." (Colin Powell and Richard Armitage oral history, Miller Center, University of Virginia, https://millercenter.org/the-presidency/presidential-oral-histories/colin-l-powell-and-richard-l-armitage-oral-history.) The Supreme Court plaintiff, Salim Hamdan, had been bin Laden's chauffeur in Afghanistan. His Guantanamo conviction for providing "material support to terrorism" was overturned in 2012.

Rodriguez and a small group of analysts, including two young women who were pushing Hayden—and through him, the president—to acknowledge that Iraq was in a state of civil war. The phrase was politically explosive. It gave the lie to the president's public assurances that democracy was abloom in Baghdad. The analysts wanted *civil war* printed in boldface in a forthcoming National Intelligence Estimate. Hayden had brought them along so they could consider their judgment. He freely acknowledged that "Iraq looked like one of Dante's circles of hell." But was the United States in purgatory, or something worse? Hayden convened the roughly five hundred members of the Baghdad station in the purloined palace the CIA had seized from Saddam, built in the baroque style best described as Early Dictator. He began with a blunt question: "What the hell is going on here?"

The station chief, Paul Nevin, six months into his second tour running the Baghdad station, was the smartest guy in the room.* He gave it to Hayden straight: The American occupation was failing. The insurgency's attacks were killing a hundred Iraqis a day; more than two hundred American soldiers would die and more than two thousand would be wounded that summer. The CIA's officers hadn't been able to travel outside the Green Zone without a military escort in full battle rattle for three years. Nevin said the prime minister, Nouri al-Maliki, would not work with the Iraqi intelligence service created by the CIA. He was part of the sectarian warfare, siding with his fellow Shia, and his interior ministry ran uniformed death squads. His government was a nest of vipers in which the virtuous lived in fear.

Hayden left Baghdad convinced that Iraq was indeed in a state of civil war, and that America had to change course and confront the chaos

---

* Nevin, in contrast to his predecessor, the acerbic D'Andrea, was a cultivated man who cared for his subordinates. A fluent Arabic speaker who sported crisp seersucker suits, he came from old money; his family kept a compound in the tony town of Blue Hill, Maine. Nevin had been a NOC—traveling the world under unofficial cover, often in disguise—before coming inside at headquarters during the late 1990s. He had served as station chief in Kabul in 2002 and 2003 and done a short stint as acting chief of station in Baghdad in 2004. He would complete his career as chief of the Near East division, and he held that post when the CIA found and killed Osama bin Laden in 2011.

head-on, rather than pulling back, as Rumsfeld and his generals kept urging.

"No good deed went unpunished"

Hayden and Rodriguez flew onward to confer with their Pakistani intelligence counterparts at the ISI, trying to spur them onward in the fight against al Qaeda. Bin Laden was issuing new calls for jihad from an unknown hideout. A new terrorist force, the Pakistani Taliban, was emerging. The CIA's officers in Islamabad, to their chagrin, remained dependent to a degree on the duplicitous ISI. The CIA station in Kabul knew that elements of the ISI secretly supported attacks against American forces in Afghanistan; its officers were running cross-border operations into Pakistan without notifying their colleagues in Islamabad, creating bad blood between them.

When Hayden took off for Kabul two days later, Rodriguez remained to confer with Gen. Ashfaq Kayani, the ISI chief. "I'm tired of you Americans saying we are not doing enough to fight the terrorists," the general told him. On August 9, he offered to show the CIA what he could do. The ISI had picked up the trail of Rashid Rauf, a British fugitive working with al Qaeda. Rauf was the linchpin of a developing plot to blow up a half dozen or more passenger jets flying from London to the United States. British intelligence had penetrated a large cell of the London jihadis and placed its members under the closest surveillance. The conspirators had sent their leader to see Rauf and an al Qaeda bomb maker in Pakistan who had devised a solution of hydrogen peroxide that could be disguised as a sports drink, carried onto a plane, and detonated with AA batteries. The plot was at least several weeks, if not months, from fruition. But Rauf could be snatched that night.

"General Kayani saw that there was a rare opportunity to roll up a terrorist and he asked me if the U.S. would support Rauf's immediate capture," Rodriguez recounted. "I made an on-the-spot decision." He always had believed it was better to ask for forgiveness than ask for permission.

He conferred with no one, acting on his own authority, "despite a vague understanding that the British authorities were hoping we would not move too rashly against Rauf." The understanding was anything but vague. The day before Rodriguez made his snap decision, Prime Minister Tony Blair had asked President Bush to ensure that the United States would do nothing to disrupt the extraordinarily sensitive investigation. Bush gave his word. At CIA headquarters, deputy director Kappes already had given that assurance to his British counterparts. At the White House, Hadley and the homeland security adviser, Fran Townsend, had done the same.

On Rodriguez's word, Rauf was arrested that night, sparking a blaze of publicity and a mad dash to roll up the London cell.* Rodriguez called Gina Haspel, his chief of staff, and asked her to inform Kappes of his decision. She called back and said: "Steve is livid." Hayden heard about the fracas in Kabul. "All hell broke loose at my headquarters," he remembered. "I was glad to be in a war zone." The British had been robbed of time to build their case against the plotters, whose subsequent trials often foundered for a lack of admissible evidence. The heads of MI5 and MI6 were furious with Rodriguez. Their trust in the CIA was damaged, as was Downing Street's faith in the White House. The debacle mattered little to Rodriguez. What counted was his bold decision to take down a terrorist. In his view, he had singlehandedly disrupted the deadliest conspiracy since 9/11.

"The liquids plot saga turned out to be emblematic of my CIA career," he reflected. "No good deed went unpunished."

The British were not the only ally at odds with the CIA.

In Germany, prosecutors were preparing thirteen arrest warrants in the case of a Lebanese-born German citizen, Khalid el-Masri, abducted in Macedonia in 2003 and flown to the Salt Pit in Afghanistan. Two months after the CIA knew it had mistaken his identity, its officers had flown him

---

* The revelation of the plot led to an instantaneous ban on passengers carrying more than 3.4 ounces of liquid on an aircraft, which remains in effect at this writing. The Pakistanis dropped terrorism charges against Rauf, who then escaped from a high-security prison under less than mysterious circumstances. The CIA killed him with a drone strike in October 2008.

to a desolate hilltop in Albania and abandoned him on a dirt road. The inspector general found that the chief of the bin Laden station, Alfreda Bikowsky, was responsible for the rendition and detention. Hayden would refuse to convene an accountability board to judge her.

In Italy, the courts had brought kidnapping charges against Jeffrey Castelli, then station chief in Rome; Robert Seldon Lady, then Milan base chief; and twenty-four other Americans in the 2003 case of a radical imam seized in broad daylight in Milan, rendered to Egypt, and released after his ties to terrorism proved flimsy. A squad of CIA officers sent by Gina Haspel, then running surveillance and rendition operations, was responsible for snatching the imam, and their tradecraft had been appalling. The Italian police had identified each of them through credit-card and cell phone records and traceable SIM cards, all revealing their true names. The snafu had gone spectacularly public. The Italian press gleefully noted that the CIA officers had stayed in $500-a-night hotels while staking out the imam in Milan. Rodriguez blocked the inspector general from investigating the blown operation and Haspel's role in it. His loyalty to his officers was widely admired at headquarters. It had helped to keep him in power.

"We were denying people their freedom, likely forever"

Hayden came home with a new portfolio of problems, all boding ill for the CIA and counterterrorism, and all paling before the immensity of what confronted the United States in Iraq. Toward the end of August, he spent a few days trying to unwind at a Navy compound in Key West, Florida, once President Truman's winter White House. One major event was on his agenda: a videoconference with Bush, Cheney, and Rice, arising from his recommendation to go public on the CIA's secret prisons. He appeared onscreen in a colorful tropical shirt straight out of Margaritaville, and he began explaining what the president should say: this was not the CIA's program, this was *America's* program, and it had protected the nation from attack. Rice, by her account, gave a passionate speech telling Bush to renounce the black sites. "Democracies don't disappear people," she said.

"Don't let this be your legacy." Cheney, in his low and reasonable voice, ripped into Rice. She called it "the most intense confrontation of my time in Washington." Hayden listened to them fight it out and then hammered home his argument. "We're not the nation's jailers," he said.

"The vice president, he didn't like that," Hayden recalled, and neither did Rodriguez. "Jose wanted to keep the harsh techniques."

Hayden told the president that the CIA could fly its fourteen remaining prisoners to Guantanamo in a few days—and then "you will be able to set forth, without apology, everything we've done."

Bush made the speech on September 2. He acknowledged the existence of the black sites. He celebrated "one of the most successful intelligence efforts in American history." He commended the CIA for wringing information from its captives through "an alternative set of procedures." Beyond that, he admitted nothing and denied everything. "The United States does not torture," he said. "I have not authorized it." Nor would he address the moral stain of America's program. Hayden did so in a memoir ten years later:

> We were denying people their freedom, likely forever, in a program of extrajudicial detention. Some people found that objectionable under any circumstances; anyone would find it objectionable if you were doing it to the wrong people. There were occasional mistakes: plain mistaken identity, or correct identity but miscalculating the detainee's knowledge of impending evil.

Once they were in Guantanamo, Hayden reflected, "there was no getting around the fact that these people were going to be in these circumstances forever."

"We need to change our strategy"

Hayden met with Bush at the White House every two or three days when he wasn't overseas, and "officially, religiously, without exception" every

Thursday morning. On the day after the annual 9/11 memorial services, the subject was Iraq. Hayden delivered the unvarnished views of his analysts as well as his own stark observations. The war was going "really, really badly," he told the president. "The situation there was very ugly . . . very dark." Though Bush said little in reply, Hayden thought he saw a flicker of sadness and a flash of remorse in his eyes. "It had an emotional impact on the President," he said. "Somebody he liked and trusted was saying this was very bad."

The morning of September 12 was one of the first times, if not the very first, that Bush had heard this message from someone in his inner circle. But he knew on some level that the greatest endeavor of his presidency was failing. He had known for a long time. In May, he had been reviewing the "blue sheet," the daily report of the morning's intelligence from Iraq, replete with death and violence. He had turned to his national security adviser and said: "Hadley, this strategy is not working."

"You're right, Mr. President, it is not," Hadley said.

"Well, we need to find a new one," Bush replied.

Five months had passed since then, and throughout the spring and summer Bush had reassured the American people that he was on the right track, and the only choice was to stay the course. But his commanders were deceiving him, he was deceiving himself, and he was deceiving the country. Finally, in early October, under Hadley's direction, Hayden and Kappes began working almost daily with key members of the National Security Council staff to formulate the essential elements of a new strategy. Their goal was to secure Baghdad so the Iraqi government could survive. This required the whole-of-government effort to impose order upon chaos, which the Kuwait conference of soldiers, spies, and diplomats had been seeking, and which the White House and the Pentagon had failed to provide.

The CIA's intelligence drove the NSC staffers toward deciding that the United States needed to send five more brigades of soldiers—thirty thousand strong—and a battalion of military and civilian intelligence officers into Iraq. There would be fresh troops under smarter generals and deeper intelligence employing new technologies from the CIA and the National

Security Agency. Since the enemy was an insurgency, they chose counterinsurgency as a strategy, and gave their stratagem a name: the surge. Their thinking was rejected by almost everyone at the top of the military and political chains of command in Washington and Baghdad. It flew in the face of what Rumsfeld and Rice and the generals had been telling Bush for the better part of two years.

Hayden was all for the surge. And so was Bob Gates. The two CIA directors, past and present, would be among the very few to make Bush understand that he was perilously close to becoming the first American president to lose a major war since Saigon fell in 1975.

Gates was serving as president of Texas A&M University when he returned an urgent phone call from the White House on October 21. Hadley asked if he would be amenable to replacing Rumsfeld as secretary of defense. Gates, stunned, said yes, instinctively. Then he hung up and thought: *My God, what have I done?* Gates had been the last CIA director to leave the job with his reputation enhanced. He was the most influential intelligence analyst in American history. His twenty-seven years in the national security establishment under six presidents gave him the status as a wise man in Washington. He had now spent seven months as a member of the Iraq Study Group, a commission created by an act of Congress to take a deep look at where the war was headed.*

In Baghdad, the study group had received what Gates believed to be a snow job from the four-star commander, Gen. George Casey. Seeking

---

* Gates struck up a friendship with one of the group's members, the gregarious and politically gifted Leon Panetta, who had served as Bill Clinton's chief of staff. They were destined to become the only two men in history to run both the CIA and the Pentagon. They made an odd couple. Gates was the son of an auto-parts salesman from Wichita, Kansas, a Reagan Republican to the soles of his wingtips, and as white as a slice of Wonder Bread. Panetta's parents were Italian immigrants who ran a restaurant in Monterey, California; he had been an eight-term congressman from his hometown, and he was a committed liberal, without the bleeding heart. They had bonded during a refueling stop at Shannon Airport en route to Iraq, making a mad dash together to the duty-free store, figuring that adult beverages would be hard to find in the Green Zone. When those bottles ran dry, Panetta wrote, "Bob suggested we try the Baghdad CIA station. We made it over there; he poured himself a vodka, and I took a scotch. It pays to know people."

enlightenment, he met privately with station chief Paul Nevin, who had worked under him at the CIA fifteen years before. Nevin told him that if the violence wasn't brought under control, the Iraqi government's palace politics wouldn't matter. They would be drowned by blood. Gates was convinced. Six days before the October 21 phone call summoning him to Washington, he had told the survey group that they should recommend sending tens of thousands more troops to secure Iraq and create the political breathing room for its leaders to establish their authority. The CIA director and the incoming secretary of defense were now both convinced that Bush had to change his mind.

Only one force could compel him to do so: the political will of the American people. The president and the Republican Party took a historic drubbing in November's midterm elections; the Democrats took control of Congress and held it for a decade. Bush's failures as commander in chief were the cause of that repudiation. Polls showed that 20 percent of the electorate thought America was winning in Iraq and 33 percent approved of his presidency. And still he clung to his illusions. He had hopes and dreams and he had called them a plan.

Hayden meant to wake him up. "Immediately after the midterms we go into a full-court press on what to do, and I mean it was full court," Hayden recounted. "Kappes and I would trade off. I'd do the morning, he'd do the afternoon, and vice versa. We were constantly meeting, and out of that comes the surge. We offered cautions about the surge. We said we agree that five brigades of professional, nonsectarian combat power will make Baghdad safer. It's going to push the violence down, but that's not your endpoint. Your endpoint is political change."

On December 8, Bush gathered the members of his war council. He found no semblance of consensus. Rumsfeld, in his last days as secretary of defense pending his successor's swearing-in, remained adamantly opposed to the surge, as were the Joint Chiefs and the top commanders in Baghdad. They all wanted out as fast as possible. Cheney thought America should stand with the Shia leaders in power and let them kill the Sunnis, a lonely position essentially aligning him with the Iranian Revolutionary Guards. Rice said the military should stand aside and let the Shia and

Sunni fight until the sectarian fire burned itself out. "It may just well be they're determined to kill each other. We just have to let them do it," Rice told Bush. He was aghast. "He was really furious—I think it was the only time he was really angry at me," Rice said. "And he said, 'So your view is you're just going to let them go at each other and they're just going to kill each other and we're just going to stand by and watch?'" The president and his secretary of state stared at each other as he seethed and she shrank from his rage. The strategic review Bush had sought for seven months was at an impasse.

Hayden helped chart a way forward. Briefing Bush on December 14, he delivered harsh judgments, informed by his analysts and the Baghdad station's reporting, that would appear shortly in the new National Intelligence Estimate on Iraq. He told the president that his strategy was failing and the situation was approaching disaster. If the American military withdrew, the Iraqi government would crumble. The chances for peace would evaporate. The scale and scope of the sectarian conflict would multiply. Massive civilian casualties and mounting political assassinations would follow. The Iraqi Army would split along religious and ethnic lines. The Sunni resistance to the government would intensify. Iran, already engaged in lethal sabotage, might intervene openly on the side of the Shia. Al Qaeda in Iraq could mount new attacks in and outside of the country. All this would "shift Iraq's trajectory from gradual decline to rapid deterioration with grave humanitarian, political, and security consequences," the forthcoming intelligence estimate warned. If the presence of the American military was no longer the principal problem in Iraq, it could become the solution by surging its forces, suppressing the violence, and stabilizing the country.

Guided by Hayden and Gates, Bush accepted the CIA's intelligence and changed his mind. He confessed his failures in a grim-faced address to the nation on January 10, 2007. "The situation in Iraq is unacceptable to the American people—and it is unacceptable to me," he said. "Where mistakes have been made, the responsibility rests with me. It is clear that we need to change our strategy." His speech paraphrased the still-secret estimate. "To step back now," Bush said, "would force a collapse of the

Iraqi government, tear the country apart, and result in mass killings on an unimaginable scale."

For three years, Bush had rejected the CIA's assessments of the war as guesswork. He now had been compelled to accept them. He had lost faith in the first two CIA directors who had served him. He now put his trust in Hayden. Bad intelligence had driven America into the war in Iraq. Good intelligence might give it a chance to find a way out.

Chapter Fourteen

"HOW FAR WERE WE PREPARED TO GO?"

On February 10, 2007, Gen. David Petraeus, the future CIA director, arrived in Baghdad as the new American commander. His mission was to stop the country from collapsing. Terrorists were slaughtering Iraqi citizens by the thousands. The prime minister sided with Shia militias and their Iranian allies in their deadly power struggle with the Sunnis, and subverted the Iraqi intelligence service created by the CIA. His government was penetrated by the spies and saboteurs of Tehran's Quds Force. The American military was under attack by the foreign fighters of al Qaeda in Iraq.

Petraeus figured he had six months to turn the war around. He quickly bonded with the CIA station chief Paul Nevin in a partnership he called "exceptional—and exceptionally close."* Nevin had been slated to leave Baghdad for the Rome station when the surge began. His reputation was so strong that Cheney intervened to keep him; the vice president had called Rodriguez and said: *This guy is staying*. Nevin and the newly appointed American ambassador, Ryan Crocker, led Petraeus's brain trust.

---

* Petraeus had worked closely with the CIA before, first as a top aide to the American general supporting the contras in El Salvador in 1986, then hunting war criminals in the Balkans in 2001, leading combat and counterinsurgency operations in northern Iraq during the first year of the war, and trying to revive Iraqi military and security forces during 2004 and 2005. He had spent most of 2006 at Fort Leavenworth, Kansas, rewriting the American military manual on counterinsurgency, which had been gathering dust since the war in Vietnam.

They worked together seamlessly. Now that the surge of troops had started, Petraeus needed a surge of ideas on how to use them. By early April, when he and his team settled on a plan, the number of terrorist attacks had escalated to more than fifty a day. The complexities were close to incalculable but the goal was simple: reduce the rampant violence to raise the chances of political progress. Petraeus would use the fresh troops to patrol Iraq's cities and villages, project power among the people, and prevent them from being killed.

The strategy depended on intelligence sharing among the military, the diplomats, the spies, and the analysts, so often at one another's throats in the first years of the occupation. *Joint* was the watchword of the day. The brain trust called itself the Joint Strategic Assessment Team. Their new strategy was christened the Joint Campaign Plan. The CIA took the unusual step of sharing intelligence gleaned from recruited Iraqi agents with JSOC, General McChrystal's Joint Special Operations Command. Petraeus, Crocker, and Nevin had joint videoconferences with Bush and the NSC every Monday at seven thirty a.m. Washington time. McChrystal convened Nevin and his fellow Middle East station chiefs every week to strategize in a secure video hookup.

"We began as a network of people, then grew into a network of teams, then a network of organizations, and ultimately a network of nations," McChrystal said.

"Everyone wanted information and intelligence"

A windfall of intelligence had arrived when Petraeus did. A small Army platoon on patrol twenty miles north of Baghdad had stopped a Mercedes sedan, captured an al Qaeda courier, and turned him over to the CIA. In the trunk of the car, they had found a laptop, hard drives, and thumb drives. It took the CIA and the NSA weeks to decipher their contents. Once made legible, the cache provided American soldiers and spies with their biggest bonanza of the war. It revealed al Qaeda's plans to attack the heart of Baghdad, pinpointed their safe houses and arms caches in villages encircling the capital, identified interlocking terrorist cells, displayed their maps of American military bases and checkpoints, and detailed orders to murder Iraqi garbagemen and bread bakers to make life in the city even more miserable than it was. The intelligence "all of a sudden changed my thought processes on how to allocate my forces during the surge," Gen. Ray Odierno, Petraeus's second-in-command, told the *New York Times* reporters Eric Schmitt and Thom Shanker three years later. He now saw the once-invisible terrorist networks ringing Baghdad and prepared to engage them in battle.

Intelligence was 80 percent of the surge, in the eyes of the Baghdad station and the special-forces commanders McChrystal and McRaven. The JSOC task force bought huge satellite dishes linked with CIA and NSA headquarters. Their airborne reconnaissance and surveillance platforms could track terrorists' phone calls and detect who was on the other line. They staked out their targets around the clock, developing a "pattern of life" profile for the night-stalking special forces and CIA paramilitary teams who sought to capture them. The relentless raids focused on reaping intelligence rather than killing the enemy. It stood to reason, as Jose Rodriguez said, that "if you blow up terrorists using a Hellfire missile, you do not get to learn from information contained in their pockets, cell phones, computers, or minds."

The raiders took the troves they seized and brought them to the task force base. CIA and NSA analysts downloaded the data and sent it through video links to their colleagues at their headquarters, who pored over it, processed it, and disseminated it throughout the world. By early 2007, some seven thousand intelligence officers and analysts were part of this effort. The take was "so rich, so timely, and so pertinent to the fight in Iraq and beyond, no one wanted to miss it," McRaven said. "Everyone wanted information and intelligence that might affect the al Qaeda threats they were chasing . . . everywhere from the U.S. to Europe, North Africa, throughout Southwest Asia."

The urgency of the surge and the unceasing search for the enemy was straining the CIA to its limits. "Counterterrorism and the war on al Qaeda were gobbling up a lot of agency focus, resources, and talent," Hayden said. He needed all the help he could get from the CIA's Arab allies. He flew to Jordan to meet with King Abdullah II and his spy chief, Gen. Mohammad al-Dahabi. The CIA trusted the king and his spies: it had created the Jordanian intelligence service, financed it with tens of millions of dollars a year, and built a new counterterrorism center on the edge of the capital. (Not all were trustworthy: General al-Dahabi was later convicted of embezzling $34 million from his agency.) The officers of the Amman station, the biggest in the Middle East save for Baghdad, saw the Jordanians as the CIA's best partner in the Arab world; they had provided the crucial intelligence that had let American forces kill their nemesis, the Jordanian terrorist al-Zarqawi, in June 2006. And they had deep connections among the Sunni sheikhs of Iraq.

Hayden urged the Jordanians to help stoke the sheikhs' slowly growing rebellion against the brutality of al Qaeda in Iraq. Their uprising became known as the Anbar Awakening.

The pipeline of foreign fighters flowed from Damascus south through Anbar Province, a Sunni stronghold stretching from the outskirts of Baghdad westward to the borders of Jordan and Syria. For two years, al Qaeda in Iraq had been terrorizing the people of Anbar. The terrorists ruled in the provincial capital of Ramadi, where they had proclaimed a caliphate under sharia law. They had killed civilians ruthlessly, assassinated political and tribal leaders, and forced families to marry their daughters to suicide bombers. By the end of summer of 2006, American military officers had all but declared Anbar a lost cause. But then an Iraqi death squad in Ramadi, guided by CIA paramilitaries, had started executing a handful of al Qaeda members. In response, the foreign fighters had murdered a prominent Sunni sheikh who opposed them, beheaded him, thrown his body into the desert, and left it to rot in the blazing sun in August 2006.

The Anbar Awakening arose three weeks later. "Those terrorists claimed that they are fighters working on liberating Iraq, but they turned out to be killers," said its leader, Sheikh Abdul Sattar Abu Risha, whose grandfather had fought the British occupiers of Iraq in 1920. "Now all the people are fed up and have turned against them."* Nevin and his officers saw what was happening with clarity. In October, the CIA's base chief in Ramadi had reported that the Sunni resistance was a force that could transform the province and defeat al Qaeda. Nevin incorporated that riveting idea into a cable to CIA headquarters. Hayden relayed it to Bush. The CIA's reporting "served as a wake-up call to the U.S. government that what was going on in Ramadi was a tectonic shift, a really decisive development," said Col. Sean MacFarland, who commanded an Army brigade in the city. "I can't overestimate the impact of it." The CIA stations in Baghdad and Amman supported the uprising in all ways possible. With their encouragement, the leaders of the Awakening recruited thousands of volunteers and sent them to Jordan for training as policemen. American forces had spent three years training the Iraqi National Police, only to see them become a brutal sectarian force; they had to be disbanded.

CIA deputy director Steve Kappes went to Ramadi and promised Mac-Farland all the money he needed to pay and equip the trainees, underwriting signing bonuses, salaries, uniforms, and guns. In response to the Awakening, al Qaeda's forces had murdered hundreds of Iraqis in and around Ramadi with heavy weapons, car bombs, truck bombs, and chlorine gas attacks. But by April 2007, they no longer controlled the city. The sheikhs had responded by gathering tens of thousands of militiamen ready to kill the terrorists and support American counterinsurgency operations. The CIA supplied money, arms, and ammunition to help the Sunni tribal leaders marshal those forces and attack their mutual enemy. The Sunni militias paid them back tenfold with intelligence on al Qaeda in Iraq.

The Awakening was a homegrown Sunni movement. The CIA didn't create it. But it nurtured, protected, and strengthened it. In May, Petraeus seized upon it. "I recognized that this is the kernel of a huge idea," he said. Acting on his own authority, he put Sunni tribesmen from across the country on his payroll and rebranded their movement. At a cost of $400 million, he created a national Sunni militia and called it the Sons of Iraq. It grew to 103,000 men, a fifth of whom were former insurgents, many

---

* Al Qaeda in Iraq murdered the sheikh on the first anniversary of the Awakening.

with American blood on their hands, all now ready to switch sides for a steady paycheck. More than the blood and sacrifice of hundreds of American soldiers who died under Petraeus's command that year, their fighting turned the tide.

When they stood up that summer, the violence started going down. American combat deaths had risen sharply in the first months of the surge; 641 troops died between March and September, and 2007 became the deadliest year of the occupation. But the foreign fighters and their Iraqi allies were dying by the thousands, and the number of terrorist attacks began slowly subsiding. Without the Sons of Iraq, the surge would not have stood a chance.

"It was a losing fight"

Its success would prove fleeting. "The surge," said Ambassador Crocker, "could not be sustained."

Petraeus's mission statement had called for "defeating the terrorists and irreconcilable groups, bringing the remainder into the political process, reducing sectarian tensions, denying Iraq as a safe haven for terrorists," and creating the conditions for the Iraqi government to function well enough to establish the rule of law, serve its citizens, and eventually allow the Americans to leave someday. "The idea here was to balance two parallel tracks of effort: effort on the security front, which arguably we could do, but at great cost—and frankly, only temporarily—and progress on the political front," said Maj. Gen. Doug Lute, Bush's newly appointed deputy national security adviser for Iraq and Afghanistan. "It was a losing fight, because we could not generate the political counterpart."

Bush had put all his chips on what he imagined to be his strong personal relationship with Prime Minister al-Malaki. Nevin believed that was a bad bet. So did General Petraeus and Ambassador Crocker. "Petraeus and I were thinking, 'I can't stand another day with this guy,'" Crocker said. "'Anybody but Maliki.' The president said, 'Not going there. . . . You've got to keep him from losing his ass.' Petraeus and I looked at each other and said, 'How exactly are we going to do that?'"

The Iraqi leader claimed to preside over a national unity government, Hayden told the president, but it was neither national, nor unified, nor a real government. Malaki saw conspiracies everywhere, especially among longtime CIA agents like his one-time ally, Ayad Allawi, the former interim prime minister, and General al-Shawani, chief of the Iraqi intelligence service. "We had made an effort with Maliki," Crocker said, "but, boy, was he frustrating, and hard to deal with, and secretive, and incapable of building alliances." Over time, Maliki reverted to his sectarian roots and his Iranian sponsors. Ultimately, Iran and its Quds Force, led by General Soleimani, would prove to be the only winners of Bush's war.

"We don't do Pearl Harbors"

In July, Bush and Cheney debated whether to start another conflagration in the Middle East. Meir Dagan, chief of the Mossad, had gone to CIA headquarters to show Hayden photographs and documents, purloined by his spies, revealing a nuclear reactor under construction three hundred miles northeast of Damacus, near the Iraqi border. "Dagan sat down, opened his briefcase, and took out color copies of the pictures," Hayden remembered. He said Syria was building a nuclear weapon at the site and that the reactor's design was North Korean. His best guess was that it would go hot by the end of the year, and if a decision to destroy it wasn't taken soon, a bombing raid would send an uncontrolled plume of radioactivity wherever the prevailing winds took it. Hayden saw the logic: "The attacker would be blamed for every thyroid problem in the Middle East for the next half-century."

The CIA and the NSA had spent May and June confirming Mossad's reporting. On July 16, Bush, Cheney, Gates, Rice, and Hayden held an off-the-books meeting in the White House residence to decide whether to launch a preemptive strike against Syria. Cheney was all for it. Gates was dead-set against it. "I am aware of no precedent for an American surprise attack against a sovereign state," he had told Bush three weeks before. "We don't do Pearl Harbors." And given the WMD fiasco, the intelligence would be regarded with skepticism.

"All right, what's the intel?" Bush asked Hayden.

"Well, Mr. President, I've got four sentences," Hayden replied. "One, that's a nuclear reactor. Two, the North Koreans and the Syrians have been fooling around with this stuff for ten years. Three, the North Koreans built it, and four, it's part of a Syrian nuclear weapons program. But bear with me. . . . I can't find the reprocessing facility. I've got no testing and developing of a warhead, so I think it's part of a weapons program, but I can only give that to you at low confidence."

Never mind that, Cheney said, the intelligence is solid, let's bomb the reactor and send a message to Syria and its terrorist allies. Gates argued furiously that an attack would be seen as another rash act by a trigger-happy president, setting off "a huge negative reaction" at home and abroad, eroding what little support remained for the wars in Iraq and Afghanistan. Bush, for the first time in six years, did not defer to Cheney's counsel for unilateral American aggression. Let's take the diplomatic track, he said, go public, expose the reactor, and shame the dictator al-Assad. But Hayden noted that Israel would not reveal their intelligence for the purpose of diplomacy with the Syrians. They wanted the reactor destroyed. Fine, let Israel bomb it, Cheney said.

"Bush effectively came down on Cheney's side," Gates wrote. "By not giving the Israelis a red light, he gave them a green one." On September 6, Israel obliterated the reactor with air strikes. Al-Assad, humiliated, said nothing. Nor did Israel or the United States. The attack remained secret until Hayden briefed Congress and the press seven months later. He reflected that the CIA had failed to detect the Syrian nuclear program until it was almost too late. "We had gotten it right," Hayden said, "but it was a near-run thing."

The American occupation of Iraq took a brutal turn on September 17. In the heart of Baghdad, nineteen Blackwater mercenaries, all military veterans under contract with the CIA, went berserk and opened fire on cars at a busy traffic circle. They killed fourteen Iraqi civilians, including two women and two young boys.*

Blackwater's private army had become an operating subsidiary of the clandestine service. Its owner, Erik Prince, had parlayed the $5 million the CIA had awarded him to guard the embassy and the station in Kabul in early 2002 into a multibillion-dollar bonanza—$600 million in contracts with the CIA, $1.2 billion with the State Department, and hundreds of millions more with the Pentagon. Blackwater personnel loaded missiles on to Predator drones, interrogated CIA prisoners, and went on paramilitary missions with officers from the special activities division, as well as serving as embassy security guards.

The company's financial success was a direct result of the power and influence of the CIA veterans who served as its executives. Cofer Black, the former counterterrorism chief, was the company's vice chairman. Ric Prado, who had been Black's operations officer, was vice president for "special government programs," meaning top secret contracts with the CIA and foreign intelligence and security services. Rob Richer, recently retired as deputy director of the clandestine service, was a vice president as well. Black, Richer, and Prado also ran a Blackwater subsidiary, Total Intelligence Solutions, which offered its services to governments, corporations, and political figures worldwide. "Cofer can open doors," Richer told the *Washington Post* a few weeks after the killings. "I can open doors. We can generally get in to see who we need to see. . . . We can deal with the right minister or person." In an October 2007 email, Prado wrote: "We have a rapidly growing, worldwide network of folks that can do everything from surveillance to ground truth to disruption operations."

Blackwater's many new contracts included a pact to provide security for Benazir Bhutto, the former prime minister of Pakistan, who had pledged to bring democracy to her country and returned from exile to campaign

---

* After years of trials, appeals, mistrials, and retrials, Evan Liberty, a former Marine, was sentenced to life in prison in December 2018; three of his fellow Blackwater gunmen received long sentences. Liberty appealed directly to President Donald Trump, saying he was a victim of a Justice Department witch hunt. Two weeks before the insurrection of January 6, 2021, Trump issued full presidential pardons to all four men.

against Musharraf. On November 3, in the face of growing street protests against him, Musharraf had declared a state of emergency, suspending the constitution, firing the chief justice of the highest court, arresting political opponents, and shutting down independent television news stations. The American ambassador, Anne Patterson, and the CIA station chief, Frank Archibald, the future head of the clandestine service, had seen this bid for absolute power coming, and they had pleaded with Musharraf not to plunge toward dictatorship. They had stalled him but not stopped him. Bhutto had written to Musharraf to warn of a conspiracy to kill her, saying a former ISI chief was behind it.

Blackwater proved powerless to protect her: she was murdered by a suicide bomber on December 27. The assassin had been sent by the leader of the Pakistani Taliban, a new coalition of some five thousand fighters in Waziristan, an ungoverned tribal province on Pakistan's border with Afghanistan. The group owed its strength to Musharraf and ISI chief Ashfaq Kayani, who had struck a deal with tribal leaders in September 2006 to cease counterterrorism operations in the province, and barred the CIA from attacking it from Afghanistan. In the Situation Room, hours after the assassination, Hayden told Bush that Musharraf, America's putative ally, had supported the forces of jihad on both sides of the border. With his help, the Taliban had returned in force in Afghanistan and al Qaeda was resurgent in Waziristan. Pakistan was now the most dangerous front in the president's war on terror.

This thought was new to Bush. Fully focused on preventing a fiasco in Iraq, he had lacked the capacity to concentrate on the perfidy of Pakistan, the war in Afghanistan, and the fight against al Qaeda. He had trusted Musharraf and failed to see that Pakistan had continued to back the Taliban, allowing it to return with the strength to attack Americans and their allies. He had failed to provide security for the people of Afghanistan, who still had no police, no military, and no army worthy of the name. He failed to act upon eighteen months of CIA reports warning that the Taliban were resurgent, tuning them out and taking comfort in the military's soothing assurances of success. The Taliban were winning, warned the CIA's hand-picked Afghan intelligence chief, Amrullah Saleh, in part because American forces were killing and imprisoning civilians in raids based on false intelligence.

"Gentlemen, we have some disconnects here," Gates told his aides at the Pentagon after a videoconference with the generals running the war. The commanders kept contradicting "report after report from the CIA saying the situation in Afghanistan is worsening at an alarming rate. Believe me," he said with a smile, "I know a thing or two about taking the Agency with a grain of salt." But Gates had a gut sense that the CIA was telling the truth and the military was lying to the president and to itself.

"We inevitably backed away"

Al Qaeda was attracting new followers from all over the world through a network of sophisticated websites, using the war in Iraq as a recruiting tool. Foreign fighters, mainly Arabs but also Muslims from throughout Europe, were arriving at al Qaeda bases in Pakistan. "A lot of the student body are people who wouldn't cause you to raise your eyebrow if they were next to you going through the passport line" in an American airport, Hayden said. The graduates were returning in force throughout Europe, and the CIA and its allied intelligence services were on high alert. A German jihadist had been arrested with fifteen hundred pounds of a hydrogen peroxide compound and twenty-six military grade detonators, which he planned to deploy in car bombs at the American air base at Ramstein. Twelve Pakistanis and two Indians were arrested in Barcelona while plotting suicide attacks in at least three European cities. Another terrorist cell was broken up as it planned to bomb the Glasgow airport. All of them had been trained by al Qaeda in Waziristan. Those camps along Pakistan's northwest frontier also served as launching pads for roadside bombs and suicide attacks in Afghanistan.

Hayden had come to see Pakistan as the ally from hell. He flew to Islamabad the week after Bhutto's assassination to confront Musharraf and Kayani, and he argued for an array of covert actions against al Qaeda and the Taliban. He proposed cross-border raids by CIA officers and special-forces operators in Afghanistan to attack al Qaeda bases in the tribal lands.

Musharraf refused: he would regard those incursions as a military invasion. Hayden countered with a plan to create a CIA base in Pakistan to launch Predator drone strikes against the enemy. Musharraf gave a provisional yes: each attack would require his prior approval. Hayden suspected the ISI would warn the terrorists beforehand. When he returned to the White House, he urged Bush to give the CIA the power to unleash the drones—with or without permission from Musharraf.

The president balked. Hayden was proposing a covert blitzkrieg in a country with which the United States was not at war, whose military possessed nuclear weapons, whose spies had the power to unleash terrorist attacks while keeping its hand hidden. Worse, for a want of intelligence, the CIA might be flying blind. Almost every major terrorist threat the CIA was tracking threaded back to the tribal areas, but its ability to tie those threads together was lacking.

"We don't have enough information about what's going on there," said the State Department's new counterterrorism chief, Lt. Gen. Dell Dailey, who had run special operations in Afghanistan and Iraq. "Not on Al Qaeda. Not on foreign fighters. Not on the Taliban." Bush dreaded the prospect of an undeclared war in the ungoverned lands of a putative ally. "How far were we prepared to go?" asked Michael Waltz, a Green Beret who served as a counterterrorism adviser to Cheney and became the White House national security adviser in 2025. "Could we really afford to make Pakistan an enemy? Were we prepared to go after insurgent training camps and headquarters in Pakistan and fight the Pakistani Army's tanks and artillery on the way in and out? Were we prepared to shoot down its Air Force, planes that the United States supplied . . . ? Whenever we began to contemplate such dark scenarios, we inevitably backed away."

The war on terror had gone adrift in 2007. Bush was gripped by a paralysis of policy and strategy and vision. The hunt for bin Laden had led nowhere. The CIA had struck blows against al Qaeda, but the forces of jihad had multiplied and metastasized all over the world. The CIA had taken no terrorists of note off the battlefield all year. "We were 0 for '07," said Hayden. He told Bush that they would never be forgiven if America were attacked again.

Chapter Fifteen

THE GOD'S-EYE VIEW

"The campaign against al Qaeda was my life and obsession," Jose Rodriguez said. Now his war on terror was over. "I was out of gas," he wrote. "It was time to step aside and let someone else lead the clandestine service."

Rodriguez was halfway through a ninety-day retirement program preparing him for life outside the CIA in mid-November 2007 when he got "a frantic call from my usually unflappable former chief of staff." Gina Haspel told him that a reporter from the *New York Times* was seeking a response from the CIA for a story about his order to destroy the videotapes of the brutal interrogations at the black site in Thailand. They both realized that if the newspaper pulled on that thread, much more would come unraveled.

It wasn't simply that Rodriguez had defied his superiors. Porter Goss had deliberately failed to inform the congressional intelligence committees about the destruction of the tapes, in violation of the rules governing their relationship. The CIA lawyer John Rizzo learned this salient fact in a phone call to the former director. "My heart sank," Rizzo remembered. He knew a scandal when he saw one.

The *Times* broke the story on December 7—Pearl Harbor Day, as Hayden noted—and the paper kept digging. Its reporting dominated the discourse about the CIA in the press and the public throughout the winter and spring of 2008. The destruction had legal as well as political implications: the CIA had failed to comply with a federal judge's order to retain all records related to its treatment of detainees. The question of obstruction of justice arose, and the Justice Department authorized a criminal investigation of Rodriguez, the highest-ranking clandestine service officer to face the threat of a felony charge in two decades. The task fell, not by chance, to the special prosecutor John Durham, who had slow-rolled the case of the CIA and the Ice Man until the statute of limitations expired. Durham dragged the new investigation out for three years. His secret report would hold that that Rodriguez had no legal authority to destroy the tapes but that the Justice Department could not prosecute him.

Four years after the story first broke, in December 2011, Mike Morell, then the CIA's deputy director, took it upon himself to render judgment. Rodriguez had defied Goss, the director of national intelligence, the White House counsel, the CIA's inspector general, and the CIA's top lawyer in destroying the tapes. There had to be a consequence for his insubordination, Morell decreed.

Rodriguez received a classified letter of reprimand. "The practical implication of the letter is nil," he said proudly, and if the CIA gave him a copy, "I'll have it framed."

He was a zealot, proud of it, and deeply admired for it by many of his officers. But he had broken the rules, and that was a dangerous thing. Hayden once said that "CIA covert actions are always on the edge. They always take place in a gray area—gray ethically, gray legally, gray operationally—they're always out there on the outer edges of executive prerogative." The reprimand Morell issued might have been a mild rebuke. But it established that Rodriguez had gone beyond the edge, and he had taken the CIA and the White House with him. The record reflected that no man save Bush was more responsible for the abuses of the war on terror that had stained the image of the United States. He wore that stain as a badge of honor.

"A cunning, resourceful, coldly calculating adversary"

"The most successful covert action I conducted while director no one knows about," Hayden said after he retired. He likely was talking about the assassination of Imad Mughniyeh, the military commander of Hezbollah, in the streets of Damascus on the night of February 12, 2008. The operation was a twofold triumph in Hayden's eyes. The CIA had killed the world's second-most-wanted terrorist. And its role had remained secret. It was an article of faith at the clandestine service that its biggest successes have always gone unheralded. "If they go heralded," Hayden said, "they're not successes."

Mughniyeh had murdered more CIA officers than any man alive. In Lebanon, during the 1980s, he and his allies had killed more than two hundred American soldiers with truck bombs. He had blown up the American embassy and killed sixty-three people—among them eight CIA personnel, including the station chief and the agency's top Mideast analyst, in the deadliest day in the agency's history—and then kidnapped the new Beirut station chief, who would die in captivity. His hostage-taking spree in Lebanon had led President Reagan to try to ransom the American captives by selling weapons to Hezbollah's military and financial sponsors, the Iranian Revolutionary Guards, igniting the biggest White House scandal since Watergate. He had been indicted for the 1985 hijacking of TWA Flight 847 shortly after it took off from Athens and the murder of a Navy diver who was on the plane. A 1986 CIA report called him "a cunning, resourceful, coldly calculating adversary for whom virtually any act of violence . . . is permissible." His subsequent crimes included the bombings of the Israeli embassy and an Israeli mutual-aid association in Buenos Aires which killed 114 people in the 1990s, along with a multitude of terrorist attacks in Israel.

In the twenty-first century, Hezbollah had grown from a terrorist band in Beirut to a state within the state of Lebanon. Its paramilitary wing, led by Mughniyeh, was more powerful than the Lebanese Army. His aims were as one with his Iranian sponsors: the destruction of the Jewish state. Mughniyeh took extraordinary measures to conceal himself; his nom de guerre was Abu Dokhan, "Father of Smoke." The Israeli intelligence services had been trying to hunt him down for twenty-five years. In September 2007, they found him.

Mossad chief Meir Dagan confided to Hayden that Israel's spies, using signals intercepts of Hezbollah's running conversations with Iran's Quds Force, had tracked Mughniyeh to Damascus. Mossad didn't have a station there. But the CIA did. And Tom Sylvester, who had departed Damascus nearly a year earlier to become chief of the counterterrorism center's Iraq group, had left behind a small but resilient network of recruited Syrian agents, safe houses, and covert communications networks for his successor.

Dagan proposed to Hayden that they collaborate on assassinating Mughniyeh. *Assassination* was a loaded word at the CIA: a legal, moral, and ethical minefield ever since Presidents Eisenhower and Kennedy had tacitly proposed the murder of Fidel Castro.* "The Agency never assassinated anybody, ever," Richard Helms said in 1988. "I was there from the day the doors opened until I left in '73, and I know the Agency never killed anybody, *anybody*." (Though in Castro's case, it wasn't for want of trying.) But the Israelis had assassinated hundreds of their enemies in the second half of the twentieth century, and hundreds more since the start of the second Palestinian intifada in 2000. Their killings had become routine and America had just as routinely condemned them. "The United States government is very clearly on record as against targeted assassinations," the American ambassador to Israel, Martin Indyk, had said in July 2001. "They are extrajudicial killings, and we do not support that." That summer, as the debate over arming Predator drones with Hellfire missiles gripped the American intelligence community, George Tenet had said it would be "a terrible mistake" for the CIA director to fire a lethal weapon like that. It

---

* A 1981 executive order signed by President Reagan read: "No person employed by or acting on behalf of the United States Government shall engage in, or conspire to engage in, assassination." But in 1984 and 1985 Reagan reversed that by signing intelligence findings—executed in direct response to Mughniyeh's terrorist rampages in Beirut—declaring assassinations lawful if undertaken "in good faith and as part of an approved operation." The congressional intelligence committees got wind of this and forced the White House to close the "good faith" loophole in 1986. Clinton's lethal finding against bin Laden in 1998 had held that killing someone posing an imminent threat to the United States was an act of self-defense, not an assassination. After 9/11, President Bush signed findings further eroding the taboo on targeted killings. The CIA still couldn't assassinate a head of state, but it could definitely assassinate the military commander of Hezbollah on orders from the president.

would happen only over his dead body. The moral equation had changed since then.

Mughniyeh was responsible for killing and maiming hundreds if not thousands of soldiers and civilians in Iraq. He had been Hezbollah's overseer for the training and arming of suicide bombers and foreign fighters flowing from Syria to Iraq since the first months of the American occupation. This let the CIA make a legal case for assassinating him in the name of anticipatory self-defense—to kill him before he kills us—under the laws of armed conflict. Hayden asked Bush for his blessings, which he eagerly gave, on the condition that no one but Mughniyeh would die. This added a degree of difficulty to an already audacious plan.

The plot to kill him took shape between November 2007 and January 2008—"a gigantic, multi-force operation, with crazy resources invested by both countries and, to the best of my knowledge, the most ever invested to kill a lone individual," a Mossad commander told the Israeli journalist Ronen Bergman. At CIA headquarters, only a handful of officers were in charge. Hayden and Kappes oversaw the work of three men: the new chief of the clandestine service, Mike Sulick, who had returned two years after Goss drove him out; the chief of the counterterrorism center, Mike D'Andrea; and the chief of the Near East division, Mike Walker, who was well acquainted with lethal covert action, having been the number two man at the special activities division on 9/11.

The CIA's officers and its recruited agents in Damascus, working with the Mossad, wove a net of surveillance around Mughniyeh as he traveled to and from Syrian intelligence offices and safe houses. They had discovered to their pleasure that he left his bodyguards behind for his frequent trysts with three Damascene women, driving a silver Mitsubishi Pajero by himself, parking in a garage, and leaving alone. They determined that they could plant a shaped explosive charge in the rear-mounted spare tire of the SUV. CIA paramilitary and technical-service officers tested prototypes at the agency's counterterrorism training base in Harvey Point, North Carolina, built on sixteen hundred boggy acres surrounded by Albemarle Sound, where the pirate Blackbeard once ruled. The murder weapon arrived at the American embassy in Syria by diplomatic pouch.

Mughniyeh was blown apart in the heart of the most heavily guarded neighborhood in Damascus. Down the street, the windows of a Syrian intelligence office were cracked by the blast. Hezbollah instinctively blamed Israel for the killing—and Syria for allowing it to happen. "Just think what this does to the Syrians," Dagan crowed. "Think of what it does to Assad, what it does to Hezbollah, when they grasp that they're not even safe in Damascus." The CIA's role stayed secret for seven years until reporters pieced it together in 2015. The agency, understandably, has never acknowledged it. Using a car bomb, a terrorist weapon, to assassinate a terrorist might have been poetic justice, but it was also, to paraphrase Hayden, very far out on the outer edges of presidential power. It crossed a threshold, framed by law, from which there was no going back.

Emboldened by the operation, Hayden said he "pushed and pushed and pushed" the president throughout the spring of 2008 to loosen the rules on targeted killings. The CIA's Predator strikes in the tribal lands of Pakistan had been few and far between—fourteen over the past four years—and some had been fatally flawed, missing their targets, killing civilians, and inflaming anti-American rage among the populace. But now, he told Bush, the CIA and the NSA had the power to focus the intelligence they had gained from spies and electronic eavesdropping, fuse it, and transform it into pinpoint firepower. Ramped-up drone assembly lines had given the CIA the capability to use a fleet of the unmanned planes to conduct surveillance of the terrorist camps for days on end.

"That persistent, godlike stare, unblinking, builds up a level of confidence," Hayden said. Armed with a God's-eye view, he argued for the unilateral authority to fire a fusillade of missiles at the CIA's targets. "It was a conscious decision to be more aggressive, believing that we had the political space to do it in our politics and in Pakistan's politics," he said. Musharraf was facing impeachment and losing his grip on power; his likely successor would be more compliant with the CIA. Bush had seven months left in office. Almost seven years had passed since Cofer Black had promised the president to deliver bin Laden's head on a pike. Here was the CIA's last chance to attack his base of power before Bush lost his own.

"What is it that we don't understand?"

By June, it was clear that the next president of the United States would be either Senator John McCain of Arizona or Senator Barack Obama of Illinois. Both prospects troubled Hayden, though he thought that "McCain would have been more disruptive to the way America produced intelligence." McCain, famously cantankerous, had clashed with Hayden more than once, and with Bush continuously since they had contested for the Republican presidential nomination in 2000.* As the son and grandson of Navy admirals, he saw the CIA as a second-echelon service whose first job was to support the military. In the heat of the 2004 elections, when right-wing Republicans were accusing analysts of leaking intelligence to subvert Bush, McCain had called the CIA "not only dysfunctional but a rogue organization." The charge that the agency had gone rogue was false—its officers were exquisitely attuned to presidential orders—but it stung nonetheless.

Most ominously, in Hayden's view, both candidates had condemned the CIA for torturing prisoners. The very mention of the word *torture* infuriated Hayden. He insisted that the United States had tortured no one. To say otherwise was to condemn the CIA for carrying out the president's commands. But McCain had the moral authority to do so; he had been tortured himself as a prisoner of war in Vietnam for five and a half years. He wanted to close the black sites and Guantanamo and compel the CIA's interrogators to abide by the Army's rules forswearing brutal interrogations. Obama wholeheartedly agreed. The CIA's lawyers feared that either man, if elected, might move to prosecute the officers responsible for renditions, detentions, and interrogations. Rizzo pressed Hayden to ask Bush for preemptive pardons for all concerned, but the director feared that would amount to a politically poisonous admission of guilt.

---

* During the 2000 campaign, Bush's operatives had smeared McCain as a closet homosexual, the father of an out-of-wedlock black child, and the mentally unstable husband of a drug addict, among other libels.

Hayden disliked McCain and he distrusted Obama, a national-security neophyte and the most liberal presidential candidate in memory. But he did see a ray of hope in him. Obama had delivered a startlingly tough speech on national security to an audience of foreign-policy panjandrums in Washington months before the presidential primaries began:

> Al Qaeda has a sanctuary in Pakistan. . . . As President, I would make the hundreds of millions of dollars in U.S. military aid to Pakistan conditional, and I would make our conditions clear: Pakistan must make substantial progress in closing down the training camps, evicting foreign fighters, and preventing the Taliban from using Pakistan as a staging area for attacks in Afghanistan.
>
> I understand that President Musharraf has his own challenges. But let me make this clear. There are terrorists holed up in those mountains who murdered 3,000 Americans. They are plotting to strike again. . . . If we have actionable intelligence about high-value terrorist targets and President Musharraf won't act, we will.

These pledges were considerably tougher than any action Bush had taken. They created the political space for Hayden to persuade the president to do what Obama had promised. Hayden wanted to escalate the CIA's war in Pakistan—and lock the next president into continuing it. He convinced the president to convene the National Security Council to hear the CIA's argument for an all-out assault.

On July 28, Bush, Cheney, Gates, Rice, Hadley, Hayden, and Kappes met in the Yellow Oval Office on the second floor of the White House residence, a location chosen to keep the meeting off the books. They had read a new National Intelligence Estimate asserting that the CIA had failed to stop al Qaeda from resurging in Pakistan, which had become the epicenter of the terrorist threat facing America. Hayden and Kappes pressed their case in the starkest terms possible.

Al Qaeda had effectively merged with the Taliban. The Islamabad station chief, Frank Archibald, had confirmed that senior Pakistani intelligence officers had given the terrorists safe havens to meet, recruit, and plot. Hayden was all but certain that bin Laden and his lieutenants were planning to hit the United States again. They posed "a threat to the homeland," he said. "They were coming at us." He delivered a dire warning: "Knowing what we know now, there's no explaining our inaction after the next attack takes place."

Bush had heard hundreds of equally terrifying red alerts since 9/11. What finally moved him was the fact that the terrorists in Pakistan were crossing the border to murder and maim his troops with a dozen attacks each day in Afghanistan. "These sons of bitches are killing Americans," he said. "I've had enough." He decided to unleash the drones.

"The President agreed to give CIA enhanced authorities to do additional things, with a little more headroom, a little more discretion," Hayden said. His deliberate understatement reflected the fact that the American government had never acknowledged that the CIA conducted lethal drone strikes.

Hayden and D'Andrea immediately began a barrage of Hellfire missiles, and they mounted plans for CIA paramilitary officers and special-operations forces to attack the terrorist bases in Pakistan. They could now kill suspected terrorists based on a reasonable suspicion rather than ironclad proof that they threatened America and its allies. They would no longer give advance warning to the ISI, whose officers had frequently tipped off terrorist suspects that they were in the CIA's crosshairs. The drone attacks would prove to be a powerful tactic, but they were not a coherent counterterrorism strategy. Air power would not defeat al Qaeda. Only intelligence could.

The drone strikes now came with a furious frequency: twenty-eight attacks in the last five months of 2008, twice as many as in the previous four years combined. The result, Hayden said, was "a dramatic spike in frequency of key al-Qaeda leadership dying." Al Qaeda responded with a dump truck filled with explosives detonated in the driveway of the Marriott Hotel in Islamabad, killing fifty-four people, including an NSA cryptologist, on September 20. Neither the CIA nor the average American fully appreciated "the resentment created by American use of unmanned strikes," General McChrystal said years later. "They are hated on a visceral level, even by people who've never seen one or seen the effects of one."

The CIA's attacks killed scores of civilians in 2008, Hayden's claims of pinpoint precision notwithstanding. More than two years passed before the quality of intelligence guiding the drones improved and the civilian death toll diminished. At the same time, American military and counterterrorism operations in Afghanistan were killing hundreds of innocent victims each year. "What is it that we don't understand?" McChrystal asked his fellow officers. "We're going to lose this fucking war if we don't stop killing civilians."

On September 26, when Obama and McCain held their first presidential debate, the conduct of the CIA was a hot topic. "We have a long way to go in our intelligence services," McCain said. "We have to do a better job in human intelligence. And we've got to make sure that we have people who are trained interrogators so that we don't ever torture a prisoner ever again. We have to make sure that our technological and intelligence capabilities are better."

Obama briefly raised the intelligence fiasco that led the United States to the disastrous invasion and occupation of Iraq, a war he had opposed from the start. Then he turned to the black sites. "It is important for us to understand that the way we are perceived in the world is going to make a difference, in terms of our capacity to get cooperation and root out terrorism. But because of some of the mistakes that have been made—and I give Senator McCain great credit on the torture issue, for having identified that as something that undermines our long-term security—because of those things, we, I think, are going to have a lot of work to do."

As Election Day approached, Bush had become one of the most reviled presidents in American history. His popularity ratings in public polls were worse than Nixon's in the depths of Watergate. He would hand his successor a howling economic crisis on top of three hot wars—Iraq, Afghanistan, and the global war on terror—without a promise of the possibility of victory.

Bush had proclaimed a "freedom agenda" in his second inaugural address, vowing that his wars would "support the growth of democratic institutions in every nation and culture, with the ultimate goal of ending tyranny in our world." But he had achieved the opposite. The terrorists had spread their ideas across the planet; Bush had been incapable of spreading his own. The success of al Qaeda's 9/11 attack was a result of his refusal to heed the CIA's warnings; the failure of his ideological crusade was a consequence of his condoning torture in the name of national security.

He had damaged America's image in the eyes of the world by his use of the CIA as an instrument of his power. The brutal techniques he authorized had "not only failed their purpose—to secure actionable intelligence to prevent further attacks on the U.S. and our allies—but actually damaged our security interests, as well as our reputation as a force for good in the world," McCain said later in life. "They stained our national honor, did much harm, and little practical good." This was the legacy Bush bequeathed to the next president of the United States.

Chapter Sixteen

NO MIDDLE GROUND

On November 4, 2008, Barack Obama won the presidency by nearly ten million votes. He declared victory just before midnight. Street parties broke out across the country and around the world. "Change has come to America," he proclaimed.

To the muted astonishment of its leaders, little would change at the CIA. "His people were signaling to us, I think partly to try to assure us, that they weren't going to come in and dismantle the place, that they were going to be just as tough, if not tougher, than the Bush people," said John Rizzo, who had briefed Obama's national-security transition team. "They signaled fairly early on that the incoming president believed in a vigorous, aggressive, continuing counterterrorism effort." He remained cautious: "It's only when the new head of the CIA comes in that you get a much clearer sense about where the agency is going to be headed."

John Brennan, the twenty-five-year CIA veteran who had been one of George Tenet's closest aides, had answered the Obama campaign's requests for advice on counterterrorism and in return received the intelligence portfolio for the transition. On November 10, to his pleasant astonishment, he was invited for a one-on-one conversation with Obama in Chicago. The black sites and cruel interrogations should never have happened, Brennan told him, and nor should the loss of innocent lives from the drone strikes continue. Three days later, Obama called him in Washington and said he wanted him to lead the CIA. Brennan was dumbfounded and delighted. But within a week, once word had leaked, the appointment was doomed. Some politicians, and many pundits, deemed Brennan guilty by association with torture, a word he refused to use. He had privately opposed it but had never had the courage to speak out when he had the chance. It quickly became clear that the Senate would not confirm anyone even remotely associated with rendition, detention, and interrogation. On November 25, Brennan withdrew.

"The whole thing played out publicly, and it was pretty ugly," Hayden remembered. He received Brennan at CIA headquarters the next day for transition teamwork. "I'm sorry, John," he said. "I know how you feel." Brennan could be brusque on a good day, and this was a bad one. "With all due respect, Mike," he barked, "no, you don't!" *Fuck you, John*, the director said to himself, silently counting to ten. Hayden was already furious when Brennan walked in. He had imagined he'd be asked to stay on—Bush had recommended that to Obama, who was retaining Bob Gates as secretary of defense—but he couldn't get an audience with the president-elect.

Obama was slowly getting up to speed on the CIA. He had received his first look at the President's Daily Brief thirty-two hours after the polls closed on Election Day.* Mike Morell, now the CIA's chief of intelligence analysis, and two other briefers continued to meet Obama almost every day during the eleven-week transition. "He was brilliant and deeply attentive," Morell remembered. "He quickly got to the heart of an issue and asked the right questions." But the PDB provided to the president-elect never covered covert operations, the most secret missions of the CIA. Hayden read Obama and his running mate Joe Biden into that world on December 9, five weeks after the election. They had planned to meet at

---

* A CIA historian's breakdown of PDB topics during the 2008 transition showed that 30 percent focused on the Middle East, in particular Iraq, Iran, and the Israeli-Palestinian conflict. Seventeen percent dealt with Afghanistan and Pakistan; 13 percent with East Asia, notably China and North Korea; and 10 percent on al Qaeda and terrorism. The remaining 30 percent covered Africa, Latin America, Russia, Central Asia, and Europe. The briefings were wide but not deep. "The PDB is a bit better than CNN Headline News in terms of depth, but it is never BBC," Hayden said.

the FBI's Chicago office that morning, but the Bureau was preoccupied: it was arresting the governor of Illinois for trying to sell an appointment to Obama's Senate seat to the highest bidder.

Across a crowded table in a hastily arranged secure conference room, Hayden laid out fourteen major covert-action programs. These included lethal counterterrorism operations across some sixty countries in the Middle East, South Asia, and Africa; targeted killings with drone strikes and paramilitary raids in Pakistan and Afghanistan; lethal raids against foreign fighters in Iraq; counterproliferation operations to disrupt the nuclear-weapons labs of Iran and North Korea; counternarcotics campaigns against cocaine cartels; and hundreds of millions of dollars for intelligence services throughout the Middle East and the former Soviet Union, along with more than a few foreign leaders, spy chiefs, and ministers.

Obama asked a few questions, "absorbing things with little visible reaction," but Biden had many. "The vice president–elect was his usual garrulous self, so one of my challenges was to get both men to the bottom of each page at about the same time," Hayden recounted. By far his biggest challenge was trying to sell the rendition, detention, and interrogation program. He did his best, but he failed.

"Your job is to restore the credibility of the CIA"

New Year's Day came and went, and Obama still didn't have a choice to replace Hayden at the CIA. His newly chosen chief of staff, the Chicago congressman Rahm Emanuel, had a brainstorm: what about Leon Panetta? They had been colleagues at the Clinton White House, where Panetta had been chief of staff and budget director, a post that had given him a mastery of the size and cost of American intelligence. More to the point, having been an eight-term congressman, he could try to repair the CIA's fractured trust on Capitol Hill. And Panetta had spoken out against the CIA's abuses in a short essay in a wonkish Washington policy journal. "How did we transform from champions of human dignity and individual rights into a nation of armchair torturers?" he had asked. And he had answered:

> One word: fear. Fear is blinding, hateful, and vengeful. It makes the end justify the means. . . . Those who support torture may believe that we can abuse captives in certain select circumstances and still be true to our values. But that is a false compromise. We either believe in the dignity of the individual, the rule of law, and the prohibition of cruel and unusual punishment, or we don't. There is no middle ground. We cannot and we must not use torture under any circumstances. We are better than that.

The idea of Panetta running the CIA was counterintuitive—"Completely out of left field," he said fifteen years later—and a shock to Mike Hayden. He was appalled at being thrown over for "Rahm Emanuel's goombah," the epithet he spat out upon seeing the news online.* "Panetta was a surprise pick to most of us," said Rizzo. "He didn't seem to have any discernable interest or expertise in national security matters. And of course, he had been a politician." And yet, "I think he turned out to be probably the most effective CIA director that I worked for." Rizzo had served ten directors over thirty-three years. Panetta had "more insight into the political realities in Washington than anyone at the table, including Obama and Biden," Gates said. "Leon was smart and tough . . . and above all, knew Congress—a perennial deficiency at CIA." He had a bond with Gates, who stayed on as secretary of defense, and one with Hillary Clinton, Obama's fierce rival for the Democratic nomination and now his choice for secretary of state. What he didn't have was any ties to the CIA or its history.

Panetta said that when Obama offered him the post on January 4, 2009, he had one demand. "Your job," the president said, "is to restore the credibility of the CIA." But the first order of business for Panetta was

---

* *Goombah* is an ethnic slur against Italian-Americans, connoting Mafia connections. Bob Woodward reported the remark and Panetta reprinted it in his memoir.

to establish his credibility *at* the CIA. He consulted all the former CIA directors, especially Gates and George Bush the elder, who advised him to listen to the old pros and learn from them. He shared a tiny space at transition headquarters with John Brennan, who had accepted a consolation prize: deputy national security adviser for counterterrorism and homeland security. Brennan schooled him over dinners of steak and good red wine. Retain the high command at headquarters, Brennan said. Absorb the culture of the agency from them. And understand that the war on terror is your highest priority. Panetta took heed. He kept Steve Kappes as his deputy and Mike Sulick as chief of the clandestine service.

On February 13, Kappes swore him into office on the seventh floor. Panetta brought his charmingly profane personality and a personalized coffee mug to his morning staff meetings (It read: CIA—CALIFORNIA ITALIAN-AMERICAN) and he expanded the inner circle of those meetings to include all the agency's divisions. "I need you to be honest with me," he told his officers. "The last thing I want is for something to be going on in the bowels of this place that I don't know about." He didn't know a great deal. No one had told him about the CIA's lethal operations until after he was sworn in. When Hayden had told him he was going to be the combatant commander of the war on terror, Panetta had thought: *What the hell are you talking about?* Hayden was talking about the drone war in Pakistan and Afghanistan.

"I really hadn't gotten fully briefed on that," Panetta recalled. It soon became clear that he would be part of a kill chain that ran from Mike D'Andrea at the counterterrorism center through the seventh-floor suites to the Oval Office. He quickly went to see D'Andrea, the Muslim convert who kept a prayer rug in his office. "You would assume a guy like Mike would be trigger-happy, but he was a professional who did not bullshit me," Panetta said. "He was totally devoted to the mission. He was totally focused. If he made a mistake, he would admit it."

Hundreds of mistakes took place, if you counted every civilian death as an unintended consequence. On his third day in office, Obama had authorized two drone strikes against training camps in Waziristan, killing five al Qaeda terrorists—and an estimated twenty civilians. Over the next eight years, he gave the execute orders for 540 more attacks, ten times the number Bush had launched, 80 percent of which were in Pakistan, the remainder in Yemen and Somalia. These killed 3,797 people, including 324 civilians, according to the Council on Foreign Relations, a firmament of the Washington establishment. Urged on by D'Andrea, Panetta requisitioned new fleets of Predators and a new, more sophisticated drone called the Reaper, knowing full well that targeted killings alone would not defeat al Qaeda. At the White House, Brennan was the action officer for lethal operations outside the war zones of Afghanistan and Iraq. He brought every plan to the president. Obama personally approved each drone strike after due deliberation, sometimes in weekly White House meetings that became known as "Terror Tuesdays." The ferocity and frequency of the attacks—more than one a week in 2009 and two a week in 2010—astonished and pleased Hayden.

"Incredible continuity between the 43rd and the 44th Presidents, despite the campaign rhetoric in 2008. I thank God for that, that's a blessing," he said. "Now, I've got some complaints. We don't detain anybody anymore, put interrogations aside. Interrogate someone? We don't capture anybody."

Obama had a clear rationale for the CIA's air war, one that he would never express in public. Al Qaeda was an existential threat. He had closed the secret prisons as a matter of law and principle. He chose to incinerate America's enemies rather than incarcerate them. The calculus wasn't that complicated to him. It was trying to kill people before they kill you. And it had the added benefit of protecting Obama's right flank from the criticism that he was too soft-hearted to command the war against al Qaeda.

On April 20, Obama visited CIA headquarters and met first with Kappes and then with a few dozen officers and analysts in a seventh-floor conference room before giving a speech in the lobby. He knew that his repudiation of torture, his release of the Bush legal memos justifying it, and his shuttering of the black sites had angered them. One officer, her voice trembling slightly, asked Obama to understand her mission. "Al Qaeda is dangerous," she said. "We need to keep after it." Her tone implied a question: did the president share her commitment? "I get it," Obama said. Now he had to prove it.

Two weeks later, Obama convened his national security team in the Situation Room. In the decade since al Qaeda had bombed the American embassies in Kenya and Tanzania in 1998, the CIA had amassed enough intelligence on bin Laden and his followers to fill a Home Depot warehouse: transcriptions of trials and interrogations and intercepts, downloaded computer and cell phone data, reports from case officers and their foreign counterparts, reconnaissance photos of safe houses and training camps and cities and villages in a dozen nations. Yet no one had a clue where bin Laden was hiding. The CIA's best guess was that he was holed up somewhere in the ungoverned tribal lands of northwestern Pakistan. Panetta brought a rack of PowerPoint slides to show the president. Several showed the names of al Qaeda couriers and communicators who might conceivably be in touch with their leader. "If we can find them," Panetta said, "we will be able to follow them to bin Laden." This in no way satisfied Obama. On June 2, he ordered the CIA to develop a detailed plan to hunt him down within thirty days.

On his first trip abroad as CIA director, Panetta met John Bennett, the station chief in Islamabad.* He promised him a large new contingent of CIA officers and targeting analysts from headquarters. Bennett needed all the help he could get. He was trying, among other responsibilities, to coordinate counterterrorism operations with the treacherous ISI, act in concert with the American ambassador as air traffic controllers in the ramped-up drone war, deal with the feckless and corrupt government of Pakistan, and find bin Laden. Panetta met him at the CIA station, which

---

* Bennett had commanded the special activities division from 2003 to 2005 before serving as station chief in Islamabad; his reporting from Pakistan had led Obama to call its harboring of al Qaeda "an international security challenge of the highest order." He was an ex-Marine and a Harvard man with a philosophy about espionage, developed while recruiting and running agents in Africa as a young case officer. The work required "deception, manipulation . . . and, ultimately, corruption," he said in a 2019 lecture. "You develop the relationship with the objective of leading this person—who may never even have thought about it—down the path of a criminal conspiracy to commit treason."

occupied the third floor of the enormous American embassy, and the two had knocked heads over what he deemed meddling micromanagement from headquarters. The argument degenerated.

"John, fuck you," said Panetta. "Fuck you," Bennett shot back. This frank exchange of views did not stop the director from making Bennett the next chief of the clandestine service.

On June 23, at headquarters, Panetta learned to his dismay that there was something in the bowels of the CIA he hadn't known about: the assassination squad that had been conceived by Ric Prado and blessed by Dick Cheney a few weeks after 9/11.

Prado, frustrated when his bosses balked at this endeavor after many months of planning, had left the CIA to become Blackwater's vice president for "special government programs" in 2004. Later that year, Blackwater and Prado's good friend Jose Rodriguez struck a deal to outsource his plans for training and deploying hits to kill terrorists. Prado had recruited brown-skinned Latinos for the task, figuring their complexions might serve as camouflage in the tribal lands of Pakistan and Afghanistan. Rodriguez had never shared these plans with the congressional intelligence committees, which by law must be kept abreast of the CIA's covert actions. Panetta immediately suspended the program, came clean with Congress the next day, and later curtailed the CIA's profligate outsourcing of its missions to private paramilitary and security contractors. None of this was popular with high-ranking members of the clandestine service.

But what really infuriated them—and the White House chief of staff Rahm Emanuel—was Panetta's decision to cooperate with the Senate intelligence committee's investigation of the rendition, detention, and interrogation program, a resolve rooted in Rodriguez's destruction of the Thailand torture tapes. "The president wants to know who the fuck authorized this!" screamed Emanuel, a small man with a big temper. Obama had said he wanted to look forward, not back, rejecting calls for a truth commission to probe the Bush administration's conduct of the war on terror. But Panetta believed Congress had the power to investigate the CIA and he had no right to refuse them. He arranged for the Senate intelligence committee's staff to read and take notes on hundreds of thousands of CIA records in a database housed in a secure reading room in Virginia. Their conclusions, published in 2014, would be devastating.

"See if they're telling the truth or not"

The summer had passed without a clue to bin Laden's whereabouts. The CIA's analysts, after five years of painstaking work, had deduced the name of a bin Laden courier, but whether he was alive or dead was anyone's guess. To strengthen the hunt, Kappes sent Greg Vogle back to Kabul for a second tour as station chief; he received fresh reinforcements of paramilitary officers, case officers, targeting officers, and analysts. Vogle gave each new arriving officer the same marching orders he had always given as a station chief. *Your mission is to destroy al Qaeda. Any questions?*

Vogle took command of a new force of Afghans recruited and trained by special-activities division officers, called Counterterrorism Pursuit Teams, which worked with the CIA station to capture or kill the enemy. He worked in tandem with General McChrystal's special-forces commandos in Afghanistan, who had the authority to kill terrorists on both sides of the border with Pakistan without the president's say-so. Vogle also oversaw a half dozen CIA forward operating bases in Afghanistan, the biggest of which was in Khost, about fifteen miles from the border. It was there—and two thousand miles to the west, in Amman, Jordan—that the first chance of a breakthrough in the hunt for al Qaeda's leaders began to take shape.

The CIA station in Amman was like an American aircraft carrier in the rough seas of the Middle East. Its allies in the Jordanian intelligence service spoke all the dialects of Arabic and had deep penetrations of radical networks among Palestinians, Syrians, Iraqis, Kuwaitis, and their own countrymen. The Americans had infinite resources to finance their work and focus their reporting. Months earlier, the Amman station chief, Lance Hamilton, and his deputy, Marc Polymeropoulos, had heard from a highly trusted Jordanian intelligence officer, Sharif Ali bin Zeid, a cousin to the king, that he had made a jailhouse recruitment of an agent prepared to betray al Qaeda.

Bin Zeid was "a tremendous ally, and our officers loved him like a brother," Polymeropoulos said. His recruit was Humam al-Balawi, a young doctor born in Palestine, an online jihadist who had created a highly popular internet persona giving violent voice to al Qaeda, praising its suicide bombers as martyrs, and amplifying the rhetoric of Ayman al-Zawahiri, bin Laden's right-hand man. Al-Zawahiri had written a decade before: "To kill Americans and their allies—civilian and military—is an individual duty for every Muslim who can do it." He was the intellectual author of the 9/11 attacks and the operational commander of al Qaeda—a target every bit as important as bin Laden to the CIA.

The doctor said he had deep connections to the al Qaeda terrorists encamped in Pakistan, and he proposed to go there and infiltrate them, using his online jihadist credentials. The Jordanians flew him to Peshawar, the capital of Pakistan's tribal lands, along with a fistful of cash and a cheap video camera. He traveled to South Waziristan and, at the end of August, he emailed bin Zeid a video clip of his conversation with Atiyah Abd al-Rahman, a top al Qaeda commander and a military and spiritual adviser to bin Laden since the 1980s.* The Amman station sent the clip to CIA headquarters. It had an electrifying effect. Another email came in November. The doctor said he was treating his mentor, al-Zawahiri, and he sent medical records matching what the CIA knew of al-Zawahiri's history of diabetes. Here was the deepest penetration of al Qaeda in history.

"We were very excited," Polymeropoulos said. "I remember writing an email to a colleague noting that this was it, this was the key lead." But a question remained: who was this doctor? "With someone of this importance, you need a CIA case officer, an operations officer to really look the asset in the eye and get a real assessment of what we're dealing with," Polymeropoulos said. "See if they're telling the truth or not."

The doctor proposed to Ali bin Zeid that they meet with a CIA contingent to discuss their next moves. But the CIA case officer who worked with bin Zeid, Darren LaBonte, had a bad premonition about that. He had

---

* Al-Rahman was killed by a CIA drone strike in August 2011.

been an FBI agent before the CIA recruited him three years earlier, and he had a healthy sense of skepticism about informants. He thought the doctor might be too good to be true. "We need to go slow on this case," he wrote to Lance Hamilton, the station chief. But Hamilton wanted to take the next step, as did everyone else up the chain of command at CIA headquarters. Their enthusiasm blinded them to the fact that no one at CIA had ever met the doctor, much less tested his veracity. Bin Zeid got the green light.

The Amman station proposed that the doctor should cross the border from Waziristan to meet the officers who ran the CIA's base in Khost. The base was led by Jennifer Matthews, a leading bin Laden analyst since before 9/11, and a highly regarded reports officer who had never run an operation in the field. She had been sent on orders from the counterterrorism chief Mike D'Andrea, who overruled the objections of the chief of station in Jordan. Vogle sent his own deputy chief of station from Kabul to support her.

The CIA contingent waited eagerly and impatiently to meet the doctor. "No one thought this was going to be sitting down and having a picnic or a barbecue," Polymeropoulos said. The doctor was "not only [someone] we had never met, but someone who had just been in—who we thought had infiltrated—the most dangerous terrorist group on the planet." One red flag, and only one, had been raised by a Jordanian officer who warned that the doctor might be a double agent. CIA headquarters had disregarded him. Matthews wanted everyone at the base to greet him as a visiting dignitary.

When he arrived on December 30, 2009, no security protocols worthy of the name were in place. The doctor stepped out of his car, mumbled a prayer, and detonated an immensely powerful suicide bomb. The fireball rose a hundred yards high. The attack—and the entire double-agent operation—had been designed by al-Zawahiri from the start. "We planned for something but got a bigger gift, a gift from Allah, who brought us, through his accompaniment, a valuable prey: Americans, and from the CIA," the doctor said in a recorded video message broadcast by al Qaeda after the attack. Matthews, LaBonte, and five more CIA officers and contractors died in an instant. Ali bin Zeid, a member of the royal family of Jordan, was killed. Vogle's deputy chief of station and five others were severely injured.

Polymeropoulos, the acting chief of station in Amman, had been linked to LaBonte in a secure chat. The link went dark. His next call came from Vogle in Kabul. They're all gone, he said. Talk to your people in your station. They're all looking to you. Keep yourself together. Polymeropoulos found it hard. "To this day, it kind of defies belief," he said. "We got beat by al Qaeda. We thought that they could not run a double agent at us with an ability to provide feeder material like you'd see from the Russians and the Chinese. But they did."

"The mission itself may have clouded some of the judgments"

Panetta would hold no one to account for the failures that allowed al Qaeda to murder seven CIA personnel; everyone was to blame, so no one was to blame. But he had asked Charles Allen, who had joined the CIA in 1958 and served for forty-seven years, to analyze what had gone wrong. In hindsight, it was clear. "There were some counterintelligence flags, probably from the outset," to which the CIA had been willfully blind, Allen said. That blindness ran all the way up the chain of command from the Amman station to the seventh floor.

No one among the dozen or so senior officers who approved the mission had seen fit to consult Cindy Webb, the chief of counterintelligence since 2006, and one of the highest-ranking women at the CIA. Webb was like the internal-affairs chief at a big-city police department, a vital necessity, yet regarded by gung-ho officers as an infernal pest. But no intelligence agency can be better than its counterintelligence service. Running an operation penetrated by the enemy was far worse than running no operation at all.

Webb was the daughter of a two-star general, raised at Army bases in Germany and South Korea during the cold war. She saw an actuarial certainty that, at any given moment, American intelligence was compromised by spies, foreign and domestic, as had been the case since the creation of the CIA. Her work was not for the faint of heart; counterintelligence investigations could last for years without resolution. If she and her colleagues didn't find the spies, they had failed. And if they did, the public perceived that they had failed by not detecting them earlier. Spy catchers were thus damned if they did and damned if they didn't, and some had good cause to doubt the existence of a just and merciful God.

From the closing days of the cold war onward, the CIA had realized, too late, that the Russians and Chinese had run spies inside headquarters—and that the Russian, Chinese, Cuban, Czech, and East German services either had dispatched double agents to deceive the CIA or doubled all the spies the agency thought it was running against them. In response, it had created a new counterintelligence center, hired FBI agents to bolster it, strengthened its offense and defense against spies, and chosen Webb to lead it in 2006.

But counterintelligence had been swamped by counterterrorism. Thousands of new officers had received little or no training in its precepts. Some officers of the clandestine service and the counterterrorism center saw Webb as an impediment, slowing the frenetic pace of their operations, obstructing their path to power. All this had meant that the doctor, and his operation, had never been subjected to counterintelligence and security protocols. The result was the deadliest day in the history of the CIA since the chief of station, the leading Mideast analyst, and six others died after Hezbollah blew up the American embassy in Beirut in 1983.

"There was a systemic breakdown with regard to the kind of judgment and scrutiny that should have been applied" to the operation, Panetta said later. "The mission itself may have clouded some of the judgments. . . . It was the intense determination to accomplish the mission that influenced the judgments that were made."

Chapter Seventeen

THE KEYS TO THE CASTLE

The world of American intelligence was like a medieval city surrounded by a moat. The city had a thousand castles. Each castle had a library with a thousand books. Each book contained a thousand secrets. The moat had a drawbridge with a locked gate. If you had the keys, a billion secrets were at your fingertips.

Once, the protocol for sharing secrets was based on the "need to know" principle. Intelligence officers had to prove that they needed access to a particular secret. A critical point of failure before the 9/11 attacks had been the CIA's refusal to tell the FBI that two of al Qaeda's hijackers were in the United States in 2000. After 9/11, the imperative to connect the dots became paramount. And the solution had seemed obvious. The need to know had been supplanted by the need to share.

Once there had been one drawbridge. Now there were a thousand. Yet the leaders of American intelligence had no idea how many keys to the drawbridge existed, or how many people were on their secure networks, strolling through the libraries and thumbing through the books of secrets. It was one thing to cross the bridge. It was quite another to loot the library, make digital copies of three-quarter of a million books, and blast them out on the internet.

"A grave and imminent risk"

On November 30, 2009, Chelsea Manning, a twenty-two-year-old Army private first class, saved a text file to an encrypted cache on her computer. It read: "Contact our investigations editor directly in Iceland +354 862 3481. 24-hour service. Ask for 'Julian Assange.'"

Manning was in a state of crisis—living as a gay man, desperate to transition, trapped in the closet of the military's "Don't Ask, Don't Tell" policy. She described herself as broken in spirit and "self-medicating like crazy." She was serving as an intelligence analyst at a military base twenty miles outside Baghdad, one among a million American government employees holding a TOP SECRET security clearance. Her assignment gave her what she described as "unprecedented access to classified networks 14 hours a day 7 days a week"—an open door to SIPRNet, the Secret Internet Protocol Router Network, used by the Pentagon and the State Department to transmit classified intelligence.

Assange was the nomadic thirty-eight-year-old warlock of WikiLeaks. His manifesto read: "The more secretive or unjust an organization is, the more leaks induce fear and paranoia in the leadership." As a teenage hacker using the name Mendax, Latin for "liar," he had been criminally charged with computer crimes in his native Australia, suffered a psychiatric breakdown, and pleaded guilty to avoid a long prison sentence. After stealing secrets for more than twenty years, he was now the verge of his greatest theft.

After Assange and Manning connected on a chat network, he sent her password-cracking software to penetrate deeper into SIPRNet, which held information classified as SECRET. She described the network as having "weak physical security" and "weak counterintelligence." She found a portal to the Joint Worldwide Intelligence Communication System and its TOP SECRET military compartments. With Assange's assistance, Manning downloaded four nearly complete databases for him: 800 Guantanamo Bay detainee records, 90,000 military and intelligence files from Afghanistan, 250,000 State Department cables, and 400,000 reports from Iraq.

On April 5, 2010, Assange stood before an audience of journalists at the National Press Club in Washington and showed them a video shot from an Apache helicopter gunship on patrol over Baghdad. The gunner had fired at both armed fighters and civilians, women and children included. Among the eighteen dead were two Reuters reporters, a cameraman and his assistant. WikiLeaks, and Assange, became famous that day. He had revealed a reality of the American war in Iraq.

Over the next year, Assange made the entire trove of purloined documents public, in four separate releases. The first were the Afghan files, which revealed the names of recruited sources who had informed the CIA and the military about the Taliban, endangering their lives. "We are studying the report," a Taliban official told the *New York Times*. "We will investigate through our own secret service whether the people mentioned are really spies working for the U.S. If they are U.S. spies, then we know how to punish them." Next came the State Department cables, which included the names of journalists, religious leaders, human rights advocates, and political dissidents living in nations like China, Iran, and Syria, who had spoken in confidence to American diplomats, often at considerable risk to their own safety. "By publishing these documents without redacting the human sources' names," the Justice Department charged when it indicted him for these leaks, "Assange created a grave and imminent risk that the innocent people he named would suffer serious physical harm and/or arbitrary detention." Among those named in Afghanistan and Iraq, "a number of people went into hiding, [and] a number of people had to move, particularly those civilians in war zones who had told U.S. soldiers about movements of the Taliban and al-Qaida," said P. J. Crowley, then the State Department spokesman. "No doubt some of those people were harmed when their identities were compromised."

The last tranche was the Guantanamo files, which included highly specific information about the discovery of Osama bin Laden's whereabouts and the name of a courier whom the CIA had determined was his contact with the outside world. Had al Qaeda's leaders read them, it could have changed the course of history.

"Thank God I'm an American citizen"

John Bennett became chief of the clandestine service, after Panetta had coaxed him out of a brief retirement, on July 30, 2010. Bennett had taken heed of the counterintelligence crisis confronting the CIA. But that could never be his first order of business, not as long as bin Laden remained at large in Pakistan. Nor could it be second, as al Qaeda plots multiplied throughout the Middle East, Europe, and the United States. Nor the third, not as long as an imam named Anwar al-Awlaki continued to plot against America.

Born in Las Cruces, New Mexico, al-Awlaki had led mosques in San Diego, California, and Falls Church, Virginia, despite having the barest religious training. Three of the 9/11 hijackers had attended his sermons. In 2002, he had fled the United States for his ancestral home in Yemen after learning, through the manager of an escort service, that the FBI had a file on him which included his frequent dalliances with sex workers. "He would always say, 'Thank God I'm an American citizen and I have a second home to go back to if things go wrong in Yemen,'" his uncle told the *New York Times*.

By 2007, he had attracted an international following—and the embrace of al Qaeda—as he called for jihad on the internet, on YouTube, and in CDs and DVDs that circulated widely in America and around the world. By 2008, he was practicing what he preached. He had become the leader of external operations for al Qaeda in the Arabian Peninsula, and the radicalizing force underlying nearly every major counterterrorism investigation by the CIA and the FBI. And by 2009, working from an isolated hideout in Yemen, he had inspired the Army major who killed thirteen people at a Texas military base, the worst terrorist attack in the United States since 9/11, and he had trained the Nigerian who had tried to blow up a Northwest Airlines flight carrying 290 passengers and crew as it prepared to land in Detroit on Christmas Day. Had the explosive sewn in the man's underwear fully ignited, it could have created the single deadliest airline crash in American history.

Every Monday, Wednesday, and Friday afternoon at four thirty, a dozen of the CIA's leaders, including Panetta, Bennett, the newly promoted deputy director Mike Morell, and the Near East division chief, Paul Nevin, met to assess the state of the war against al Qaeda. The meetings were led by Mike D'Andrea.

D'Andrea and an ever-growing contingent of CIA officers and analysts—first a few dozen, then a few hundred, now a few thousand—had been pursuing al Qaeda for twelve years, ever since the African embassy bombings in August 1998. He commanded the largest component of the CIA, overseeing some three thousand officers, analysts, technicians, support staff, and contractors. His counterterrorism center was spending roughly $3 billion a year, a sum equal to the CIA's entire budget a decade before. He worked sixteen-hour days, often sleeping in his office, pausing only to wolf down a meatless halal meal and chain-smoke cigarettes in the courtyard. He was admired by his superiors and ruthless to his subordinates, some of whom had nicknamed him "Ayatollah Mike." D'Andrea would launch 117 drone strikes in Pakistan in 2010 alone. By then, he was responsible for killing perhaps two thousand terrorists and, by the CIA's admission, many scores of civilians; human rights groups counted hundreds. He was by any measure the most lethal American officer in the war on terror. But he was more than a relentless executioner. No one at the CIA had done more to analyze and understand al Qaeda.

D'Andrea now proposed to kill al-Awlaki, if he could be found at his mountain hideout in northern Yemen. Obama thought it an easy call. But the president was well aware of the Fifth Amendment's commandment that "no one shall be deprived of life, liberty, or property, without due process of law," and he sought a classified opinion from David Barron at the Justice Department's Office of Legal Counsel. Barron's view was that the president had the right to order the death of an American citizen whom an "informed, high-level official"—like D'Andrea—had determined was posing an "imminent threat of violent attack." The war on terror now pushed deeper into the dark fringes of the law. No

American citizen had been killed on the order of a president, without a trial, since the Civil War.*

"We have found a guy"

The CIA loved to call its invasion of Afghanistan a magnificent success. But bin Laden and almost all of his commanders had escaped, first to the teeming cities of Pakistan, then to safe havens in the remote villages of Pakistan's tribal lands. By 2006, al Qaeda was as dangerous a threat as it had been on the day it attacked America.

And then the CIA had started to know its enemy. Some of this knowledge had come from interrogations. Some had come from capturing computers and documents in raids conducted after missile strikes. But it wasn't torture and it wasn't drones that had turned the tide. The CIA had been recruiting and running al Qaeda agents in the tribal lands of Pakistan from 2006 onward. This achievement, which has gone unheralded, was a singular success of the CIA station in Islamabad under John Bennett. He had a squad of CIA and ISI officers who ran a stable of recruits reporting on the al Qaeda network and the lives of bin Laden's lieutenants. Having a team of spies in the enemy's camp was a rare accomplishment.

"Exquisite human sources with firsthand knowledge who are close to decision-makers are the exception, not the rule," Mike Morell said. "The exception being al Qaeda. That is the great success story" of the CIA after 9/11. "It required an immense amount of resources, our best people, and focused leadership." Scores of al Qaeda and Taliban leaders were captured or killed in Afghanistan and Pakistan during 2009 and the first half of 2010 alone.

And now the CIA had picked up the scent of a trail to the world's most wanted man.

---

* Al-Awlaki died in a drone strike in Yemen in September 2011. The attack also killed Samir Khan, an American citizen born in Pakistan, and an editor of *Inspire*, al Qaeda's English-language online magazine. The next month, a mistaken drone strike killed Awlaki's sixteen-year-old son—also an American. In 2014, Obama appointed Barron to the federal appeals court in Boston, where at this writing he presides as chief judge.

One afternoon in August 2010, when the counterterrorism meeting was over, D'Andrea and two of his top analysts asked to see Panetta and Morell alone in the director's suite. After more than eight years of futility, they had a potential lead as to the whereabouts of Osama bin Laden— the name of a man who might serve as his courier, his connection to the outside world. The clue did not, to their surprise, point to a mud hut in Waziristan but to a small city 150 miles away.

"We have found a guy we know as Abu Ahmed," D'Andrea told the director. "He is living in the town of Abbottabad."

The briefers laid satellite reconnaissance photos on Panetta's desk. They showed a compound on a dead-end street in a well-to-do neighborhood. It was enclosed by eighteen-foot-high walls, crested with barbed wire. Within them stood a tall white house whose third story had a balcony shielded by another wall, fully seven feet high. Panetta stared at the pictures. "Who puts a privacy wall around a patio?" he said. "Exactly," one of the analysts replied. The CIA station in Islamabad soon reported that the house had no telephone or internet connections, that its occupants burned their trash instead of putting it out on the street, and that the children in the compound never left to go to school. All this led Panetta, Morell and D'Andrea to brief Obama in the White House Situation Room on the auspicious date of September 10.

"We don't know much about the compound," Panetta told Obama. Collecting intelligence on it might prove tricky, he warned. "The goddamn Pakistan Military Academy is in Abbottabad," a stone's throw from the walled house, and the city was "a goddamn retirement area for senior Pakistani military officers." He speculated that the ISI might be harboring bin Laden, an ominous thought: the CIA had been coordinating counterterrorism operations with its leaders for eight years while placing little trust in them.*

---

* John Bennett, as station chief in Pakistan, had developed a good sense of the ISI's priorities. First was spying on the president of Pakistan, Benazir Bhutto's widower, Asif Zardari. Second was penetrating and attacking the Pakistani Taliban, though the ISI never had the sources and the informants in the tribal areas that they claimed. Third was spying on India, their nation's mortal enemy, against whom Pakistan had fought and lost three wars. Finding bin Laden and attacking al Qaeda were not on the ISI's to-do list, as far as Bennett could determine.

Obama listened intently, his chin in his left hand, his finger pointed at his temple. Then he gave Panetta two orders: Find out everything you can about that place and report back to me. And brief no one else about what you've found until I say so. Fourteen full-dress meetings followed with increasing frequency and intensity over the following eight months, the most crucial series of conversations about a covert action between a president and his spy chiefs in the history of the CIA.

"The station was not happy"

Two weeks later, Cameron Munter made the rounds in Washington before departing to take up his post as the new American ambassador in Pakistan, a nation he perceived as less a country with an army than an army with a country. He visited CIA headquarters for intelligence briefings, including a visit with the taciturn D'Andrea, and then went to the White House to discuss the drone program. Brennan and his fellow deputy national security adviser, Maj. Gen. Doug Lute, explained that the CIA had a bright green light to intensify the strikes. He went to see the president. The drone program matters, Obama told him. We need to prevent a catastrophic terrorist attack.

Ambassador Munter learned that the CIA conducted three kinds of attacks in Pakistan. The first, against "high-value targets," were relatively rare; the CIA had been picking them off one by one for years, and fewer and fewer remained. The second, for "imminent threats," were less uncommon. The CIA or the NSA would overhear the chatter of terrorists talking about attacking Berlin or Amsterdam, and then the conspirators would die. The third were "signature strikes"—attacks on what seemed to be a group of terrorists, based on the pattern of their lives detected by persistent surveillance, even if the CIA didn't know who the targets were, if they were plotting against the United States, whether they intended to use the bags of fertilizer they were hauling to build a truck bomb or to grow their crops. These were far more frequent than they had been a year or two earlier. In their aftermath, the ISI often fed stories to Pakistani journalists that the Americans had massacred a village, wantonly killing women and children and progovernment tribal leaders. Some of these accounts, though far from all, were factual. The drones were only as accurate as the intelligence guiding them, and when they killed innocent people, they fueled the continuous state of political crisis in Pakistan, whose civilian leaders were feckless and powerless, none more so than its president.

When he arrived in Islamabad, Munter met the recently arrived station chief, Jonathan Bank, a tightly wound officer who had served as an executive assistant to Pavitt and at CIA stations in the Balkans, Russia, and Iraq. The ambassador told him that he needed to be fully informed on what the CIA was doing in Pakistan. "The Agency guys worked for us. They were advisors and not policymakers," Munter said. "I appreciated their extraordinary expertise, expertise I couldn't match. But I expected them to understand that their role, both in intelligence-gathering and operations, was clearly subordinate to mine." This rule was not unwritten. It was the clearly stated policy of every president since Kennedy, and the CIA broke it at its peril. Munter insisted—as had his predecessor, Anne Patterson—on signing off on each drone strike approved by D'Andrea and Brennan. Ambassador Patterson had never turned the CIA down. That changed.

"On a couple of occasions, they requested a signature strike, and I said no," Munter said. "We were IDing people whom we did not know, in a country with which we have diplomatic relations. Five or six times I said it didn't feel right. And the strike was called off. The station was not happy."

These tensions were starting to rise in the fall of 2010, as platoons of new CIA officers and contractors arrived in Pakistan with diplomatic passports, swelling the station's ranks. The ambassador didn't always know who they were and what they were doing. Nor did the ISI, despite its best efforts. Its chief, Ahmed Shuja Pasha, had become infuriated when the American embassy had announced a year before that it was expanding from five hundred to eight hundred people. He had demanded to know the names of the officers working at the CIA station and held up the imports of the armored vehicles they drove. He saw the dramatic increase of the numbers of American spies and special-operations soldiers as a threat to the integrity of his nation. He did not want Pakistan to become a CIA country.

In December, Pasha decided to burn the station chief, and some of the ISI's remaining bridges to the CIA along with him. Bank was identified first in a lawsuit filed on behalf of the family of two men killed by a drone strike in Waziristan, and then, repeatedly, in the Pakistani press. Death threats against him hurled by bloggers flooded the internet. A prominent newspaper and a national television station published not only his name but his home address, along with photos of the homes where the CIA's officers and contractors lived. All of this flowed from the ISI.

Panetta was outraged: allied spies did not do that to one another. Morell flew to Islamabad in a CIA Gulfstream jet and hustled Bank out of the country on December 16. Six weeks passed before his successor arrived. Mark Kelton had served as station chief in Moscow from 2002 to 2004; he knew what it was like to operate under the gaze of a hostile intelligence service. But two days after he took over in Islamabad, he faced an unforeseeable crisis.

The CIA maintained a base in the city of Lahore, 170 miles to the southeast. A hot-tempered CIA contractor named Ray Davis, who had worked for Blackwater and whose job was to provide on-the-job security for case officers, was driving through the city on January 27, 2011, when two men on a motorcycle pulled up and flashed a gun at him. He shot them dead, and called the base for help. The CIA men racing to the scene crashed into another motorcyclist and killed him in a hit-and-run. Davis was arrested, and a police search of his car revealed, among other evidence, a bank statement listing the CIA as his employer. A major scandal erupted in Pakistan, igniting calls to convict and execute Davis for murder.

Kelton went to see Ambassador Munter to announce that the CIA would stonewall the police. Pasha called Panetta to ask: is this guy yours? Panetta denied it. After that, Pasha refused to talk with the new station chief, making the ambassador his intelligence liaison instead.

The relationship between the ISI and the CIA reached a new low. Pasha demanded that more than three hundred Americans, all of them either CIA officers and contractors or special-operations forces, leave the country forthwith. Obama ordered Secretary of State Hillary Clinton to find a diplomatic solution to the political disaster created by Ray Davis. The president and Panetta had a far bigger problem to resolve in Pakistan.

"We did not have a single piece of hard intelligence"

The CIA was now certain that the courier at the compound was working for al Qaeda, and quite possibly for its leader. "We were so convinced that the house in Abbottabad harbored a valuable target that we began to fashion a plan for taking it," Panetta said. Morell and Bennett doubted that the CIA's paramilitary officers alone could infiltrate the town, carry out a raid on the walled compound, and capture the building and its occupants. A joint operation with the ISI was out of the question. Panetta thought it was time to call in the military. On the evening of February 25, he had dinner at CIA headquarters with the three-star SEAL who now led the Joint Special Operations Command, Vice Adm. William McRaven, and told him everything he knew about the compound. McRaven and his SEAL teams had conducted hundreds of night raids in Afghanistan and Pakistan. He was confident they could take the compound, if the CIA truly believed that it was bin Laden's hideout. The meeting was a dress rehearsal for the full-scale briefing Panetta and Morell delivered on March 14 in a Situation Room meeting attended by Obama, Biden, Gates, members of the president's national security team, a senior military contingent, and the CIA's top analysts.

"The session," wrote Morell, "was one of the most important with a president that I ever attended." At its outset, the CIA told Obama there was a strong possibility that Abu Ahmed was harboring bin Laden at the Abbottabad compound. But that assessment depended on inference and guesswork. The Joint Chiefs and McRaven were weighing two plans of attack, each with potentially grave problems. The Air Force could blow the compound to smithereens with thirty-two 2,000-pound bombs. That would make gathering DNA evidence identifying bin Laden exceedingly hard, obliterate a potential trove of intelligence on al Qaeda, and outrage the nuclear-armed Pakistani military. Or McRaven's commandos could swoop into the compound on helicopters, storm the house, guns blazing, and kill bin Laden. The possibility that Pakistani soldiers and intelligence officers stationed nearby would detect the raid and counterattack was not low. Then the SEAL team would have to fight its way out.

Gates and Biden expressed grave doubts. The vice president worried about the lethal political fallout from a failed raid. The secretary of defense pointedly questioned the intelligence. "The case for bin Laden being at the compound was entirely circumstantial," Gates said. "We did not have a single piece of hard intelligence he was there." He asked point-blank: how confident were the CIA's experts? Morell said he had been surer about the WMD estimate than he was about bin Laden's being in Abbottabad. This wasn't comforting. The analysts' guesstimates ranged widely. A 40 percent chance? Eighty percent?

"I knew those numbers were based on nothing but gut instinct," said Gates, the career CIA analyst. Nor was he the only skeptic. From Islamabad, Mark Kelton had weighed in with his own doubts about the intelligence. He wanted hard proof, not an analytical assessment, he told D'Andrea. He wanted an agent to lay eyes upon bin Laden. The chances of that sighting were vanishingly small. The tension between headquarters and the Islamabad station intensified. Kelton and D'Andrea fought furiously.

Nor was this the only friction grinding away at Obama's national-security team. The State Department was on the verge of a deal to free Ray Davis from prison by paying $2.3 million in blood money to the families of the men he had killed, but "white-hot public anger in Pakistan against the United States had not abated," Gates recounted. He remembered vividly that in 1979, when he was the executive assistant to the CIA director, a mob of Pakistani students inflamed by Iranian propaganda had stormed and burned the American embassy and the CIA station in Islamabad, killing four people and taking a handful of hostages. Now, three decades later, the United States was planning a military assault on Pakistani sovereignty, and the blowback, Gates predicted, "would almost certainly get very ugly" if the mission went awry. Then he summoned a dreadful ghost into the Situation Room.

Gates repeatedly invoked the searing memory of the 1980 mission to free the hostages held at the American embassy in Tehran. Eight helicopters carrying Delta Force soldiers had flown to a desolate site in eastern Iran code-named Desert One. Five were in working order, one had a cracked rotor, the second had a hydraulic leak, the third had been snarled by a sandstorm. Gates had been in the Situation Room when the commanders advised President Carter to abort the operation. Minutes thereafter, one chopper had collided with a C-130 refueling plane, killing eight American commandos in the Iranian desert. The failure effectively ended Carter's presidency. Gates called it "a crushing humiliation that took years for our military to overcome."

Mindful of Murphy's Law—whatever can go wrong will go wrong—Gates advised Obama and McRaven to add two backup helicopters for the Abbottabad assault, and to cloak the raid in "a fig leaf—granted, a very small fig leaf—of deniability." The chain of command would run from Obama to Panetta to McRaven, whose forces would become CIA officers for the purpose of the mission. If disaster struck, the CIA somehow would try to deny all, and surely take the hit for the military and the commander in chief. Panetta ordered the CIA's public affairs office to prepare two briefing books, each one thirty-three pages thick: one for success and one for failure.

Obama thought it came down to a coin toss, a fifty-fifty chance that bin Laden would be captured or killed. Panetta fingered his rosary beads. McRaven consulted the lunar calendar to see which night would be the darkest. It was fitting that the timing of the mission would be ruled by the phases of the moon. On Friday, April 29, Obama gave the go order. Gates still had deep doubts but ultimately went with the decision. Biden had argued the question both ways but came out against it. McRaven reported from Jalalabad, Afghanistan, that SEAL Team Six could execute the order on Saturday or Sunday; the moon would be rising late in the night sky over Abbottabad. One last bit of lunacy remained.

Saturday night was the annual White House Correspondents' Association dinner, an event of pomp and comedy, where reporters in formal wear commingled with famous guests. What would it look like if Obama was onstage laughing it up while SEALs were dying in combat? Then Saturday morning came a weather report from McRaven: too much cloud cover. The mission would take place on Sunday afternoon Washington time. Obama put on his tuxedo and headed up Connecticut Avenue for the Hilton Hotel. The White House speechwriters had prepared a portfolio of zingers for their boss, including a searing roast of Donald Trump, the television celebrity who had been putting out the lie that Obama had not been born in the United States and was thus an illegitimate president. "He just skewered Trump and brought the house down," said James Clapper, the director of national intelligence.*

May Day dawned. Obama and his national-security aides convened at the White House, and the president played nine holes of golf to preserve the illusion of an ordinary Sunday. Panetta and Morell turned the director's conference room into a command post. D'Andrea presided at the counterterrorism center as McRaven's SEAL team took off for the one-hundred-minute trip of 160 miles to Abbottabad. When one of the choppers stalled out on landing and crashed at the edge of the compound, the counterterrorism center fell silent. Everyone thought: *Desert One*. Then came the sound of gunfire. Then fifteen minutes of silence. Then the SEALs brought a man out in a body bag, his face half blown off. After scooping up everything that looked like it might be intelligence, they took off for Afghanistan.

McRaven declared to those gathered at the White House and the CIA that Osama bin Laden was dead. Are you sure it's him? Obama asked. When the team returned, McRaven unzipped the body bag. The Kabul

---

* The president nailed Trump as a conspiracy theorist. "No one is prouder to put this birth certificate matter to rest than the Donald," Obama said, his eyes flashing. "And that's because he can finally get back to focusing on the issues that matter—like, did we fake the moon landing? What really happened in Roswell? And where are Biggie and Tupac?" Clapper glanced at Trump. "He wasn't laughing—he was glowering. I'll never forget that."

station chief, Chris Wood, stood by his side. He had been hunting bin Laden since 1997. That's him, Wood said. The sense of exhilaration inside the counterterrorism center was as strong as an electric current. Panetta and Morell embraced and headed down from the seventh floor to go see the president. Obama addressed the nation and the world at 11:35 p.m. A crowd gathered in Lafayette Square across the White House at midnight, many of them college students. They chanted "USA! USA! USA!" and then took up another cry: "CIA! CIA! CIA!" More than a few officers saw that on TV and thought: *Well, that'll never happen again.*

Seven thousand miles away stood Shkin, the CIA's most dangerous outpost in Afghanistan, high on a mountain ridge three miles from the frontier with Pakistan. The base had its own T-shirt: *Hell Is Only Shkin Deep.* Constant attacks from both sides of the border had killed two CIA officers and three special-forces soldiers over the years. Mick Mulroy, the CIA commander at the base, had been up all night listening on a secure link with Kabul as the Abbottabad attack unfolded. And then, as Americans celebrated outside the White House, the first of a barrage of hundreds of rockets from Pakistan began raining down on his position. Bin Laden's life was over, but his war was not.

Chapter Eighteen

THE RIGHT SIDE OF HISTORY

The trove of intelligence seized by the SEAL team in Abbottabad revealed that the CIA had been wrong about bin Laden, in one regard. It thought he had become an isolated figurehead, no longer in day-to-day command of al Qaeda. But as the analysts combed through the windfall, they saw that he had been planning new attacks, appointing new commanders, conceiving new strategies. And in the last months of his life, as the CIA plotted to kill him, he had been watching the unfolding events of the Arab Spring with undisguised pleasure.

One of al Qaeda's enduring goals had been the overthrow of secular Arab leaders. That description fit the three most powerful men threatened by the popular uprisings that had started in Tunisia and spread to ten nations. Muhammar Qaddafi had misruled Libya since 1969. Bashar al-Assad and his father before him had been the dictators of Syria since 1971. Hosni Mubarak and his generals had run Egypt since 1981. *The people want to bring down the regime* was the cry of the oppressed in their capitals. As the demonstrators took to the streets demanding freedom, they had no weapons but their voices, and no one leading the charge. "This chaos and the absence of leadership in the revolutions is the best environment to spread al-Qaeda's thoughts and ideas," bin Laden said in a journal he had dictated to his daughter. To the horror of the Obama administration, this proved to be true.

"We missed the boat on the Arab Spring," Panetta said. "We were unable to anticipate it. We didn't see the impact that social media had, its ability to unify the protests, and we didn't see that young people with no hope for the future had been mobilized by social media. And we dropped the ball later on, when there was a chance for stability."

The CIA had not sensed the tremors of the uprisings and the power of their first reverberations, nor foreseen that street protests could shake the foundations of authoritarian governments across the Middle East and North Africa. Its officers and analysts relied on the CIA's liaisons with the strongmen and spymasters of the Arab world to tell them what was happening out on the street. These leaders, the CIA's most trusted sources of intelligence, were aging men with clouded vision.

In Egypt, Omar Suleiman, Mubarak's intelligence director and right-hand man, had been the most valued interlocutor for the CIA and the State Department for twenty years. Every CIA director since Bob Gates had taken his counsel on counterterrorism; Mike Hayden called him "the most knowledgeable go-between we had" on Israel's battles with the Palestinians. The CIA's liaison with him was the most successful element of Washington's diplomatic relationship with Cairo, the American ambassador had reported in 2006. But now Suleiman was old and ill, increasingly isolated, and unaware of the tidal wave about to engulf Mubarak. The CIA's vision was further impaired by its failure to see through the eyes of millions of young people in the Arab street. The CIA did not understand that the demonstrations flowed from the interconnected ideas and hopes of protestors connected, inspired, and mobilized by messaging one another on Facebook and Twitter. It was blind to what those people were thinking and saying. It did not truly value open-source information until years later. If it wasn't secret, it wasn't intelligence, and if it wasn't intelligence, it wasn't important.

"Shoot first and talk later"

In late January 2011, huge crowds of demonstrators began gathering at Tahrir Square in downtown Cairo, calling for Mubarak to step down. The

United States had supported him for three decades, sending his army close to $50 billion ever since Israel and Egypt had signed the Camp David accords in 1978. American leaders had always regarded him as they had once seen the Shah of Iran: an island of stability in the Middle East. Now even John Brennan was among the national-security aides urging Obama to stand with the people against Mubarak. Bob Gates was appalled at the thought. He had been a CIA staffer at the National Security Council in 1979 when student revolutionaries overthrew the shah of Iran, whom the CIA had installed in a coup a quarter century before. Islamic zealots had quickly seized political power in Tehran and still held it. Now, as Gates saw it, the idealists in the White House were siding with the protestors in the name of regime change—and in effect, without realizing it, aiding the forces of jihad.

As the protests grew, Obama weighed whether to tell Mubarak to step down, knowing that his handpicked successor was Suleiman, who had imprisoned and tortured his political enemies in the past, and who was angling for political power. The president chose Morell as his interlocutor with Suleiman, a clear sign of the suasion the CIA was thought to have in Egypt. Morell drafted a message with the understanding that Mubarak would read it in a televised address. Its gist was: *I have heard the voice of the people. I am giving up my power. A representative council will run the country and conduct elections to choose a new leader.* Mubarak went on the air and said nothing of the sort. "I felt horrible," Morell said, "mostly for Egypt but also because my personal diplomacy had failed so miserably."

On February 1, hours after Mubarak's speech, Obama convened the National Security Council. Biden and Clinton cautioned him against calling for Mubarak to resign. Gates was more forceful. Humiliating Mubarak, he warned, would send a message to every other ruler in the region to "shoot first and talk later." (In fact, Mubarak's forces began killing demonstrators in Tahrir Square the following day. He would be tried for murder, convicted, retried, and acquitted.) And what if he did leave? Gates asked. What then? A military dictatorship?

Obama overruled his elders and took heed of his younger aides, who had warned against his being on the wrong side of history. What side was that? Gates fumed. The history of revolutions began with hope and ended in bloodshed. And how could you know where the right side of history lay when you didn't know what was happening in the present day? Bad intelligence, like good intentions, could pave a road to hell.

Obama called Mubarak, urged him to step down, and told the world what he had done. The army took over, dissolved the parliament, and suspended the constitution. Elections were held, Islamists won, and then the minister of defense took power in a coup d'etat.

"The Somalia of the Mediterranean"

On February 15, four days after Mubarak resigned, the Arab Spring reached the shores of Tripoli.

After Qaddafi's thugs shot and killed protestors calling for human rights, a separate armed resistance movement began to grow in Benghazi, four hundred miles to the east. The longtime Libyan intelligence chief Musa Kusa had seen the chaos and destruction coming. He had worked closely with the CIA for twelve years, mounting operations against Libyan fighters returning from Afghanistan and Iraq who aimed to overthrow Qaddafi. Kusa had made Libya "a strong partner in the war against terrorism," and his cooperation was "a key pillar of the U.S.-Libya bilateral relationship," Ambassador Chris Stevens had reported in 2008. He had packed his bags in March and fled the country. The CIA had lost its chief liaison in Libya and an alliance against al Qaeda as a consequence of the uprising.

The regime continued killing its citizens, and Obama stated flatly that Qaddafi had to step down. His United Nations ambassador, Susan Rice, won a resolution authorizing the Security Council to use force to stop an "imminent massacre" in Libya. Obama was dead set against putting American boots on the ground in Libya. But he was all for American sneakers. In March, he signed a finding that sent CIA case officers and paramilitaries into Libya to aid the Benghazi rebels and guide British air strikes against Qaddafi's tanks, artillery, and antiaircraft weapons. Months later, they located his caches of chemical weapons, made a beeline for the bunkers, secured them, cocooned the missiles and warheads, and helped smuggle them out of the country to be destroyed. By then, Qaddafi had fled into hiding, where a mob of rebels would track him down, sodomize him with a bayonet, and kill him.

Bin Laden had predicted that he could open up a beachhead in Libya if and when Qaddafi fell from power, and that al Qaeda would turn the nation to "the Somalia of the Mediterranean." From there, his forces could spread jihad throughout North Africa and across the sea. He was once again prescient. Libya's once-fearsome security and intelligence forces collapsed under attacks by militias, whose ranks included radical Islamists aligned with al Qaeda, and the defeat of the Libyan military opened its weapons stockpiles, putting a huge amount of firepower in the hands of jihadists in a three-thousand-mile swath from Somalia to Mali.

"Assad is no Qaddafi"

The Arab Spring came to Assad's police state on March 6. Fifteen Syrian teenagers from well-do-to families in the southern city of Daara were arrested and tortured for writing antigovernment graffiti on a public wall. Peaceful protests calling for their freedom escalated in Damascus and Aleppo. Syrian security forces shot and killed four protestors outside a Daara mosque after Friday prayers on March 18. By the following Friday, the movement against the regime was nationwide. The dictator began to order the arrests of thousands in April 2011.

The kings of Saudi Arabia and Jordan told the State Department's Bill Burns that Assad was finished and, as Burns noted, "the U.S. intelligence community didn't push back against that assessment." The CIA had an accomplished station chief in Damascus, Mark Pascale, who would go on to serve as chief in Moscow and Beijing. The State Department had a courageous ambassador to Syria, Robert Ford. Neither had the power to predict the future. "Assad is no Qaddafi," Ambassador Ford reported in a White House meeting at the end of March. "There is little likelihood of mass atrocities. The Syrian regime will answer challenges aggressively but will try to minimize the use of lethal force." As he came to realize, he could not have been more wrong. "No one understood how far the Syrian government was willing to go to maintain its control in Damascus," he later reflected. Assad's crackdown soon became a regional war that would kill at least three hundred thousand Syrians, send thirteen million into exile, and breed the most violent and virulent brand of Islamic jihad the world had ever seen. He remained in power for thirteen more years, thanks in part to the Russian military and Iranian intelligence.

The CIA's analysts had told Obama that the Arab Spring would hurt al Qaeda by showing people that political change was possible without violence and death. In this it was again less perceptive than bin Laden. Mike Morell soon concluded that by destabilizing dictatorships and disrupting the CIA's longstanding liaisons with their intelligence chiefs, the Arab Spring had given al Qaeda and its followers the chance to build safe havens and gather their forces.

Obama had broken the tradition of unswerving support for pro-American autocrats in the Middle East by telling Mubarak that his time was up. The tradition was soon reestablished. When the Egyptian army seized power two years later, Morell—by then on his second stint as the acting CIA director—breathed a sigh of relief. "This is a good thing," he said. He was keeping to the customs of American foreign policy in the Middle East.

"He'd attained this kind of godlike charisma"

A politically charged changing of the guard now took place at the CIA. Gates wanted out as secretary of defense, and he thought Panetta should replace him at the Pentagon. Biden had tried to seal that deal during the final days of the planning of the attack on Abbottabad. Panetta had worked for presidents going back to Nixon, he understood the political rituals of succession, and he knew it wasn't a real offer unless it came from Obama.

"Who do you have in mind for CIA?" he asked.

We're looking at David Petraeus, Biden said.

"You sure?" Panetta said.

There were several ways of looking at Petraeus, the soldier-scholar with a PhD from Princeton who had returned to battle as commander of the war in Afghanistan on July 4, 2010. As Obama surged thirty thousand more troops into the fight, Petraeus had ramped up the bombings, special-operations attacks, and targeted killings against Taliban leaders, and he had told Congress that he had broken the enemy's momentum. He was held in such high esteem that few doubted his word, which proved false. Petraeus was the nation's most popular and politically adept general. Senator McCain had called him one of the greatest military leaders in American history. He had assiduously cultivated the war correspondents who covered him, and they had sung his praises in bestselling books. "Mr. Obama is retaining a celebrated soldier with extensive knowledge of intelligence gathering in both Afghanistan and Iraq. His reputation was so formidable, officials said, that it was difficult to rotate him to another military post," the *New York Times* reported when the president nominated Petraeus as CIA director on April 28, three days before the bin Laden raid.

Some of this acclaim had gone to his head. There were few greater romances in American public life than the love affair between David Petraeus and David Petraeus. His ego was reflected on the walls of his headquarters office, where scores of pictures of himself in the theaters of war hung like vanity mirrors. Some officers who served beneath him called him King David, though not to his face. Some of his ardent admirers in the Republican Party thought he might follow in the tradition of Ulysses S. Grant and Dwight D. Eisenhower, who rose from battle to become commanders in chief. The idea that the general could run for the White House in 2012 dismayed Obama's political advisers. Panetta surmised that they wanted Petraeus at the CIA "to distract him, at least for a while, from the presidential ambitions he was believed to harbor."

Petraeus had been the four-star general running Central Command in Florida before going to Afghanistan. The CENTCOM post had exquisite perquisites, including an immense retinue of subservient aides-de-camp, valets, chefs, bag carriers, and a twenty-eight-motorcycle escort when he went out to dinner. With all that came a sense of entitlement and the headiness of having great power. "He'd attained this kind of godlike charisma," Panetta said. "But everybody also knew what the hell he was like." Gates offered him some salient advice: when you pull up to CIA headquarters on your first day, get out of the car alone and check your generalship at the door.

"Years of vengeance"

Petraeus wasn't sworn in until September 2011, so Morell ran the CIA as it tried to contain the resurgence of al Qaeda and foresee what would happen when American forces left Iraq.

The December deadline had been set three years earlier by Bush and the fractured government in Baghdad. As it approached, "we disengaged not only militarily," said Ambassador Ryan Crocker, "we disengaged politically. The war was over. We were out. Let the chips fall where they may. Well, I don't think we thought through exactly how many chips were going to fall and what the consequences of that would be." After Bush's father had walked away from Afghanistan in 1989, seven years of fighting among the CIA-backed warlords who had defeated the Soviets led to the rise of the Taliban and al Qaeda. It happened again, but this time in months, not years. The 2011 American withdrawal led directly to the emergence of ISIS, the Islamic State of Iraq and Syria—another unintended consequence of Bush's war.

The troop surges Petraeus had sought and won in Iraq and Afghanistan had always been a gamble. They didn't pay off precisely as he had hoped. On June 22, after Petraeus returned to Kabul to close out his command, President Obama announced that he was keeping a pledge to bring ten thousand troops home from Afghanistan for Christmas, and twenty-three thousand more by the following summer. Petraeus protested. "That invalidates my campaign plan, Mr. President," he said. This was arrogance, and his impulse to make policy above his pay grade would not serve him well at the CIA.

Despite the empty promises of the three-stars and two-stars who swore that victory was at hand, the Afghan war went on into its second decade. President Hamid Karzai, empowered by the CIA, supported by hundreds of billions of Pentagon dollars, isolated from reality, and increasingly erratic, now professed to oppose the Americans. The feeling was mutual. The CIA's operators and analysts knew that Karzai, his governors, and his ministers were either corrupt or incompetent or both. But they also knew he had a point when he criticized the occupation. The United States was not winning hearts and minds in Afghanistan. The American military training of Afghan soldiers and national police was a multibillion-dollar fiasco. American troops kept killing innocent civilians with mistaken attacks or, in one case, an unprovoked mass-shooting massacre. They defiled the Koran in public, burning it, pissing on it. Afghans whose loyalties had not been bought had begun to despise the Americans. The Taliban knew this. They lived among the people. They knew the Afghans had repelled every foreign invader over the course of their six-thousand-year history. They knew one day the United States would get tired and leave. *The Americans have the watches*, the Taliban's more worldly leaders always said, *but we have the time.*

The CIA's station chiefs, base chiefs, operations officers, and paramilitaries fought on. "We were there to kill Taliban and al Qaeda, period," said Marc Polymeropoulos. In July, he took over the Shkin base, at the tip of the spear aimed at the tribal lands of Pakistan. "Send me to the worst place, the hardest place, the toughest place on the whole planet," he had told his superiors after recovering from the shock of the fatal disaster in Khost. The remorse and guilt he felt drove him to Shkin, to avenge those seven deaths and "to turn that place into a killing machine." He and the fifteen men with him were under constant attack. Six miles eastward, the Pakistani military supported Al Qaeda and Taliban fighters who shelled the base with 107-millimeter rockets. Polymeropoulos told his highest superiors at headquarters that they needed to strike back:

"We're in armed combat with the Pak military every day, not just with al Qaeda," he told them.

It's complicated, came the reply.

"Not for me," he said. He won the argument. American forces returned fire against the Pakistani positions. In the course of a year, "we did some huge damage to al Qaeda and senior Taliban members, taking them off the battlefield," he said. "Which was good."

Eight years earlier, two CIA officers, William Carlson and Christopher Mueller, both special-forces veterans, had been killed in a six-hour firefight outside the wire at Shkin. "We tracked down the Taliban members responsible, recruited sources, and took them out," Polymeropoulos said. "And that night, sitting around the campfire, we called one of the deceased officer's widows in Fort Bragg and told her we had avenged her husband's death." Word spread quickly among CIA officers around the world. Polymeropoulos came back from twelve months in Afghanistan with a battlefield promotion. He became a senior deputy at the counterterrorism center, overseeing lethal operations in the Middle East, from 2012 to 2014.

"These were my years of vengeance. Of justice," he said. "Zero moral qualms."

Chapter Nineteen

"SOMEONE IS ALWAYS WATCHING"

David Petraeus had gotten off to a good start at the CIA, or so he thought. "This is the best job I've ever had," he told Morell in November 2011. "The people here are the best I've ever worked with." He believed he bonded with the barons of covert action and counterterrorism, some of whom he knew from his years in Afghanistan and Iraq, and almost all of whom were veterans of the Marines or a SEAL team. He decided that the warfighters were the people who made the CIA click.

But the CIA was not CENTCOM. "It's not at all like a military organization, where the commander has a huge staff right underneath him," Petraeus said. "At the very top, there's actually very little capability directly under the director, as there is in a military command." He wanted a big staff, in part, because he wanted to make big decisions and do big things. But there were always more tasks than people to do them, as Petraeus saw it, and there was never enough money. When he first saw the CIA's annual budget, which had just hit an all-time high of close to $15 billion, he was taken aback. That's it? he said. That's all? The Pentagon spent almost that much every week.

He said he loved the CIA, but the love was unrequited. "He did not connect with most of the people," Morell said. "Part of it was that he created the impression through the tone of his voice and his body language that he did not want people to disagree with him.... And part of it was that his expectations of what a staff would do for him—borne of being a four-star general—were inconsistent with the Agency culture." A grinding tension grew as Petraeus repeatedly ordered the creation of what he called "a strategic campaign plan" to reshape the CIA for the future. He wanted big questions answered: "What are the enduring missions? What are the emerging missions? And then how do we need to adjust the resources devoted to each mission?" He found the CIA did not have the time or capacity for that kind of big-picture thinking.

The Army in which Petraeus had served for thirty-seven years was a huge, top-heavy hierarchy. The CIA was a flat and nimble organization by comparison; the chief of the clandestine service oversaw more than two thousand people but the chain of command was two deep. Petraeus gave a mission to the clandestine service, they devised a plan, he approved it, they set out to execute it, and then it was on to the next crisis. "Which is fine," he said, "except that it means that you don't have any real strategic planning capacity at the top." His new campaign plan never took shape. But it didn't take a PhD to see that some enduring missions had eroded and other emerging missions were urgent. The CIA under Petraeus looked much more like a paramilitary organization than a spy service. Ever since 9/11, thousands of the most talented and experienced officers and analysts, and thousands more newly minted ones, had thrown themselves into the war on terror. The CIA's traditions of espionage and counterintelligence had dwindled for a decade while its old enemies were gathering force.

At the start of the twenty-first century, it had seemed that the United States would shape the world. China's leaders would strike alliances with corporate America as it joined the World Trade Organization. Putin would partner with NATO even as President Bush promised to extend the American-led military alliance "eastward and southward, northward and onward" along Russia's western frontier. American power had grown in a rising wave since the end of the cold war as it projected its strengths: democracy, capitalism, military dominance. Now the wave had crested and broken. The long wars had slowly sapped the nation's strength, its wealth, and its moral authority. Its days as the world's sole superpower were over now. Russia and China were rising up against the United States.

"I think Putin is not a democrat anymore"

Bush had said he had looked into Putin's eyes and seen his soul, so he didn't need intelligence assessments on his intentions. Seeing him as an ally in counterterrorism, he ensured that spying on the Kremlin would not be among the CIA's highest priorities. But he had come to a striking realization after five and a half years in office: he had misplaced his faith and trust. "I think Putin is not a democrat anymore," he had said in July 2006. "He's a tsar. I think we've lost him." Since then, it had become increasingly clear that Putin was going to threaten America's global authority as he sought to recapture the lost glory of the imperial Russian empire. Wherever Bush had gotten the idea that he once had been a democrat—or ours to lose—it wasn't from CIA headquarters.

Some of the CIA's best insights into Putin's thinking had come from its future director, Bill Burns, the American ambassador to Moscow from 2005 to 2008. In those years, Putin accused the United States of trying to use its military might to create a world in which there was "one master, one sovereign," and he began pushing back against its global influence. He believed the CIA was a hidden force behind the expansion of NATO, which placed its frontline forces on his borders, and he was certain that its spies had fueled the prodemocracy forces in former Soviet states like Ukraine.

Putin employed his own spy services as blunt instruments of sabotage and subversion. He had used them to devastating effect in 2007, launching a crippling cyberattack on Estonia as it threw off the last vestiges of its years as a Soviet vassal, and again as weapons of cyber and information warfare in 2008, during a hydra-headed military invasion of Georgia. He had started murdering his opponents, like Alexsandr Litvinenko, a Russian security officer who was poisoned after defecting to England, and Anna Politkovskaya, a prominent journalist shot to death in the stairwell of her Moscow apartment building on Putin's fifty-fourth birthday. Burns had attended her funeral. His reporting during his four years in Moscow had depicted an increasingly hostile Russian leader projecting his power through overt acts and covert action.

Burns, now the deputy secretary of state, found Putin in a foul mood when he traveled to Russia in March 2012, and particularly furious at Burns's boss. Secretary of State Clinton had sharply criticized his rigging of parliamentary elections in December, saying "Russian voters deserve a full investigation of electoral fraud and manipulation." Thousands of demonstrators had taken to the streets chanting "Putin is a thief!" and "Russia without Putin!"

The uprisings of the Arab Spring haunted Putin, who had watched and rewatched the cell phone videos of Qaddafi's death at the hands of a mob and the point of a bayonet. The Russian leader surmised that Obama was behind it all. He claimed publicly, repeatedly, that Clinton was working in secret to subvert him. Both Burns and the CIA station in Moscow had warned that trouble lay ahead for the United States after Putin's imminent and inevitable reelection. He would seek revenge against America.

"We were under a constant intelligence attack"

In February 2012, Xi Jinping, soon to be the president of China, toured the United States and dined with America's leaders in Washington. Obama and Biden found him hard to read. Reformer? Hardliner? Potential friend or implacable foe? The CIA's assessments of his political thinking and his potential strengths were unusually vague. The reason its vision was cloudy soon would be revealed with a terrible clarity.

The CIA station in Beijing had many missions—developing a detailed picture of the intentions of Chinese leaders, recruiting agents within the Communist Party and the People's Liberation Army, and spying on North Korea; in that last task it received an occasional assist from its Chinese counterpart, the Ministry of State Security. The MSS had been created in 1983, and it had first focused on rooting out internal enemies within China. It didn't become a global spy agency until 1998. But since then, it had expanded exponentially and now employed at least a quarter of a million people, making it twelve times the size of the CIA. Its complex of four big offices on the northwest side of Beijing included a safe house where the CIA station chief could meet its senior officers every few months to discuss subjects of mutual interest, like the North Korean nuclear-weapons program.

The MSS had eighteen bureaus, and the CIA had no good idea what half of them did. It knew that the first bureau trained thousands of spies to work under nonofficial cover in the United States, typically in the guise of businessmen or graduate students. They served two causes: traditional espionage and transnational repression, the targeting of dissidents and critics of the state among the Chinese diaspora. The eleventh bureau ran highly successful political influence operations, convincing Washington think tanks, prominent academics, and members of Congress that China was moving toward democracy, or something like it, and bore no ill will toward America. The thirteenth bureau was a science and technology laboratory developing ways to collect intelligence through the internet, smartphones, and social media. Chinese spies had run email spearphishing attacks, data-mined Facebook and Twitter, hacked the Obama and McCain campaigns in 2008, and incessantly attacked the CIA's servers. These three bureaus were part of the immense and intensifying effort by the MSS and the intelligence divisions of the People's Liberation Army to penetrate the American military-industrial complex, the American intelligence establishment, and the American government.

On his final trip to China as secretary of defense, Bob Gates had received a stinging slap in the face. Shortly after he landed, the People's Liberation Army rolled out its new stealth fighter—a knock-off of the Air Force F-35, which was being developed under lock and key at a cost of $406.5 billion. Chinese spies and hackers had stolen gigabytes of data on its design and technologies from the giant military contractor Lockheed Martin. China's brazen theft of American industrial knowledge, intellectual property, and secret intelligence during the twenty-first century became the biggest transfer of wealth the world had ever seen.

The eighteenth bureau of the MSS aggressively spied on more than twenty thousand Americans in China. Its work was a small facet of the world's most powerful surveillance state. The Chinese government was in the fifth year of a long-running project to install hundreds of millions of closed-circuit television cameras to monitor citizens and foreigners alike, using big-data computing and cell phone tracking to build digital dossiers. The eighteenth bureau used CCTVs and facial-recognition technology to surveil the intelligence officers and diplomats working in the American embassy and its consulates. The Americans already knew that their phones were tapped and their homes were bugged. Now they were being followed by the all-seeing eyes of Chinese intelligence everywhere they went.

"We were under a constant intelligence attack," said Robert S. Wang, the deputy chief of mission at the U.S. embassy in Beijing from 2011 to 2013. "They were tracking everyone who went in and out of the embassy. Everyone was a target."

Despite this incessant surveillance, the CIA had achieved a remarkable and unprecedented penetration of China's government during the past decade. Its officers had managed to recruit and run close to thirty well-placed Chinese agents over the course of seven years, beginning in 2003. They were part of the middle and upper levels of the government, including the Chinese Communist Party, the People's Liberation Army, and the MSS itself. These recruitments were a remarkable accomplishment growing out of a deep understanding of the political culture of China. The CIA saw that the corruption of the Communist Party was the flaw in China's armor. People who wanted to rise quickly in the ranks of the Chinese government had to pay huge bribes—"promotion fees"—to their superiors. The CIA had that kind of money readily at hand. After meeting and cultivating its recruits, CIA officers had financed their ascent through the ranks, giving them millions of dollars to help them claw their way up the greasy pole of Chinese politics. The Beijing station bought access to the thinking of the Chinese government. Recruiting and paying those agents was an exquisitely delicate job, and yet it proved the easier part. Communicating with them securely and protecting them from detection was far harder. Case officers know that their agents' lives are in the CIA's hands. The agents knew that too.

"Nothing about espionage is straightforward"

They were captured, imprisoned, tortured, and executed, one by one by one, in a series of arrests beginning at the end of 2010 and lasting for two excruciating years. The creation of the Chinese spy network was one of the highest achievements in the history of the clandestine service, its destruction an unsurpassed debacle, a disaster the CIA still struggles to understand.

"Nothing about espionage is straightforward," said Paula Doyle. She became the deputy national counterintelligence executive* in 2012, nine years after she celebrated the triumphant takedown of A. Q. Khan, following three tours as a station chief in Europe, the Middle East, and Asia. "It was really hard to describe a direct line"—a clear chain of facts explaining what had happened in China. But over time, Doyle and the CIA came to see that the deaths were part of a larger pattern.

The story began not in Beijing, but in Tehran. A source inside Iran's Ministry of Intelligence and Security had warned the CIA that some of its agents inside the Islamic republic's nuclear-weapons program had been compromised. But how? It wasn't clear. Then the Iranians and their Lebanese partner, Hezbollah, announced that they had arrested upward of forty recruited CIA agents and unmasked forty-two more working overseas during the summer of 2011. And then the deaths of the Chinese agents came in an accelerating cascade.

"That was a huge issue. And we were very heavily focused on it," Petraeus said. "A very, very substantial effort went on to uncover what was happening." The CIA knew that "what the Chinese do really, really well, is vacuum up data, anywhere, doesn't matter what it is," he said. "They're very good at using it to pull a digital needle out of a digital haystack by

---

* In that post, Doyle also oversaw the damage assessments of the WikiLeaks release of classified documents and Edward Snowden's disclosures and defection to Russia. She coordinated the counterintelligence work of all American military and civilian intelligence agencies.

connecting various dots. So if you have one individual exposed, then perhaps there's something that links that individual to somebody else who might be linked to another."

A joint CIA and FBI team mounted an investigation which the Bureau code-named HONEY BADGER, after a savage predatory mammal. They began with a mole hunt, the biggest and most complex search for a spy since the CIA's Aldrich Ames and the FBI's Robert Hanssen sold out the dozen most highly valued Soviet and Russian agents working for the United States in the 1980s, sending them to their deaths or to prison, and crippling American intelligence operations against the Kremlin. Those investigations had taken nine years and sixteen years, respectively, and one reason they took so long was that the CIA and the FBI had a hard time believing that one of their own could betray the United States.

The investigators interviewed nearly everyone who had worked in the Beijing station since 2001. Suspicion quickly fell on a retired case officer named Jerry Chun Shing Lee, a forty-seven-year-old Army veteran who had resigned from the CIA and settled in Hong Kong. Lee had reapplied to the agency after an April 2010 meeting with two MSS officers who gave him $100,000 and offered to set him up for life if he spied for them from inside the CIA. In August 2012, the agency lured him to Hawaii with a bogus job offer. When the FBI searched his hotel room, they found handwritten notes with the names and telephone numbers of eight agents he had once handled. They could have made an open-and-shut case—if any of those names had belonged to the betrayed Chinese. Lee eventually pleaded guilty to conspiring to commit espionage and received a nineteen-year sentence.

The investigators kept following three trails in 2012. Was there another CIA officer working for the Chinese? Were case officers careless in their clandestine meetings with their agents? Had the MSS cracked the covert communications systems—the "covcom"—through which the CIA corresponded with the network? The third path led back to Tehran. The CIA discovered that Iranian intelligence had compromised the covcom created for recruited agents. The covert channels looked like rudimentary websites about news, weather, sports, and other innocuous topics. When an agent typed a password into a search bar, the sites opened up a hidden communications link to his CIA case officer.

The forensic investigators of Citizen Lab, a Toronto-based organization working at the intersection of information technology, human rights, and global security, discovered a decade later that the covcom system was fatally flawed. They probed the coding on a single website, still extant on the Internet Archive's Wayback Machine, which had been used by an Iranian agent arrested in 2010 and jailed for nine years. They found the coding linked to a network of 885 covcom websites in twenty-nine languages, among them Chinese and Russian. Almost all had been active between 2004 and 2013. "Blocks of sequential IP addresses registered to apparently fictitious US companies were used to host some of the websites," Citizen Lab reported. "All of these flaws would have facilitated discovery by hostile parties." In other words, the CIA's global covcom were like a loosely knitted sweater. If you pulled one strand, the whole thing started to unravel.

"The covert communications system was the only thing that really mattered," Doyle said.

By the end of the summer of 2012, it had started to dawn on the investigators that the Iranians had broken the flimsy cover of the covcom and shared their discovery with the MSS. But that still didn't fully explain the disaster: the CIA's covcom in China were more sophisticated than the ones uncovered in Iran, less susceptible to failure. While the broad outlines of the case slowly became clearer, a mystery remained at its heart. "It was the covcom, plus Lee, plus an X factor," said William Evanina, the CIA's chief of counterespionage in 2013 and 2014 and the national counterintelligence executive for seven years thereafter. "The story has not been told up to this day."

When Xi Jinping took power in China in the fall of 2012, he immediately began a campaign that led to the arrests of senior party members and the severe discipline of tens of thousands of high-ranking officials for taking payoffs. Xi had learned that the corruption of the party, where bribery was the means of ascent, had been the key to the CIA's penetration of its ranks. Politically corrupt leaders were a threat to national security, as Americans would learn for themselves four years later.

"Someone is always watching"

The downfall of David Petraeus was the most humiliating scandal of its kind since President Clinton had sex with a White House intern fifteen years before.

Two FBI agents came to see Petraeus at his seventh-floor suite on Friday, October 26, 2012. The FBI's deputy director, Sean Joyce, had told Petraeus they wanted to talk to him about a cyber-stalking case involving Paula Broadwell, who had published a highly flattering book about him in January. She had harassed a Petraeus groupie whom, Broadwell believed, was a rival for his attention. But the agents had another agenda. The FBI had searched Broadwell's computer and discovered her voluminous correspondence with Petraeus. The agents asked the CIA director if he had shared classified information with her. Petraeus flatly denied it, knowing that lying to the FBI is a felony. He was keenly aware that if the truth were known, he could be charged with a more serious crime, the unauthorized disclosure of classified information, carrying a penalty of ten years in prison. His judgment might have been clouded by the fact that the FBI men also told him they knew he had had an extramarital affair with Broadwell.

"Character is what you do when no one is watching," Petraeus had always told his soldiers. "And remember, someone is always watching."

Petraeus hoped the secret of the liaison might hold. He telephoned Joyce on a secure line and asked if there was any way to keep this delicate matter quiet. There wasn't. The next day, a third FBI agent, styling himself a whistleblower, leaked the sordid details to the House Republican majority leader, Eric Cantor, insisting that a political cover-up was afoot to ensure the imminent reelection of Barack Obama. Cantor called FBI headquarters, trying to sniff out a scandal. The call compelled Joyce and the FBI director, Robert S. Mueller III, to consider if and when and how they should inform Petraeus's immediate superior, the director of national intelligence, Gen. James R. Clapper. The agents reinterviewed Petraeus on October 31, assuring him that the FBI did not probe people's sex lives and had no interest in investigating his passionate fling with Broadwell.

She was the cheerleader he had never had in high school. She was a lot like him—West Point graduate, fitness fanatic, zero body fat, infinite ambition—though twenty years younger. She had asked him to be her mentor six years before. She was writing a PhD thesis on Petraeus, and she wanted to turn it into a bestselling book. He had invited her to Afghanistan to work together. She had come out four times. They jogged six-minute miles in the morning and spoke at length at night. In July 2011, at the end of his command, they had flown out of Kabul together on his Gulfstream jet. A few weeks later, Petraeus had given Broadwell eight black notebooks he had compiled in Afghanistan, and she had photographed about one hundred pages from them.

The notebooks contained details of covert operations, the identities of CIA and special-forces officers, the deliberations of the National Security Council, and the general's discussions with the president of the United States. "They are highly classified, some of them," he told her. "I mean there's codeword stuff in there"—*codeword* signifying a classification above top secret. None of this made it into her book. But the sharing of these secrets evidently deepened their sense that they could share another. Their tryst had started in November 2011, two months after he took over at the CIA.

A year later, on Friday, November 2, 2012, the FBI had confronted Broadwell and learned some details about the documents Petraeus had given her. The agents' report reached FBI headquarters on Monday. On Tuesday, Election Day, Obama ran strong but Republicans kept the House. That afternoon, Mueller called Clapper, who in turn called Petraeus and advised him to resign forthwith over his illicit affair. The director still thought he might brazen it out. On Wednesday, he marked his sixtieth birthday at home, and he talked things over with his wife of thirty-seven years. He didn't show up for work on Thursday. That morning, Clapper and Joyce came to the White House with the news that Petraeus was under investigation—not for his love life, but for leaking secrets. That evening, at about nine p.m., the director called Morell to disclose the extramarital relationship.

"He walked me through the entire story of the affair," Morell recounted. "He told me, 'Michael, I am going to resign,' saying he had made a terrible mistake and his resignation was a first step toward redemption." Morell was all but speechless. "I understand" was all he said.

Part of the power of the CIA director comes from claiming the moral authority to command amoral acts. He has to ask his officers to work at the outer limits of what law and politics permit—like the drone strike that killed the American citizen Anwar al-Awlaki in Yemen shortly after Petraeus took over the CIA. In turn, his officers need to know they can trust his judgment. Now they knew they could not.

On Friday, November 9, Obama accepted the resignation of David Petraeus. The shock of the American political and military establishment was immense. Its leaders sputtered praise for Petraeus in public and privately fumed at the Bureau for airing his dirty laundry. Some were mystified that he would resign over violating his marriage vows. They only knew half of the story. On Monday, the FBI executed a search warrant at Broadwell's house and discovered the trove of intelligence Petraeus had handed over to her. He hired the highest-priced lawyer in Washington and asserted repeatedly that he had never broken the secrecy statutes that are the CIA's holy grail. After more than two years of denials, during which he landed a lucrative job in private equity, he pleaded guilty in March 2015 to a misdemeanor charge of mishandling classified materials, received two years' probation, and paid a $100,000 fine.

"The more stars you have, the higher you climb the flagpole, the more of your ass is exposed," Mark Clark, the youngest four-star Army general during World War Two, had once observed. Petraeus had failed to cover his own.

The president began the search for the fifth director of the CIA in little over eight years. He didn't need to look far. John Brennan had been at his side from the start as his counterterrorism adviser and, in effect, his national intelligence director. He eagerly accepted Obama's offer, and he determined to take his oath of office with his hand not on the Bible but on an original draft of the Constitution of the United States.

White House colleagues who knew Brennan as the drone czar were surprised to learn that he had spent most of his twenty-five years at the CIA as an analyst, and that he held decidedly mixed views about the clandestine service, covert action, and the agency's conduct in the war on terror. "The CIA as an institution, and CIA officers as individuals, had made some serious mistakes," Brennan believed. He would spend much of the next four years dealing with the consequences.

Chapter Twenty

LETHAL AND LEGAL

A decade before, when Brennan served as the CIA's deputy executive director, he had learned for the first time what his officers were doing to their prisoners of war. Reading the cables from the black site in Thailand had made him physically ill. He had grabbed an open pack of stale cigarettes he kept in his desk in case of emergency, headed downstairs, walked out of headquarters to the far edge of the parking lot, and started chain-smoking. *My God, what are we doing?* he had thought. He had found the waterboarding and naked shackling and dog-kenneling of the prisoner Abu Zubayda "morally repugnant . . . brutal and inhuman . . . un-American."

After climbing the stairs back to the seventh floor, Brennan had gone to talk with George Tenet. But he had lacked the courage to say what he was thinking. "I pulled my punches," he recalled. "I never said to him, 'George, this program is unethical. It is wrong.'" Nor did he talk to his trusted legal counsellor. "He never expressed any concerns to me—and my office was fifteen feet away from his," said John Rizzo, who had retired as the CIA's top lawyer in October 2009. "I just never heard from him directly or ever heard that he had expressed any concerns to colleagues. I've talked to other agency veterans. And I can't find anybody who remembers that." Brennan was a devout Catholic who had dreamed in his youth of becoming the first American pope, and he came to consider his failure to speak out his life's most egregious sin of omission.

His chance to speak his mind came when the Senate intelligence committee held his confirmation hearings on February 7, 2013. Eight weeks earlier, the committee had completed the Torture Report, a painstaking account of the detention and interrogation program. Its staff had spent nearly four years combing through the CIA's files—some six million pages of operational cables, internal emails, situation reports, inspector general's investigations, oral histories, and more. Obama had made it clear from the start of his presidency that he did not want to look back in anger at Bush's war on terror. The Democrats on the Senate intelligence committee had defied his wishes. Its chair, Senator Dianne Feinstein, had convinced Leon Panetta, an old friend in the politics of Washington and California, to turn over the evidence. That decision had flabbergasted Brennan in his role as White House intelligence consigliere. "In my twenty-five years at the CIA, I had never heard of such a thing being contemplated, much less done," Brennan said. "And I certainly had no premonition that this arrangement would become a source of tremendous conflict between Democrats on the committee and a future CIA director, namely me."

"There is no middle ground"

The trouble had started with Jose Rodriguez and his defiant decision to destroy the videotapes of the torture of Abu Zubayda. When the *New York Times* was about to publish the story in December 2007, Rizzo had asked Porter Goss if he, as director, had informed the congressional intelligence committees about the destruction. Goss had known very well he had the legal duty to do so, having been the House intelligence chairman for seven years. He had kept silent. He hadn't had the nerve. A lack of candor. "It was the ultimate nightmare scenario," Rizzo recounted. "The *New York Times* was about to break a huge, holy-shit sensational story about the CIA, and our congressional overseers would be finding out about it for the first time. For three decades, I had been an eyewitness to the Agency's complex relationship with Congress, and I immediately knew what the reaction would be. Congress would go berserk."

After the initial outcry, the Senate intelligence committee's staff had spent a year looking into the tale of the tapes, and it had determined by reading the CIA inspector general's reports that the abuses at the black sites had been far more brutal than the CIA's leaders had admitted in their classified briefings. In March 2009, the committee had voted 14–1 to conduct a full-scale investigation of the detention and interrogation program. Its completed report, which ran to more than 6,700 pages, with some 38,000 footnotes, has never seen the light of day, and likely never will. But Brennan had read the draft of its book-length summary before his confirmation hearings. He found it "rather damning," he had testified. "There clearly were a number of things—many things—that I read in that report that were very concerning and disturbing to me." Chief among them were the conclusions that the interrogations had been ineffective in gathering intelligence on al Qaeda, that the CIA had misled not only the committee but the White House and the Justice Department about the program, and that its prisoners had been abused in ways that no one had imagined. CIA officers and contractors had exceeded the expansive legal limits of the Bush White House torture memos by threatening prisoners with death, depriving them of sleep for up to 180 hours, shoving hoses into their rectums to force-feed them, and, as had happened twice, killing them.*

"I don't know what the facts are, or the truth is," Brennan told the senators. "I really need to look at that carefully and see what CIA's response is."

The reputation of the CIA now depended how it handled the report. If and when its findings became public, it threatened to inflict a public relations disaster on an intelligence service that had suffered too many. When newspaper reporters first began to expose the black sites in 2005, Phil Mudd, then the deputy counterterrorism director, had told a colleague that the CIA had to push back, and hard, by telling its version of the interrogation program to the press and the American people: "We either get

---

* The rectal force-feedings had little to do with nutrition. They were a form of sadism, and they were inflicted to gain "total control over the detainee," as an interrogator reported to CIA headquarters.

out and sell, or we get hammered, which has implications beyond the media," he had argued. "Congress reads it, cuts our authorities, messes up our budget. . . . We either put out our story or we get eaten. There is no middle ground." In one among several instances of selective declassification, a CIA spokesman spun the story of the interrogation of Abu Zubayda to the author Ronald Kessler, chief Washington correspondent of the right-wing cable outlet Newsmax, in order to convince him of "the enormously valuable intelligence . . . gleaned from CIA's intelligence program."

Immediately after the assault on Abbottabad and the killing of bin Laden, with the agency's standing with the American people at an all-time high, the CIA's Office of Public Affairs had sold a far more compelling tale about the efficacy of torture to Hollywood. The result was *Zero Dark Thirty*, a thriller which had premiered three days before the report was completed in December 2012. The CIA's public affairs staff had wooed and won the movie's screenwriter, granting him extraordinary access to CIA officers and headquarters. In turn, he had wined and dined Alfreda Bikowsky, the al Qaeda analyst who was an enthusiastic debriefer of waterboarded prisoners, a militant proponent of the harshest techniques, and a forceful witness before the Senate intelligence committee, swearing that torture worked. The committee report said her impassioned cables from her black-site confrontations with Khalid Sheikh Mohammed, 9/11's mastermind, had created "a template on which future justifications for the CIA program and the CIA's enhanced interrogation techniques were based." Bikowsky became a model for the leading character in *Zero Dark Thirty*. The film was a huge box office hit, won a best-picture Oscar nomination, and shaped public opinion about the interrogation program's righteousness. But its message had been too much for Mike Morell, then serving his second stint as acting director, pending Brennan's confirmation. He had emailed everyone at the CIA to warn that the film created "the strong impression" that torture had blazed the trail to bin Laden's door.

"That impression is false," he wrote. "Whether enhanced interrogation techniques were the only timely and effective way to obtain information from those detainees, as the film suggests, is a matter of debate that cannot and never will be definitively resolved." This nuanced critique proved to be the most measured position the CIA would take on the question of whether torture worked.

"A blight on our nation's soul"

Brennan, sworn in as director on March 8, 2013, returned to the CIA feeling supremely self-confident, determined to "hit the ground running and even call bullshit when I saw it." But to his dismay much of the next twenty months were consumed by an escalating war with the Senate intelligence committee over the Torture Report. He later called this struggle the biggest problem he faced in his four years running the agency—a striking statement, considering the challenges of Russia and China, the war in Afghanistan, the rise of ISIS, and his excruciating effort to reshape the CIA in the face of bitter resistance from within.

The twenty-first-century CIA had been consumed by counterterrorism and the demand for tactical intelligence. It needed to be able to look over the horizon at the long-term challenges of great-power conflicts and tectonic shifts in geopolitics. "With billions of dollars invested in CIA over the past decade, policymaker expectations of CIA's ability to anticipate major geopolitical events should be high," he had observed during his confirmation hearings. Its inability to understand the Arab Spring and its aftermath, he had admitted, showed "that CIA needs to improve its capabilities and its performance still further."

When Brennan arrived on the seventh floor, Morell was already preparing the preliminary response to the Torture Report's twenty conclusions, led by senior analysts who had not participated in the program, and Brennan sent it to the Senate intelligence committee over his signature. Faced with an overpowering indictment of its leaders, their counterterrorism chiefs, and their officers, the CIA admitted that it had been unprepared to run the black sites, unable to manage them at the outset, unwilling to analyze the effectiveness of its interrogation methods, unable to justify imprisoning a fifth of its 119 detainees, and unenthusiastic about holding its officers and contractors accountable for their abuses. It maintained that most of these failings had been recognized, and many corrected, after John Helgerson's inspector general reports in 2003 and 2004. Morell underscored what he had told the workforce: the CIA took no position on whether the intelligence wrung from detainees by beatings, starvation, sleeplessness, and waterboarding could have been obtained through other means. The answer was and forevermore would be unknowable, he wrote.

But the CIA fought back against the Torture Report's central conclusions with all the strength it could muster. It insisted that had not had willfully withheld information about the program from the White House. It denied that it had deliberately misrepresented to the State Department, the FBI, the Congress, the media, and the American people what went on at the black sites. It rejected the report's charge that the black sites did not produce unique intelligence that saved lives, foiled plots, and imprisoned jihadists. The CIA's most prominent veterans of the war on terror reacted to that accusation with seething fury.

Among them was Gina Haspel, who had become acting chief of the clandestine service one week before Brennan's arrival at headquarters, following the retirement of John Bennett. Brennan was painfully aware of how few women had ascended to the CIA's top ranks. But he had known that Feinstein would fervently oppose her, for Haspel was forever linked to the waterboarding at the black site in Thailand.* Instead, he made her London station chief—a post traditionally awarded to aging officers on their last tour—and in her stead promoted Frank Archibald, the veteran of Pakistan and the Balkans, then serving as chief of the Latin American division. This mollified the intelligence committee, but not for long.

Feinstein wanted the Torture Report declassified in its entirety, allowing for the protection of the identities of the CIA's officers, sources, and foreign liaisons. Brennan demanded far more deletions, and Obama

---

* Brennan also considered making Mike D'Andrea chief of the clandestine service. He believed that D'Andrea was the CIA officer most responsible for the fact that America had not suffered a direct hit from al Qaeda since 9/11. He also knew that elevating him might produce an intense public outcry, which was the last thing the CIA needed at the time.

backed him. The CIA began a long battle with the Senate staff to redact the report and refute its findings. Then its officers and lawyers became alarmed when the staff director, Daniel Jones, asked them to hand over the Panetta Review—a thousand-page set of written reports prepared by CIA analysts for the former director in 2009, summarizing the documents he was sharing with the committee.

Very few people knew about the Panetta Review. Fewer knew that its gist was—in Panetta's own words—"not all that different" from the Senate report. Among its findings was that the CIA in its briefings had inflated the importance of the intelligence wrung from Khalid Sheikh Mohammed, its most highly valued prisoner, undermining its argument that 183 waterboard sessions and 180 hours shackled to the ceiling without sleep had worked wonders. Worse, as Brennan ruefully noted, some of the officers preparing the review had added their own thoughts to the summaries— "personal comments reflecting their individual outrage and disgust about what they had read." Worst of all, the CIA suspected that Jones had somehow already seen the review. It did not know that he had secretly printed out its key passages and stored the pages in the committee's safe. The review eviscerated the agency's rebuttals, Jones later said, with "a damning argument against the CIA's torture program."

Mark Kelton, now the CIA's chief of counterintelligence, decided to play hardball with Jones. He sent a squad of IT specialists to hack into the Senate staff's computers, where they found the Panetta Review, and read the emails of five staffers in their search. Brennan was shocked—"My heart skipped a few beats"—when Kelton briefed him on what he had done. The CIA's charter forbade it from spying on Americans, and the mission of the counterintelligence staff decidedly did not entail snooping on the United States Senate. Brennan wisely asked his inspector general, David Buckley, to step in. Buckley reviewed the facts and decided to make a criminal referral to the Justice Department, seeking an investigation of Kelton and the counterintelligence techs. In turn, the CIA's acting general counsel, Robert Eatinger, who had been the interrogation program's top lawyer, and whose name appeared some 1,600 times in the full Senate report, made a criminal referral against Jones for unauthorized possession of classified information. That act, Brennan said, "had the very unfortunate effect of pouring gasoline on an already raging fire."

Feinstein took to the Senate floor for a forty-five-minute speech denouncing the CIA for "illegal and unconstitutional" acts of counterespionage on Capitol Hill. Brennan, unwisely, publicly denied it. "As far as the allegations of CIA hacking into Senate computers, nothing could be further from the truth," he falsely asserted. "We wouldn't do that. I mean, that's just beyond the scope of reason in terms of what we would do." The dispute was becoming a full-blown political crisis when Vice President Biden summoned them for a come-to-Jesus meeting.

"We have to get this behind us, folks," Biden said. "I know that John will find out what his people did," he told Feinstein. "He'll tell you exactly what happened and will apologize to you if an apology is called for."* The senator, still furious, told Biden and Brennan that the interrogation program was "a blight on our nation's soul. I want to make sure it will never be repeated, under a Democratic or a Republican president."

"That's for damn sure," Biden replied.

"Is this who we are?"

"I believe we compromised our basic values by using torture to interrogate our enemies and detaining individuals in a way that ran counter to the rule of law," Obama said on May 23, 2013. In his speech at the National Defense University at Fort McNair in Washington, he made promises which, if kept, would wind down the war on terror.

---

* When Brennan saw the inspector general's conclusive report that the CIA had indeed spied on Feinstein's staff, he privately apologized to the senator and publicly issued a statement that he himself called "ambiguous and confusing," admitting next to nothing. As it developed, the CIA seemed to have misconfigured the search program for the documents, which were stored on a CIA-run network designed to be accessible to the Senate staff. It was never clear if the CIA had inadvertently shared the Panetta Review, though the CIA clearly thought the Senate staff had purloined it. Attorney General Eric Holder declined to bring any charges against CIA officers or Senate staffers. A CIA accountability board, keeping with tradition, found no reason to hold Kelton or his officers accountable.

"America is at a crossroads," he said. "We must define the nature and scope of this struggle, or else it will define us. We have to be mindful of James Madison's warning that 'No nation could preserve its freedom in the midst of continual warfare.'" He pledged to limit the drone strikes he and Brennan and D'Andrea had launched in Pakistan and Yemen and Somalia—roughly 380 to date, killing more than 2,800 people, including hundreds of civilians.

"It is a hard fact that U.S. strikes have resulted in civilian casualties, a risk that exists in every war," he said. "And for the families of those civilians, no words or legal construct can justify their loss. For me, and those in my chain of command, those deaths will haunt us as long as we live, just as we are haunted by the civilian casualties that have occurred throughout conventional fighting in Afghanistan and Iraq. The necessary secrecy often involved in such actions can end up shielding our government from public scrutiny. It can also lead a president and his team to view drone strikes as a cure-all for terrorism."

By the time he gave that speech, he was already sharply curtailing the strikes by demanding a higher standard of intelligence on their targets. The new rules authorized the targeted killing of people who posed a continuing and imminent threat to the American people, whose capture was not feasible, where the host country would not or could not stop them, and with a near certainty that no civilians would be killed or injured. A great deal of the credit for that decision went to Avril Haines, whom Brennan chose as the CIA's deputy director after Mike Morell retired in June 2013. She had been a deputy national security adviser to Obama, serving principally as Brennan's legal confidant on intelligence matters, and she was a steadfast advocate for dialing down the drone war.

"Avril and I bore the scars of a lot of the pushback that we received from counterterrorism proponents that wanted to have more latitude in carrying out strikes," Brennan said—chief among them D'Andrea, who had been running the counterterrorism center for seven years. Haines had challenged him constantly, and she often won. "More innocent civilians would have died and a far wider set of targets would have been pursued without the changes that she secured," said Samantha Power, then United

Nations ambassador. "Avril sought to put a lethal instrument of U.S. power into a legal framework . . . and to give a program shrouded in secrecy far more transparency." But as Haines herself observed, "just because something is legal doesn't make it right. . . . I think it is crucial to consistently consider the human and ethical consequences of your work. There is no question that doing so takes its toll."

Haines was an outsider—the first woman to serve as the CIA's deputy director, and the first in sixty-two years who was neither a senior military or CIA officer. She was forty-four years old, a trained theoretical physicist, a judo brown belt, an amateur pilot who once nearly crashed a light plane into the North Atlantic with the man she would marry, and the onetime owner of an independent bookstore in a bohemian Baltimore neighborhood. She had become an insider—a State Department lawyer for political and military affairs and deputy counsel to the Senate Foreign Relations Committee under Biden before joining Obama's national security team. Haines had put in a hundred hours a week at the White House; Obama publicly praised her "intelligence, work ethic, and humility." The deputy Washington director of Human Rights Watch called her the nicest person she had ever met in the government. Humility and kindness were rare qualities in the CIA's suites, perhaps because no woman ever had been second-in-command.

At the White House, and at the CIA, Haines had pushed Obama to fulfill his pledges to close Guantanamo. The biggest stumbling block was the question of how to try terrorists with evidence obtained by torture. That question could not be raised. The judges at the military tribunals and the lawyers before them were gagged by secrecy; without the findings of the Torture Report, they could not speak about what had gone on in the black sites. "History will cast a harsh judgment on this aspect of our fight against terrorism and those of us who fail to end it," Obama had said at Fort McNair. "Imagine a future—ten years from now or twenty years from now—when the United States of America is still holding people who have been charged with no crime on a piece of land that is not part of our country. . . . Is this who we are? Is that something our Founders foresaw? Is that the America we want to leave our children?"

"They claimed that all this was a rogue operation"

The Torture Report was the deepest congressional investigation of the CIA since 1975, when a committee led by Senator Frank Church had exposed the assassination plots, right-wing coups, and mind-control experiments mounted under presidents from Eisenhower to Nixon. The Church committee had interviewed scores of the CIA's top officers and captured the dreadful sense of emergency that had gripped them as they faced the Soviet threat. "We are facing an implacable enemy whose avowed objective is world domination by whatever means and at whatever cost," read a top secret 1954 report to Eisenhower on the sprawling covert operations of the CIA. "There are no rules in such a game. Hitherto acceptable norms of human conduct do not apply." The CIA, it said, might have to resort to methods "more ruthless than that employed by the enemy." The cold war leaders of the CIA were never nearly as cruel as the KGB and its Kremlin commissars. But they were cold-blooded. They believed that "the country was in desperate peril and we had to do whatever it took to save it," in the words of Hugh Cunningham, a founding member of the CIA who ran the training of its recruits under Eisenhower and returned to that post in the Nixon years.

The leaders of the twenty-first-century CIA thought Islamic terrorism was as dangerous as Soviet communism, that it posed an existential and enduring threat to America, and that they had acted with the greatest morality to destroy it by any means necessary. They believed to the marrow of their bones that their brutality had produced indispensable intelligence that had led to the deaths of terrorist leaders, deepened the CIA's theretofore sketchy understanding of al Qaeda, and foiled devastating attacks against America and its allies. "We understood what harsh and difficult interrogations would look like in later years," Tenet wrote in his rebuttal to the Torture Report, his first public statement after eight years of silence. "Those moral and ethical choices in preventing the loss of American and allied lives were enormously difficult." They were made out of "a moral obligation to protect a just society in order to save thousands of

Americans or our allies from another mass-casualty attack." Morell was more philosophical. "Is it moral to subject other human beings, no matter how evil they are, to harsh interrogation techniques, particularly when done by the country that stands for human dignity and human rights?" he asked. "What is the morality of doing so? What is the morality of believing that, if you do not use the harsh techniques, you may well be making a decision that leads to the death of Americans in a terrorist attack that you could have otherwise prevented?"

But defending torture required political language, as George Orwell defined it, "designed to make lies sound truthful and murder respectable, and to give an appearance of solidity to pure wind." The waterboard wasn't torture, for "the United States does not torture," as Bush had insisted. Rodriguez spoke for many of his fellow counterterrorism officers when he wrote: "I am convinced that when in later years President Obama and his Attorney General said that waterboarding is torture, they were referring to the waterboarding methods used by the Spanish Inquisition, or by the Japanese during World War II, or the Khmer Rouge in Cambodia"— not to the techniques of the CIA. "I cannot tell you how disgusted my former colleagues and I felt to be labeled 'torturers' by the President of the United States." To say the word was to call Bush a liar and the CIA's officers war criminals. Brennan had refused to speak it at his confirmation hearings. And yet there it was, in black and white, in footnote 727 of the Senate report, in an interview with the director of central intelligence by the inspector general on September 8, 2003: "Tenet believes that if the general public were to find out about this program, many would believe we are torturers."

The Torture Report was thus named with good reason. But its authors had made some bad judgments. They had failed to interview anyone who could convey how the sense of cataclysmic fear, created in no small part by the CIA's threat reports, had led to the cruel interrogations. Highlighting how the counterterrorism center had hyped its black-site intelligence, they downplayed the possibility that some of it was indeed precious. And they repeated a mistake made by Senator Church, who had declared that the CIA "may have been behaving like a rogue elephant on a rampage." But the CIA, with rare exceptions, was not a rogue elephant. When people were trampled, it wasn't the elephant's fault. It was the fault of the mahout—the elephant driver. And the mahout was the president of the United States. The CIA wasn't a loose cannon, but a sword and shield wielded by the commander in chief. The Torture Report argued that CIA had foisted the interrogation program on Bush with falsehoods. It failed to address the political, legal, and moral issues raised by the fact that he had embraced it.

"They claimed that all this was a rogue operation and that the White House was intentionally kept in the dark about important aspects about it," Mike Hayden said in his own rebuttal to the report. That conclusion was reached without a single conversation with anyone from the Agency involved with the program (or from the Bush White House, for that matter).* The report ignored Bush's public commentary that he was briefed on and approved techniques like waterboarding. It obscured the fact that its work was curtailed by the Obama administration's refusal to share Bush White House documents on the program, in the name of executive privilege.

The report was silent on the years of quiet acquiescence by Congress to the CIA and the White House. Tenet had secretly briefed the leaders of the Senate and the House intelligence committees six times about the interrogation techniques, though in what detail was in hot dispute. The first briefing was for Porter Goss and Nancy Pelosi, the future Speaker of the House, on September 4, 2002. Declassified CIA records show that they were told that "enhanced interrogation techniques had been employed" against Abu Zubayda. They were not told he had been waterboarded

---

* The intelligence committee staff had conducted no interviews with the roughly two hundred CIA officers who ran the interrogation program—a glaring omission. But none would voluntarily testify. Attorney General Eric Holder had opened a criminal investigation into the program in August 2009. Holder gave the case to the prosecutor John Durham, who advised the CIA's general counsel to keep CIA officers from talking to the Senate investigators. He closed his investigation without charges in August 2013. The Senate staff could have insisted on interviews after that, but they thought that time had run out.

eighty-three times. Pelosi said seven years later that she was never told about any of the techniques. Goss responded that she must have had amnesia. Hayden had briefed the full committees and the congressional leadership repeatedly after he became CIA director in May 2006. The following month, the Supreme Court had ruled the prisoners were covered by the Geneva Convention, and Justice Sandra Day O'Connor had opined that "a state of war is not a blank check for the President." Congress had given him that carte blanche. The Constitution gives war powers to Congress—including the right "to make Rules concerning Captures on Land and Water"—but the intelligence committees had lacked the will to invoke it. Their leaders could have found the courage to assert the power to shut down the black sites if they believed they were an abomination. They had left the job to Obama.

"In the immediate aftermath of 9/11 we did some things that were wrong. We did a whole lot of things that were right, but we tortured some folks," Obama said at a press conference on August 1, 2014, with the report's publication still four months away, after a year of wrangling over its declassification. "I understand why it happened. I think it's important when we look back to recall how afraid people were after the Twin Towers fell and the Pentagon had been hit and the plane in Pennsylvania had fallen, and people did not know whether more attacks were imminent, and there was enormous pressure [on the CIA] to try to deal with this. And it's important for us not to feel too sanctimonious in retrospect about the tough job that those folks had. . . . [But] when we engaged in some of these enhanced interrogation techniques, techniques that I believe and I think any fair-minded person would believe were torture, we crossed a line. And that needs to be understood and accepted."

It required an open mind and an even temper to consider that two opposing ideas might be true: that the CIA had tortured prisoners, and that it also had saved lives. Perhaps immoral means had served a moral purpose. But the argument was like a religious schism, a clash of absolutes. Either the CIA's success was measured by plots foiled and terrorists killed, or its failure to obtain unique intelligence without torture had inflicted incalculable damage to America's honor. There was no middle ground.

Chapter Twenty-One

FACE-EATING BABOONS

A series of seismic shocks shook the pillars of American intelligence throughout 2014 and 2015, and their force resounded for the following decade. The epicenters of these tremors lay in Moscow and Beijing. The damage they inflicted compelled a host of senior CIA officers to return to espionage after devoting their lives to counterterrorism. Twenty-five years after the fall of the Berlin Wall, the great-power conflicts of the cold war were returning with a vengeance.

The CIA came to see that China and Russia had very different stratagems in their intelligence wars against the United States. The Chinese wanted to import their all-pervasive surveillance systems to America and gather data on its citizens to achieve information dominance should a war break out in some distant decade. China wanted to know their enemies. The Russians simply wanted to screw them.

The CIA's new station chief in the Netherlands was among the first to grasp the growing Russian attack on the United States. The son of a decorated Green Beret, he had picked up some seventh-floor polish as an executive assistant to Avril Haines after seven hard years of counterterrorism operations in Afghanistan, Iraq, Pakistan, and Jordan. Upon arriving in the Hague in the summer of 2014, he found an extraordinary partner: Rob Bertholee, the former commander of the Royal Netherlands Army.

Bertholee led the Dutch civilian intelligence agency, the AIVD. That service was less than a tenth of the size of the CIA, but it punched far above its weight, with a particular expertise in how Russian cyberweapons were targeting the governments, military forces, and security organizations of Europe. Working with his military intelligence counterpart, Bertholee had formed a new signals-intelligence office, the Joint Sigint Cyber Unit, and the core of that fifty-member team was a group of young hackers recruited out of the nation's best technological universities. They had taken aim at the Kremlin that summer, and with good reason.

On July 17, 2014, five months after Putin's special-operations forces attacked Ukraine and seized the Crimean Peninsula without firing a shot, Russian soldiers occupying a swath of the nation's eastern frontier had destroyed a civilian airliner with a surface-to-air missile. The attack killed all 298 people aboard, and two-thirds of the dead were Dutch. The shootdown of Malaysia Airlines Flight 17 was the deadliest in the history of aviation. Putin had denied any responsibility, and the United States had no response. Its silence emboldened Putin, strengthening his sense that America was a feckless opponent in his war on truth. "We had a massive information gap," said the assistant secretary of state for Europe and Eurasia, Victoria Nuland. "We didn't have the kind of intelligence assets where we could prove he was lying" about what the Russians were doing in Ukraine. For a want of insight on Putin's thinking, Obama misread Russia's intentions and capabilities. "Russia is a regional power," he said, no longer the superpower of old nor "the number-one security threat to the United States." This calculated insult, delivered in a March 2014 speech in the Hague, was a serious misjudgment, based on bad intelligence and wishful thinking.

Putin had built a powerful arsenal for political warfare—a war of disinformation, espionage, sabotage, and subversion—and he was taking aim at America. One of his weapons was malware wielded by a group of hackers working for the Russian foreign intelligence service. Cybersecurity firms codenamed them Cozy Bear.

Spurred by the deaths of their compatriots, the Dutch intelligence service opened a new window into this netherworld with a remarkable technical penetration. They identified the malware and began hacking back to seek its source. Then they wormed their way into the computer network of a university building next to Red Square in Moscow. The network included a security camera overseeing the room where the Russian hackers gathered. The Dutch peered through its lens. With the help of facial-recognition software supplied by the CIA, they determined that the people in the room weren't students. They were intelligence officers. The Dutch had penetrated the lair of Cozy Bear. By August, they had detected the beginnings of a Russian cyberattack on the American government. As summer turned to autumn, they learned precisely what the Russians' targets were.

Bertholee took this unique intelligence to the CIA station chief. The gift came with a warning. He was taking a calculated risk in sharing it with the Americans, and if they compromised the operation, he would see to it that the station chief would be declared *persona non grata* and sent packing. This created an excruciating dilemma for the station chief. How would he share this secret with his superiors—and their counterparts outside the CIA—without someone in Washington burning the source? All spies worth their salt knew Ben Franklin's aphorism from *Poor Richard's Almanac*: three may keep a secret if two are dead.

"Hand-to-hand combat"

The CIA's man in the Hague entrusted the information to Mark Kelton, who had been his station chief in Pakistan and now headed counterintelligence operations. Kelton told James Comey, the FBI director. Comey alerted the Department of Homeland Security, which did not know how to respond, and the National Security Agency, which did. The NSA and the FBI saw that a barrage of emails, which looked like they had come from American think tanks and universities, had arrived in the inboxes of staffers at the Pentagon, the White House, and the State Department, with malware secreted in their links. Anyone who clicked a link let the Russian hackers' command-and-control system enter an American government domain. Cozy Bear started reading Obama's mail and the Joint Chiefs' agendas, harvesting thousands of email addresses for more spearphishing attacks across official Washington.

"Those attacks were against the unclassified systems, the email systems, and related systems," Brennan said. "And this was typical of what the Russians and others tried to do, which is to penetrate those unclassified networks and gain access so they can gather information, understand who is key on what issues, try to find compromising information on individuals. They tried to collect as much information as they can, and gaining the real email addresses helps, because then they can contact other people and purport to be somebody in the White House or in the State Department . . . to gather as much information as they can so that they can leverage it for intelligence activities."

The Russians achieved their deepest penetration in the State Department's computer archives.* That breach that led to a battle unlike any other in the history of warfare. Richard Ledgett, the deputy director of the National Security Agency, later said that his cybercommand had fought "hand-to-hand combat" with the hackers in November. To his surprise, Cozy Bear fought back instead of disappearing when detected. "We would take an action; they would then counter that," he said. "It was about a 24-hour period of parry/riposte, parry/riposte, measure/countermeasure. That was new. That's a new level of interaction between a cyber attacker and a defender."

The NSA discovered that Cozy Bear controlled a multitude of servers around the world. It had to play digital Whac-A-Mole with the enemy: no sooner did it remove their command-and-control channel to the malware than the Russians moved to a new channel. No one at the NSA had ever seen anything like it. "Those guys were really dug in," Kevin Mandia, a leading cybersecurity expert, told the *New York Times* reporter David Sanger. "They weren't planning on leaving. Usually, you shine a light on the malware, and the guys on the other end scatter like roaches. Not the Russians."

---

* Two years later, when the FBI finally understood the scope of the Russian attack, it saw the purpose of the State Department hack. Putin wanted to dig up dirt on someone he personally despised: Hillary Clinton, the former secretary of state and the frontrunner for the Democrats' presidential nomination in 2016.

Seven months later, Cozy Bear burrowed into the computer networks of the Democratic National Committee in Washington. After its cousin, Fancy Bear, the hacking component of the GRU, Russia's military intelligence service, joined the cyberattack, Putin would launch the most devastating covert operation against the United States since 9/11.

"As devastating a breach as any in American history"

A more devastating penetration was taking place four blocks from the State Department. Undetected, the intelligence officers of the Chinese Ministry of State Security had been raiding the files of the Office of Personnel Management, the repository of dossiers on 22 million federal employees, including 19.7 million who had applied for a security clearance, and the fingerprint files on 5.6 million of those applicants. This gold mine included nuggets of information on everyone who had worked for the CIA in the twenty-first century. The data, once sifted and assayed, gave the Chinese many ways to unmask them. "The OPM hack was as devastating a breach as any in American history," William Evanina, the CIA's chief of counterespionage before becoming the national counterintelligence director in 2014, said a decade later. "It will affect us for the next twenty years."

Gaining a government security clearance required filling out a 121-page application called Standard Form 86. The SF-86 required detailed biographical information, foreign travel records, summaries of psychological and emotional health counseling, a history of drug and alcohol use, personal financial records, and a list of computer passwords, all stored in indexed databases: "Information about everybody who has worked for, tried to work for, or works for the United States government," FBI director Comey said. "Just imagine if you were a foreign intelligence service and you had that data."

The CIA didn't have to imagine. The hack struck a devastating blow against the clandestine service. The Chinese Ministry of State Security gave the data to Alibaba, one of the most powerful artificial-intelligence and cloud-computing companies in the world, which had just launched the biggest initial public offering in history on the New York Stock Exchange, giving it a market value of $231 billion. Alibaba crunched it all in ninety days. Then the MSS integrated the intelligence on people it suspected to be CIA officers with passport records and biometric data like iris scans, stolen from immigration kiosks in the world's major airports. (During 2014, the Chinese also stole the passport and credit card data of 383 million people from the Marriott hotel chain and the personal records of 78 million Americans from the health-insurance giant Anthem.) All this data created sophisticated algorithms for Chinese counterespionage that would last until the present generation of CIA officers retired.

"There's no fixing it," Mike Hayden said. The intelligence nightmare continued for years. Emboldened by success, the Chinese spy service eventually penetrated all the major American telecommunications companies, recording the phone calls of American leaders and hacking into the database for court-authorized national-security wiretaps against Chinese targets, a counterespionage disaster without precedent.

"The ability to spy on China was neutered" by 2014, Evanina said. The CIA postponed new assignments for officers bound for China under diplomatic cover. The possibility that they might spend the rest of their careers behind a desk was high. Worse yet, when American spies flew to their posts throughout the world, they were increasingly placed under immediate and intense surveillance by Chinese officers, and on occasion physically confronted at airport baggage carousels throughout Europe, Africa, and Asia. The CIA station in Moscow concluded that the Chinese had almost certainly shared the fruits of their exploits with the Russians.

Gone were the days when a fake passport and a cover story were all a spy needed to get by. The age of ubiquitous technical surveillance had arrived. "The foundations of the business of espionage have been shattered," said Duyane Norman, a three-time station chief. Now that everyone created an indelible residue of digital dust, clandestinity was a fading memory. "Folks are going to have to live their cover in a whole different way," said Dawn Meyerriecks, who became the CIA's deputy director for science and technology. "It's extremely difficult now to run cover operations when so much is known and can be known about almost everybody," said Joel Brenner, the first national counterintelligence executive under Obama. "Now you show up at the border of Russia, they've got your high school yearbook out there where you wrote about your lifelong ambitions to work for the CIA."

Andrew Hallman, the first chief of the CIA's newly created Directorate for Digital Innovation, said upon taking office in 2015: "The days of attending a cocktail party and writing up your notes are over.... We have to come up with new ways to operate." His successor, Jennifer Ewbank, said that Americans had to grasp the fact that "digital autocracies" like China and Russia were "at the controls of highly developed, well-resourced cyber programs pointed like daggers at U.S. interests at home and abroad." This public understanding came only after the daggers had pierced the CIA and the government of the United States.

"Don't take me away from the mission"

As the spies tried to reimagine the art of espionage, Brennan decided it was high time to knock them off their pedestal. He began the biggest reorganization of the CIA since its creation in 1947.

But as soon as he set his plans in motion, he said, he encountered ferocious resistance: "Many CIA officers became quite vocal in their opposition to what they anticipated might be a change to the traditional headquarters array of four separate directorates"—operations, analysis, science and technology, support—and he found it difficult to sell them on his grand vision of a twenty-first-century CIA. The heavy lifting started when Brennan assigned nine officers, led by Greg Vogle, the special-activities division chief and thirty-year CIA veteran of paramilitary missions, to lay the foundation for the new architecture. He told them that the CIA was segregated, with spies, analysts, and techies walled off in the silos of the directorates, and he gave them three months to integrate them. Break down the walls, he said, and build up unified commands based on missions. As Vogle's team did the groundwork, Brennan awarded a no-bid contract of more than $10 million to the management consultants McKinsey & Company to sketch a blueprint.* McKinsey's mumbo-jumbo about *metrics* and *operationalizing* did not sit well with many officers. Nor did the way "they shattered longstanding structural constructs that people had invested their whole careers in," said Larry Pfeiffer, who had served six directors and two acting directors at the CIA.

"During the ninety-day study," Brennan recalled, "I frequently heard the question, 'What's broken that you're trying to fix, John?'" The reorganization was regarded as a disruption, in the spirit of Silicon Valley's "move fast and break things" morale, but not in a good way. "We really don't want to talk about or do anything unless it has to do with the mission," Mike Morell observed. "Trying to get somebody to go to a leadership training course, for example, or focus on anything like that is really, really hard. . . . People are saying, 'Don't take me away from the job. Don't take me away from the mission.'"

Brennan unveiled the renovated CIA on March 6, 2015. The Directorate of Digital Innovation—the first new directorate in a half century—rewired the networks of the clandestine service and crafted new cyber tools for collecting intelligence by hacking computers and cell phones. The CIA's computer network operations budget had been $685 million in 2013; the digital directorate spent $3 billion in 2017.

Adding the new directorate was far easier than fusing fourteen thousand operators and analysts into ten new "mission centers." Six of these mapped the world: Europe and Eurasia (including Russia), the Near East, South and Central Asia, East Asia and the Pacific, Africa, and the Western Hemisphere. Four covered transnational issues: counterterrorism, counterproliferation, counterintelligence, and technology. Crucially, each mission center would be run by a newly appointed assistant CIA director in charge of every facet of the centers' work: espionage, covert operations, liaison with foreign intelligence services, analysis, tech sup-

---

* McKinsey, the world's most powerful and amoral consulting firm, since has become notorious for helping opioid manufacturers sell more drugs and aiding authoritarian crackdowns in China and Saudi Arabia. Its work for the CIA was more benign, unless you count the mind-numbing infliction of vacuous management-speak.

port, and logistics. Brennan had created a new layer of bureaucracy in the name of efficiency. "Before, because there was one person in charge of analysis and one person in charge of operations, they could set a standard, and they could hold everybody to it," Morell said. "And now there's ten, eleven, twelve people doing that. There is a risk to that, and you just have to mitigate it."

Brennan had a hard time convincing the spies that any of this was a good idea. Some feared that their chief would become an empty suit, an espiocrat solely responsible for training and assigning officers to serve in the mission centers. Brennan, in turn, believed those officers were guilty of "insularity, parochialism, and arrogance" in their conduct of espionage. He thought they saw "the clandestine collection of intelligence from human sources as the be-all and end-all of national security, and they had little understanding and even less appreciation for the importance and role of other disciplines and capabilities outside the espionage world." The clandestine collection of intelligence from human beings—HUMINT, in spook-speak—had been the heart and soul of the CIA for seven decades. Despite that, Brennan's message was clear: be multidisciplinary or be gone.

Frank Archibald, the chief of the clandestine service, told Brennan face-to-face that he fervently opposed the changes. Brennan fired him. No director in the history of the CIA had ever summarily dismissed his spy chief for resisting an order. "I told Frank that I had decided it was time for new leadership of the DO and that I would be replacing him," Brennan recounted.* "I then called Greg Vogle into my office and told him I wanted him to be the new DDO. I figured that if Greg was able to survive the ninety days leading the study group, he probably also could withstand whatever flak he was likely to take from his DO colleagues as he directed them to get aboard the reorganization train." Vogle took the friendly fire and stood by the director. "Brennan had guts. He saw what we needed to do, and he pulled the trigger," he later told the *Washington*

---

* Brennan renamed the clandestine service the directorate of operations, the DO, as part of the reorganization. Its chief, the deputy director of operations, was thus the DDO. This simply reinstated the names which had been in place from 1973 to 2005. Some officers appreciated this as a return to tradition. Not all.

Post's David Ignatius on deep background. A columnist with CIA sources cultivated over three decades, Ignatius reported: "Among retired case officers I talked to, there was near-universal scorn for what Brennan tried to do. One described the reorganization as a political 'reeducation camp.'"

The old boys inside and outside headquarters didn't like Brennan for a lot of reasons—he was Obama's man, he wore a rainbow lanyard on his badge in support of gay and lesbian employees, he pushed hard for racial diversity and inclusion, he promoted women to high-ranking positions and made the liberal-minded Avril Haines as his deputy director—but they really hated his reorganization and his firing of Frank Archibald. Two of his division chiefs and Mark Kelton, the head of counterintelligence, resigned in solidarity. But Kelton had another reason for quitting. His ambition to replace Archibald had been dashed.

So had Mike D'Andrea's dreams of commanding the clandestine service. A few days later in March, Brennan told D'Andrea his time was up. In his decade as the CIA's counterterrorism chief, he had never wavered in his militance. *Kill them all, let God sort them out* was his way of thinking, and when his fellow officers said, *Mike, you can't kill them all*, he'd reply, *Well, let's try*. He was a hero to many at the CIA, the man who had best defended the homeland from attack. He was responsible for the deaths of more than two thousand al Qaeda terrorists and the destruction of its operational leadership. He was also responsible for the deaths of many scores of civilians. Among them was Warren Weinstein, a veteran American aid worker killed in January 2015. Kidnapped in Lahore and held hostage for three years by al Qaeda near the Afghan border, he had died by a CIA drone strike conducted on D'Andrea's authority. The same missile killed an Italian aid worker, Giovanni Lo Porto. The United States did not acknowledge their deaths until Obama personally apologized in a grim formal statement at the White House on April 25. By then D'Andrea had been demoted to a desk job, in charge of reviewing ongoing covert operations. He would live to fight again after Obama left office. Brennan named Chris Wood, the former Kabul station chief who had identified bin Laden's body after the Abbottabad raid, as the new counterterrorism chief. The CIA's drone strikes diminished significantly thereafter.

"I don't want our intelligence agencies being a paramilitary organization. That's not their function," Obama said a year later. "As much as possible this should be done through our Defense Department so that we can report, here's what we did, here's why we did it, here's our assessment of what happened. And so slowly we are pushing it in that direction."

Obama brought Haines back to the White House as his deputy national security adviser, and Brennan replaced her with another outsider, David Cohen, the Treasury Department's secret weapon in the war against ISIS. Cohen would become the longest-tenured deputy director of the CIA in sixty years, serving out the Obama years and returning under Biden. Brennan, who had devoted more time and energy to the reorganization than anything else save the Torture Report, charged the newcomer with making it work. "It was disruptive," Cohen said. "The agency is very mission-focused and doesn't like to do things other than put their head down and charge ahead. It required people to lift their head up and think about working at the agency in a different way." It took the rest of 2015 and all of 2016 before the changes began to gain traction.

For years, Cohen said, the CIA had sacrificed long-term strategic thinking for the daily grind of tactical victories in the war on terror. "Where I think the agency could do better is to look over the horizon to understand challenges, really significant challenges that are coming but that have not yet fully ripened into a crisis," he said. "Because of the intense focus on mission, and on the crisis of the day . . . that sometimes gets left behind."

"The most amazing information-warfare blitzkrieg we have ever seen"

One of the overlooked dangers on the horizon was Russia's covert warfare against the United States.

The CIA had tried to work with the Russians on counterterrorism since the end of the cold war. Every CIA director from Tenet to Brennan had ordered his officers to try to cooperate with Putin's intelligence services. Every effort at liaison had elicited little more than drunken toasts and empty promises from the Russians. They used the pretext of cooperation to undermine the CIA and share the identities of its officers with its enemies; they would offer their right hand for a handshake and try to pickpocket the Americans with the left. Doug Wise, a four-time station chief, had a pithy description of America's repeated efforts to enlist the Russians in the war on terror: A man buys a baboon as a pet. The baboon rips his face off. Then he goes out and buys another baboon. How many times did America have to let the Russians rip off its face? How long until presidents understood that Putin saw the United States as the main enemy, as had the Soviets?

Time after time, said Steve Hall, a former Moscow station chief, the Russians would propose a counterterrorism conference in Moscow. "And, of course, for them, that's a targeting event . . . designed to be able to look at CIA officers who spend most of their time in Washington and perhaps don't have as much counterintelligence savvy as somebody who's deployed to Moscow—and they're looking at ways to get at them."

"I once had a Russian intelligence officer tell me, 'You probably think, and you probably thought in the '90s, that Russia was going to become a Western democracy,'" Hall said. "'You guys continue to think that we want to be like you, we want to be like the West. We don't. I bet you don't make that same mistake with the Chinese, do you?' Until we're really willing to look at Russia, willing to see that they really are focused on the destruction of Western democracies, we're not going to get our policies right. That cold, hard look has been really hard to do for most presidents."

Bill Burns, as the American ambassador to Moscow, had warned Bush about Putin's plots against democracies; the autocrat had convinced himself that "the best way to create space for Russia as a major power in the world is to chip away at an American-led order." NATO was the emblem of that order. Its expansion to include nations once under Soviet rule was "the brightest of all red lines" for Putin, Burns had cautioned the president. Bush had ignored him and pressed ahead.

In April 2007, Putin had attacked Estonia, which had joined NATO three years earlier, in the world's first cyberwar. The Baltic nation of 1.3 million, occupied by Soviet troops until 1994, had been brought to its knees for three weeks. Russian hackers had crashed the government, banks, businesses, telecommunications, and the media of the world's most wired nation; Estonians couldn't use cash machines, pay their bills, or watch the news. Seven weeks later, Bush had hosted Putin for a weekend of lobster and sailing at his family's compound in Kennebunkport, Maine. He had done nothing in response.

In August 2008, Putin had started Europe's first twenty-first-century war by sending his tanks and troops into the former Soviet republic of Georgia. In the first five minutes of the war, he had launched a massive coordinated cyberattack against the government and the nation's news websites. His propaganda outlet, RT, leapt into the void. Putin had flown from the Beijing Olympics to the outskirts of the war zone to stage a video accusing the Georgian soldiers of war crimes. Two women played the roles of terrorized refugees.

> FIRST WOMAN: They burned our girls while they were still alive!
> PUTIN: *Alive?*
> SECOND WOMAN: They stabbed a baby. He was one and a half. . . . An old woman with two little kids—they were running and a tank ran over them.
> PUTIN: They must be crazy. This is genocide.

Putin had initiated a new form of warfare by using cyberattacks and disinformation to shape the world's perceptions of the battlefield. His lies were convincing enough—and America's reluctance to confront him strong enough—that the Bush administration reacted to the invasion with little more than expressions of concern. "Putin got away with it," said Daniel Fried, then the assistant secretary of state for Europe and Eurasia. "And I say that without pride or pleasure. The Bush administration after the war understood that its policy of reaching out to Putin had failed." Obama's attempts to get along with the Russian leader were doomed as well.

"Georgia was a turning point," Mike Morell observed, "a really important moment, and maybe that should have been the wakeup call—that moment where he was willing to invade a neighbor." Obama did not get that call until it was too late. After Putin began his third term as president in 2012, he reverted to "what was essentially Russian behavior during the Cold War, which is 'challenge the United States everywhere you can in the world, and do whatever you can to undermine what they're trying to accomplish. Do whatever you can to weaken them,'" Morell said. "Putin's view of us is that we want to undermine him, and that we are actively working to do so. He really believes that. And he points to things that are absolutely true. The State Department pushing for democracy in Russia openly. And then he points to things that aren't true, like the CIA was behind the street protests in Kiev that led to all the problems in Ukraine."

Putin's invasion of Ukraine and his seizure of the Crimean Peninsula in 2014 was a hydra-headed attack of disinformation, cyberwarfare, and special-operations forces. As the Russians landed in Crimea, they shut down government and media websites in Kyiv and hacked the cell phones of parliamentarians. As Ukraine held an election to replace a Kremlin-backed president who had massacred protesters and fled to Moscow, the Russians broke into the central election commission's network and, just before the polls closed, posted the fake news that a fringe pro-Putin candidate had won.

The election hack in Kyiv was the work of Cozy Bear's cousin, Fancy Bear, the weapon of the GRU, the Russian military intelligence service. It came seven weeks before the downing of Malaysia Airlines Flight 17 and the ensuing onslaught of disinformation designed to disguise Russia's responsibility. Putin's trolls put out a conspiracy theory on the internet: the CIA had loaded hundreds of corpses on that plane and then shot it down. This outrageous falsehood was part of an onslaught of disinformation designed to defend the Russian occupation of Ukrainian soil. "People were repeating that story again and again," said Sri Preston Kulkarni, a director of the Ukraine Communications Task Force. "And I realized we had gone through the looking glass. . . . If people could believe that, they could believe almost anything."* The NATO commander, Gen. Philip

---

* On the campaign trail in October 2015, Donald Trump belittled the American intelligence community's conclusion that Russians and Russian-backed separatists had shot down the plane: "Putin and Russia say they didn't do it, the other side said they did. No one really knows."

Breedlove, called Russia's cascade of lies "the most amazing information-warfare blitzkrieg we have ever seen." The work of the Russian intelligence services was designed to undermine the integrity and the legitimacy of democratic nations. Putin wanted to attack democracy itself. He was an architect of an alternative world in which an autocratic leader could tell his people there were no facts and there was no truth and they would believe him. Obama should have seen what had happened to Ukraine as a warning. He did not.

The CIA station chief in the Hague had given American intelligence a window into Cozy Bear's lair, but it closed late in 2015, after the Russian hackers realized they had been detected by the Dutch. By then, they had gained access to the Democratic National Committee's computer networks. Fancy Bear soon joined it. The Russians stockpiled gigabytes of data for their intelligence operations and created a clandestine arrangement with Julian Assange and WikiLeaks to weaponize what they had stolen.

Their audacious act of political warfare aimed to help elect a demagogue as the next president of the United States. "He is an absolute leader of the presidential race, as we see it today," Putin said on December 17, seven weeks before Donald Trump won the first Republican primary election. "He says that he wants to move to another level of relations, a deeper level of relations with Russia. . . . How can we not welcome that? Of course, we welcome it."

Looking back, Leon Panetta put it bluntly: "Putin looked at Trump and immediately determined that he was a perfect candidate."

Chapter Twenty-Two

THE USEFUL IDIOT

John Brennan went to Moscow in March 2016 on a mission to urge the Russians to help end the bloodshed in Syria. Nearly four years earlier, as Assad began to crush his opponents, Clinton, Panetta, and Petraeus had pressed Obama to sign a covert-action finding authorizing the CIA to support the fractured resistance. He had balked. In the Situation Room, Bill Burns, the deputy secretary of state, had warned that the CIA "tended to overstate how fast and effectively it could arm the Syrian rebels," and that "no one really knew what it would mean when the Iranians and the Russians doubled down in response."

After Assad had used chemical weapons against his own people in August 2013, killing some 1,400 civilians, Obama signed that finding. Under a major paramilitary program code-named TIMBER SYCAMORE and backed by the Saudis, the CIA had been training and arming the Syrian resistance in Jordan and sending them into battle, supported by American air strikes and special-operations soldiers. While their combined force had beaten back ISIS strongholds in Iraq and Syria, the CIA had failed to begin to achieve the rebels' aims of overthrowing Assad. Putin had now intervened with warplanes and mercenaries to support the regime. The battle for Syria had threatened to become a proxy war between the United States and Russia.

Brennan met with his intelligence counterparts and with Putin's chief of staff, Sergei Ivanov, a former KGB officer and a chief overseer of the growing attack on the 2016 presidential election. He got nowhere with the Russians. "American policies are allowing the Islamists to gain strength," Ivanov told him. "You are supporting terrorists." Nor did Igor Korobov, the new head of Russian military intelligence, offer any hope for a resolution in Syria.

The GRU chief had struck Brennan as anxious when they spoke. Perhaps that was because "he wondered whether I knew at the time that his organization had successfully conducted its first round of election-related cyberattacks," Brennan reflected. "I wish I had known, but I didn't."*

"Putin will eat your lunch"

On March 17, while Brennan was in Moscow, Donald Trump secured the Republican nomination for president. "When it became clear that there was going to be a race between Trump and Clinton," Brennan said, "I think that is when they really stepped up their efforts—not only to denigrate Hillary, but also to promote his prospects."

The Russian intelligence services turned their full force on the election on March 29, when Trump hired Paul Manafort as a campaign strategist. He had offered to work for free—Trump liked that—and he would become chairman of the Trump campaign in May. When Victoria Nuland, the State Department's top Russia hand, heard the news, she was thunderstruck. "Manafort!" she said to herself. "He's been a Russian stooge for fifteen years." Russia had been his client, on and off the books, ever since he had signed a political consulting contract in 2005 promising to "greatly benefit the Putin government."

---

* In late March 2016, GCHQ, the British counterpart of the National Security Agency, detected that Fancy Bear was calling home to Russia from within the Democratic National Committee's networks in Washington. The British alerted the NSA. But it was old news—the NSA had told the FBI six months before. An FBI agent had phoned a DNC tech to alert him. The tech thought the caller might be an impostor. He had done nothing, nor did the agent follow up. The DNC didn't take the threat seriously until late May.

Manafort had come to the attention of the CIA station in Kyiv no later than 2013. He and his business partner, a Russian intelligence operative named Konstantin Kilimnik, were in Ukraine working for the pro-Kremlin president, who had paid him $17 million, of which Manafort had illegally laundered $12.7 million. The Russian intelligence services had a dossier of compromising information on him, including his debt of many millions to a Kremlin oligarch and close Putin confidant for a business deal gone bad. Manafort tried to barter down that debt by trading internal polling data from the Trump campaign. Manafort said it showed that Trump had a narrow path to victory in November if the campaign mounted fierce attacks on Clinton's reputation in traditionally Democratic states like Michigan, Pennsylvania, and Wisconsin. He gave it to Kilimnik, who gave it to Russian intelligence officers at the GRU, who focused their work accordingly. Kilimnik, in turn, wanted Manafort to sell Trump on a "peace plan" for Ukraine giving Putin control of an autonomous republic in the heart of the country's east, occupied since 2014 by Russian troops.

As the CIA and FBI belatedly discovered, "there were extensive contacts between individuals affiliated with the Trump campaign and Russians, whether they be Russian citizens or Russian intelligence officers or Russians who had contacts with Russian intelligence," Brennan said. "It was clear that the Trump campaign was seeking assistance from Russia." The Russians held thirty-eight meetings and made 272 email or telephone connections with members of the Trump team, including his future national security adviser, retired lieutenant general Michael Flynn, and his future attorney general, Senator Jeff Sessions of Alabama. All told, thirty-three high-ranking campaign officials either held these conversations or knew about them. And every one of them, including Trump, lied or dissembled about these liaisons when questioned by the FBI, Congress, or reporters.

On March 31, in Washington, Trump gathered his tiny circle of foreign policy advisers. Among the five was an underemployed twenty-eight-year-old energy consultant named George Papadopoulos. He said he could help arrange a meeting between Trump and Putin, brokered by an acquaintance named Joseph Mifsud, a Maltese professor with extensive contacts in the Russian Foreign Ministry. The two conferred on April 26 at the Andaz Hotel in London. Mifsud told him he had just returned from Moscow, where he had learned from high-ranking Russian officials that the Kremlin had compromising information on Clinton in the form of thousands of her emails. Mifsud, a recruited Russian agent, had learned this secret from a contact at the Internet Research Agency, a Russian intelligence front whose operatives posed as Americans online from an office building in St. Petersburg. Since 2015, and with increasing force once the campaign was under way, the IRA had been flooding social media with disinformation and propaganda savaging Clinton and supporting Trump; it reached 126 million American Facebook users and spewed forth fifty thousand fake Twitter accounts. The CIA was unaware of its existence.

On May 10, over gin and tonics in a London bar, Papadopoulos shared the story of the stolen emails with a man he had just met: a diplomat named Alexander Downer, Australia's envoy to the United Kingdom. Downer didn't know what to make of him, or his information, but he briefly noted it in a cable to his foreign ministry in Canberra. His report was filed and forgotten for ten weeks.

On May 26, Trump clinched the Republican nomination, and on the next day, he publicly proclaimed his admiration for the Russian leader for the twenty-eighth time. Clinton fired back. "He praises dictators like Vladimir Putin," she said. "I will leave it to psychiatrists to explain his affection for tyrants. I just wonder how anyone could be so wrong about who America's real friends are. Because it matters. If you don't know exactly who you're dealing with, men like Putin will eat your lunch." The feast began soon after she clinched the Democratic nomination on June 6. But it was Clinton whom the Russians devoured.

On June 8, a GRU front called DCLeaks, hosted by an online GRU persona named Guccifer 2.0, began posting the first of thousands of emails stolen from the Democratic National Committee. Some revealed infighting and friction in the Clinton camp. These carefully calibrated document dumps from the GRU would go on until Election Day. The

DNC's leaders, in full panic, shut down their network, scrubbed it over a weekend, and decided to tell the *Washington Post* that Russian cyberhackers had penetrated their systems and stolen the files.

Then Julian Assange chimed in.

Assange had long claimed to be a journalist, an editor, and a publisher on a courageous crusade against secrecy. This cloak of respectability had worn thin. It had frayed in 2012 when he became a paid talking head for RT, the Russian propaganda network. After RT's editor in chief visited Assange at the Ecuadorian embassy in London, where he had sought asylum after jumping bail on a rape charge in Sweden, Russian media had announced in 2013 that RT had struck a deal with WikiLeaks to receive "new leaks of secret information."

On June 12, 2016—three days after Donald Trump Jr., Paul Manafort, and Trump's son-in-law Jared Kushner met at Trump Tower with a Russian lawyer who had promised dirt on Clinton—Assange told a British television reporter: "WikiLeaks has a very big year ahead. We have emails related to Hillary Clinton which are pending publication." He had received his first installment and awaited much more. On June 21, Guccifer 2.0 posted another set of DNC documents, some detailing Clinton's political vulnerabilities. Assange then wrote in a private message to the GRU front: "If you have anything Hillary related we want it," saying the stolen goods would have "a much higher impact" if WikiLeaks released them. There were so many emails that the Russians had trouble transmitting them, until the London bureau chief of RT came to the Ecuadorian embassy and slipped Assange a capacious USB drive.

On July 14, the GRU successfully sent him a gigabyte of encrypted files. Its Guccifer persona announced: "The main part of the papers, thousands of files and emails, I gave to WikiLeaks. They will publish them soon." On July 22, three days before the start of the Democratic convention in Philadelphia, Assange tweeted: "Are you ready for Hillary? We begin our series today with 20 thousand emails from the Democratic National Committee."

From that day on, the Trump campaign built a strategy around Assange, encouraging WikiLeaks, celebrating its work, and receiving in return a heads-up on what was coming next. The campaign had advance knowledge of every major WikiLeaks release thanks to Roger Stone, a political dirty trickster since the Nixon years, Manafort's former business partner, and Trump's longtime lobbyist—which he obtained via a back channel to Assange.* The National Security Agency soon detected and tracked a multitude of direct messages sent via Twitter between the GRU and WikiLeaks. If it hadn't been evident before that Assange was working with Putin's spies, it was now.

"This was uncharted territory"

Brennan saw, for the first time, that the Russians weren't simply conducting espionage, but mounting a campaign of sabotage, a political warfare attack unlike any the United States had ever seen.

On Monday, July 25, his black SUV pulled up to CIA headquarters at dawn. Over the weekend, he had called for everything his officers and analysts knew about the Russian operation to be gathered on his desk that morning. He wanted both their formal reporting and the raw intelligence underlying it: unfiltered information from recruited agents, friendly foreign intelligence services, and electronic intercepts. He reviewed what the NSA and the FBI and the Department of Homeland Security had on the Russians. Stacks of three-ring binders filled his suite. He met with the leaders of the CIA's Russia House, the epicenter of operations against the Kremlin, along with top counterintelligence and digital-directorate officers. He read case histories of Russian espionage against the United States going back decades. The Russians had tried to manipulate politics in the United States since the 1930s, when their spies had put a New York congressman on their payroll. The FBI recently had warned the right-wing

---

* Stone was sentenced to forty months in prison for witness tampering, obstruction, and false statements in the special counsel's investigation of the Russian role in the 2016 campaign. Trump commuted his sentence before he was jailed and then pardoned him in 2020.

California congressman Dana Rohrabacher, a pro-Putin firebrand, that the Russian were trying to recruit him. "There's two people I think Putin pays: Rohrabacher and Trump. Swear to God," the House majority leader, Kevin McCarthy of California, had told a handful of his Republican colleagues in June.

Brennan found that the CIA was not up to speed on Russian information warfare. It did not fully grasp that "the cyber sphere is a tremendous venue to influence people's views, perspectives, votes, attitudes," he said. "But we knew that the Russians were navigating into some of the electoral systems in individual states, basically mapping that infrastructure," he said. "And we were concerned that the Russians might try to take down the voter registration rolls on the day of the election. And we were mindful of that, watching it, and really hoping they were not going to do anything on the technical front. But the more extensive and the more impactful area of Russian interference was the influence operation. And I learned"—belatedly—"a lot about just how extensive and successful the Russians were in the social-media environment."

As Brennan was absorbing the intelligence, the torrent of emails Assange had unleashed jogged the memory of Alexander Downer, the Australian diplomat in London. On July 26, he went to the American embassy at the Court of St. James's. He told the deputy chief of mission about Trump's foreign policy adviser confiding in him that the Russians wanted to share dirt on Clinton derived from cyberespionage. She, in turn, briefed two people at the embassy. One was the FBI's legal attaché. The other was the CIA station chief—Gina Haspel.

The next day, at a press conference, Trump appealed to the Russian intelligence services to hack and release an archive Clinton had deleted from a private account she had used as secretary of state. "Russia, if you're listening," he said, "I hope you're able to find the 30,000 emails that are missing." Hours later, for the first time, the GRU spear-phished email addresses used by Clinton's personal office, and targeted seventy-six of her campaign's accounts.

On the morning of July 28, after spending three long days and nights reviewing the intelligence, Brennan called his trusted confidant Avril

Haines, now Obama's principal deputy national security adviser. "I need to see the president," he said. "It is really important that I do so today." The White House set a table for four—Obama, Haines, national security adviser Susan Rice, and chief of staff Denis McDonough—and laid out a light lunch of soup and salad in the small dining room off the Oval Office at 1:45 p.m. Brennan minced no words. "Mr. President, it appears that the Russian effort to undermine the integrity of the November election is much more intense, determined, and serious than any we have seen before," he began. "Putin has authorized these activities"—and he intended to elect Trump by eviscerating Clinton. The CIA knew that the operation was directed by Putin because a recruited agent in the Kremlin named Oleg Smolenkov had told them so, confirming intelligence obtained by communications intercepts. Brennan shared the fact that the CIA had a spy in Putin's camp, a remarkable achievement, in the strictest confidence, insisting that the secret could not leave the room.*

The president asked if the Russians could really try to change the popular vote tally, as they had done in Ukraine in 2014, or find ways to sabotage the state-by-state Electoral College count with electrons. Could they obliterate voter registration rolls? Make names disappear? Prevent people from voting? What about money? Obama wondered. Were they secretly financing Trump? There was only one way to find out, Brennan told the president: "The CIA, FBI, and NSA need to work together on this." He would create a team at CIA headquarters from all three agencies, and they would seek to understand the attack so the president could decide how to fight back.

"We had our work cut out for us," Brennan recalled. "It was going to be a very, very challenging intelligence effort. It was going to be a very

---

* Smolenkov was a longtime aide to Putin's principal foreign policy adviser on American affairs, Yuri Ushakov, who had served as Russia's ambassador to the United States from 1999 to 2008. He likely was recruited not long after the fall of the Soviet Union, before he joined the ambassador in Washington at the turn of the century. Russian media outed him, with an assist from Putin's intelligence officers, two years after the CIA, fearing for his life, smuggled him out of Russia and into the United States via Montenegro in 2017.

challenging policy effort as well, from the standpoint of what to do. This was uncharted territory in many respects." What should Brennan say to the Russians? What should Obama tell the American people? What could the CIA bring to bear against Putin's spies? "We were navigating shoals that I had never encountered before," he said.

"An unwitting agent of the Russian Federation"

On Friday morning, July 29, Brennan called FBI director Comey and pledged to tell him everything the CIA was learning about the Russian operation, including anything about the involvement of Americans. That weekend, the FBI opened a counterintelligence case code-named CROSSFIRE HURRICANE. The investigation had to confront an appalling question. Were members of the Trump campaign—or Trump himself—working with the Russians? On the next Friday, Mike Morell addressed it with an essay endorsing Clinton in the *New York Times*. What Morell published was extraordinary in two respects. The CIA's chieftains, even in retirement, did not publicly pick sides in presidential races. And he told millions of people what many of his peers were thinking: Trump was acting as if he were a Russian asset.

"In the intelligence business," the CIA's former deputy director wrote, "we would say that Mr. Putin had recruited Mr. Trump as an unwitting agent of the Russian Federation." He was after all a pure product of the KGB, trained to identify and exploit a person's weaknesses. "That is exactly what he did early in the primaries," Morell pointed out. "Mr. Putin played upon Mr. Trump's vulnerabilities by complimenting him. He responded just as Mr. Putin had calculated. Mr. Putin is a great leader, Mr. Trump says, ignoring that he has killed and jailed journalists and political opponents, has invaded two of his neighbors and is driving his economy to ruin. Mr. Trump has also taken policy positions consistent with Russian, not American, interests—endorsing Russian espionage against the United States, supporting Russia's annexation of Crimea." Morell, who had read scores of the CIA's profiles of foreign leaders in his day, portrayed the presidential contender as a potential despot. "Trump is not only unqualified for the job, but he may well pose a threat to our national security," he concluded. "He would be a poor, even dangerous, commander in chief."

Mike Hayden soon weighed in with his own assessment: maybe Trump wasn't a Russian agent, but he was something close to it. "I'd prefer another term drawn from the arcana of the Soviet era: *polezni durak*," Hayden wrote in the *Washington Post*—a useful idiot manipulated by Moscow. Leon Panetta went one step further. "There wasn't any question in my mind that Trump and Russia were, quote, working together, unquote, in ways to try to improve Trump's chances of winning," he said. "Russia was manipulating Trump and Trump was behaving in a way that clearly protected the Russians as well."

Trump mounted his own assault on his opponent's character as he accepted the Republican nomination: "This is the legacy of Hillary Clinton: death, destruction, terrorism, and weakness." Throughout August, Trump assailed her with increasing intensity. She was a stalking horse for ISIS. She was mentally ill. She was going to steal the vote, rig the results, seize power by fraud. Assange echoed Trump in a Facebook interview with the *New York Times*, calling Clinton "a demon that is going to put nooses around everyone's necks as soon as she wins the election." The Internet Research Agency pushed identical themes and conspiracy theories on the internet. The Kremlin's tools and trolls were on the campaign trail alongside Trump, his invisible surrogates.

The Russian assault on democracy once would have united American leaders. No longer. Obama had told Brennan to inform the Gang of Eight—the leaders of the Senate and the House and the intelligence committees—about Putin's operation. But when he briefed Senate Minority Leader Mitch McConnell of Kentucky on September 6, he received a startling rebuff. "He said, 'Well, it sounds as though you and the CIA are trying to prevent Donald Trump from being elected,'" Brennan remembered. When Obama summoned the congressional leaders to the White House and asked them to sign on a joint statement decrying the

Russian attack, McConnell refused. "The stronger the bipartisan outrage about Russian interference could be, the more weight and the more credibility it would have with the American people," Brennan said. "McConnell resisted that. He put his party above national identity and national loyalty. . . . He was very concerned that if there were revelations that the Russians were involved in the election it could undermine Trump's chances. He wanted to prevent that from happening."

Obama agonized about whether to accuse the Russians. How was he to tell the American people that the CIA had concluded that Putin was trying to elect Trump? He didn't find the will to do it. He was afraid of seeming to put his thumb on the scales of the election, though the Kremlin was putting its boot on it. And he didn't want to provoke an all-out cyberwar with Putin: Lt. Gen. James Clapper, the director of national intelligence, had warned him that the Russians had implanted malware—Energetic Bear—in the American electrical grid. With a few well-placed keystrokes, they could black out cities and bring down networks on election day, sowing chaos and obliterating the count.

"The president always felt as though, if he needed to take more aggressive action against Russia, he could," Brennan said. "But what would the Russians have done to counter that? And if they were going to counter it, how could that have further interfered in the election?" As he put it dryly, an escalation really could run the risk of war: "The ecosystem of the international arena now has a very large digital component to it. And it is that component where intelligence, security, and military services are very active prior to an increase in tension or military conflict."

Five weeks of nonstop Situation Room meetings among the guardians of American national security failed to produce a presidential statement on the Russian attack. Finally, early in October, Clapper had had enough. They had to say *something*. If they didn't, there'd be hell to pay someday. He and Jeh Johnson, the Homeland Security secretary, struggled to find the right words. *Trump* and *Putin* were not among them. Over three days, they fashioned a three-paragraph press release that they believed would alert the American people. It began:

> The U.S. Intelligence Community is confident that the Russian Government directed the recent compromises of e-mails from US persons and institutions, including from US political organizations. The recent disclosures of alleged hacked e-mails on sites like DCLeaks.com and WikiLeaks and by the Guccifer 2.0 online persona are consistent with the methods and motivations of Russian-directed efforts. These thefts and disclosures are intended to interfere with the US election process. . . . We believe, based on the scope and sensitivity of these efforts, that only Russia's seniormost officials could have authorized these activities.

The statement went public at three p.m. on Friday, October 7. Sixty-three minutes later, the Washington Post revealed the *Access Hollywood* tape, in which Trump boasted about sexually assaulting women. Half an hour after that, WikiLeaks unleashed another barrage of Clinton campaign emails, stolen by the Russians six months before and stockpiled like an arsenal of flash-bang grenades ever since. The battalions of Washington reporters covering politics were dazzled and transfixed by the fusillade. The handful who covered intelligence fought their editors to find space for the Russia story, which wound up on the back pages.

"I am shocked," Morell said, "that there wasn't a bigger outcry from Congress, the executive branch, the media. People just kind of accepted . . . an attack on our democracy."

On October 19, when the candidates held their final debate, Clinton delivered another warning against the Russian assault. Trump rejected the idea outright and absolved Putin of responsibility:

> TRUMP: He said nice things about me. If we got along well, that would be good. He has no respect for her. . . .
> CLINTON: Well, that's because he'd rather have a puppet as president of the United States.
> TRUMP: No puppet. No puppet. You're the puppet!
> CLINTON: It's pretty clear you won't admit—

TRUMP: No, you're the puppet!

CLINTON: —that the Russians have engaged in cyberattacks against the United States of America, that you encouraged espionage against our people, that you are willing to spout the Putin line, sign up for his wish list, break up NATO, do whatever he wants to do, and that you continue to get help from him, because he has a very clear favorite in this race.... We have seventeen intelligence agencies, civilian and military, who have all concluded that these espionage attacks, these cyberattacks, come from the highest levels of the Kremlin and they are designed to influence our election. I find that deeply disturbing. And I think it's time you take a stand...

TRUMP: She has no idea whether it's Russia, China, or anybody else. She has no idea. Hillary, you have no idea.... And our country has no idea.

He was close to the mark on that last point. It wasn't enough for the intelligence community to have sounded the alarm. The president had to make sure the people heard it. Obama had failed to tell the country what he knew to be true.

"We made America great"

On November 9, 2016, a sleepless night was ahead of us, wrote a Russian troll at the Internet Research Agency's headquarters in St. Petersburg. *When around 8 a.m. the most important result of our work arrived, we uncorked a tiny bottle of champagne . . . took one gulp each and looked into each other's eyes. . . . We uttered almost in unison: "We made America great."* Trump had won Michigan, Pennsylvania, and Wisconsin—three swing states specifically targeted by Russian intelligence officers armed by their *polezni durak* Paul Manafort—by 10,704, 46,765, and 22,177 votes, respectively. That gave him forty-six electoral votes; if Clinton had done fractionally better in each state, she'd have won the Electoral College as well as the popular vote. Fewer than eighty thousand ballots had made Trump the next president of the United States.

The barons of American intelligence believed the Russian attack had been a key to his victory. "I am confident that the Russians changed some votes," Brennan said. "I don't know whether it was one vote or two million . . . but there were a sizable number of votes that were changed as a result of Russian influence operations." Clapper concluded: "Knowing what I know about what the Russians did, how massive the operation was, how diverse it was, and how many millions of American voters it touched . . . it stretches credulity to conclude that Russian activity didn't swing voter decisions, and therefore swing the election." Pete Strzok, who led the CROSSFIRE HURRICANE investigation as the deputy assistant director of the FBI's counterintelligence division, concurred: "Without Russian assistance," he said, "I don't think Trump gets elected."

Some of their colleagues thought that Russian intelligence had set its sights on Trump long ago. He had first visited Moscow in 1987, seeking to build a luxury hotel across Red Square from the Kremlin in partnership with the Soviet government, and he was already dropping hints about running for president. His real estate deals around the world, and his solvency after bankruptcy, depended in part on Russian money. He fancied Slavic women, and he was cheating on his wife. He had returned to Moscow to run a beauty contest he owned in 2013. "Do you think Putin will be going to The Miss Universe Pageant," he had tweeted, and "if so, will he become my new best friend?"

The Russia House veteran Rolf Mowatt-Larssen, a Moscow station stalwart and a highly experienced mole hunter, said: "I have no doubt that Donald Trump was a target" of Russian intelligence officers during these years. "The vulnerabilities are there. The Russians would not have missed them. I can assure you they would never have missed an opportunity to approach such an influential American businessman, regardless of whether they thought he'd ever be president or not. They would have." Trump's greed, his corruption, and his egomania had made him a mark for three decades.

In 2016, Trump was still trying to build a Moscow hotel, still shamelessly flirting with Putin, and stampeding toward the White House with covert support from Russian intelligence. Putin, as an experienced KGB officer, knew how to handle Trump. He influenced him with praise and political support, and won influence in return. "He believes that he can manipulate Donald Trump," Morell said a month after the election, "not because he holds financial dealings or anything else over his head, but because Vladimir Putin as a former intelligence officer knows that when you have a narcissistic personality it is very, very easy to play to that person and get them to do what you want them to do simply by flattering them. That's what Putin did and Trump responded." Fiona Hill, the Putin biographer who served as the National Security Council's director for Russia and Europe in the Trump White House for two and a half years, said: "That's exactly what a case officer does. They get a weakness, and they blackmail their targets. And Putin will target world leaders. . . . I firmly believe he was also targeting President Trump."

The ultimate target of what Mike Hayden called the most successful covert operation in history was the American people. Morell later told the journalist Robert Draper: "This is the only time in American history when we've been attacked by a foreign country and not come together as a nation. In fact, it split us further apart. . . . It deepened our divisions. I'm absolutely convinced that those Russian intelligence officers who put together and managed the attack on our democracy in 2016 all received medals personally from Vladimir Putin."

They couldn't have done it without Assange. "I love WikiLeaks!" Trump had proclaimed on the campaign trail. And so did Mike Pompeo, the man chosen as his CIA director.

"BUSTED: 19,252 Emails from DNC Leaked by WikiLeaks," Pompeo had exulted on Twitter during the Democratic convention. Like Trump, he promoted the work of Assange and ridiculed the idea that the Russians were his source. "Frankly," he told Fox News, "it's pretty clear who invited the Russians to do damage to America, and it was Hillary Clinton." Pompeo was a pugnacious, soaringly ambitious, archconservative Kansas congressman who had attacked Clinton for three years from his seat on the House intelligence committee. "There is no doubt that American lives are at risk today because of her actions," he had written in a July letter to Clapper. Pompeo had disdained Trump, too, and in no uncertain terms. In March, during the Republican primaries, he had warned that Trump would be "an authoritarian president who ignored our Constitution" if elected. But once he was the nominee, Pompeo attached himself to Trump as a remora fastens onto a shark. Steve Bannon, the president-elect's cynical strategist, promoted Pompeo for CIA director, and won him an audience with Trump, who hadn't vetted him, on November 16. The meeting was short and without substance. The next day, his phone rang. Trump offered Pompeo his dream job.

"It's going to be great and wild!" Trump told him.

"Are we living in Nazi Germany?"

On December 11, the *New York Times* and the *Washington Post* reported the CIA's conclusion that the Russians had aimed to elect Trump. "I don't believe it," said the president-elect. "These are the same people that said Saddam Hussein had weapons of mass destruction." He also said he would read the President's Daily Brief only if and when it suited him. It didn't suit him. "He touched it. He doesn't really read anything," said Ted Gistaro, the veteran CIA analyst assigned to brief Trump. He was prone to "fly off on tangents," Clapper said. "There might be eight or nine minutes of real intelligence in an hour's discussion." (In a break from tradition, the CIA did not brief the president-elect on covert-action programs until a few weeks after his inauguration.) Trump constantly railed about the "Russia hoax" with Gistaro, blaming the CIA for leaking to reporters in an effort to undermine the legitimacy of his election. At one briefing, Gistaro said, "he vented for ten minutes about how we were out to destroy him." The Russian attack on the election, a CIA historian wrote, had become "the most politically charged issue in the history of presidential transitions."

Obama directed the CIA, FBI, and NSA to present him with a final report on the operation and then share it with Trump. The CIA's Russia, cyber, and counterintelligence experts drafted a top secret version—eyes only for Obama, Trump, and the Gang of Eight. Beth Sanner, a heralded CIA analyst who became Trump's White House briefer two years later, said she led "a rigorous effort to declassify that very classified report" for the public. The CIA had to "really consider what should be declassified and what should remain classified in order to protect sources and methods," Sanner said. "You want the people who really understand the risks involved in each sentence." The source most in need of protection was the CIA's recruited agent in Moscow.

On January 6, 2017, Brennan, Clapper, Comey, NSA director Mike Rogers, and Ted Gistaro met at Trump Tower with the president-elect, Pompeo, the national security adviser–designate Mike Flynn, the vice president–elect Mike Pence, and four other members of the Trump transition team. Clapper said the evidence that Russia had monkey-wrenched the election and that Putin was in charge of the operation was so solid that Trump never even tried to dispute it. The meeting almost came off without a hitch.

But when Brennan described how the CIA's human source had reported the direct role of Russia's intelligence services, Trump sneered. Such people, he said, were "sleazeballs" who'd say anything for a buck. Then FBI director Comey—against the advice of Brennan and Clapper—took Trump aside for a one-on-one talk about a dossier prepared for the Clinton campaign by Christopher Steele, a former British intelligence officer who had led the Russia desk of MI6. The report began: "Russian regime has been cultivating, supporting and assisting TRUMP for at least 5 years." Comey had been given a copy by Senator John McCain, and the dossier had circulated among Washington reporters, though none had published it. Neither the CIA nor the FBI had verified its raw intelligence—some of it very raw. It alleged, among other things, that the Kremlin could blackmail Trump over his financial and sexual misdeeds, including a covertly taped assignation with prostitutes in a Moscow hotel during the Miss Universe pageant in 2013. Comey rationalized his decision to discuss the dossier by reasoning that it inevitably would become public, and Trump didn't deserve to be sandbagged by it.

The dossier surfaced in the press five days after the briefing and the unclassified public report. Trump conflated them. It was all a hoax. "I think it was disgraceful that the intelligence agencies allowed any information that turned out to be so false and fake out," Trump said. "That's something that Nazi Germany would have done and did do. . . . Are we living in Nazi Germany?" Brennan told the *Wall Street Journal* that Trump had no business calling his spies an American Gestapo. "Tell the families of those 117 CIA officers who are forever memorialized on our wall of honor that their loved ones who gave their lives were akin to Nazis. I found that to be very repugnant."

Pompeo told Trump that he needed to go to the CIA on Saturday, January 21, the day after he would be sworn in as the forty-fifth president, and mend his fences. The press had asserted that "Trump hated the intelligence agencies. I knew better," Pompeo said. He called CIA headquarters on January 19 and told Meroe Park, the CIA's number three official, who would be the acting director on the day of the transition, that Trump would be coming to Langley in forty-eight hours. He ordered her to set the stage before the memorial wall and ensure a good turnout for his speech. Their conversation was awkward. Pompeo hadn't been confirmed by the Senate. He was still a congressman from Kansas. Park was taken aback.

"She said we needed to cancel," Pompeo recalled. "'Too late,' I said."

Chapter Twenty-Three

RING-KISSING AND KNEECAPPING

There is nobody that feels stronger about the intelligence community and the CIA than Donald Trump," the president said as began his televised speech at CIA headquarters on Saturday afternoon, January 21, 2017. The memorial wall of honor stood behind him. Its stars are sacred icons at the CIA, as is the passage from the Gospel of John engraved in large letters on the opposite wall: And Ye Shall Know the Truth and the Truth Shall Make You Free.

"The reason you're my first stop is that, as you know, I have a running war with the media," he said. "They are among the most dishonest human beings on Earth"—the crowd laughed and applauded—"and they sort of made it sound like I had a feud with the intelligence community. And I just want to let you know, the reason you're the number one stop is exactly the opposite—exactly." He beamed at his audience. "Probably almost everybody in this room voted for me." Awkward silence ensued. He praised Pompeo. "He's a gem." Scattered applause rose and faded. "Many of you know him anyway. But you're going to see. And again, we have some great people going in. But this one is something—is going to be very special, because this is one, if I had to name the most important, this would certainly be perhaps—you know, in certain ways, you could say my most important." Then he praised his national security adviser. "General Flynn is right over here. Put up your hand. What a good guy." More applause. Mike Flynn would be forced to resign three weeks later for lying to the FBI about his secret conversations with the Russian ambassador.

And then Trump praised himself. He said 1.5 million people had attended his inauguration. That was a lie. He said he had been on the cover of *Time* magazine fifteen times. That was a lie. He concluded telling the crowd of four hundred in the CIA's marbled lobby: "I love you. I respect you. There's nobody I respect more." And that was a lie too. Trump's speech was a desecration. Soon bouquets of flowers appeared in front of the memorial wall. No one had died. But something had.

Pompeo soon became the one of the most influential figures of Trump's presidency. Throughout his fifteen months at the CIA, he broke a taboo by trying to shape the foreign policy of the United States. "CIA does not make policy," the agency's website avows. Pompeo did, at every chance he got. Anything that Obama and Brennan had done, he would undo when he could. He played the role of secretary of state—until he won the job. Pompeo was the only member of the president's core national-security team who wasn't fired or compelled to quit; Trump ran through six national security advisers, four secretaries of defense, and four directors of national intelligence in four years. How did he do it? By his own account, he trusted in God, worked hard, kneecapped his enemies, and kissed the president's ring, smiling at his every utterance, and swaying him with his swaggering style. His loyalty verged on fealty; it called to mind James Schlesinger, who had been President Nixon's budget chief before replacing Richard Helms as CIA director in 1973. Schlesinger "really had *R.N.* tattooed on him," said Helms. His first words to the seventh floor upon taking office were succinct: "I'm here to make sure you don't screw Richard Nixon."

Pompeo spent every possible moment with Trump without ever once disagreeing with him. "I argue with everyone," the president said. "Except Pompeo." Unless he was overseas meeting foreign spymasters, his first stop in the morning was a hideaway at the Eisenhower Executive Office Building next to the White House. When the president received an intelligence briefing in the Oval Office, Pompeo delivered it, giving a running commentary and lingering by the president's side for hours thereafter. He elbowed out Dan Coats, the new national intelligence director, who by rights was in charge of the brief. "Each day, we're in there," Pompeo said proudly. "It's like clockwork." This was not precisely true. "Trump received a briefing only two or three times a week," an official CIA history noted. The president typically spent four or five hours each morning watching TV and tweeting, coming to work around eleven o'clock; the briefing usually took place late in the morning or early in the afternoon. Only after his time with Trump was over did Pompeo arrive at CIA headquarters.

He was "a heat-seeking missile for Trump's ass," as a former American ambassador told *The New Yorker*'s Susan Glasser. His passionate embrace of the president was seen as a smart move by the CIA's top officers, on the principle that you should hold your friends close and your enemies closer. The CIA's standing in the American government rested in great part on the director's proximity to the power of the president. But there was a catch. Though Pompeo sometimes served as a heat shield for the CIA, protecting it against the president's smoldering wrath, he also shielded Trump from intelligence he didn't want to hear. And he never once spoke up in public to defend the CIA against the president's fierce attacks.

"The president could blunder us into war"

Pompeo's first personnel decision was making Gina Haspel his deputy. They had met when she was the London station chief and hosted members of the House intelligence committee when they toured European capitals. The only thing the public knew about her was that she had overseen torture in Thailand and had executed Jose Rodriguez's order to destroy the tapes recording it. Pompeo took her on because she had impressed him as "aggressive, patriotic and brilliant," and "a conservative's conservative"—and above all to show that he supported what the CIA had done at the black sites. He had said that Senator Feinstein's publication of the Torture Report had "put American lives at risk," that the waterboarders were not torturers but patriots, "heroes, not pawns in some liberal game being played by the ACLU and Senator Feinstein. Her release of the report is the result of a narcissistic self-cleansing that is quintessentially at odds with her duty to the country." He had meant it, though he had privately apologized to Feinstein at his Senate confirmation. "I was wrong to have essentially accused her of treason," he admitted. He thereby won her vote.

Pompeo gave Haspel the broadest authority to run the CIA at headquarters, oversee its operations, and choose her top subordinates. She selected Tomas Rakusan as the new chief of the clandestine service in August 2017. He was the officer who had infiltrated Baghdad months before the American invasion of Iraq, posing as a Czech security officer by day, locating Saddam's air defense systems and troop concentrations at night, and winning the rarely awarded Distinguished Intelligence Cross for his bravery and cunning. Rakusan, whom everyone called Tom, was unknown to the public, and still is. His appointment was a secret and remains so. At this writing, his name has never appeared in a newspaper or a book. The only speck of digital dust about his past showed that he had a high school diploma from the American University School in Beirut, Lebanon, whose student body included the children of diplomats and spies. Rakusan had joined the CIA in 1981, at the age of twenty-one, and had served four stints as chief of station, most recently in Jordan, before becoming the chief of the Near East division in 2013 and the deputy chief of the clandestine service under Greg Vogle in 2015. Against strong competition, he had long been regarded as one of the smartest and toughest officers in the CIA.

Pompeo said he loved "pipe-hitters"—cold-blooded killers in combat, take-no-prisoners allies in government—and his second major personnel decision was to bring Mike D'Andrea back into battle from his desk job reviewing ongoing covert operations. Haspel had warned him that many people who had worked for "Ayatollah Mike" feared or despised him. Pompeo sized him up face-to-face: "They tell me you're an asshole, a shithead, and impossible to work with. He smiled and gave a perfect reply: 'Mr. Director, I am *not* impossible to work with.' I hired him on the spot," and put him in charge of a new mission center, devoted to aggressive covert operations against Iran.*

Pompeo was unalterably opposed to the multinational deal the Obama administration had struck with Iran in 2015, which had imposed tight restrictions on its nuclear programs, including strict international surveillance, in exchange for the limited relief of economic sanctions. The pact had been signed after extraordinarily complex negotiations at a beach resort in Oman, led by Bill Burns, the deputy secretary of state, a handful of American diplomats, and Norm Roule, a thirty-four-year CIA veteran who served as the national intelligence manager for Iran. The Iranian nuclear issue was, as Burns saw it, "the most combustible challenge on the international landscape." His negotiations had been as secret as the planning for the bin Laden raid; the outcome was highly favorable for the United States. The agreement had unanimous support from Secretary of Defense Jim Mattis, Secretary of State Rex Tillerson, Joint Chiefs chairman Gen. Joseph Dunford, and national security adviser H. R. McMaster. They all believed that breaking it would run the risk of war.

Pompeo called the deal "sheer madness" and set his sights on its destruction. "The first step," he argued, "was tuning out the overwhelmingly pro–nuclear deal analysts" at the CIA. They had consistently reported that Iran was in compliance with its restrictions, which had demonstrably slowed its progress toward building a bomb. Pompeo trashed their work. After a series of National Security Council sessions, he told Trump that the CIA's intelligence was irrelevant and advised him to renounce the pact.

---

* On January 3, 2020, D'Andrea and the CIA—in concert with Central Command and at the urging of Secretary of State Pompeo—assassinated Qasem Soleimani, for twenty years the commander of the Iranian Revolutionary Guards' Quds Force, the godfather of Hezbollah, and the mastermind of countless roadside bombings that killed and maimed Americans soldiers in Iraq. Soleimani was obliterated by a drone strike outside the Baghdad airport. D'Andrea had targeted him through relentless surveillance, and fixed his location at the hour of his death through an agent network at the airport. Trump said Soleimani had planned to blow up four American embassies in four Mideast capitals, including Baghdad. Pompeo said these attacks were "imminent." It later became apparent that no intelligence supported that claim, though Soleimani without question had plenty of American blood on his hands.

He was convincing: the president called it "the worst deal ever" and unilaterally withdrew. In a memoir he was writing at the time, after he retired from the State Department, Burns called Trump's demolition of the Iran deal "exactly the kind of risky, cocky, ill-considered bet that had shredded our influence before, and could easily do so again."

Pompeo applauded the president's unhinged musings on foreign policy. Trump asked him at one intelligence briefing: "How would we do if we went to war with Mexico?" Pompeo said he thought that Trump was "simply testing and expanding the range of ideas that might be useful in fulfilling his essential promises to the American people." He countenanced Trump's threat to rain nuclear "fire and fury" on North Korea. "Kim Jong Un just stated that the 'Nuclear Button is on his desk at all times,'" the president tweeted. "I too have a Nuclear Button, but it is a much bigger & more powerful one than his, and my Button works!" Pompeo wrote that "the strategy of matching Kim's incendiary rhetoric was brilliant. No other administration would ever have done this." Trump threatened to "totally destroy North Korea" in his first speech to the United Nations General Assembly. Before that vow, Mike Hayden wrote, "I had worried that the president could blunder us into war with his language. Now I was afraid he would order us to start one."

Throughout Trump's first year, to the surprise of the CIA's analysts, "North Korea tested missiles of all kinds almost every other month and tested the largest nuclear weapon to date," said Andy Kim, whom Pompeo called out of retirement to serve as chief of the CIA's new Korea Mission Center. "Critics were very vocal about the lack of U.S. engagement with North Korea. Many were concerned about the situation and asked the U.S. to engage with North Korea to defuse the tension." Pompeo convinced Trump to send him to meet Chairman Kim in Pyongyang and lay the groundwork for a summit meeting with the president. Their conversation began with Kim saying: "Mr. Director, I didn't think you'd show up. I know you've been trying to kill me." Pompeo says he replied, "Mr. Chairman, I'm still trying to kill you." Smiles all around. The tyrant swore he would give up his nuclear arsenal. Kim was lying, of course, but Trump believed him.

"Our operations were immediately at risk"

On April 13, 2017, Pompeo gave his first public speech as CIA director, at the Center for Strategic and International Studies in Washington. It wasn't one he wanted to deliver. The subject was WikiLeaks and Julian Assange, whom he and Trump had celebrated for sabotaging the Clinton campaign. They had now sabotaged the CIA.

"WikiLeaks walks like a hostile intelligence service and talks like a hostile intelligence service and has encouraged its followers to find jobs at the CIA in order to obtain intelligence," Pompeo said. "It overwhelmingly focuses on the United States while seeking support from anti-democratic countries and organizations. It's time to call out WikiLeaks for what it really is, a non-state hostile intelligence service, often abetted by state actors like Russia."

Assange had conspired in the largest theft and disclosure of secrets in history. In March, he had begun to unleash thirty-four terabytes stolen from the CIA—about two billion pages' worth of data—under the rubric "Vault 7." They described in detail more than one thousand hacking tools and malware weapons the agency had developed. They included cyberespionage systems giving spies and recruited foreign agents the ability to infiltrate the smartphones and computer networks of foreign governments, hostile intelligence services, and terrorist groups. The thief was Josh Schulte, a borderline sociopath and avid child-pornography collector whom the CIA had hired in 2012, at the age of twenty-one. He helped to make these tools at the Operations Support Branch of the CIA's Center for Cyber Intelligence, where a frat house atmosphere prevailed. Schulte was such a disruptive force, raging at his colleagues and superiors, that his powers as a systems administrator had been revoked. Furious at the loss of his privileges, he had secretly restored them, broken into the developer network, and stolen the entire toolbox. He had sent everything to WikiLeaks in late April and early May 2016, just as Assange was preparing to publish the first set of documents the Russians had stolen from the Democratic National Committee.

The thievery devastated the CIA. "The capabilities we had been developing for years that were now described in public were decimated," said Sean Roche, the number two man at the CIA's digital directorate. "Our operations were immediately at risk." Scores if not hundreds were curtailed or shut down, including espionage against Russian, Chinese, North Korean, Iranian, al Qaeda, and ISIS targets. Many of the operations depended on recruited foreign agents who had, at great danger, done things like placing a CIA thumb drive into an adversary's computer. The loss "immediately undermined the relationships we had . . . with vital foreign partners, who had often put themselves at risk to assist the agency," Roche said. Rebuilding the cyberespionage arsenal would cost the CIA hundreds of millions of dollars in the coming years.

A CIA task force reported in October, two months after the FBI arrested Schulte: "We did not realize the loss had occurred until a year later, when WikiLeaks publicly announced it." Worse yet, "had the data been stolen for the benefit of a state adversary and not published, we might still be unaware of the loss." The report assumed that Assange had shared everything, including the source code for the hacking tools, with the Russians. "The WikiLeaks Vault 7 disclosures have brought to light multiple ongoing CIA failures," the task force continued. The CIA's officers had "prioritized building cyber weapons at the expense of securing their own systems. Day-to-day security practices had become woefully lax. . . . We failed to empower any single officer with the ability to ensure that all Agency information systems are built secure and remain so throughout their life cycle. Because no one had that ability, no one was accountable."

Trump was intrigued by a self-styled intelligence community whistleblower named William Binney whom he had seen on Fox News arguing that the CIA had used the hacking tools to frame the Kremlin for its role in the 2016 election. The conspiracy theory was endorsed by Fox hosts Sean Hannity and Ann Coulter, as well as the Russian foreign minister Sergei Lavrov. The president ordered Pompeo to invite Binney to CIA headquarters and hear him make the case that the attack on American democracy was an inside job. By Binney's account, Pompeo listened carefully for an hour and suggested that officials at the FBI and the NSA would be interested in his story. "The intelligence community wasn't being honest here," Binney said. "I am quite willing to help people who need the truth to find the truth." The CIA director did not record this encounter in his memoir.

Pompeo struck back against WikiLeaks throughout the summer and fall of 2017. By calling it a hostile intelligence service, he freed the CIA to undertake aggressive counterintelligence operations to disrupt it, and from the time of the Vault 7 hack onward, the group did not obtain American government secrets. He said that "you only need to go to WikiLeaks' Twitter account to see that every month they remind people that you can be an intern at the CIA and become a really dynamite whistleblower. . . . I think our intelligence community has a lot of work to figure out how to respond to them." Then he went after Assange as best he could. The CIA's London station spied on him at his Ecuadorian embassy hideout and learned that Russia planned to smuggle him out to Moscow, according to William Evanina, the national counterintelligence chief. This led Pompeo to consider a kidnapping plan to render him into American custody. Nothing came of it. Assange had not yet been indicted for espionage, and the idea of carrying out an extrajudicial rendition in London was anathema to the CIA's lawyers. He remained holed up in a three-hundred-square-foot room at the embassy.

In the spring of 2019, Ecuador revoked its grant of asylum to Assange, the British police swiftly executed an arrest warrant, and the United States indicted him on espionage charges for stealing secrets in concert with Chelsea Manning. ("I know nothing about WikiLeaks," Trump said after Assange's arrest.) He spent the next five years in a British prison fighting extradition to America. Finally, four months after Josh Schulte received a forty-year sentence, Assange agreed to plead guilty and went free.

He never was charged for his role in the Vault 7 theft. Trump never said anything about the cyberattack on the CIA. His last words about Assange were: "I think he's been treated very badly."

"A surrender agreement with the Taliban"

As a candidate, and in his first months as commander in chief, Trump had railed against the war in Afghanistan, calling for an immediate and unilateral withdrawal of American troops. The CIA warned of the consequences: the Taliban would return to power instantly, and al Qaeda would revive as a threat to the United States within a year or two. Now his stance had changed. He still wanted out, but he wanted to win. He didn't trust his generals—whom he called "a bunch of dopes and babies" to their faces—to defeat the Taliban.* So he called in the CIA.

Pompeo met with Trump in mid-July 2017 at his club in Bedminster, New Jersey, bringing top officers from the special activities division, the counterterrorism center, and the South and Central Asia mission center. They proposed spending tens of millions of dollars to beat the Taliban into submission. This proved, in the short run, politically expedient for the president. "The American people don't mind if there are CIA teams waging a covert war there," said Ken Stiles, a veteran counterterrorism officer. "They mind if there's 50,000 U.S. troops there." Thus Afghanistan became Pompeo's war in the summer of 2017, and so it remained. He took charge of drone strikes as soon as Trump abrogated Obama's rules designed to avoid killing civilians. He ordered a small battalion of paramilitary officers to attack the leadership of the Taliban and the Haqqani network, a terrorist mafia created by a veteran of the CIA's war against the Soviets during the 1980s, which ran military operations and sent suicide bombers against the Afghan government and its American allies.

---

* This tirade, during an all-hands meeting at the Pentagon on July 20, 2017, prompted Secretary of State Rex Tillerson to mutter that Trump was "a fucking moron." The remark was duly reported by the press and Tillerson did not disavow it. Trump had hired Tillerson, a globe-trotting oil executive, on the recommendation of none other than Bob Gates, who had met him when they served on the board of the Boy Scouts of America. Trump had taken note of the rebuke, and he had determined to fire Tillerson and replace him with Pompeo when the right moment arrived.

Pompeo publicly vowed that the CIA was going to break their backs. "We can't perform our mission if we're not aggressive, vicious, unforgiving, relentless," he said in an October 12 speech. "We have to be focused on crushing our enemies." The new motto of the CIA's Kabul station, posted on the wall, was "Win Quickly"—to change the course of the war before Trump changed his mind again. The new strategy lasted less than six months. By the spring of 2018, the American military estimated that the Taliban's forces had grown to roughly sixty thousand fighters, more than twice what they had been seven years before, and four times the size of the American military in Afghanistan.

Now Trump wanted out again. He made Pompeo secretary of state on April 26, 2018, and ordered him to make a deal with the Taliban. The plan had been to force the enemy to come to the negotiating table. Pompeo delivered the negotiating table to the enemy. He chose Zalmay Khalilzad—the Afghan-born American diplomat who had served as Bush's ambassador in Kabul, Baghdad, and the United Nations—as his envoy. ("I hear he's a con man," Trump said at an Oval Office meeting with Pompeo, Haspel, and the rest of his national security team. "Although you need a con man for this.") Khalilzad's negotiations with the Taliban at a luxurious hotel in Doha, the capital of Qatar, duplicitously excluded the Afghan government. Pompeo also did his best to conceal the details of the deal he was striking from everyone else in the American government.

But he let the Taliban know that "the United States was ready to cut and run from the country and provide international legitimacy to the enemy while doing so," said Lisa Curtis, a longtime CIA analyst, the National Security Council's senior director for South and Central Asia from 2017 to 2021, and a leading member of the American delegation at Doha. "Everything about the way in which the United States negotiated with the Taliban signaled desperation for a deal that would cloak its troop withdrawal in the guise of a negotiated peace settlement." When the existence of the negotiations leaked, Pompeo and Khalilzad repeatedly vowed that the Taliban would break ties with al Qaeda, tuning out the CIA's reporting that this belief was a delusion. Trump wanted to invite the Taliban's leaders to Camp David to seal the Doha accord—right before the anniversary of the September 11 attacks. (His briefer, the CIA veteran Beth Sanner, sardonically asked her colleagues: "Is Ivanka going to wear a burqa?") That photo opportunity never happened. But the deal was done nonetheless.

Two days before the pact was signed, Trump received a report in the President's Daily Brief that Russian military intelligence officers had paid Taliban fighters millions of dollars to attack American and NATO troops in Afghanistan. The bounties were Putin's payback for the CIA's multibillion-dollar support for the Afghan resistance during the Soviet occupation of the 1980s. The going rate was $200,000 for a dead American. Trump and Pompeo studiously ignored the CIA's reporting in the name of their own devious deal with the Taliban.

"The Doha agreement had a really pernicious effect on the government of Afghanistan and on its military—psychological more than anything else—but we set a date certain for when we were going to leave and when they could expect all assistance to end," said Gen. Frank McKenzie, the head of Central Command. The agreement also committed the United States to ending air strikes against the Taliban. As the Taliban got stronger, the Afghan government and its army faced an unrelenting attack.

In executing the president's orders, Pompeo was paving the way for the most devastating American defeat since Vietnam. Seeing the consequence, Trump's second national security adviser, H. R. McMaster, said bluntly: "Our secretary of state signed a surrender agreement with the Taliban."

Chapter Twenty-Four

THE ENEMY OF INTELLIGENCE

"I know CIA like the back of my hand," Gina Haspel said at her confirmation hearing before the Senate intelligence committee on May 9, 2018. "I know what we need to be successful in our mission."

Haspel was the first career clandestine service officer chosen to lead the CIA in forty-five years, and the first woman ever. Half of her life as a spy had been spent running or overseeing operations against the Russians, their allies, and their agents. As deputy director, she had spent weeks before the hearing working with her British counterparts to prove that Putin's spies had tried to kill a former Russian intelligence officer in England with a military-grade nerve agent. She had personally convinced Trump to strike back against Russia's covert operations by expelling sixty spies from their diplomatic posts in Washington and New York, by far the strongest action his administration ever took against the Kremlin. Putin retaliated tit-for-tat against Americans at the Moscow embassy and the St. Petersburg consulate, a severe but temporary setback for the CIA's espionage mission in Russia.

She painted a romantic portrait of her first years as a spy. "I recall very well my first meeting with a foreign agent," she recounted. (This had been in Ethiopia, in the late 1980s, when the nation was still in the Soviet orbit, and the CIA-backed guerillas were fighting the socialist government in a long and brutal civil war.) "It was on a dark, moonless night, with an agent I'd never met before. When I picked him up, he passed me the intelligence and I passed him an extra five hundred dollars for the men he led. It was the beginning of an adventure I had only dreamed of."

Haspel had been the chief of station in New York in 2011 and 2012, where she had maintained an extraordinary liaison with David Cohen, the New York City Police Department's deputy commissioner of intelligence and a thirty-five-year CIA veteran.* Haspel worked with a secret NYPD team, the Demographics Unit, created by a CIA officer who became Cohen's right-hand man. The unit was staffed by cops of Pakistani and Arabic heritage who ran informants and infiltrated Muslim communities throughout the city and its suburbs in the name of counterterrorism. The CIA's charter forbids it from spying on Americans, but Cohen could do it on Haspel's behalf. He had been her patron at the CIA. In 1996, when Cohen was the chief of the clandestine service, he made Haspel the station chief in Azerbaijan, a former Soviet republic wedged between Russia and Iran; she then became a deputy chief of Russian operations in 1998. She thanked Cohen, without naming him, in her testimony: "When a very tough, old-school leader announced that I was his pick to be chief of station in a small but important frontier post, a few competitors complained to me directly: Why would they send you? I owe that leader much for believing in me at a time when few women were given these opportunities." Haspel eventually would promote three women to the top of the CIA's chain of command—Beth Kimber to run the clandestine service, Didi Rapp as chief of intelligence analysis, and Dawn Meyerriecks to head the science and technology directorate.

Now she was at the apex of her thirty-three-year career. Any other nominee with her experience might have been confirmed unanimously. But the question of torture nearly derailed her. Haspel's stint at the black site in Thailand, where she had presided over brutal waterboarding fifteen

---

* Not to be confused with the David Cohen who had been the CIA's deputy director under John Brennan. After the Associated Press ran a Pulitzer Prize–winning series on the CIA-NYPD liaison in 2011, reporting that they had "blurred the bright line between foreign and domestic spying," the CIA's inspector general conducted an investigation that cleared Haspel and her officers.

years before, consumed most of the two-and-a-half-hour hearing, her first public appearance before the American people.

Senator Kamala Harris of California, drawing on her training as a prosecutor, interrogated her sharply:

> Q: Do you believe that the previous interrogation techniques were immoral?
>
> A: Senator, I believe that CIA officers, to whom you referred—
>
> Q: It's a yes or no answer. Do you believe the previous interrogation techniques were immoral? I'm not asking do you believe they were legal. I'm asking do you believe they were immoral?
>
> A: Senator, I believe that CIA—
>
> Q: It's a yes or no.
>
> A: —did extraordinary work to prevent another attack on this country, given the legal tools that we were authorized to use.
>
> Q: Please answer yes or no. Do you believe in hindsight that those techniques were immoral?
>
> A: Senator, what I believe sitting here today is that I support the higher moral standard we have decided to hold ourselves to.
>
> Q: Can you please answer the question?
>
> A: Senator, I think I've answered the question.
>
> Q: No, you've not.

Haspel's amoral answers turned nearly half the Senate against her. She was confirmed by a margin of five votes only after sending the intelligence committee a letter saying: "With the benefit of hindsight and my experience as a senior agency leader, the enhanced interrogation program is not one the CIA should have undertaken."

The senators had given almost every other issue short shrift. They had one question about Trump's hostility toward American intelligence. Haspel had deflected it. They asked no questions about Russia. Soon there would be a multitude. As he had from the start of his campaign, Trump continued to show that he was in Putin's thrall. He kept trashing the CIA and the FBI, disparaging their espionage and counterintelligence work, calling it a conspiracy aimed at undermining the legitimacy of his election and sabotaging his presidency. Over the following thirty months, Haspel would have to confront the fact that Trump was a priceless geopolitical ally to Putin, supporting his policies, parroting his propaganda, and denying the evidence of his political warfare against American democracy.

She was the first director who ever had to grapple with a terrible dilemma: what should the CIA do when the president of the United States is a threat to national security?

"A fictional narrative"

On July 13, Dan Coats, the national intelligence director, told Congress that the Russians threatened to sabotage America's computer networks and governmental systems, including the coming midterm elections. He invoked 9/11: "The warning lights are blinking red again," he said. "The digital infrastructure that serves this country is literally under attack." The same day, Robert S. Mueller III, the special counsel leading the investigation of Russia's role in the 2016 election, indicted twelve GRU officers for Putin's assault on American democracy. Mueller had the Russians' true names, their American aliases, their ties to Assange and, through him, to the Trump campaign. Some of his evidence came from the CIA's counterintelligence center and their Russia House colleagues. The special counsel already had won convictions against Trump's first national security adviser, Mike Flynn, for lying about his secret dealings with the Russians, and Trump's first campaign chairman, Paul Manafort, for crimes including his corrupt dealings with pro-Putin politicians in Ukraine. Mueller also had indicted Manafort's business partner, the Russian intelligence operative Konstantin Kilimnik.

Manafort had long promoted a conspiracy theory, first voiced by Kilimnik, that the Russians were not to blame for hacking the computer server of the Democratic campaign. The Ukrainians had done it, framed the Kremlin for it, and conspired with the Democrats to smuggle the server into the hands of a Ukrainian oligarch. This outrageous lie was "a fictional narrative that has been perpetrated and propagated by the Russian security services themselves," said Fiona Hill, the National Security Council's senior director for Russia and Europe. But Trump said he knew it was true, because Putin had told him so during a private meeting at the Group of 20 summit in Hamburg in July 2017. Fixated on the falsehood, he had ordered his personal lawyer, Rudy Giuliani, the former mayor of New York, to go to Ukraine and find proof that the lie was the truth.

On July 16, 2018, Trump stood side by side with Putin at a press conference in Helsinki. A reporter asked: "Just now, President Putin denied having anything to do with the election interference in 2016. Every U.S. intelligence agency has concluded that Russia did. My first question for you, sir, is who do you believe? My second question is would you now, with the whole world watching, tell President Putin, would you denounce what happened in 2016 and would you warn him to never do it again?" Trump said he had "two thoughts." He began: "Where is the server? I want to know where is the server and what is the server saying?" And then he said: "My people came to me, Dan Coats came to me, and some others. They said they think it's Russia. I have President Putin. He just said it's not Russia. I will say this: I don't see any reason why it would be. . . . I will tell you that President Putin was extremely strong and powerful in his denial today. But I really do want to see the server," he said. "Where are those servers? They're missing. Where are they?" The press corps was first mystified—what servers?—then astonished. The president had cut the throat of American intelligence while Putin looked on smirking.

Trump's kowtow set off an explosion. "I've seen Russian intelligence manipulate many people over my professional career and I never would have thought that the U.S. President would become one of the ones getting played by old KGB hands," said Congressman Will Hurd, a veteran CIA officer and a Republican member of the House intelligence committee. Brennan said that Trump's performance was "nothing short of treasonous." Panetta called it "one of the most tragic moments in the history of the relationship between a United States president and the intelligence community."

Coats and his colleagues wondered aloud what Putin had on Trump. They had no answer. Pompeo kept his silence, and so did Haspel. When she spoke with Trump in the Oval Office in the months after Helsinki, she did not contradict or confront him. She kept a gimlet eye on intelligence briefings about Russia which might inflame Trump's simmering fury at the CIA, and never spoke out in public to defend her workforce in the face of the president's attacks. "Those of us who have worked with Haspel over the years had little expectation that she would push back against this president," said the senior counterterrorism officer Douglas London, a thirty-four-year CIA veteran who had run operations against the Russians across the Middle East and Asia.

But Haspel pushed back hard against Trump after the October 2 murder of Jamal Khashoggi, a crusading journalist who wrote opinion columns for the *Washington Post* criticizing the repressive Saudi regime. Khashoggi was killed and dismembered with a bone saw at the Saudi consulate in Istanbul on orders from the kingdom's de facto ruler, Crown Prince Muhammad bin Salman. The prince had wooed and won the Trump White House by cultivating the president's son-in-law, Jared Kushner, who received a $2 billion investment for his start-up private equity firm from the Saudis in 2021. Their bromance, along with the Saudis' promises to purchase hundreds of billions of dollars of American weapons, was a pillar of Trump's foreign policy in the Middle East. Trump brushed off the charge of murder, defending the Saudi ruler in public and in private meetings with members of Congress. "I saved his ass," Trump later told the *Washington Post*'s Bob Woodward. "I was able to get Congress to leave him alone. . . . He says very strongly that he didn't do it."

The CIA said he did do it. "The Crown Prince viewed Khashoggi as a threat to the Kingdom and broadly supported using violent measures if necessary to silence him," the agency concluded, and he had sent his personal security force to carry out the killing. After Haspel reported what the CIA knew to Congress behind closed doors, she authorized her officers to tell the *Post* precisely how they knew. Their evidence included an audio recording from an eavesdropping device the Turks had planted inside the Saudi consulate. "The Turks gave the CIA a copy of that audio," the *Post* reported on November 16, "and the agency's director, Gina Haspel, has listened to it." (Two decades before, Haspel had served as deputy chief of station in Turkey. She spoke the language, she had maintained deep ties to Turkish intelligence, and she had flown to Ankara to hear the tape for herself.) "The audio shows that Khashoggi was killed within moments of entering the consulate," the *Post*'s story continued. "Khashoggi died in the office of the Saudi consul general, who can be heard expressing his displeasure that Khashoggi's body now needed to be disposed of." The fact that Haspel had put her name on the *Post*'s account underscored that the intelligence was ironclad. Trump flew into a rage when he saw the story. "They did not come to a conclusion," he lied. "The CIA doesn't say they did it." The CIA didn't have facts, he said, but "feelings"—another outrageous rebuke. He believed the prince, just as he had believed Putin, more than his intelligence service. He never trusted Haspel after that. Nor could she trust him.

Trump's hostility boiled over after Haspel testified to Congress about the threats facing the United States on January 29, 2019. She directly contradicted the president's claims that he had defeated ISIS ("They're still dangerous," she said), that Iran was defying sanctions against its pursuit of the bomb ("They are in compliance"), and that he had personally defused the North Korean nuclear threat (Kim remained "committed to developing a long-range nuclear-armed missile that would pose a direct threat to the United States"). The president struck back with barbed insults. "Perhaps Intelligence should go back to school!" he tweeted. "The Intelligence people seem to be extremely passive and naïve. . . . They are wrong!"

His mind was made up. He did not want to be confused with facts. He was an ideologue—if rants and rages could be called ideas—and ideology was the enemy of intelligence.

"The existential danger to the nation"

By attacking Haspel and the CIA, and embracing dictators and despots, the president was exerting "a strong and inappropriate public political pressure to get the intelligence community leadership aligned with his political goals," said Doug Wise, the four-time CIA station chief whose missions had ranged across the world. "The existential danger to the nation is when the policymaker corrupts the role of the intelligence agencies, which is to provide unbiased and apolitical intelligence to inform policy."

Trump now steered the ship of state not by the compass of his counsellors but by his zigzag impulses and zealous grievances. By early 2019, after two years in office, he had rid himself of the people who had restrained his worst instincts, such as Secretary of Defense Jim Mattis and White House chief of staff John Kelly, both retired four-star generals who pointedly noted that they had sworn allegiance to the Constitution, not to the president. "He's an idiot," Kelly concluded, and a fascist to boot. "It's pointless to try to convince him of anything. He's gone off the rails." His third national security adviser, John Bolton, an ardent hawk, found he could not reason with the president, and soon gave up trying.*

After sacking Attorney General Jeff Sessions for failing to derail the Mueller investigation, Trump replaced him with Bill Barr, who had led the Justice Department under the first President Bush. Barr, as a junior at the elite Horace Mann prep school in New York in the late 1960s, had startled a college guidance counsellor who asked about his ambitions. "I told him that my career goal was to become director of the CIA," Barr recounted. "It was a short interview." He had indeed worked for the CIA in the 1970s, as an intern, an analyst, and a low-level liaison to Congress, before joining the Justice Department in the Reagan and Bush administrations. Like Dick Cheney, whom he had known well, he was a fervent believer in the unitary executive theory of presidential power. The theory holds that the president has absolute authority over the entire federal

---

* Mattis wrote in 2020: "Donald Trump is the first president in my lifetime who does not try to unite the American people—does not even pretend to try. Instead, he tries to divide us." Kelly said in 2023 that Trump "has no idea what America stands for and has no idea what America is all about, [and] has nothing but contempt for our democratic institutions, our Constitution, and the rule of law." Bolton wrote in 2024: "Trump is unfit to be president. If his first four years were bad, a second four will be worse." It's still astonishing today to read the memoirs of Bolton and Barr, which record the unhinged ravings of the president and his detachment from reality, and remember that they kept a conspiracy of silence while he remained in office.

government, and that Congress and the courts cannot restrain him, especially in matter of national security. Trump took this to mean that he had, as he said, "the right to do whatever I want as president." And that included using the Justice Department to destroy his political enemies, real and imagined, inside and outside the government.

Trump thought the CIA was the capital of the "Deep State," a cryptocracy of spies and soldiers and diplomats usurping his powers and hellbent on destroying him. His conspiratorial mind had contorted the Russia investigation—led by the lifelong Republican and longtime FBI director Robert Mueller—into an immense plot secretly run by the Obama administration's intelligence chiefs. He said Obama had wiretapped Trump Tower during the previous campaign—and that the CIA might be spying on him still. He charged that Brennan had used the British electronic-eavesdropping service, GCHQ, as a cut-out to keep the CIA's fingerprints off the surveillance. This would have taken place while Haspel was the London station chief. GCHQ issued a rare public statement calling the accusation "utterly ridiculous."

Barr was a cynical man, and though he knew better, he played along with the president's delusions. "I think spying did occur," Barr said. "I need to explore that." First, he did his best to suppress Mueller's special counsel report and sow doubt about its conclusions: the Russians had worked to help Trump win, the Trump campaign worked with them, and Trump tried to obstruct justice during the investigation. Second, he assigned John Durham—the same federal prosecutor who had declined to file charges in the killings and torture of CIA prisoners—to investigate the investigators of the FBI and the CIA. Durham grilled Brennan, along with senior CIA analysts and counterintelligence officers, about their conclusions that Russia had come to Trump's aid. Brennan correctly surmised that Trump wanted him tried for treason. And third, Barr argued on Trump's behalf for opening the CIA's operational files on the Russian election attack for the president's review. Trump somehow believed they would expose the evils of the Deep State.

Haspel repeatedly refused to release them. She infuriated Trump by repelling his assaults on the citadel of secrets. The CIA had a well-founded fear that the president might expose its sources and methods to the world. Trump had a habit of taking top secret documents to his White House residence and never returning them, including files on covert operations and the recruited foreign agents of the clandestine service. He believed they belonged to him.

"The whole scheme was bound to backfire"

By the spring of 2019, many of Trump's thoughts on foreign policy issues of life and death depended not on the CIA's analysis or the NSC's advice, but on the cajoling of Vladimir Putin.

The Russian leader had talked him into thinking that North Korea posed no nuclear threat, a falsehood which the CIA's reporting refuted. More ominous, Putin had persuaded the president to withdraw American forces from Syria and leave the conflict to Moscow. That decision led Defense Secretary Mattis to resign in protest, enraged CIA officers who had risked their lives to support the Syrian opposition, and opened the door for Russia to return to its cold war status as a power broker in the region. "In Syria, the president had, over the course of a single week, reversed decades of successful U.S. government efforts—which I participated in on the ground in multiple Middle Eastern countries as an operations officer—to remove Russia as a major player in the Middle East," said Marc Polymeropoulos, who served as the CIA's deputy chief for Russia at the time. He was enraged to see video footage of Russian soldiers hoisting their flag over an abandoned American base in Syria, symbolizing "the total public humiliation of the U.S. government. Russian propaganda organs celebrated this picture, understanding too well how far the U.S. has fallen."

At Helsinki, in their private one-on-one, Putin had convinced Trump that Ukraine had hacked the 2016 election to help Clinton. Thus indoctrinated, Trump now believed that the Ukrainians had not only purloined the phantom Democratic National Committee server but formed a crooked alliance with Joe Biden, a contender for the 2020 election. This fantasy, fueled by Russian disinformation and stoked by the frenetic Rudy Giuliani, began to consume Trump. He seethed over it and commanded Pompeo and Bolton to do something about it. Meanwhile, Giuliani was sending the president and the secretary of state packages of propaganda delivered by Kremlin-backed politicians in Ukraine. Barr thought Giuliani was an "unguided missile," his mission "idiotic beyond belief," and his reports to the White House a ticking time bomb. "The whole scheme was bound to backfire," he wrote three years later, though he never breathed a word at the time. The only leading figure in Trump's world who spoke up was his first homeland security adviser, Tom Bossert, another man of expertise and experience whom Trump had driven out of office. "That conspiracy theory has got to go," he said. "If he continues to focus on that white whale, it's going to bring him down."

The CIA station in Kyiv had a keen and continuing interest in the Russian intelligence agents who fed lies to Giuliani and, through him, to Trump and the American people. Haspel was well aware of the president's obsession and knew he was chasing an illusion. The CIA's analysts later concluded that Putin himself was overseeing the disinformation operation, as part of a new political warfare campaign to help Trump win reelection in 2020.

On April 25, the United States ambassador to Ukraine, Marie Yovanovitch, picked up her phone in Kyiv at one a.m. and heard a State Department officer ordering her to quit her post and fly home on the next plane. The command had come from Trump, at the insistence of Giuliani, and it had been executed by Pompeo, who feigned innocence as he fed the ambassador to the wolves. The president's lawyer swore that she had been undermining his efforts to persuade the government of Ukraine to investigate Biden, who had kicked off his campaign for the White House later that day. Her ouster had "a really devastating effect on the morale of all the teams that I work with" at the NSC, the CIA, and the State Department, Fiona Hill said.

The ambassador left Kyiv on the day of the inauguration of Volodymyr Zelensky, the new president of Ukraine, an actor who had played that role in a popular television comedy. Zelensky now commanded a beleaguered army that had been fighting the Russians and Kremlin-backed separatists in eastern Ukraine for five years and had lost some thirteen thousand soldiers in battle. The United States had committed more than $1.5 billion in arms and materiel to Ukraine since the Russians first attacked in 2014. The Pentagon and the State Department had promised to send $391 million more before September 30, including sniper rifles, rocket-propelled grenade launchers, counter-artillery radars, night-vision equipment, and more.

Trump spoke with Putin again on May 3. Fiona Hill was on the call; a transcript went to CIA headquarters. She told her colleagues that Putin had "extensively talked Ukraine down, said it was corrupt, said Zelensky was in the thrall of oligarchs." The Russian autocrat had by now shaped Trump's perception on how to use power. "In the course of his presidency," Hill later wrote, "Trump would come more to resemble Putin in political practice and predilection than he resembled any of his recent presidential predecessors." He wasn't making America great again. He was making it more like Russia.

Trump told the acting White House chief of staff, Mick Mulvaney, a founder of the right-wing House Freedom Caucus who once had called Trump "a terrible human being," to hold up the $391 million in military aid as leverage on Zelensky. On July 10, Gordon Sondland, a wealthy campaign donor whom Trump had named ambassador to the European Union, braced the Ukrainian national security adviser, who was at the White House seeking to arrange a face-to-face talk between Zelensky and Trump. In the presence of Hill and a close aide, Sondland said Mulvaney could make that meeting happen—if the Ukrainians joined Giuliani in pursuit of the white whale.

Hill was aghast. So was a senior CIA analyst in his thirties, a slender man with a wispy beard and a 2010 master's degree from Harvard in Russia, Eastern Europe, and Central Asia studies. He had risen rapidly as a Ukraine expert at the CIA and he had been detailed to the National Security Council staff in 2017. He had returned to the agency after finding the Trump White House untenable. More than a few idealistic young people join the CIA with the romantic notion that they might be a witness to history, and perhaps even change its course. He was about to have that chance.

Trump called his July 25 conversation with Zelensky "a perfect phone call." First, he dangled the promised military aid. Then he said: "I would like you to do us a favor, though." Ukraine would get the weapons once his government dug up dirt on Biden. He told Zelensky that Giuliani and Barr would be calling him to follow through. Trump was acting like a mob boss, practicing extortion posing as statecraft. Pompeo had heard every word of the conversation. Hill's NSC deputy for Europe, Alexander Vindman, was on the call too, listening in from the Situation Room. Unlike Pompeo, he did not hold his peace. Vindman, a Ukraine-born U.S. Army lieutenant colonel awarded a Purple Heart in Iraq, told his twin brother, Eugene, the NSC's ethics lawyer: "If what I just heard becomes public, the president will be impeached." Trump later fired both of them.

The CIA analyst read Kyiv's official report on the call, including Trump's demands, on a Ukrainian government website. He began digging into the case. He spoke by phone with Fiona Hill, who had just resigned and was unwinding in Hawaii. He went to the White House to consult Vindman, whom he knew from his time at the NSC. Vindman described Trump's tactics as "crazy" and "frightening"—as the analyst reported in a whistleblower's complaint he sent, anonymously, to the office of the intelligence community's inspector general, Michael Atkinson, a career Justice Department lawyer. The August 12 letter began:

> In the course of my official duties, I have received information from multiple U.S. Government officials that the President of the United States is using the power of his office to solicit interference from a foreign country in the 2020 U.S. election. This interference includes, among other things, pressuring a foreign country to investigate one of the President's main domestic political rivals. The President's personal lawyer, Mr. Rudolph Giuliani, is a central figure in this effort. Attorney General Barr appears to be involved as well.

None of what the whistleblower reported was a secret within Trump's inner circle. They all knew he had strong-armed the leader of Ukraine, who was fighting Russia for his nation's survival, to help himself win re-election as president of the United States. Trump explicitly told Bolton he was freezing the military aid unless and until Ukraine delivered the dirt. Pompeo, as always, stayed silent and complicit. Only Barr took action: when he learned about the whistleblower's letter from the CIA's general counsel, he did his best to bury it, since Trump had implicated him in the scheme. But he failed.

After taking the time to deem the accusations both credible and urgent, Atkinson determined that the law commanded him to send the letter to the congressional intelligence committees, which he did four weeks later. Trump soon fired him too.

"The intelligence agencies have run amok"

Dan Coats knew his days as director of national intelligence had been numbered ever since Helsinki, and he had privately decided to resign at summer's end. The president threw him overboard beforehand. On July 28, three days after the perfect phone call, Trump had tweeted Coats out of office without warning and announced his replacement: John Ratcliffe, an archconservative three-term Texas congressman. Ratcliffe had run for election with a campaign biography that invented his accomplishments as a federal prosecutor in terrorism cases. He had been a personal-injury lawyer and the mayor of Heath, Texas, population seven thousand, before winning his seat. Ratcliffe had been on the House intelligence committee for less than a year, his attendance spotty and his grasp of the issues scant. But the president had seen him on Fox News railing against "the Russia hoax" and he liked the way he looked on TV.

Trump said Ratcliffe was going help him bring the CIA to heel: "I think we need somebody like that that's strong and can really rein it in. As you've all learned, the intelligence agencies have run amok. They've run amok." This pronouncement was the first clear sign that the president was prepared to place political hacks in control of American intelligence to protect his power. But within a week, Trump was forced to withdraw the nomination. The Senate's leading Republicans told the White House they would not confirm Ratcliffe; he was a lightweight and a blowhard, unfit for the office. They would change their tune come the spring of 2020, when Trump resurrected Ratcliffe as the nation's intelligence czar, ramming his nomination through the Senate and setting him on a course to control the CIA at Trump's command.

On September 10, after the congressional intelligence committees received the whistleblower's letter from the inspector general, House Democrats launched an investigation of the president, which led swiftly to an impeachment inquiry. Trump suspected a mole within the National Security Council. "I want to know who's the person who gave the whistleblower the information because that's close to a spy," he said on September 26. "You know what we used to do in the old days when we were smart? Right? With spies and treason, right? We used to handle them a little differently than we do now."

The whistleblower was publicly savaged in Congress and online after House Republicans leaked his name to right-wing trolls. His life was threatened repeatedly; the CIA assigned him bodyguards and advised him to leave his home for a succession of hotel rooms. He recorded in writing his "extreme apprehension about the backlash against me" and his fear that "I will be stuck with Trump's ire." He wasn't the only person who faced violent harassment for standing up to Trump, who could marshal a mob with a tweet. "Many people were hounded out of the National Security Council because they became frightened about their own security," Hill testified at the impeachment inquiry. She herself was receiving death threats and vicious telephone calls at her home from Trump supporters accusing her of "colluding with all kinds of enemies of the President."

After Congressman Adam Schiff of California, a former prosecutor and chairman of the House intelligence committee, took the lead in the impeachment hearings, Trump assaulted him in hundreds of tweets—*corrupt, maniac, deranged*—and the ensuing threats against his life earned Schiff a twenty-four-hour security detail. The president ordered his aides to stonewall the hearings and ignore subpoenas commanding them to appear. Ambassadors, senior State Department officials, and NSC officers nonetheless testified under oath about the president's shakedown of Ukraine. Trump called them "human scum."

On December 18, the House impeached the president for his abuse of power and his obstruction of Congress. Conviction required a two-thirds vote in the Senate, where the Republicans refused to hear a single witness and, inevitably, acquitted him. Before they did, Schiff gave then a warning.

"He has betrayed our national security and he will do it again," he said. "He has compromised our elections and he will do so again. You will not change him. You cannot constrain him."

Chapter Twenty-Five

"WE ARE ON THE WAY TO A RIGHT-WING COUP"

Tom Rakusan was on a mission to penetrate the Kremlin. The CIA's spymaster had fought against Saddam Hussein and al Qaeda, but the Russians were his greatest enemy. His hatred was bred in the bone. His parents were Czech; he was nine years old when Soviet tanks and troops crushed the Prague Spring uprising in 1968. He saw Putin's attack on America as another 9/11. And the CIA had been blindsided by it.

Rakusan had taken over the clandestine service when Greg Vogle retired in August 2017, after serving as his deputy for two years. He had already vowed to undertake a gut renovation of the CIA's Russia House, established seven decades before to gather intelligence on the Soviet Union and run covert operations to undermine Soviet influence around the world. Penetrating the high councils of the Kremlin had been the greatest aspiration of the early CIA, a goal never achieved. The mission was revived with a vital urgency.

Rakusan began by bringing in scores of counterterrorism officers who had fought al Qaeda and its descendants over the course of fifteen years. He told them: *The Russians manipulated our fucking elections. How do we make sure this never happens again?* He didn't care if they didn't speak Russian or had never set foot in Moscow. Neither the new deputy chief of the Europe and Eurasia Mission Center, Marc Polymeropoulos, nor the new leader of Russia House, Patrick Weninger, had the benefit of that experience. He said they needed to take their expertise in targeting and recruiting terrorists and turn it against Russia spies, diplomats, and oligarchs. Their goal was to obtain intelligence on the intentions of the Russian leader and his inner circle through espionage.

In addition to sabotaging American democracy, "the Kremlin was attempting to kill dissidents abroad, fomenting unrest across the democracies of Europe, and pursuing a zero-sum policy when it comes to the United States, meaning anything that hurt the U.S. and its allies was good for Russia," Polymeropoulos recounted. "This was the adversary that we faced and we were obliged to counter it in every corner of the globe."

The transformation of Russia House required "a change of mindset, harking back to what we had learned in the past seventeen years during the long wars, and applying that," Weninger said. He had made his name at the CIA ten years before by recruiting and running a midlevel al Qaeda terrorist in Iraq, using the intelligence the agent revealed to take out his fellow jihadists, and then saving his life when his commanders suspected his betrayal. Like Polymeropoulos, he had served in the ultimate hardship post, the Shkin base in Afghanistan, with Vogle as his station chief, and he had been deputy chief of station in Jordan under Rakusan. He had seen the scope of Putin's sabotage of America and its allies as a station chief in Europe from 2014 to 2017. But when the Russia House post came open, a longtime mentor on the seventh floor had warned him: "You don't want that job. We're going to have to make massive changes there. It's going to be hard. People aren't going to want to change." The next day, he said, his mentor called him back: "I thought about it overnight. I want you to take that job. I'm going to change it. You're going to help me change it."

Some among the old guard at Russia House had held "this kind of age-old notion that Russians were not easily recruitable," Polymeropoulos said. "Those of us coming from outside that world said: 'Look, we respect your expertise. But let's take a crack. Be more aggressive. Maybe it's not as hard a target as we think.'" The new leaders wrote a manifesto entitled "A Call to Arms" and sent it to the CIA's workforce. They took their playbook from the counterterrorism center's rapid and resourceful mobilization against al Qaeda in Afghanistan. "We understood that the Russian threat was as serious as the national security challenge we faced on Sept. 12, 2001," Polymeropoulos said. "We could not afford to lose this fight."

Rakusan and Weninger enlisted the chiefs of American national security—secretaries of defense, national security advisers, the directors of the NSA and the FBI. They went to see the leaders of the Senate intelligence committee, whose staff was writing a devastating bipartisan five-volume report on the Russian attack and the Trump campaign's role in it. "There was unanimity on both sides of the aisle about getting off our back foot," Weninger said. How much money do you need? the senators had asked. Go get the bastards. The intelligence committees had delivered tens of millions of dollars, and Russia House had doubled in size in less than two years.

Haspel had given Rakusan all the people he required, cyber tools from the digital directorate, deep dives from the analysts, and her moral support. Rakusan was so dead-set on his goal that he had traded jobs with Beth Kimber in December 2018. Though both were headstrong, and sometimes clashed, they were of one mind about this mission. She became the new clandestine service chief and he took direct command of the Europe and Eurasia Mission Center and, with it, Russia House. On paper, it looked like a step down. In reality, he was stepping up. "What he had done was to reimagine, and get us out of, a paradigm where we're stuck in the early Cold War," said Tom Sylvester, who would go on to lead the clandestine service in 2023. "The heart of the issue was the concrete decisions by which to ensure that we would put daylight into Russia House."

Russia House had long been the most clandestine and cloistered part of the CIA. For forty-five years, until the end of the cold war, it had been the heart of the Soviet Division. The division's previous chief, Milt Bearden, likened it to an isolated village, far back in a high mountain valley, that had been snowed in for decades. The Russia House conference center at headquarters was still decorated with Soviet propaganda posters depicting muscular peasants and handsome soldiers. One-third of Russia House was a back room where operators and analysts had toiled throughout their careers in the greatest secrecy; the nature of their work had not changed fundamentally since Winston Churchill called Stalin's Russia "a riddle, wrapped in a mystery, inside an enigma." They guarded and hoarded intelligence reaped through years of painstaking, difficult, dangerous operations. They were reluctant to share their secrets with outsiders, and everyone was an outsider. They were proud, to the point of arrogance. To their shame, they had failed to see the Kremlin's attack on the 2016 election until it was too late.

Rakusan thought far outside the box as he imposed his will on Russia House. He ordered the old guard in the back room to unseal their secret files, sanitize them to protect sources and methods, and share them with the clandestine service—and, more importantly, America's allies overseas. In the past, those secrets always had been deemed too sensitive; the CIA's intelligence-sharing on Russia had been a one-way street. That all changed, and the result was nothing less than revolutionary. This transformative moment marked the return of espionage to its traditional place of preeminence at the CIA after twenty years in eclipse.

Rakusan and his officers now worked in the closest liaison with the British, the Dutch, the Ukrainians, the Poles, the Czechs, the Estonians, and other services throughout Europe and around the world, cross-fertilizing intelligence, choreographing operations, and recruiting Russian sources. "Morale was extremely high," Polymeropoulos said. "The infectious passion and drive of Rakusan, Kimber, and Weninger reminded many of us, including me, of the harrowing yet invigorating days after 9/11, when the CIA had a similarly clear and laser-focused mission."

Polymeropoulos flew to Moscow for meetings with the CIA station and his Russian counterparts. The Russians knew he was coming and told him stay away, advice he ignored. Before dawn on December 5, 2017, he awoke with a start in his bed at the Marriott Hotel. The room was spinning, he was overcome with nausea and vertigo, he couldn't walk. He had become one among some fifteen hundred Americans—principally spies, diplomats, and military officers—to be struck down in nations including Cuba, Poland, Georgia, Australia, and Taiwan. Was the still-unexplained phenomenon called Havana Syndrome caused by Russian attacks with directed-energy weapons? The CIA's Office of Medical Services didn't think so, but its work was so inept, so widely disparaged within the agency's ranks, that its director, Keith Bass, was compelled to retire. (At this writing, Bass has been nominated by Donald Trump to run the Pentagon's $54 billion Office of Healthcare Systems, and the syndrome's origins remain uncertain.) The debilitating migraines Polymeropoulos suffered forced him to retire from the CIA in December 2018.

"The wild card was sitting in the Oval Office"

By 2019, after two years of rejuvenation, "the CIA was in fact in a very strong position to push back against the Russian threat," Polymeropoulos said. It kept gathering and reporting intelligence on the Russians' political warfare and propaganda campaigns, recruiting new sources on the edges of Putin's inner circle, and gaining momentum as 2020 began. But its counterattack confronted an immense obstacle.

"The wild card was sitting in the Oval Office," Polymeropoulos said. The wrath of the president had made the present day "perhaps the most difficult time to be an intelligence officer since the creation of the CIA in 1947." While the CIA did battle with the Kremlin, its war could not be won, not as long as Trump remained commander in chief and retained his strange alliance with Putin.

The Senate acquitted Trump on February 5, 2020; all but one Republican rejected his impeachment. The absolution unleashed his vengeance. "It clearly did embolden him," John Bolton said. "This is Trump saying, 'I got away with it.' And thinking, If I got away with it once, I can get away with it again." Bolton, who had departed abruptly as Trump's third national security adviser five months before, had never found the integrity or the courage to testify against him.

The White House now became a madhouse, a place "where everything was like a clown car on fire running at full speed into a warehouse full of fireworks," in the words of Stephanie Grisham, then the president's press secretary. Trump began to purge the government of anyone he deemed disloyal, beginning with the State Department ambassadors, National Security Council staffers, and Pentagon officials who had testified in the impeachment inquiry. He raged at the CIA and the national intelligence directorate for reporting that Putin was out to reelect him. He saw them as the pillars of the Deep State and the perpetrators of the Russia hoax. He set out to infiltrate the American intelligence establishment with MAGA foot soldiers who would serve as saboteurs, seeking to kill the messengers or, failing that, the message. Bill Burns, the future CIA director, wrote that Trump was tearing at the foundations of American government: "Taking aim at an imaginary 'deep state,' he has instead created a weak state, an existential threat to the country's democracy and the interests of its citizens."

First Trump keelhauled Joseph Maguire, the acting director of national intelligence. Maguire, a longtime SEAL commander who had retired as a vice admiral and led the National Counterterrorism Center, had taken over the directorate six months before. On February 14, Maguire and Haspel were in the Oval Office trying to tell Trump about the threats to the 2020 election when he erupted without warning. "Hey, Joe," the president said to Maguire, "I understand that you briefed Adam Schiff and that you told him that Russia prefers me." Maguire hadn't been the briefer, but it hardly mattered. With a tweet, he was out, and Trump's henchman Ric Grennell was in as the acting DNI—nominally, Haspel's boss. A right-wing Twitter troll whom the president had appointed ambassador to Germany, where his imperious sniping had outraged the host government, Grennell had no qualifications to be the American intelligence czar save his fealty to Trump, which was absolute, as was his capacity for backstabbing.

At the president's command, Grenell pushed out the leaders of the national intelligence directorate, ridding its top ranks of expertise, and making a devoted MAGA fanatic named Kash Patel his right-hand man. Two years before, Patel had been a Republican aide on the House intelligence committee, assigned to undermine the Russia investigation. Then Trump had appointed him to the NSC staff where, to the great discomfort of his superiors, he had served as the president's mole during the impeachment inquiry. Now the president intended to use Grenell and Patel to spy on the spies for him.

In April, to the horror of Attorney General Barr, Trump tried to make Patel the deputy director of the FBI. "The very idea of moving Patel into a role like this showed a shocking detachment from reality," Barr observed. He vowed that the appointment would happen "over my dead body." After three failed attempts at this subversion, Trump backed down, but not for long. In seven months, he would seek to install Patel as the deputy director of the CIA.

Trump knew the Senate would never confirm Grenell as intelligence czar, so he revived the failed nomination of the Fox News favorite John Ratcliffe to be the nation's intelligence czar, and he rammed the congressman through the once-resistant Republicans in the Senate on May 21. The vote was 49 to 44, the narrowest margin ever for the post. The result put Ratcliffe atop the American intelligence community, with Patel remaining as his principal deputy, both overseeing Haspel, and primed by the president to retaliate against the CIA for its reporting.

They set out to ransack Russia House, rifling through top secret files for anything that might fulfill Trump's desire to deny that he was Putin's chosen candidate, and to support his attack on the CIA as the headquarters of the Deep State conspiracy, the laboratory where the idea that Russia had influenced the election had been invented. Throughout the summer and into the fall, they kept trying to find fragments of raw intelligence in a flailing attempt to score political points for the president's reelection campaign. Haspel resisted them as best she could.

Ratcliffe refused to release the intelligence community's traditional annual threat assessment, which had for three years running surveyed Putin's attacks on the United States. He cut off the flow of classified information to Schiff and his fellow Democrats on the intelligence committee, assailing them as leakers. His own directorate told Congress at the end of his short reign that he had delayed, distorted, and obstructed reporting on Russia's election interference. Above all, he fed Trump's obsession that the Democrats had used the CIA and the NSA to undermine him.

"Obama knew everything. Vice President Biden, dumb as he may be, knew everything," Trump told Fox on August 13. "Brennan and Clapper . . .

spied on my campaign, which is treason. They spied, both before and after I won, using the intelligence apparatus of the United States to take down a president, a legally elected president, a duly elected president of the United States. It is the single biggest political crime in the history of our country."

On August 29, on the president's orders, Ratcliffe canceled all oral intelligence briefings to Congress on the subject of Russian election interference. Schiff and House Speaker Nancy Pelosi howled in protest. "The American people have both the right and the need to know that another nation, Russia, is trying to help decide who their president should be," they said. Biden voiced his objections as well. "President Trump is hoping Vladimir Putin will once more boost his candidacy and cover his horrific failures to lead our country through the multiple crises we are facing. And he does not want the American people to know the steps Vladimir Putin is taking to help Trump get reelected."

But the CIA knew.

"Russia is playing us all like a fiddle"

"We assess that President Vladimir Putin and the senior most Russian officials are aware of and probably directing Russia's influence operations aimed at denigrating the former U.S. Vice President, supporting the U.S. president and fueling public discord ahead of the U.S. election in November," began the August 31 edition of the *WIRe*—formally, the *Worldwide Intelligence Review*. The *WIRe* is a CIA newsletter, classified Top Secret, which circulates among roughly three hundred people at the White House, the Pentagon, and the State Department, along with members of the intelligence committees and the congressional leadership. It's a digest of reporting from the CIA's officers and analysts, the National Security Agency, the FBI, and the departments of State, Treasury, and Homeland Security, along with open-source intelligence.

The influence operations had infected Washington at the highest levels, ensuring that Putin's deceptions were part of Trump's deliberations and Republican discourse. The Russians had picked their useful idiots with precision, and they struck gold with people who could get the president's attention, in person or on television. The Russian spies—along with their Ukrainian agents, Russian state media, trolls, and online proxies posing as Americans—laundered their disinformation about Biden and the coming election through Rudy Giuliani, Fox News, and Republican members of Congress who had the president's ear. Mainlining their lies into the MAGA media empire run by right-wing TV hosts and their guests was a better way of reaching an American audience than Facebook and Twitter had been four years before.

The August 31 *WIRe* cited as an example the work of Andriy Derkach, a Ukrainian lawmaker and longtime Russian intelligence agent. (Derkach was sanctioned ten days later by the Treasury Department for running "a covert influence campaign" to undermine the election, and later indicted for money laundering.) He had worked for many months with Giuliani to libel Biden as corrupt. He had fed his lies to Senator Ron Johnson, the Republican chairman of the Homeland Security committee. In turn, the senator had held theatrical hearings, spewing falsehoods about Biden, his family, and Ukraine. Among them was the charge, which Trump repeated forty-two times on the campaign trail, that Hunter Biden had received $3.5 million from a Russian oligarch.

FBI agents had warned Senator Johnson that he was a target of the influence operation. He blew them off, saying they wanted only "to offer the biased media an opportunity to falsely accuse me of being a tool of Russia." He wasn't the only prominent politician dancing to the Kremlin's tune by amplifying its disinformation in Congress and on television. As Trump's favorite senator, the Republican Lindsey Graham, had noted ruefully: "Russia is playing us all like a fiddle." Graham himself got played. In late September, five weeks before the election, Ratcliffe backhanded the senator a sheaf of documents—previously rejected as baseless by Republicans on the Senate intelligence committee—purporting to show that Hillary Clinton had had a hand in the Russia hoax. Graham released it. Few fell for it.

"Where are all the arrests?"

Coronavirus had been crushing the country since March and the president had been lying about it ever since. He had wanted the CIA to call it a Chinese bioweapon, which it evidently wasn't. He had downplayed the pandemic with a cascade of incoherent speeches. More than four hundred thousand Americans died during the last ten months of his presidency, a toll greater than all the Americans killed in World War Two, and many of those lives were lost as a consequence of Trump's invincible ignorance and incompetence.

Trump was diagnosed with a serious case on October 1. The White House had been a Covid vector for weeks. He had tested positive fifteen days before and, after denying the results, he had infected his wife, more than a few close aides, and a handful of reporters. When he returned to the White House after a three-day course of steroids and experimental drugs at the Walter Reed National Military Medical Center, he was more deranged than ever.

His pursuit of the white whale was pathological. He wanted his opponents imprisoned for conspiring to concoct the Russia hoax. "Where are all the arrests?" he tweeted on October 7. "BIDEN, OBAMA, AND CROOKED HILLARY LED THIS TREASONOUS PLOT!!! BIDEN SHOULDN'T BE ALLOWED TO RUN—GOT CAUGHT!!!" He specifically wanted John Brennan charged with treason for using the CIA to spy on his campaign in 2016, which it hadn't. He buttonholed the attorney general: Why hadn't he indicted the bastard? "As far as we can tell, the CIA stayed in its lane in the run-up to the election," Barr told him. "You buy that bullshit, Bill?" Trump shouted. "Everyone knows Brennan was right in the middle of this." Barr lost his cool. "Well, if you know what happened, Mr. President, I am all ears. Maybe we are wasting our time having an investigation. Maybe all the armchair quarterbacks telling you they have all the evidence can come in and enlighten us."

They did just that. The Trump whisperers were moving into the president's innermost orbit. Chief among them were Rudy Giuliani, his personal lawyer, lost in an alcoholic fog; and Mike Flynn, Trump's disgraced national security adviser, now a devoted adherent to the dark conspiracies of QAnon.* Both were allied with Flynn's lawyer, Sidney Powell, another QAnon aficionado. Flynn called her the guardian angel of American justice; she convinced Trump to pardon him for lying to the FBI about his covert conversations with Russian leaders. "From early in the Trump administration," Barr recounted, "Powell had appeared frequently on Fox news shows challenging the Russiagate narrative." Trump watched her and became a big fan.

Throughout October, Powell furiously attacked the CIA and its director as a subversive force. She was enthralled by a fantasy, which she first publicly espoused on Fox on November 6, three days after the election. She said the CIA had a supercomputer codenamed HAMMER, and a software system called SCORECARD, with the capability to hack the election and steal votes. The CIA had used this diabolical machine to ensure that Obama and Biden won in 2012. John Brennan had used it to advance their agenda of turning America communist. Biden had used it to win the Democratic presidential nomination. And Gina Haspel had programmed it to defeat Trump in 2020.

Haspel already had a prominent place on Trump's enemies list. She had blocked his attempts to ransack the Russia House files on Putin's support for the president. She had resisted his calls to seek out and destroy the CIA whistleblower who had lit the fuse for his impeachment. She had never taken the loyalty oath. She had refused to become part of his campaign. She had not been complicit.

The president determined to fire her, along with the defense secretary

---

* QAnon was an online vortex of insanity. Chief among its tenets was that the Democratic Party was a cabal of Satanic, blood-drinking pedophiles running a child sex-trafficking ring at the core of a criminal racket aimed at defeating Trump. Its adherents believed that Trump was a savior, secretly fighting the cabal of child molesters, and planning to arrest and execute thousands of its members, including leading Democrats, on a day known as "the Storm." A reputable poll conducted in October 2020 found that half of Trump's supporters believed in QAnon. Trump had told Senator Mitch McConnell: "My understanding is they basically are just people who want good government."

and the FBI director. He wanted to decapitate the deep state once and for all before it could destroy him. He planned to do it soon after he declared victory in the election.

"The whole thing is insanity"

Americans had three ways of reading the election returns, which took an agonizing ten days to complete. It might have looked like a landslide. Joe Biden had won by more than seven million votes and a 306-to-232 margin in the Electoral College. It was anything but. The Electoral College went for Biden by fewer than 45,000 votes in all of Georgia, Arizona, and Wisconsin.

And then there was Trump's way. "There will be a smooth transition—to a second Trump administration," Secretary of State Pompeo smirked at a press conference on November 10: "All right? We're ready."

Barricaded in the White House, crying fraud, Trump fired the secretary of defense with a tweet: "Mark Esper has been terminated." Esper's primal sin was warning that the wholesale declassification of intelligence which the president had demanded would do great damage to national security. Trump had now churned through three secretaries of defense, four national security advisers, and four White House chiefs of staff in his quest for blind loyalty.

The next morning Haspel called Gen. Mark Milley, the chairman of the Joint Chiefs of Staff. "Yesterday was appalling," she said. "We are on the way to a right-wing coup. The whole thing is insanity." Haspel and Milley stayed in constant contact, keeping watch against a surprise attack by the president—whether abroad or at home. She knew from her own experience in nations like Turkey and Azerbaijan and Ethiopia how autocrats acted. Her prediction that Trump planned to overthrow the American government in an *autogolpe*, a coup from the top, was precise. And she sensed, not without reason, that hers might be the next head to roll.

Trump now installed a troika of MAGA men at the apex of the American military. The clown car had come to the Pentagon.

Kash Patel, the new chief of staff and shadow secretary of defense, immediately distinguished himself by presenting General Milley with a fabricated presidential order to withdraw American forces from Iraq and Somalia forthwith; the general saw it for what it was and countermanded it. Soon Haspel received a letter from the Office of the Secretary of Defense: on orders from the president, the Pentagon was cutting off support for the CIA's special-activities division and its paramilitary operations. Patel's mission at the Pentagon included finding top secret National Security Agency records proving that Obama and Brennan had eavesdropped on Trump. He had failed. They did not exist.

The new undersecretary of defense for intelligence was Ezra Cohen, a young protégé of Mike Flynn's whom McMaster had fired as senior director of NSC intelligence after six months for his insolence. To his consternation, Cohen had discovered that QAnon's adherents thought he was "Q"—the Trump administration official secretly working to expose the Deep State cabal of child rapers and Satan worshippers. The new undersecretary of defense for policy was Anthony Tata, a retired Army brigadier general catapulted to power after the president saw him on Fox, raving that Barack Obama was a Muslim terrorist and that John Brennan should be arrested for conspiring to assassinate Trump. Tata had tweeted at the former CIA director: "Pick your poison: firing squad, public hanging, life sentence as prison b*tch, or just suck on your pistol. Your call."

The president thought that smoking guns, an arsenal of them, had been cached and concealed at the CIA by Haspel.* Trump decided on a plan to get rid of her and install Patel in her place. "The idea was to put Kash in as the deputy, which doesn't require Senate approval, and then to fire Gina

---

* During this chaotic month, or shortly thereafter, Trump got his hands on a thick binder that once had been stored in a safe inside a secure vault at CIA headquarters. It contained raw intelligence that the CIA, the NSA, the FBI, and America's NATO allies had complied on the Russians, including the sources underlying the January 2017 intelligence assessment that Putin had tried to help Trump win. This trove of secrets disappeared and has not been seen since. (Jeremy Herb et al., "The Mystery of the Missing Binder: How a Collection of Raw Russian Intelligence Disappeared Under Trump," CNN, December 15, 2023, https://www.cnn.com/interactive/2023/12/politics/missing-russia-intelligence-trump-dg/.)

the next day, leaving Kash in charge," Cohen said. This scheme bore the influence of Mike Flynn and Sidney Powell, who were now at the center of Trump's swirling world.

On November 14, Trump put Giuliani and Powell in charge of his legal team seeking to overturn the election. They appeared on Fox the next day. Powell claimed that Haspel had stonewalled her search for its election-manipulating software—"which makes me wonder how much the CIA has used it for its own benefit in different places. And why Gina Haspel is still there in the CIA is beyond my comprehension. She should be fired immediately." She continued: "President Trump won by not just hundreds of thousands of votes, but by millions of votes, that were shifted by this software that was designed expressly for that purpose." The nation's top election-security officer, Chris Krebs, director of the Cybersecurity and Infrastructure Security Agency, called this utter nonsense and assured Americans that the election had been unmarred by fraud. Trump fired him immediately.

At a press conference on November 19, Giuliani ranted for thirty-eight minutes about fraudulent Biden ballots he claimed to have uncovered, as black rivulets of commingled sweat and hair dye ran down his face. Then Powell elaborated on her case: the election had been stolen by "the massive influence of communist money through Venezuela, Cuba, and likely China" flowing to Dominion Voting Systems; the ballot-counting company had been bribed by the communists to flip votes to Biden through a secret algorithm. "This is the consummate foreign interference in our election in the most criminal way you can possibly imagine," she said.

A reporter from a right-wing news outlet asked her about "reports that there was a piece of hardware, probably a server, picked up in Germany. Is that true, and is it related to this?"

"That is true," Powell said.

Powell then called Ezra Cohen at the Pentagon with an urgent demand. "Gina Haspel has been hurt and taken into custody in Germany," Powell said. "You need to launch a special operations mission to get her." Her story centered on the server for HAMMER, the secret CIA computer system, the engine of the scheme to steal the election from Trump. She said Haspel had undertaken a secret mission to seize and destroy the server, seeking to eliminate the evidence of the conspiracy. She wanted the Pentagon to launch a commando raid to arrest her and expose the CIA's role in the election fraud. Cohen, to his credit, did not call in SEAL Team Six. He thought Powell was insane.

Tinfoil-hat fantasies about the all-powerful CIA were standard fare for deluded souls who in the past would have hallucinated about saints and demons, but rarely if ever had they afflicted the high councils of American national security. Variations on Powell's story soon spread throughout QAnon. One version held that Haspel had been imprisoned at Guantanamo and charged with treason. Another said she had died in service of the CIA's plot against America.

Trump's own plot against Haspel began taking shape on December 8, when he ordered Patel to return to Washington from a trip to Asia. The president then braced the White House chief of staff, Mark Meadows, a weak-willed House Freedom Caucus founder. He told Meadows he would have to man up and break the news to Haspel: Trump was firing the CIA deputy director, Vaughn Bishop, and replacing him with Patel. The president assumed Haspel would resign quietly; if not, he would remove her. Either way, Patel would become the CIA's leader on December 11. He planned to fire the FBI director after decapitating the CIA. He was driven by his delusion that somewhere in the back room of Russia House was a secret dossier that could convict Obama, Biden, Clinton, and Brennan for crimes against the state.

Haspel got wind of this scheme and she went to the White House for the president's intelligence briefing that day, for the first time in many weeks. She reminded Trump how tough she was, how adept the CIA was at killing terrorists, how vital it was to his power. She left the Oval Office, went to the chief of staff's office, and confronted Meadows, who told her for the first time that Patel would be installed that day. She wouldn't tolerate it, she told him. If she was going to be fired, or forced to resign, she needed to hear it from the president. Meadows left his desk and came back in a few minutes to say that Trump had backed down. Word quickly spread in the West Wing that Haspel had brandished a political hand grenade and was prepared to pull the pin. If she were going down, the leaders of the American intelligence community would go down with her, rebuking Trump with a mass resignation in protest.

"Gina, who's a very savvy operator and an incredible public servant, already had what I call a suicide pact in place," said Trump's White House communications director, Alyssa Farah Griffin. "The entire IC would walk with her if that happened . . . the entire intelligence community. So, they were able to stop it."

On December 14, Attorney General Barr came to the White House to hand in his resignation to Trump. The president gave him a report from a self-styled election security expert—the same man who had fed Powell and her far-right allies the story of the secret CIA server in Germany. "This is absolute proof that the Dominion machines were rigged," Trump said. "This report means I won the election and will have a second term." Barr skimmed it and saw that it was nonsense. He thought that if Trump "actually believed this stuff he had become significantly detached from reality."

Shortly before seven o'clock on the night of Friday, December 18, Flynn and Powell sneaked into the White House uninvited and sat down with the president in the Oval Office. The cashiered general and his crackpot lawyer proposed a military coup to overturn the election. Flynn, who had said on television the day before that Trump should declare martial law, presented him with a draft three-page executive order for his signature. Written in the language of a covert-action finding, it read: "Effective immediately, the Secretary of Defense shall seize, collect, retain and analyze all machines, equipment, electronically stored information, and material records" from the election by calling out the National Guard. Four weeks after Inauguration Day, the Pentagon, where Patel still presided as chief of staff, would present its findings to Ratcliffe at the national intelligence directorate. To carry out the order, Trump would appoint Flynn as his field marshal and anoint Powell as his special counsel, armed with the power to indict the Americans who had plotted to topple Trump from power. It was the most conspiratorial conversation in the Oval Office since the smoking gun tape, in which President Nixon ordered the CIA to help him cover up the Watergate break-in back in 1972. But it was crazier than anything Nixon ever contemplated.

A White House lawyer who had seen Flynn and Powell skulking into the Oval Office called for backup from his colleagues, including Pat Cipollone, the White House counsel. They interposed themselves at the president's side, and a foul-mouthed screaming match ensued, as Flynn cursed them as quitters and they cursed him for a fool. Trump sided with the coup plotters and declared he was appointing Powell as his legal ringleader. The argument went for six hours, well past midnight, and the White House lawyers left thinking they might have lost it.

An hour later, at 1:42 a.m. on December 19, Trump tweeted out an invitation to an insurrection. *Statistically impossible to have lost the 2020 Election. Big protest in D.C. on January 6th. Be there, will be wild!* The right-wing coup Haspel had foreseen would come to the Capitol on that day, a violent assault on American democracy led by the president of the United States.

Chapter Twenty-Six

THE GLORY GATE

Throughout the twentieth century, every commander in chief had believed in what President Woodrow Wilson had said when he took the nation into World War One: "The world must be made safe for democracy. Its peace must be planted upon the tested foundations of political liberty." This too had been a credo for the CIA.

The means to that end had been brutal at times. The CIA's coups had overthrown freely elected leaders, swung elections with suitcases of cash, and supported dictators in the name of the United States. These missions were a foundation of American foreign policy for presidents from Truman to Reagan. So was the struggle against Soviet communism, and the CIA fought that battle around the world. Its veterans believed they had been on the side of the angels when they shipped missiles to the Afghan mujahideen and smuggled printing presses to Solidarity in Poland during the 1980s. These covert operations had undermined the Kremlin, which was the whole point of the cold war, and had been ever since the CIA's foundation. And once the Russians lost, the world was transformed, or so it had seemed. By the turn of the twenty-first century, the number of democracies in the world was roughly equal to the number of autocracies. Never before in the history of civilization had so many free nations flourished.

The moment was fleeting. Ever since, the arc of freedom in the world had flatlined and then fallen. The global decline of democracy had started when Bush invaded Iraq, justifying the war with the CIA's false warnings, and befouling the image of the United States as a beacon of freedom. Trump's rise to power had made the world take note that American democracy itself was in deep trouble, its politics descending into tribal warfare, its power to inspire the oppressed a distant memory. In office, the president attacked the freedom of the press, freedom of religion, and the legitimacy of free elections. He stripped the State Department of ambassadors, scorned his military commanders, and embraced dictators who killed and jailed their opponents. By the time of Trump's insurrection, autocracy was once again the rule across great swaths of the globe. The number of democratic nations had plunged to its lowest levels since the 1950s. Freedom had died through the corruption of political dialogue and the gradual erosion of civil liberties, human rights, and equal justice under law.

Trump had brought America to the brink of anarchy. The fear that America was a failing nation lingered like the stench of tear gas as clean-up crews began repairing the broken windows of the Capitol and hauling away the discarded banners of the coup.

"Scatological realities"

The CIA had endured four years of Trump's misrule and emerged largely unscathed, in no small part due to Gina Haspel's efforts to barricade headquarters against the president's wrath. He likely never knew about the call to arms, and with good reason. "Gina deserves enormous credit, and more credit than she often gets, for protecting this place," said her successor, Bill Burns. "She did a great deal to help insulate this place, particularly towards the latter months" of the Trump administration.

Biden had nominated Burns to lead the CIA on January 11, 2021, five days after the insurrection at the Capitol. The choice would be among the most consequential of his presidency. Regarded by his peers as the greatest Foreign Service officer of his generation, Burns had been running the Carnegie Endowment for International Peace, America's oldest think tank, founded in 1910 with the goal of abolishing war, before Biden chose him. He bore a passing resemblance to its first president, Elihu Root, who had been President Theodore Roosevelt's secretary of state, a winner of the Nobel Peace Prize, and a grandmaster of American foreign policy in the decades when the United States became a world power. The journalist Robert Draper described Burns memorably, if melodramatically: "A tall discreet figure with weary eyes, ashen hair, and a trim mustache. A sort you could easily imagine in a John le Carré novel whispering into a dignitary's ear at an Embassy party that the city is falling to the rebels and a boat would be waiting in the harbor at midnight."

Burns had never been a spy, but he was no stranger to the CIA. He had worked closely with its officers and analysts for the better part of forty years. His close friend and longtime State Department colleague Ryan Crocker once observed that ambassadors and station chiefs had been "together everywhere in the world since the end of World War Two. We live the same kinds of lives. Our kids grow up together. We run the same kinds of risks. We understand each other. In terms of cultural affinities, I think we're very close." Burns exemplified this kinship. He had been at the nexus of intelligence and diplomacy from the start of his career; he had worked with station chiefs in the Middle East and Russia who later held top ranks at the CIA, including Steve Kappes, deputy director from 2006 to 2010; Mike Sulick, chief of the clandestine service under Kappes; and Tom Rakusan, Haspel's choice for spymaster. These officers had "a really deft touch for working with people who may have had natural suspicions about Americans," Burns observed. "Intelligence is about human interactions, just like diplomacy is."

In his four years as CIA director, Burns wove intelligence and diplomacy together into a force intended to replace weapons as the highest expression of American authority abroad. He believed that the United States had been tethered to a fundamentally flawed strategy throughout the twenty-first century, too narrowly focused on counterterrorism tactics and too wrapped up in magical thinking about America's power to transform the world at gunpoint.

Born in 1956 at Fort Bragg, North Carolina, the son of an Army major general who had led the Arms Control and Disarmament Agency under President Reagan, he had joined the Foreign Service in January 1982 and served for thirty-three years.* His rise at the State Department had been meteoric; his fluency in Arabic and Russia was matched by his mastery of muscular diplomacy in the decade of American global dominance after the cold war. He had arrived in Jordan as the American ambassador in August 1998. On his third night, a terrorist attack on his compound in Amman was foiled in the nick of time. A few days later, al Qaeda bombed the American embassies in Nairobi and Dar es Salaam, the opening battle of the war that would consume the soldiers, spies, and diplomats of the United States.

Burns had returned to Washington to lead the State Department's Near East Bureau in April 2001. He and his colleagues had questioned the CIA's warnings about Saddam's arsenal, anticipated that the invasion of Iraq would be a disaster, and warned of its dangers in a formal memo titled "The Perfect Storm." But they pulled their punches, and Burns failed to take a lonely stance against the war. "That remains my biggest professional regret," Burns reflected. "The Iraq invasion remains the original sin. It was born of hubris . . . the heady, irresponsible, and unmoored notion that shaking things up violently" would bring peace and democracy to the Arab world. For the next two decades, "we continually found ourselves sucked back into the morass of our misadventures in the Middle East," while China and Russia gathered global power.

In August 2005, he had secured what he thought was his dream job, ambassador to Russia; he had served at high rank at the Moscow embassy a decade before. "The Kremlin is meant to intimidate foreigners," he recounted. "You come into these great halls in the Kremlin with massive ceilings. You walk down a very long corridor. These two-story bronze

---

* "My career didn't get off to a rocket-propelled start," he recounted. As a very junior officer in Jordan, he had volunteered to drive a supply truck six hundred miles over rutted roads from the Amman embassy to the American outpost in Baghdad during the war between Iraq and Iran. "It just seemed like an interesting adventure," he said. "I got to the border. An Iraqi security official on the Iraqi side of the border—who bore a striking resemblance to Saddam Hussein—confiscated the truck." Burns was driven to Baghdad under police escort, the truck and its cargo vanished, and "I spent the next three and a half decades in dread fear that my salary was going to get docked."

doors open and you're waiting to present your credentials as ambassador for Vladimir Putin to walk out. And Putin himself is not a particularly imposing figure. He's about five foot six, I think. But this is meant to shock and awe . . . and it actually succeeds." One of his first guests in Moscow had been Barack Obama, a freshman senator from Illinois, stopping in Moscow en route to Ukraine. After an informal dinner, they talked until midnight about Putin and the Iraq war; they were of one mind about the folly of the American invasion and the disaster of the occupation.

Burns had sized up Putin as a vengeful man seeking to restore Russia's status as an imperial nation. Toward the end of his tour, in March 2008, Putin had summoned him to the presidential dacha outside Moscow, and told him to come alone. Incensed at Bush's overtures toward admitting Ukraine into NATO, the autocrat harangued the ambassador: "Doesn't your government know that Ukraine is unstable? Don't you know that Ukraine is not even a real country?" And why did the United States want to undermine Russia? He had left Moscow for Washington that summer with a sense of foreboding, as relations between Russia and the United States plunged to their lowest depths since the early 1980s.

Burns had served under Obama as the State Department's undersecretary for political affairs, the third-ranking post, and then as the deputy secretary of state from July 2011 until retiring in November 2014; he was succeeded by Tony Blinken, who had been Vice President Biden's deputy national security adviser and would become his secretary of state. He looked back on those last three years as a time of lost opportunities. "After the recklessness of his predecessor, Obama's mantra of 'don't do stupid shit' was a sensible protocol," Burns wrote in his 2019 memoir, *The Back Channel*. "But there were other scatological realities in foreign policy. Shit happened, too"—especially in the ruins left by two long wars and the grim aftermath of the Arab Spring—and, ultimately, "Obama could not overcome his inheritance in the Middle East."

In his final diplomatic mission, Burns had worked in the greatest secrecy to complete the world-changing accord compelling Iran to curtail its nuclear weapons program—then watched as Mike Pompeo, making policy as CIA director, had convinced Trump to rip it up, over the strongest objections from the rest of his national-security team. As a parting gift, Trump and Pompeo had handed Biden and Burns a poisoned chalice: the Doha accord they had struck with the Taliban.

"An instrument of surrender"

"It's an instrument of surrender, not a peace agreement," said David Petraeus, the American commander in Afghanistan before becoming CIA director. "The worst diplomatic agreement I have ever seen," said Douglas London, the CIA's chief of counterterrorism for south and southwest Asia, including Afghanistan, under Trump. (Burns did not disagree.) "Trump will be responsible for the consequences, politically and militarily," the former national security adviser, John Bolton, had warned in June 2020. But it would be Biden who carried the burden.

Pompeo and his envoy Zalmay Khalilzad had met with the Taliban unilaterally, excluding the Afghan government. They negotiated the agreement with the de facto leader of the Taliban, Mullah Abdul Ghani Baradar, the deputy defense minister in the Taliban government before the CIA and the American military overthrew it in December 2001. Baradar had coordinated attacks on American forces for years thereafter. The CIA and the ISI had captured him in Karachi in 2010; Khalilzad, acting on Trump's behalf, convinced Pakistan to set him free in 2018. Trump had telephoned Baradar in Doha after he signed the accord and said: "You are a tough people and have a great country and I understand that you are fighting for your homeland. . . . The withdrawal of foreign forces from Afghanistan now is in the interest of everyone." Then he asked: "Do you need something from me?" Baradar replied: "We need to get prisoners released."

At Trump's behest, the Afghan government freed some five thousand of them, including senior war commanders. The CIA station in Kabul reported that their release had instantly regenerated the Taliban's military strength. Neither Pompeo nor Khalilzad had consulted the Pentagon or the National Security Council, nor warned them in advance that they had signed a secret protocol barring the United States from supporting the Afghan army in combat. By the time Trump left office, he had withdrawn all but about twenty-five hundred American troops from Afghanistan. The Taliban now had more than thirty times that number of fighters ready for battle. Their sole obligations under Doha were to refrain from attacking Americans and to refuse to shelter al Qaeda. They would keep the first promise.

The Doha deal required all American forces to leave Afghanistan on May 1, 2021—six weeks after Burns took office, following a rare unanimous Senate confirmation. Playing for time, Biden announced on April 14 that the United States would start the withdrawal on May Day, but wouldn't complete it until the twentieth anniversary of al Qaeda's attacks on America. September 11 still haunted the nation like an incubus.

Later in April, Burns flew in secret to Kabul to confer with Dave Pitts, the CIA station chief. Pitts, a special-forces veteran and longtime paramilitary officer in his late fifties, had held high rank in the Baghdad station and had served in Afghanistan from 2012 to 2015. He now commanded close to two hundred officers and oversaw the Zero Units, three thousand Afghans, nominally attached to their government's national-security directorate, who worked for the CIA as counterterrorism troops, translators, and bodyguards. Pitts knew without a doubt that the Taliban would keep their promise to resume fighting if the May Day deadline wasn't kept, and he predicted with impressive precision how and where they would carry out their campaign.*

Burns asked how the war might end. What was the worst-case scenario? What if it were worse than that? The CIA's tactical intelligence was good. Its strategic intelligence—its capacity to anticipate surprise—was not.

Shortly after Biden was sworn in, the CIA's analysts had estimated that

---

* CIA officers and analysts and their colleagues in Kabul used an artificial intelligence tool called Raven Sentry to predict enemy attacks on Americans and their Afghan allies with surprising accuracy. Their office was called the "nerd locker." The tool incorporated open-source reporting, including historical data going back to the Soviet occupation, when the CIA backed the Afghan guerrillas. The journal of the U.S. Army War College reported: "In some cases, modern attacks occurred in the exact locations, with similar insurgent composition, during the same calendar period, and with identical weapons to their 1980s Russian counterparts." (Thomas W. Spahr, "*Raven Sentry*: Employing AI for Indications and Warnings in Afghanistan," *Parameters*, Summer 2024.)

the Taliban could not win their war until the end of 2022, a grievous error in judgment. They had failed to see the damage that Doha had done to Afghan morale, and thus overestimated the staying power of the government. In June, they revised their thinking. Their consensus now was that Kabul would not face a serious assault until late in 2021, well after American troops departed. Their confidence in their own reporting was not high, and with good reason. How long the Afghan military would hold out was a mystery. The CIA could assess its strength in numbers, but not its will to fight.

On July 2, in the dead of night, the United States pulled out of the Bagram air base, where more than one hundred thousand American troops once had been stationed, turning off the lights and locking the gates without telling the Afghan government. The decision was more demoralizing than Doha. The soldiers of the Afghan military began laying down their arms and taking off their uniforms, and the Taliban started sweeping through provincial capitals in the countryside.

By July 6, the CIA had raised the alarm that Kabul could not withstand a Taliban assault when it came. Its briefers evidently did not convince the president. Biden continued to insist that the Afghan government would not fail, and that Americans would not be forced to flee the country at gunpoint. He grew angry during a July 8 press conference:

> Q: Is a Taliban takeover of Afghanistan now inevitable?
> THE PRESIDENT: No, it is not.
> Q: Why?
> THE PRESIDENT: Because you—the Afghan troops have 300,000 well-equipped—as well-equipped as any army in the world—and an air force against something like 75,000 Taliban. . . .
> Q: Your own intelligence community has assessed that the Afghan government will likely collapse.
> THE PRESIDENT: That is not true. . . . That is not true. They did not—they didn't—did not reach that conclusion. . . .
> Q: Do you see any parallels between this withdrawal and what happened in Vietnam?
> THE PRESIDENT: None whatsoever. Zero.

Some of this was generals deceiving Biden, and some was Biden deluding himself. On July 13, a coalition of the diplomats remaining at the American embassy, spurred by the CIA station's reporting, filed a rare protest through the State Department's dissent channel, a direct line to Secretary of State Tony Blinken. They warned that the United States was unprepared for a Taliban takeover and the embassy lacked an escape plan. The State Department had never seriously considered a large-scale evacuation before, because it had never believed the Taliban could invade Kabul anytime soon. The dissenters also protested that red tape had snarled the special visa applications of more than twenty thousand Afghans who had worked with the United States and whose lives would be in danger if the Americans left without them.

By the night of August 3, the Taliban had taken over half the country. They would control the rest in eleven days. But the CIA and the Pentagon still had made "no intel assessment that says the government's going to collapse and the military's going to collapse" imminently, said General Milley, the Joint Chiefs chairman. "As late as the 3rd of August—and there's another one on the 8th of August—they're still talking weeks, perhaps months."

After the city of Kandahar fell on the night of August 11, Haines convened a crash seven a.m. meeting of the national-security team and warned that Kabul might be next. Biden finally came to grips with the cascading crisis, and on August 12, he ordered the American embassy, which housed the CIA station, to prepare to shut down. The State Department formally requested that the Pentagon begin the evacuation in earnest. Diplomats and spies alike began burning classified files and helicoptering to a secure building at the Hamid Karzai International Airport, where some three thousand American soldiers and Marines were flying in for the evacuation that would end the American military occupation of Afghanistan.

Kabul fell on August 15. The Afghan military and security forces, trained and equipped by the United States at a cost of hundreds of billions of dollars, had "put their weapons down and melted away in a very, very short period of time," General Milley said. The Taliban had picked up the arms they had laid down and entered the capital without firing a shot. Ashraf Ghani, the Afghan president, fled the country for Abu Dhabi. The last diplomats to leave the American embassy hauled down the flag and hightailed it to the airport in a Chinook helicopter. At Eagle Base, the nearby CIA paramilitary outpost, officers blew up their vehicles, deleted their hard drives, gathered the Zero Units from across the country, and ordered the abandonment of the CIA bases at Khost and Shkin, where their comrades had lost their lives to al Qaeda.

The last CIA officer to leave Shkin set the base ablaze. The skull of a Texas Longhorn that once had looked down from the wall above the bar stared up from the charred rubble. When the Taliban arrived, one of their fighters said: "They only left us bones."

"The Taliban didn't defeat us. We defeated ourselves."

In the last days of April 1975, as the army of North Vietnam laid siege to Saigon, the station chief, Tom Polgar, led the evacuation of American embassy staff, along with CIA officers and their recruited agents, as Marines flew helicopters onto the embassy grounds and atop the station to lift them to safety aboard ships offshore. Despite his valiant efforts, the United States left behind many thousands of South Vietnamese who had served the American cause, abandoning them to a cruel fate at the hands of the enemy. At the final hour, Polgar wrote a cable to CIA headquarters, and then smashed the machine that had sent it:

> It has been a long and hard fight and we have lost. This experience, unique in the history of the United States, does not signal necessarily the demise of the United States as a world power. The severity of the defeat and the circumstances of it, however, would seem to call for a reassessment. . . . Let us hope that we will not have another Vietnam experience and that we have learned our lesson. Saigon signing off.

Thirty years later, Polgar remembered: "As we stepped up the narrow metal steps to the helicopter pad on the roof, we knew we were leaving behind thousands of people in the embassy's logistics compound. We all knew how we felt, leaders of a defeated cause."

In Kabul, on August 16, tens of thousands of Afghans began gathering at the gates of the civilian terminal on the south side of the international airport. A handful were shot by American soldiers trying to contain the surging crowds. Hundreds more clambered over razor-wired walls onto the runways, frantically seeking a flight out. Some climbed on the wings of jets awaiting takeoff. A few clung to the fuselage of a giant C-17 military transport as it fired its engines. They fell from the airborne plane to the tarmac, their final moments indelibly recorded by Afghan journalists. The *New York Times* reported: "The images evoked America's frantic departure from Vietnam, encapsulating Afghanistan's breathtaking collapse in the wake of American abandonment."*

The United States was attempting one of the largest airlifts in history, and the most complex since the fall of Saigon, with too few troops and too little planning. As the temperature reached ninety-five degrees, the gunmen of the Taliban, the United States Marines, and the Zero Unit troopers pushed back against the seething throngs of desperate people, some of whom died as they were shot and trampled at the airport gates. "I live with memories of women and men walking through razor wire, slicing up their bodies, for a chance that I would allow them into the airport," said Sam Aronson, a State Department consular officer. "I remember giving a horrible choice to a young mother whose husband got stopped by the Taliban: Get on the plane and never see your husband again, or exit the airport and lose your only chance at freedom."

The worst horror was the crush of terrified people at the Abbey Gate, by American military decree the only way out for Afghan civilians, guarded by young marines, many on their first deployment in a combat zone. Thousands upon thousands, some waving passports with newly validated visas, begged for days on end for a chance of escape.

---

* The evacuation was a political disaster for President Biden, whose approval ratings plunged steeply during the August airlift, falling below 50 percent and never recovering thereafter.

Bill Burns flew into this maelstrom on Sunday, August 22, and bunked at the military terminal on the airport's north side. He said his mission was "simply to persuade the Taliban to let us conduct an evacuation and not get in the middle of it"—trying to ensure that the Americans and their allies would not be shot in the back as they left Afghanistan. Having the CIA director negotiating on behalf of the United States mattered, if only "because if you had sent the Secretary of State or a senior diplomat, it would have connoted a kind of recognition" that the Taliban was a legitimate government. Not for the first time, and not for the last, Burns was conducting intelligence diplomacy, a fine art few others ever mastered.

"So I'm going to meet Mullah Baradar," Burns said. "He has his bodyguards and I have my bodyguards, all of whom two weeks before had been shooting each other, fingers on the trigger. . . . I thought, 'Oh, great, we're going to go to a meeting and this is going to turn into a firefight.' Fortunately, things calmed down. They understood the message and by that point, I think, Baradar's view was we were kind of raining on their parade. This is the moment of national triumph for the Taliban, and instead of being able to bask in victory, they had this scene out at the airport that was distracting attention." He saw that the Taliban were all too eager for the Americans to leave. They didn't need to be convinced.

Burns asked station chief Dave Pitts about the CIA's evacuation plan. Fortunately, he had one, although the State Department didn't until after the Taliban had taken Kabul; its envoys were making it up on the fly, amid the fear and chaos. Pitts had a shuttle of Russian-built helicopters flying from Eagle Base to the airport, but that was the least of it. He had devised his own escape route. It was called the Glory Gate, a grandiose name for a corridor of concrete blast walls at the north side of the airport, controlled by CIA paramilitaries, Delta Force commandos, and Zero Unit troops. The CIA's Afghan soldiers, a host of recruited Afghan agents from across the country, and their families made it out of Kabul through that passageway. So did several hundred Afghan civilians whose lives were in danger. "When I saw that the American operators at Glory Gate were bringing in their high-value assets on foot, I had this idea that I could do the same," said Aronson, the State Department consular officer. With the help of a young Afghan he'd befriended, who'd worked as a translator for American special forces, Aronson brought fifty-two people from thirteen Afghan families through the Glory Gate to safety.

The CIA got almost all its people out. "One of our most profound obligations is to our Afghan partners," Burns said. "We managed to get out thousands of our partners and their family members"—some thirty thousand people in all. But to the undying shame of the United States, the majority of Afghans who had worked for the American cause over the course of two decades would be left behind. More than seventy thousand abandoned allies—including tens of thousands of people holding visas or awaiting them—would remain in mortal danger of the Taliban's vengeance.

Burns flew out of Afghanistan on August 25 with a sense of foreboding. "I remember driving around Kabul International by Abbey Gate," he said. "A threat stream at that time that we were collecting intelligence on was as intense as any as I have ever seen."

The CIA was picking up alarming signs of an impending car bomb attack at the airport by ISIS-K, the terrorist group based in Kabul.* At four thirty that afternoon, the American military commanders in Afghanistan held a conference call with Defense Secretary Lloyd Austin and General Milley at the Pentagon and CENTCOM's generals in Qatar. "I don't believe people get the incredible amount of risk on the ground," Austin said, warning of an imminent "mass casualty event." The commanders on the ground said Abbey Gate faced the greatest danger, and they detailed their plans to close it in twenty-hour hours. They didn't make their deadline.

---

* Formed in 2015 by Pakistani and Uzbek jihadists, ISIS-K fought the Taliban for control of Afghanistan, attacking a maternity hospital, a university, and aid groups in its terror campaign, killing or injuring thousands. It expanded in size and lethality after the fall of Kabul. In January 2024, it murdered ninety-six Iranians at a memorial for Qassem Soleimani, the Revolutionary Guard Corps leader killed by a drone strike by the CIA and the Pentagon in 2020. Soleimani had led Iran's fight against ISIS-K and its affiliates. In March 2024, the group killed 145 people at a Moscow concert hall. The CIA had warned both the Iranians and the Russians beforehand but it was unheeded. The "K" in ISIS-K stood for Khorasan, a medieval empire incorporating Afghanistan and parts of Iran, Pakistan, and Central Asia.

The next day, at 4:40 p.m., a squad of special-forces soldiers pulled up to Glory Gate and ordered everyone to leave immediately: a car bomber was headed for the airport. That order did not reach the American troops at Abbey Gate, and even if it had, the crowds were so thick and the situation so beyond control that nothing they could have done would have saved the day. And it wasn't a car bomb that struck. A black-clad ISIS-K terrorist exploded a suicide vest at Abbey Gate at 5:50 p.m. Twenty pounds of ball bearings tore through the sea of humanity, killing 170 Afghan civilians and thirteen members of the United States military—eleven marines, a soldier, and a sailor, the last Americans to die in Afghanistan.

The hunt for the phantom car bomber continued. For eight hours on August 29, intelligence analysts and drone operators at Central Command's newly created Over-the-Horizon Strike Cell in Qatar tracked a white Toyota Corolla through the streets of Kabul. Two sets of mechanical eyes stared down at the car: a CIA surveillance drone with a camera and a military Reaper drone armed with a Hellfire missile. The Reaper fired at a white Toyota Corolla which had just parked at a house in a residential neighborhood near the Kabul airport. General Milley called it "a righteous strike" against ISIS-K. This was a lie. The last American drone attack of the war had killed Zemari Ahmadi, a longtime worker for a food charity based in California, and nine more innocent civilians, including seven children in his extended family.

One minute before midnight on August 30, the last American military plane took off from Kabul. The United States had fled Afghanistan, following in the footsteps of the armies of the Soviet Union, the British Empire, Genghis Khan, and Alexander the Great. Twenty years gone, a trillion dollars spent, 2,448 American soldiers killed, 20,722 more wounded, and many thousands more whose minds would be haunted forever. Among the dead were 3,846 American contractors, 1,144 allied service members, 66,000 Afghan national military and police, 444 aid workers, 72 journalists, at least 13 CIA officers—and tens of thousands of Afghan civilians who had worked for the United States. Once it had been the good war, the just war, the war the Bush White House called Operation Enduring Freedom. Now it was a lost cause. As America took flight, Gen. H. R.

McMaster had the final word: "The Taliban didn't defeat us. We defeated ourselves."

Dave Pitts was among the last to leave Kabul. In October 2021, Burns made him the CIA's chief for South and Central Asia, covering thirteen countries, including Afghanistan and Pakistan. He had one last mission to complete in the land of the Taliban.

A few months after he returned to headquarters, his officers and their counterterrorism colleagues brought him good news. They had discovered that Ayman al-Zawahiri, the leader of al Qaeda since the killing of Osama bin Laden, was living in an elegant four-story safe house in an upscale Kabul neighborhood, about two miles from the abandoned American embassy. Al-Zawahiri, now seventy years old, never left the house except to take in a little sun and fresh air on its expansive third-floor balcony in the morning. The building was owned by a senior aide to Sirajuddin Haqqani, the interior minister of the Taliban government and a man the United States called a global terrorist. Haqqani was the son of a preeminent Afghan warlord backed to the hilt by the CIA during the Soviet jihad, a man praised by President Reagan as a freedom fighter.

Burns brought a scale model of the safe house to the Situation Room and briefed Biden on the CIA's plan to kill al-Zawahiri. Biden approved it on the condition that no innocents would die. The operation was "a result of countless hours of intelligence collection over many years," said the CIA veteran Mick Mulroy. Burns kept the scale model in his seventh-floor suite as a totem.

On a midsummer morning, as the sun rose over Kabul and the call to prayer rang out from the minarets, al-Zawahiri stepped outside to greet the dawn. Two Hellfire missiles obliterated the emir of al Qaeda. And in that moment, a long chapter in the history of the CIA came to a close.

Chapter Twenty-Seven

HUMAN INTELLIGENCE

Five weeks after the fall of Kabul, Tom Sylvester foresaw that Russia was preparing to invade Ukraine. No eureka moment, no flash of insight, no single source had led to this revelation. Many streams of intelligence, flowing through myriad channels, had become a mighty river by the beginning of October 2021. The CIA, riding that current, had arrived at the conclusion that Putin was going to war.

As the CIA's new chief for Europe and Eurasia, Sylvester had taken charge of the call to arms against the Kremlin, inheriting three years of work by his predecessor, Tom Rakusan, whose renovation of Russia House had doubled and redoubled the recruitment of Russian sources. "There are two ways in which what Tom did in those years, I think, really made a difference," Bill Burns said. "One was simply to restore focus and significance to what Russia House was doing, because we had managed over the years to sustain a fair amount of expertise on Russia, good Russian-language speakers. And then the second thing that Tom did with that effort was to push back against the Russian services, who hadn't had as much pushback" before the call to arms, "working with liaison partners overseas to expose and disrupt Russian intelligence activities. Both of those things, I think, created a really good foundation" for the CIA's assault on the Kremlin.

"And then what we tried to build on that, starting in the spring of

2021, was the recruitment dimension of this," Burns said. "This was really, especially once the war drums started beating, a once-in-a-generation opportunity, given the disaffection in some parts of the Russian elite and Russian society" against Putin's regime. Dave Marlowe, whom Burns had appointed chief of the clandestine service in June 2021, said the CIA started "looking around the world for Russians who are as disgusted with [Putin] as we are." It found more than a few.

The CIA was able to run its newly recruited Russian agents—and dare to share their intelligence with allied spies— thanks in part to Paula Doyle, who had helped take down A. Q. Khan's nuclear-weapons network fifteen years before. She had identified and fixed the fatal flaws in the covert-communications systems that had led to the deaths of agents in China and Iran. Doyle said she and her teams had "shaped the ability for CIA to handle sensitive new spies using techniques designed to keep them productive and safer. We were absolutely focused on winning the tradecraft war for those who followed us" after she retired as the CIA's associate deputy director of operations for technology.

Sylvester said she had answered an urgent question asked by case officers transmitting and receiving secret intelligence: "How do we ensure that it is not immediately penetrable by the Russians?" Thus reassured, station chiefs around the world had convinced foreign services—including some who never before had been allies—to help them spy on Russia's military, intelligence, and diplomatic officers.

"There was the strategic decision on how we would share intelligence," Sylvester said. "We used it as an influence mechanism, in and of itself, to get governments to start cooperating with us that had not done so" in the past. "The fact that we shared accurate information with many, many of our partners that accurately predicted the fact that Russia came into the war, they told us, was the most powerful thing the CIA had done with them and for them for the last eighteen years." The intelligence sharing paved a two-way street with foreign services, and "allowed them to open up taps of cooperation and intelligence that they had theretofore not shared with us. It was a huge leap of faith for many of them. But a lot of them went out on a limb, based on what we were sharing."*

Burns had called upon every arm of American intelligence to back the CIA in its quest. The FBI's national-security and counterintelligence divisions had stepped up their efforts to spy on the Russians. Paul Nakasone, the four-star general in charge of the National Security Agency and its Cyber Command, had trained his eavesdropping powers on Putin's people. Defense Secretary Lloyd Austin had focused the Pentagon's spy satellites on Russia military movements. Avril Haines, the former CIA deputy director, now led the national intelligence directorate, and she had invested many millions in the effort, coordinating the seventeen agencies she oversaw and assigning scores of her analysts to sift and assay what they had gleaned.

As it gathered strength, the call to arms itself had become that once-in-a-generation opportunity of which Burns spoke, a chance for a sea change at the CIA, a return to its central mission: espionage. For twenty years, its officers had fought a counterterrorism war, and a counterinsurgency campaign that had flowed from the counterterrorism war. "We were focused on *that*, and China and Russia were focused on *us*," Mike Morell said in an oral history released on September 11, 2021.

The CIA had failed to deduce the military intentions of the Russians during the cold war. Now, thirty years after the hammer and sickle was struck for the last time over Red Square, its spies had seen inside the Kremlin, and divined the secrets only espionage could reveal.

---

* In one key meeting, Patrick Weninger, representing Russia House, convened his counterparts from spy agencies inside and outside NATO, including the British, the Ukrainians, and the Dutch, all gathered in The Hague, where he had once been station chief. The intelligence flowed both ways; the Dutch service had developed a network of recruited agents both in Russia and Ukraine in their long hunt for proof of the Russians' guilt in the 2014 shootdown of Malaysia Airlines Flight 17, in which 193 Dutch citizens had died. The work of Dutch intelligence officers led to convictions of two Russians and a Ukrainian collaborator in 2022.

"I'm convinced the Russians are going to invade"

"By the eleventh of October, I'm convinced the Russians are going to invade Ukraine," General Nakasone said. "The preponderance of intelligence was different than anything we'd ever seen before."

On that morning, Burns and Haines went to the Oval Office to present the intelligence to President Biden and Vice President Harris. Secretary of State Blinken, Defense Secretary Austin, and General Milley joined them. The CIA's spies and recruited agents, the NSA's communications intercepts, and the Pentagon's photoreconnaissance satellites all told one story. "We actually made the call on Russia" based on "a lot of really exquisite collection" of intelligence "and the deep expertise . . . to interpret that, and know what it meant," said Linda Weissgold, once Bush's White House briefer, now the CIA's director of intelligence analysis.

Burns told the president that Putin intended to invade when winter came. "We saw not only the massing of forces on the borders of Ukraine, we also—through the information that we got—had an understanding of what the Russian leadership was actually thinking and planning for those forces," Blinken said. Haines pointed out that Putin was pouring money into military contingency plans and beefing up his reserve forces. "There were things that really made this a much more compelling case—budget decisions that were taken, other forms of intelligence surrounding it, the information campaign that they were playing," she said. "It wasn't until you brought it all together, you start to see how the picture pulls together."

Burns and his colleagues laid out in fine detail the Russian military's order of battle and its operational strategies. Assuming the CIA was right about the magnitude of the coming invasion, he said, "it would be the biggest ground war in Europe since the Second World War." The Ukrainians would put up a valiant struggle—but the CIA reckoned that the chances that they could defend their country were slim to none. (Having overestimated the staying power of the Afghan military, its analysts now underestimated the will of the Ukrainians to fight.) The intelligence pointed to an assault roughly equal to the 1968 Soviet invasion of Czechoslovakia, in which 250,000 troops had taken one hundred hours to achieve their military objectives. The CIA figured that Kyiv could fall as quickly.

Why would Putin do it? Biden asked. What was he thinking? Burns knew. For twenty-two years, he said, he had watched him stewing in a toxic brew of grievance and insecurity and ambition. He believed that the CIA had overthrown the Soviet empire he had sought to resurrect and supported the subsequent uprisings in nations, like Ukraine, once under the Kremlin's control. He was an apostle of payback. Burns had heard firsthand from Putin that he was obsessed with Ukraine, insisting that it was not a country, but an integral part of imperial Russia going back a thousand years. He had now convinced himself that his duty was to seize it by force, to fulfill his destiny to restore Russia as an empire.

The president sent Burns on a mission to Moscow with orders to talk Putin out of it, if he could. The director walked into the immense grandeur of the Kremlin on November 2 and met with Yuri Ushakov, Putin's foreign policy adviser; Nikolai Patrushev, Putin's longtime KGB cohort and director of his Security Council; and Sergei Naryshkin, the head of his foreign intelligence service. Putin wasn't present. He called in from his mansion in the Black Sea resort of Sochi, where he was in isolation during a fourth coronavirus wave in Moscow. Burns laid out in precise detail what the CIA knew about his plans, and warned of the consequences if he went ahead with his attack on Ukraine, including severe economic sanctions meant to cripple Russia's banking system and crush the value of its currency.

"He was utterly unapologetic," Burns recounted. "You could see the absolute conviction that they were going to roll over, that he had modernized the Russian military to the point where the Ukrainians were no match. I came back virtually convinced that he was going to invade. And it was partly because of what we could see, what we had collected through human and technical intelligence. But it was also partly just the fixation that I had seen Putin build up over the years that Russia couldn't be a great power, he couldn't be a great Russian leader without controlling Ukraine and its choices. And he thought this was the window for him to accomplish that."

On January 12, 2022, Burns flew to Kyiv. "The president sent me out to talk to Zelensky," he said. "We had collected by that point some fairly precise intelligence on what the Russians were planning, including to decapitate the regime and killing Zelensky, and a lightning strike, as they saw it, across the Belarus frontier to take Kyiv." From that day forward, "we shared intelligence quite systematically with the Ukrainians to help them get ready to defend themselves."

Putin had badly misjudged the strength of his military, blind to the lies and corruption that corroded it and the incompetence and arrogance of the generals who commanded it. But Ukraine could not fend off the Russians by force of arms alone. Secret intelligence would be its strongest weapon.

"You were in the trenches together"

The CIA station in Kyiv had been working with the Ukrainians for eight years, ever since the February 2014 popular revolution that had overthrown Putin's puppet president in Kyiv. The Ukrainian intelligence services had to be torn down and rebuilt; their ranks had been riddled with Russian agents who had ransacked their offices and set fire to their files during the uprising. That April, after Putin had seized and annexed the Crimean Peninsula and sent special-forces units to back a separatist battle in eastern Ukraine, John Brennan had flown to Kyiv in secret, or so he had thought. A mole inside Ukrainian intelligence had relayed his arrival to Russian state media. They had immediately reported on his visit, calling it proof that the CIA was running the politics of Ukraine, and publishing a photoshopped image of Brennan costumed as a clown.

The reality was deadly serious. From that day forward, four successive station chiefs, backed by a large and growing task force at Langley, worked to help Ukraine create a twenty-first-century spy service. The CIA provided everything from a new headquarters complex to paramilitary training at the special activities division's base in Harvey Point, North Carolina. A small unit of Ground Branch officers went to occupied eastern Ukraine to school their embattled allies in long-range sniper techniques, antitank warfare, covert communications, and camouflage. At CIA headquarters, the mission to make the Ukrainians intelligence services trusted partners was overseen by five successive chiefs of the clandestine service: Greg Vogle, Tom Rakusan, Beth Kimber, David Marlowe, and Tom Sylvester, who took the top post in June 2023. The investment would pay an enormous return.

"The CIA was very prompt and professional in assisting us in our goal of rebuilding Ukraine's intelligence capabilities," said Valentyn Nalyvaichenko, who had been appointed in 2014 to lead the Security Service of Ukraine, the SBU. "We had to first root out any of the traitors, moles, or other pro-Russian actors at the SBU. It meant that within a week, we fired over ninety percent of top SBU leadership. This also meant that we had to quickly find new people to replace them. It was difficult, of course. However, without first cleaning up the Russian *agentura* at SBU, it would have been impossible to build up trust with CIA. . . . Quickly we began training with our American partners to build up a new counterintelligence force in Ukraine—something that we accomplished within a few months."

That force was created by Lt. Gen. Valeriy Kondratiuk, who led the military intelligence service, the HUR. His officers had penetrated their Russian rivals, the GRU, and helped the CIA uncover the hackers who had plotted to help elect Trump in 2016. The CIA provided spy gear to create surveillance networks in eastern Ukraine and tap the cell phones of top Russian military and intelligence officers visiting the frontlines from Moscow. General Kondratiuk ran a new paramilitary unit, created by the CIA station and trained by Ground Branch officers, which ran sabotage operations behind enemy lines. Since 2017, he had been sending undercover spies, trained by the CIA in Germany and Poland, on espionage missions inside Russia. His successor, Lt. Gen. Kyrylo Budanov, had run some of those operations himself. The alliance with the CIA "only strengthened" over the next five years, Budanov said. "It grew systematically. The cooperation expanded to additional spheres and became more large-scale."

By the time Burns took charge at the CIA, the Ukrainians had proved as adept as the CIA at convincing Russians to betray their country, perhaps more so. "We say that we spy," David Marlowe reflected. "But what we really do is we have relationships with people who spy, and we give them some kind of compensation in exchange for that. And so, if we're going to invite somebody into a relationship where they're risking prison or death, when they're betraying their tribe or their institution or their country because they believe in what they're doing with us, we have to be very judicious about that."

The Ukrainians were less judicious, and with good reason. "For a Russian, allowing oneself to be recruited by an American is to commit the absolute ultimate in treachery and treason," General Kondratiuk said. "But for a Russian to be recruited by a Ukrainian, it's just friends talking over a beer."

The spy services of Kyiv, resurrected by the CIA, were becoming one of America's best sources of intelligence on the Russians; the CIA was becoming the Ukrainians' best defense against them. "It was probably one of the best investments that the CIA, the U.S. government, has made," Sylvester said; it had created "the trust, the confidence, the ability in times of need to feel like you were in the trenches together." By the fall of 2021, the CIA had given the Ukrainians a graduate course in espionage and paramilitary operations, along with the ability to understand and utilize a steady stream of American intelligence.

"If you ask me the two biggest factors" that allowed Ukraine to hold out against the Russians, Sylvester said, "one was the decisions in 2014 onwards to invest, put in people and money and training continuously, all the way up to the war. And second was this ongoing decision on the intelligence sharing and the repeated travel by our director all over Europe," working to unite the spy services of NATO in advance of the Russia invasion.

"This is the nation's intelligence"

Burns and Haines now led a revival of the long-dormant tradition of American political warfare as they helped create a whole-of-government plan against a Russian invasion. American intelligence had identified hundreds of spies posing as diplomats in Russian embassies across Europe; all would be outed and expelled by allied nations. America economic warfare would hit Putin's oligarchs and power brokers where it hurt, starting with sanctions that froze $5 billion of the Russian central bank's assets in the United States, blocking the use of foreign reserves to prop up the Russian ruble. Burns and Blinken began working in tandem to unify the NATO nations, shoring up the alliance Trump had undermined.

Crucially, Burns helped convince Biden to launch a dramatic information-warfare blitz. The United States would announce that it knew beyond a doubt Russia would invade Ukraine.

The ability to anticipate a surprise attack was one thing. The decision to share the intelligence detailing Putin's war plans with the world was quite another. The case had to be ironclad: The acrid stench of the CIA's disastrous reporting on Saddam's arsenal still lingered, eighteen years after it had blazed the trail to war in Iraq. American allies had questioned the CIA's judgment on world events ever since. When Haines presented a watered-down intelligence brief to NATO ministers in mid-November, she was met with deep skepticism. "Really? Are you, in a way, hyping up the threat?" she said they had asked. "Is this going to lead us into the situation, as opposed to actually helping us to prepare for it?"

Burns thought a steady drumbeat of top secret intelligence, openly presented as irrefutable facts, would shape public perception about Putin's intentions, convince dubious NATO allies, unite Europe against Russian aggression—and, conceivably, deter the attack, though that was a very long shot. He and Haines got unanimous consent from their colleagues. General Nakasone said: "This is the nation's intelligence. This isn't an agency's or the intelligence community's or anyone else's intelligence. When it benefits our national security, why do we not do that?"

Biden instructed his national security adviser, Jake Sullivan, to orchestrate the selective declassification of secrets, edited to protect intelligence sources and methods. In late January and early February 2022, the press secretaries of the White House, the State Department, and the Pentagon detailed Russian troop movements, a plot to install a pro-Russian leader in Kyiv, and a false-flag attack staged by the Kremlin. The sharing of secrets "enabled the president to build a strong coalition" within NATO, Burns said. "It helped the Ukrainians defend themselves. And it helped disarm the false narratives that I had watched Putin erect and we had never caught up with so many times in the past."

On February 17, the information-warfare campaign reached a crescendo when Blinken went before the United Nations Security Council and laid out the gist of the intelligence. His speech, being true, was the mirror image of Colin Powell's presentation to the Security Council in 2003. Blinken said the false-flag attack could be "a violent event that Russia will blame on Ukraine, or an outrageous accusation that Russia will level against the Ukrainian government. It could be a fabricated so-called 'terrorist' bombing inside Russia, the invented discovery of a mass grave, a staged drone strike against civilians, or a fake—even a real—attack using chemical weapons." The Kremlin had prepared a video depicting explosions, corpses, and mourners for victims of a Ukrainian terrorist attack, all of it done to create a pretext for war. "In response to this manufactured provocation," Blinken said, "the highest levels of the Russian Government may theatrically convene emergency meetings to address the so-called crisis. The government will issue proclamations declaring that Russia must respond to defend Russian citizens or ethnic Russians in Ukraine. Next, the attack is planned to begin. Russian missiles and bombs will drop across Ukraine. Communications will be jammed. Cyberattacks will shut down key Ukrainian institutions. After that, Russian tanks and soldiers will advance on key targets that have already been identified and mapped out in detailed plans. We believe these targets include Ukraine's capital, Kyiv, a city of 2.8 million people."

He concluded: "Now, I am mindful that some have called into question our information, recalling previous instances where intelligence ultimately did not bear out. But let me be clear: I am here today, not to start a war, but to prevent one."

One week later, Russia invaded Ukraine. Biden had ordered the evacuation of the embassy, but Burns insisted to the president that a core of CIA officers would remain in-country. They provided the Ukrainians military and spy services crucial intelligence on where the Russians would attack and the weapons systems they would use. "Without them," said Ivan Bakanov, then chief of the SBU, "there would have been no way for us to resist the Russians, or to beat them."

"Fight fire with fire"

General Milley had called his counterpart in Moscow days before the war began. "This is an enormous strategic mistake that you're making," he told Gen. Valery Gerasimov, chief of staff of the Russian armed forces. "You'll get in there in fourteen days, you won't get out for fourteen years, and you will have body bags flowing back to Moscow the entire time." As the war went on, with no end in sight, all signs suggested that he had been right.

Biden signed a covert-action finding immediately after the invasion authorizing the CIA to provide intelligence support for lethal operations against Russian forces on Ukrainian soil. Burns visited Zelensky and the CIA station in Kyiv thirteen times thereafter, a journey requiring a flight to Poland and a twelve-hour train ride from the border to the capital. Burns often went to the front lines of the war to see the struggle for himself. With each trip, the American intelligence liaison with Ukraine deepened. Some aspects were at arm's length: the CIA didn't command or micromanage its counterparts. Others required the use of a ten-foot pole, including a striking number of sabotage missions on oil depots and military targets deep inside Russia, whose accuracy depended on more than Google Earth. And a few were beyond the pale. The Ukrainians didn't tell the CIA when they set out to assassinate their enemies in Russia and in occupied Ukraine. Though the CIA supplied the intelligence that let the Ukrainians put Russian military commanders in their crosshairs, it tried to dissuade the Ukrainians from a targeted strike on May Day 2022 that barely missed Gerasimov, whose brutal indifference to the lives of innocent civilians had set the tenor of the Russian assault.

Five weeks later, an excruciating tension arose at the Kyiv station. The Dutch military intelligence service had warned the CIA that Ukrainian commandos planned to blow up the $20 billion Nord Stream pipelines. The lines ran from Russia to Germany under the Baltic Sea; Germany's energy bills were a bulwark of the Russian economy. The CIA's objections served only to delay the plot by three months. In early September, a six-man team used a Polish front company to charter a sailing yacht in Germany; a deep-sea diver plunged into the sea to place explosive charges on the pipelines.

On September 26, the bombs went off. The SBU colonel who led the sabotage, Roman Chervinsky, later said he had also "planned and implemented" operations to kill pro-Russian separatist leaders in Ukraine. The undersea explosions inflicted grave economic damage on Russia, sparked outrage in Germany, and led to an international criminal investigation. But given Moscow's unceasing attacks on schools, hospitals, orphanages, playgrounds, hotels, and apartment houses, along with energy plants and other civilian targets in Ukraine, the Nord Stream bombing did not alter the moral equation of the war for the CIA.

To the contrary, the war had brought the clandestine service back to its roots.

The covert operations of the CIA and the concept of political warfare as an instrument of power owed their existence to George Kennan, the diplomat who had helped establish the American embassy in Moscow in 1933 and served as its deputy chief of mission during World War Two. Kennan was regarded as America's preeminent Kremlinologist for two generations thereafter. He had returned to the United States after the war to serve as the State Department's policy planning chief, reporting directly to the secretary of state, General George C. Marshall, and the secretary of defense, James Forrestal. Stalin was on the warpath to seize half of Europe, and the United States had no plan to stop him.

In September 1947—seventy-five years to the day before the world heard about the Nord Stream bombing—Kennan had proposed to Forrestal that the newborn CIA "fight fire with fire." Soon thereafter, he called for the inauguration of political warfare against the Soviets: the coordinated use of espionage, economic sanctions, diplomacy, and information operations intended to achieve victory over adversaries without firing a shot. For the newborn CIA, the missions would include spying, sabotage, propaganda, and support for underground resistance movements. All of that and more was now being carried out by the Ukrainian intelligence services trained, equipped, and emboldened by the CIA. Burns and his colleagues at the Pentagon, the State Department, and the National Security Council were projecting American power against the Kremlin, without the president sending in the marines. The declassification and publication of secret intelligence had exposed and effectively blunted Putin's plans to use disinformation and lies as instruments of war.

Throughout the summer and fall of 2022, the CIA's Moscow station was reporting dismay and disbelief among Russia elites at the failures of the invasion. Putin had intended to show the world that Russia was a great power by conquering Ukraine. He had exposed the rottenness of his regime for the world to see. The United States had regarded him as "a very savvy gangster, unbound by facts, law, morals or truth," in the words of John Sullivan, the American ambassador in Moscow from October 2019 to September 2022. The invasion had revealed that he was neither a savvy nor a strategic thinker. "He really thought he could take Kiev in less than a week, and he thought he could establish his dominance over Ukraine very quickly," Burns said. "Putin's fond of saying that Ukraine is not a real country. Well, real countries fight back, and that's just what President Zelensky and my intelligence counterparts in the Ukrainian military have done."

The Ukrainians would survive as a free people, he said, "so long as we continue to support them."

Chapter Twenty-Eight

THE MORALITY OF ESPIONAGE

On November 14, 2022, Burns flew to Ankara for an urgent talk with Sergei Naryshkin, his Russian counterpart. Their meeting, at the headquarters of the Turkish intelligence service, was the first between high-ranking American and Russian officials since the invasion of Ukraine. Biden had sent Burns on a mission to prevent a nuclear war.

Putin had made thinly veiled threats to use nuclear weapons in battle against Ukraine and for political blackmail against NATO and the United States. Since the invasion, he had placed his nuclear forces on high alert, tested a new intercontinental ballistic missile, and warned that Russia would use all the means at its disposal, including nuclear weapons, if he so chose. Burns knew the danger was real. "Given the potential desperation of President Putin and the Russian leadership, given the setbacks that they've faced so far, militarily, none of us can take lightly the threat posed by a potential resort to tactical nuclear weapons or low-yield nuclear weapons," he had said in April, two months after the invasion. "We watch for that very intently. It's one of our most important responsibilities at CIA."*

---

* The explosive power of "low-yield" nuclear weapons in the Russian arsenal ranged from about 0.3 kilotons—roughly 300 tons of TNT—to 10 kilotons. The bomb the United States dropped on Hiroshima was about 15 kilotons. Most tactical nukes are designed for artillery shells, but the smallest could fit in a backpack.

In September, the CIA and the NSA had intercepted chatter among Russian battlefield commanders suggesting that Putin might not be bluffing. A thorough analysis of these intercepts had appeared in the President's Daily Brief. Some at the CIA assessed the chances of a nuclear strike at fifty-fifty. "We have a direct threat of the use of the nuclear weapon if, in fact, things continue down the path they've been going," Biden had told a group of wealthy fundraisers in New York on October 6. Blinken and Milley had called their Russian counterparts to protest, to no avail. Defense Secretary Lloyd Austin rang up the Russian defense minister, Sergei Shoigu, twice in three days. Shoigu maintained that Ukraine was prepared to use a dirty bomb against his forces, a clear sign of plans to concoct a false-flag pretext for Russia's using tactical nuclear weapons in battle. Austin told him he was lying. Burns shared the intelligence on the threat with China's Ministry of State Security; President Xi publicly admonished Putin against the saber-rattling shortly thereafter.

Naryshkin had arrived in Ankara thinking that Burns was ready to negotiate a ceasefire under which Russia would keep the land it had seized from Ukraine. Burns disabused him of that delusion. He told him to tell Putin to knock off the threats and provocations. He warned, in the strongest words possible, of the consequences if Russia broke the nuclear taboo. The Pentagon had war-gamed it: if Putin exploded a weapon of mass destruction, the United States military would destroy Russia's army on the battlefield in Ukraine.

Putin responded by moving an arsenal of tactical nuclear weapons into Belarus, whose southern border lay sixty miles north of Kyiv. He took pleasure in psychological warfare at home and abroad, and he continued to use the specter of World War Three to rally his citizenry and rattle the nations of NATO. "State propaganda is preparing people to think that nuclear war isn't a bad thing," noted the Russian journalist Dmitry Muratov, a Nobel Peace Prize laureate. "On TV channels here, nuclear war and nuclear weapons are promoted as if they're advertising pet food."

"A full-frontal assault"

Burns and Naryshkin moved on from the threat of Armageddon. They agreed on a deal to free Brittney Griner, the American basketball player, who was locked up in a penal colony, once part of Stalin's gulag archipelago, a hellhole even by Russian standards. This marked the beginning of twenty-one months of intense intelligence diplomacy conducted by Burns and CIA officers in Moscow, Berlin, Warsaw, Riyadh, Istanbul, and Washington. It led to a grand bargain: a prisoner exchange surpassing the spy swaps of the cold war in its complexities and intrigues.

Burns previously had proposed to Alexander Bortnikov, the career KGB officer who led the Russian federal security service, the FSB, that they open a formal intelligence channel for prisoner exchanges. The CIA and the KGB had started a hotline for back-channel discussions in 1983, at the height of cold war tensions between Washington and Moscow, but it had fallen into disuse after the Soviet Union dissolved in 1992. Biden and Putin, at their first and only summit meeting in June 2021, had agreed to revive it, and the CIA's Moscow station became the American switchboard for the prisoner negotiations. The hope was that after its station chief and case officers outlined a deal with their Russian counterparts, Burns could do the hard bargaining to seal it.

Griner, who had joined a Russian league during the Phoenix Mercury's offseason, had been arrested nine months earlier at the Moscow airport for possession of less than a gram of medically prescribed hashish oil, convicted of drug smuggling, and sentenced to nine years. Burns offered to exchange her for one of the world's most notorious merchants of death—Viktor Bout, once a GRU cadet, who had sold Soviet-made arms to warlords, terrorists, and rogue states around the world since the 1990s. Bout had been arrested in Thailand, in a sting executed by U.S. drug-enforcement agents posing as Colombian guerrillas, convicted in Manhattan in 2011, and sentenced to twenty-five years' imprisonment. The deal was a straight-up trade: the arms dealer for the star athlete. On

December 8, twenty-four days after Burns and Naryshkin met in Ankara, Griner and Bout were set free at an airport in Abu Dhabi.

In January 2023, six weeks after Griner was freed, the CIA proposed trading the American Paul Whelan for two Russian spies, a married couple who had just been arrested in Slovenia, the nation nestled between Italy, Austria, Hungary, and Croatia; the pair, posing as Argentinians, had been trying to penetrate the intelligence services of those countries. Whalen, a dishonorably discharged ex-Marine working as a corporate security consultant in Moscow, had been arrested on an espionage charge in 2019 and sentenced to sixteen years in prison. The FSB rejected the deal. In mid-March, Burns called Bortnikov to press for a resolution, but he was intransigent. The CIA soon found out why.

Putin was playing for greater stakes. On March 29, the FSB arrested Evan Gershkovich, a correspondent for the *Wall Street Journal* based in Moscow, and accused him of being a spy.* Gershkovich's reporting on the Russian military and its failures in Ukraine had made him a visible target, a valuable hostage, and a pawn in a vicious game. That harsh fact became clear to Biden and Burns after his arrest. "There was just a general recognition across the entire government, whether it was us, the CIA, the White House, that it was going to take more than just a one-for-one swap," said Ambassador Roger Carstens, the State Department's special envoy for hostage affairs; the CIA "played an outsized role" in "a full-frontal assault" by Biden, Burns, and Blinken to resolve the American prisoners' dilemma.

Burns now proposed to up the ante. The CIA's call to arms had led to the arrests of deep-cover GRU spies in Norway and Poland, along with the pair in Slovenia, during 2022. The CIA's Moscow station proposed to add them to the bid for Gershkovich and Whelan during its next meeting with the FSB in November 2023. The station chief reported that Putin wanted to extort a higher price.

---

* The charge was absurd. The CIA had foresworn using journalism jobs as cover in 1977, though posing as a reporter had been splendid camouflage for cold war case officers over the course of thirty years. It was easy to see why: the job of an American foreign correspondent was to go to other countries and put penetrating questions to utter strangers.

The Russians insisted on the release of Vadim Krasikov, a high-ranking FSB colonel serving a life sentence in a German jail. Krasikov had shot and killed an exiled Chechen rebel with a silenced handgun at a children's playground in the Tiergarten, the elegant leafy park in central Berlin, in 2019. For Putin, springing him was a matter of loyalty: he had been part of the president's security detail at the Kremlin and his orders had come from the top. For the German chancellor, Olaf Scholz, the idea was abhorrent, unless there were a higher moral imperative. And that was winning freedom for the political prisoner Alexey Navalny, the Russian dissident whom Putin had tried to murder with a nerve agent, jailed on trumped-up charges after a sham trial, and then thrown into solitary confinement in a freezing cell at a desolate penal colony forty miles north of the Arctic Circle. The chancellor faced intense resistance from his national-security team and his political counsellors. Would he overrule them and release Krasikov for the greater good of freeing Navalny?

Biden put the question to Scholz in the Oval Office on February 9, 2024. "For you, I will try to do this," he replied.

A week later, the Kremlin announced that Navalny was dead at the age of forty-seven. His death knocked the secret negotiations with the Germans sideways. The news broke on February 16, in the opening hours of the annual Munich Security Conference, where Vice President Harris led the American delegation. In a private meeting, she urged Scholz to keep the fate of Putin's assassin on the table despite Navalny's death. Harris also had a one-on-one talk with Prime Minster Robert Golob of Slovenia, who assured her that he would free the two Russian spies in his country's custody when the time came for a prisoner exchange. Scholz held out until June 7, relenting only after receiving a personal letter from Biden persuading him to relent.

This set the stage for a climactic meeting convened with the strictest secrecy in—of all places—the capital of Saudi Arabia.

Burns himself had been in and out of the Middle East constantly, taking on the thankless task of making peace. With $18 billion of American military aid, the Israelis were slaughtering tens of thousands of Palestinians, their vengeance for the killing by Hamas of twelve hundred Israelis in October 2023, an attack unforeseen by political, military, and intelligence leaders in Israel and the United States. A week earlier, the national security advisor Jake Sullivan had said the Middle East was quieter than it had been in two decades. With American bombs, Israel now laid waste to Gaza, destroying hospitals and universities, terrorizing two million civilians. Biden mulled withholding weapons from the Israelis to moderate their conduct, but he delayed only one shipment. He tacitly approved their attacks in Lebanon, Syria, and Iran to destroy the military leadership of Hezbollah and Hamas. Perhaps he thought the success of Israeli intelligence in assassinating terrorist commanders was a counterweight to the remorseless killing of women and children by the Israeli military.

Over the course of a year, Burns made fourteen trips—to Doha, Cairo, Amman, Tel Aviv, Paris, and Warsaw—trying to broker a ceasefire and the release of hostages in Gaza, meeting with the chiefs of the Mossad and the Egyptian intelligence services, the president of Egypt, and the prime minister of Qatar, among others. (The Qataris spoke with the political chieftains of Hamas, who lived in exile; they, in turn, spoke with their military leaders in Gaza.) Burns was the lead American negotiator, and not only for the fact that he had known many of the key players in the Middle East during his twenty-five years as a diplomat. More than a few leaders in the Arab world, including terrorist chiefs, thought the CIA was the preeminent power broker in American foreign policy. Burns believed this was a case where the mythical sway of the CIA was not a bad thing. But the force of logic failed to convince the intransigent Benjamin Netanyahu and the dwindling numbers of die-hard Hamas leaders who survived the Israelis' relentless efforts to kill them. They all believed in the logic of force.

"We've come close at least a couple of times, but it's been very elusive," Burns said as the slaughter in Gaza ground on. "In the end, it's not just about brackets in texts or creative formulas when you're trying to negotiate a hostage and ceasefire deal. It's about leaders who ultimately have to recognize that enough is enough, that perfect is rarely on the menu, especially in the Middle East." Burns had put a concrete ceasefire proposal to Netanyahu and his war cabinet in May 2024. They took eight months to sign it and two months to break it.

"I could think of nothing more consequential"

The CIA and the Russians sat down in Riyadh on June 25. The Americans brought a framework for a prisoner swap to the table.

They named their price for the assassin Krasikov: freedom for Vladimir Kara-Murza, a Russian-British journalist whose work had won him the 2024 Pulitzer Prize for commentary—and a twenty-five-year prison sentence for treason—along with six jailed Russian activists who had worked with Navalny, human rights organizations, or the political opposition; Alsu Kurmasheva, a Radio Free Europe/Radio Liberty reporter and an American citizen, charged with acting as an unregistered foreign agent; Sasha Skochilenko, a creative artist; and a high school student, an immigration lawyer, and a political scientist. All had been locked up for crimes against the state. In exchange for Evan Gershkovich and Paul Whelan, the Russians would receive six jailed spies, including Krasilov, and two cybercriminals imprisoned in America. The key to unlocking the cells holding Russia's political prisoners was the value Putin placed on the life of a cold-blooded murderer. On June 27, the FSB officers flew back to Moscow to deliver the terms of the proposal to Putin.

That night, fifty-one million people watched Biden stumble and flail through a televised debate against Trump in Atlanta; some soon turned away in shock. When he spoke, his train of thought derailed; when he stood silent, his jaw was slack, his eyes vacant, as if he had forgotten who he was. He was eighty-one, a tired and tongue-tied old man, and it was impossible to imagine him serving for four more years. Overnight, he had made Trump a prohibitive favorite to win back the White House. The coming days would bring the deepest humiliation of his life and one of the highest moments of his presidency.

Burns spoke with Bortnikov over the July 4 weekend and urged him to take the offer. Late the next week, the CIA and the FSB met in Istanbul, where the channel first had opened, and where the deal would be consummated in a series of choreographed flights from six nations. Putin accepted the terms on July 17, with one catch: he would release only convicted prisoners. Two days later, the judges in the sham trials of Gershkovich and Kurmasheva sped their cases to conclusion, handing down guilty verdicts and harsh sentences. That set everything in motion, save for one last detail. Slovenia hadn't issued a formal pardon to the Russian spies it held; their release required it and the deal would fall apart without it.

On Sunday, July 21, the president of the United States, sick with Covid and deep in despondency, sat isolated at his vacation home in Rehoboth, Delaware. At 12:09 p.m., he placed a call to the prime minster of Slovenia and secured the pardons. Ninety-seven minutes later, he posted an announcement on social media: *I believe it is in the best interest of my party and the country for me to stand down and to focus solely on fulfilling my duties as President for the remainder of my term.* After fifty-two years of political life, he was giving up power. Then he announced that he wanted Harris to run in his place.

Burns flew back to Ankara a few days later to arrange the logistics of the prisoner flights with the Organization, as the Turkish intelligence agency was known. Over the years, the Organization had arrested and tortured dissidents and journalists while working with the Americans against al Qaeda and ISIS. Few intelligence services that the CIA counted as partners were great respecters of human rights. But Turkey was the only NATO nation that maintained a close political dialogue with Russia, often at the expense of its international reputation, and it was the logical nexus for the prisoner exchange.

The CIA and the State Department choreographed flights arriving from Moscow, Washington, Berlin, Warsaw, Oslo, and Ljubljana. On the morning of August 1, one plane left Ankara heading north over the Black Sea to Russia, another west over the Atlantic to America. Upon their return, Krasikov and his comrades received a hero's welcome from Putin. And then, a few minutes before midnight, after a thirteen-hour trip on a State Department Gulfstream G550, Gershkovich, Kurmasheva, and Whelan stepped onto the tarmac at Joint Base Andrews, twelve miles southeast of the White House. Biden and Harris were there to meet them. "I could think of nothing more consequential" than their freedom, the president said.

"To try and change the world around them"

As the days and weeks of Biden's presidency dwindled, along with his powers of thought and speech, the world was approaching a state of total war. Russia, China, North Korea, and Iran were allied against America and NATO in the battle for Ukraine. The four nations had formed an axis of autocracy for a new cold war against the West. Putin was attacking civilian targets in Ukraine with Iranian kamikaze drones, sending ten thousand North Korean soldiers into battle, and buying Chinese machine tools and microelectronics to build new Russian missiles and tanks.

China, in turn, purchased Iranian oil to underwrite Tehran's support for the Kremlin, collaborated with Russia on developing new weapons, and conducted joint military drills with Russia in the South China Sea, raising alarms in Taiwan and South Korea, not to mention CIA headquarters. Burns had created a new China Mission Center in 2021, and three years later it consumed a fifth of the CIA's budget, roughly $3 billion a year. Its analysts had concluded that the Chinese were on a campaign "to supplant the United States as the preeminent global power," David Marlowe said after retiring as chief of the CIA's clandestine service. "They have not been the least bit coy about it. They have declared it openly, and their actions have consistently reflected their intent."

Biden did not grasp that the world as he knew it was ending, that the system of law and principles built after World War Two to keep the peace was shattering. He had no strategy for a new age of global conflict. And he had never articulated a war plan for the arming of Ukraine, simply framing it as an existential struggle between democratic principles and authoritarian power. But Russia always had explicit aims: to conquer Ukraine and obliterate the identity and culture of its people. So the CIA kept concentrating on helping the Ukrainians kill the enemy.

Zelensky said the Russians had lost 198,000 dead and more than 550,000 wounded, while the Ukrainians had suffered 43,000 battlefield deaths and 370,000 injuries. The reported number of Russians killed in thirty-four months was more than triple the number of Americans who died during sixteen years of war in Vietnam. The United States had delivered more than $135 billion worth of military aid to Ukraine, its lethality multiplied by real-time intelligence on the Russians' locations, much of it provided by the CIA station in Kyiv. But "U.S. and NATO weapons took too damn long to arrive in Ukraine, and they came with far too many restrictions," Paula Doyle said. When Republicans in Congress blocked the weapons shipments for five months, holding Ukraine hostage to their demands to stop migration at the southern border of the United States, the tide of war had shifted to Russia's advantage until after the Republicans finally relented in April 2024.

"Putin's view has always been we have attention deficit disorder, and we'll get distracted," Burns said. "And I believe and my colleagues at CIA believe that Putin is wrong about that, as he was profoundly wrong in his assumption about the Ukrainians' will to resist, and the will of the West, of the United States, and all of our partners, to support the Ukrainians." But the weapons America provided fell far short of helping Zelensky fulfill his hopes for victory, including the return of all Ukrainian land. Until the last weeks of his presidency, Biden barred Ukraine from using American long-range missiles to strike Russian airfields, which led to continuous catastrophic attacks on apartment houses, schools, hospitals, and power plants, each one a war crime. Yet for all the pain and suffering Putin had inflicted, he had not come close to victory.

"In a sense, Putin has already suffered a strategic defeat," Burns said in July 2024. "If Ukraine's goal is to be an even stronger, more independent, more sovereign country, able to make its own choices, they've already won and Putin's lost." Two weeks later, the Ukrainian army, led by the SBU, launched an audacious counteroffensive, seizing dozens of Russian villages around the city of Kursk, taking hundreds of soldiers as prisoners, and forcing the evacuation of 120,000 civilians. Putin's dismay, and his army's disarray, was impossible to conceal. The impact of Ukraine's counterattack on Kursk was immense, and for good reason. Its forces had carried out the first invasion of Russia since World War Two, striking a blow against Putin's twenty-five-year campaign to paint Russia as a resurgent superpower, wounding not only the army but the state itself. "Putin was at his best moment the day before he invaded because he had all the power that he's ever going to have," Marlowe said. "His objectives were to squeeze things out of Ukraine, to threaten NATO and affect NATO unification, and to show off to the world that Russia is powerful militarily, economically, diplomatically. He squandered every single bit of that."

Sylvester called the survival of Ukraine a triumph of HUMINT— human intelligence, the heart and soul of espionage. The term was coined early in the cold war to distinguish the work of human spies from SIGINT, signals intelligence collected by the newborn National Security Agency, and IMINT, imagery obtained by the U-2 plane and photoreconnaissance satellites. These technologies had undermined traditional espionage, the former CIA director Richard Helms had warned in 1983. "With the passage of time, a distortion threatened to change the character of our work," he said. "The collectors with technical gadgets began to disparage the work of human collectors. The new cry from the gadgeteers was, 'Give us the money and leave it to us.' And, indeed, why take risks running spies when gadgets would tell you what you wanted to know? But therein lay a fallacy. And the debate over the elements of that fallacy is with us today and inevitably will crop up from time to time in the future. Why? Because gadgets cannot divine man's intentions. Even if computers can be programmed to think, they will not necessarily come to the same conclusion as Mr. [Yuri] Andropov," the longtime KGB chief who was then the leader of the Soviet Union.* "If there is a weakness in our intelligence apparatus," Helms concluded, "it is in our ability to figure out what the leaders of a foreign power are going to do in any given situation."

All this remained true four decades later. If the CIA had ten analysts studying the transcript of an intercepted conversation, "they're going to come to ten different analytic assessments on what happened," Sylvester said. But "if you actually talk to somebody who was in the room," you

---

* Here Helms foresaw by forty years the problems the CIA now faces in harnessing artificial intelligence for tasks beyond summarizing information in a sea of data. The predictive powers of AI remain no better than the human mind. It still lacks common sense or the ability to deal with ambiguity.

might know the truth, or something close to it. "When we talk about human intelligence, it really is the collection of everything that goes into how our adversaries are thinking, acting, and the context in which those decisions are being made."

Some officers in the clandestine service had long held "a very stunted view of what espionage is, what human intelligence is, that it's solely measured by the number of reports that you disseminated and the number of clandestine agents that you've recruited," he said. "Well, that might have been important in 1982." No longer. The people the CIA had recruited to penetrate the Kremlin "are not case numbers. They are not numbers in a file. They're human beings who've decided to make some incredibly bold and courageous things to try and change the world around them."

America's ability to warn the world about the coming Russian invasion and blunt its force after the war began had rested in great part with the CIA. "That was based on espionage, human intelligence, the collection of insights from people to effect policy," Sylvester said. So too was the CIA's decade of covert support for Ukraine. That mission depended on the ability "to build up human relations" with its military and intelligence officers. "Is that espionage? Absolutely. That's what HUMINT is. . . . And I think this should be so revelatory," he said. "It's a compilation of all the traits that make a human service."

"The greatest immorality and the greatest morality"

The thought that a humanity lay at the heart of espionage clashed with the tenet that American intelligence was at best amoral and at worst immoral to the core. Yet the idea was essential to the enlistment of foreign agents, the endeavor at the heart of the CIA's mission. The CIA had been fortunate that the United States, for all its flaws, had held a higher moral ground than its worst enemies. For many years, it had claimed to stand for democracy and human rights, against tyranny and oppression. Today this stance might seem like a myth.

But throughout the twenty-first century, "when authoritarian leaders in Moscow, Beijing, and Tehran used coercion and lethal force to bend their citizens and other countries to their will, they invariably inspired otherwise patriotic subjects to protest and get thrown in jail or be killed, conform but secretly seethe, or get up the courage to clandestinely work behind the scenes with Washington and our closest allies," said Paula Doyle, an architect of the beautiful operation to stop rogue nations from gaining nuclear weapons. "Some of the latter came to CIA seeking revenge. Some sought the power to change their systems. Some wanted money in order to achieve a lifestyle or retirement that would have otherwise been impossible. Some did just about anything to be in a position to bring their families to the West to live in freedom. They were the reason we had a CIA. *They* brought us war plans and intentions. *They* brought us nuclear plans and intentions. *They* brought us physical access in dangerous places and cultural details that made covert action possible and—in some cases—wildly successful."

The alliance between a CIA case officer and a foreign recruit was an alloy of trust and betrayal, founded in the agent's faith in the United States and his choice to commit treason. "Like war, spying is a dirty business," observed William Hood, a charter member of the CIA who spent twenty-eight years running missions against the Soviets. "Shed of its alleged glory, a soldier's job is to kill. Peel away the claptrap of espionage, and the spy's job is to betray trust." And yet the relationship between officer and agent was built on their trust in one another. It was "a covenant, not unlike marriage . . . a bond forged in hardships and risks, for a greater good," said Juan Cruz, chief of the Latin American division in the Obama years.

"The business is schizophrenic," said Luis Rueda, the author of the covert-action plan Tom Sylvester had executed with the Kurds to subvert Saddam. "At the tactical level, it deals with humans. We find out what the prospective agent needs, whether money, validation, or something else, and help him or her achieve it. We devote great effort to protecting them. We stand by them. However, at the strategic level, it is all about protecting and advancing U.S. national interests. Are we helping the Ukrainians? Yes. But we are doing it because it weakens Russia and strengthens our position, not out of some sense of morality or humanitarian impetus. We help and use people at the same time. We have sacrificed people at the end of that human relationship to advance U.S. interests."

The litany of those sacrifices was long. The eldest Kurdish fighters still remembered how they had been betrayed by Secretary of State Henry Kissinger, who had cut off the CIA's covert support for their armed struggle against Saddam and left them to face his pitiless wrath. The Kurdish leader Mustafa Barzani had appealed to Kissinger in a letter: "Your Excellency, the United States has a moral and political responsibility to our people." He received no answer. Kissinger had been cold-blooded about it. "Covert action," he had said in 1975, "should not be confused with missionary work."

The Rev. William Sloan Coffin Jr. would agree. A fiercely committed opponent of the Vietnam War in his years as the chaplain of Yale University, Coffin had been an equally intense anticommunist as a CIA officer in Munich in the early 1950s. The Pentagon had ordered the clandestine service to obtain the Kremlin's plans for World War Three, a mission at the time akin to asking it to plant spies on Mars. Coffin had recruited and trained Russian exiles who formed four-man parachute teams and flew over the Iron Curtain into the Soviet Union, as far east as the outskirts of Moscow. None survived. Coffin knew these were suicide missions. He had no qualms about it.

"The ends don't always justify the means," he said in 2005. "But they are the only things that can."

In the twenty years between the end of the war in Korea and the end of the war in Vietnam, legions of young officers had graduated from the U.S. Military Academy at West Point and by choice or chance entered the clandestine service not long thereafter. During those decades, they were schooled by the CIA's director of training, Hugh Cunningham, who was like Bill Coffin and his friend George H. W. Bush, a Yale man and a member of its most secret society, Skull and Bones. The West Point honor code was clear: "A cadet will not lie, cheat, steal, or tolerate those who do." Indoctrinating his students into their own secret society, Cunningham had taught them another ethos.

"We must have the greatest immorality, and we must have the greatest morality," he had told them. These words could serve as a credo for the CIA. To hold both those ideas to be true required an abiding faith in the righteousness of the mission.

"I spent my entire CIA career lying, cheating, stealing, manipulating, deceiving," said James Olson, the cold war leader of Russia House and the chief of counterintelligence during his three-decade career. He was a devout Catholic who used the just-war theory of the medieval theologian Thomas Aquinas as a moral compass: if it were morally sound for a soldier to kill in a just war, then lying, cheating, and stealing were justified to subvert the Russians and the rest of America's enemies. They were requisite when recruiting agents to commit treason and betray their leaders on the behalf of the United States. "If we're going to defend our country against the evils that are out there, we can't go out there with our hands tied behind our back," Olson said in 2021. "We've got to fight tough. And *that's* the issue. How tough is too tough? When do we cross the line? When do we betray those values that we're fighting so hard to defend? When do *we* become *them*?"

"The infantry of our ideology"

The CIA had crossed the line in the first twenty years of the twenty-first century, serving a tool for torture and an instrument of death, running cruel prisons and executing innocent people, though the moral responsibility lay with the presidents who gave the marching orders, not with the officers who executed them. It had targeted and assassinated an American citizen, albeit a terrorist, at Obama's command. "The precedent of an American president being able to kill an American citizen under any circumstances, on just his signature, is dangerous," Bob Gates had warned. The CIA's analysts had provided the abysmal intelligence to justify the invasion of Iraq, though the bloodshed of the war forever stained the hands of the man who had started it. On September 11, which now seemed like the first day of the new millennium, Americans had seen to their sorrow that when intelligence fails, people die.

A quarter of a century later, they were still learning that when intelligence succeeds, it can save lives. And the CIA had saved thousands more lives than it had taken during the four years that Bill Burns led them. It did so on a single day in the summer of 2024. Its officers had stopped a potentially cataclysmic attack by four young ISIS-K adherents intent on bombing a Taylor Swift concert in Vienna, at a venue that held an audience of seventy thousand. "They were plotting to kill a huge number, tens of thousands of people at this concert, I am sure many Americans," the CIA's deputy director, David Cohen, told the world on August 28, 2024. He said the arrests of the suspects had been "a really good day" for the CIA.

Harder days lay over the dark horizon. The threats facing America and its allies were as grave as any since the cold war. "The world is getting increasingly complex and increasingly dangerous," Tom Sylvester said. "Across the globe our adversaries are doing everything they can" to undermine American power and instill authoritarian rule. Russia and China depended on "other countries that fear their dominion, fear their tyranny, and only cooperate from a sense of either intimidation, or that it's business, or they're bought off"—but America had allies around the world who "identify with us and what we want to do in this globe." Over the course of eight decades, the CIA had done what it could to protect the United States, by means both moral and immoral. Its officers had seen themselves as a secret army in the battle for what once was known as the free world. Now the most immediate danger facing the country was one the CIA was powerless to prevent. And that was the threat to American democracy itself.

A nation's intelligence officers, John le Carré observed, are "the infantry of our ideology." In America, they follow the command of presidents and presidents alone. Now the Supreme Court had ruled that presidents were protected from prosecution for crimes committed in the ambit of their power. A president "who admits to having ordered the assassinations of his political rivals or critics . . . has a fair shot at getting immunity," Justice Sonia Sotomayor had written in dissent from the court's 6–3 decision. "The president is now a king above the law." The CIA veterans John Sipher and James Petrila observed: "If a president should choose to declare a political rival guilty of treason, deploy a paramilitary group to assassinate that rival and direct the attorney general to sign a document saying that said rival's death is necessary for 'the securing of liberty,' these would be official acts for which the president is immune." This fear was not that far-fetched.

A lawless chief executive could command the CIA to serve as his secret police, to spy on Americans, and to support right-wing dictators, as it had done in the greatest secrecy during the cold war. He could demand that it cease spying on Russia and subvert American allies instead. He could order it to conduct political warfare against the citizens of the United States, and to assassinate his enemies at home and abroad. The officers of the CIA would be the only line of resistance. Unless they rebelled against him, the CIA would no longer be an intelligence service under law, but a secret weapon wielded by a man above it.

Tom Sylvester served for three days as the acting director of the Central Intelligence Agency at the start of the new year, returning to lead the clandestine service into the spring. In that short time, America's role in the world was forever altered, its alliances shattered, its enemies emboldened. And when he looked back at his thirty-four years as an American spy, he reflected on the power of tyrants to shape the fate of nations. He had fought, an unknown soldier, against Saddam and Assad and Putin, and he now bore witness to what he had seen. "I've had this catbird seat in watching, over the past decades, what has happened in world history. And what continues to horrify me, shock me, is the fact that single individuals have within their power the ability to wreak pain and suffering," he said. "So many innocent people. Such pain, such destruction, such suffering. . . . And I think that's the hardest part for me."

EPILOGUE: AUTOCRACY IN AMERICA

On January 20, 2025, Donald Trump took the oath of office in the Capitol Rotunda, where his mob had rampaged four years before.

His inaugural speech praised the memory of President William McKinley, the chosen candidate of the robber barons who ran the country at the turn of the twentieth century. McKinley had made America an empire by taking over the Philippines, Hawaii, Guam, Cuba, and Puerto Rico, and striking the deal that created the Panama Canal. And through him, Trump invoked the spirit of Manifest Destiny, the ideology that God gave the United States the divine right to seize land with guns and money. In days to come, he promised to make America greater, expanding its dominion, the sovereignty of other nations be damned. He wanted to seize the canal, annex Canada, and buy Greenland. If Russia could take great swaths of Ukraine, why couldn't he remake the map of the world—by force, if necessary?

The question was among the first to confront the CIA's new director, John Ratcliffe. He was likely to tell the president whatever he wanted to hear; he had promised to align the CIA with Trump's view of the world. Candidates for the CIA's top ranks faced loyalty tests. Their interrogators asked three questions: Had they voted for Trump? Wasn't the 2020 election stolen? What did they think about the January 6 insurrection? CIA officers and analysts feared they would be fired as Ratcliffe enforced Trump's ideological purge. Sylvester's heir apparent lost his chance to lead the clandestine service when the White House learned of his ardent support for Ukraine.

"We will clean out all of the corrupt actors in our national-security and intelligence apparatus," the president had vowed. The new secretary of defense was Pete Hegseth, a Fox News host who had convinced Trump to absolve American war criminals and stood credibly accused of sexual assault and alcohol abuse. He quickly fired all of the Pentagon's top lawyers, the judge advocates general with the power to say that a president's order was unlawful and must be disobeyed, and hired his personal attorney in their stead. The Putin apologist and conspiracy theorist Tulsi Gabbard became director of national intelligence. The thought that she would oversee the President's Daily Brief was appalling to CIA officers; the likelihood that allied intelligence services would balk at sharing secrets with her was high. Trump's favorite political saboteur, Kash Patel, took over the FBI, ousting its leaders and promising to empty its headquarters, dismantle its national-security and intelligence divisions, and investigate the president's political enemies.*

These three represented the disastrous rise of misplaced power. Giving them authority over America's national security was madness in the eyes of professional intelligence officers. But placing Ratcliffe atop the CIA made perfect sense, if you were Trump.

Ratcliffe had won the job on the strength of his eight months as director of national intelligence during 2020, when he had distorted reporting and analysis about the Russians in order to please the president. "This idiot is abusing his office," Mike Hayden had tweeted back then. "The head of the intelligence community should be hands off on politics. This is reprehensible!" (If Trump won a second term, Hayden had predicted, the United States "will be just like Russia or China. A tin-pot dictatorship.")

---

* The founding father Alexander Hamilton believed that no right-minded president would nominate people "who had no other merit than . . . being in some way or other personally allied to him, or of possessing the necessary insignificance and pliancy to render them the obsequious instruments of his pleasure." (*Federalist* No. 76, April 1, 1788.) But these were precisely the qualities Trump demanded. "Totalitarianism in power invariably replaces all first-rate talents, regardless of their sympathies, with those crackpots and fools whose lack of intelligence and creativity is still the best guarantee of their loyalty," as Hannah Arendt wrote in *The Origins of Totalitarianism* (1951).

The Russia House veteran John Sipher had warned that Ratcliffe regarded the CIA as "a place to hunt for nuggets that can be used as political weapons—sources and methods be damned," thereby "creating a fictional narrative for political purposes." He said that it was "child's play to concoct any story you wish by plucking selective details from the millions and millions of pages held by the intelligence agencies."

Ratcliffe's record as an intelligence chief was a harbinger of what was to come at the CIA. "Disaster comes to policymakers who insist that intelligence conform to some politically pleasing standard," the CIA's former acting director and deputy director John McLaughlin wrote in January 2025, and "disaster comes to intelligence officers who are tempted to discern that standard and play to it."

The president had vowed vengeance against the imaginary deep state. On Ratcliffe's recommendation, Trump stripped security clearances from fifty CIA veterans—including the former directors and acting directors Hayden, Panetta, Brennan, McLaughlin, and Morell—whom he deemed deep statesmen. The agency could no longer call upon their experience and expertise. Then Trump abolished the armed security details protecting three men facing death threats for their roles in the 2020 assassination of Qasem Soleimani, Iran's Revolutionary Guard commander. His decision threatened the lives of Mike Pompeo, once his doggedly loyal CIA director and secretary of state; John Bolton, his former national security adviser; and Mark Milley, the just-retired Joint Chiefs chairman. Trump's vindictive act mortified Tom Cotton, the archconservative chairman of the Senate intelligence committee, who wondered aloud whether intelligence officers would now balk at dangerous missions targeting Iran, China, or North Korea. Testifying to the committee, Ratcliffe flirted with perjury as he whitewashed his role in a Signal chat which disclosed American military and intelligence secrets to the world.

Ratcliffe abolished the CIA's policies mandating a diverse workforce and fired the people assigned to fulfill them. The most recent directive, signed by Gina Haspel and renewed by Bill Burns, said that the "CIA's ability to achieve its critical mission of collecting foreign intelligence . . . and conducting covert action . . . requires us to attract America's best," regardless of race or gender. This decision augured badly. For more than forty years, the clandestine service had been trying to recruit and retain African American, Arab American, and Asian American officers, on the sound basis that sending an all-white cadre to spy in places like Somalia, Pakistan, or China was terrible tradecraft. In an age of ubiquitous technical surveillance, the CIA desperately needed spies who could blend into the human terrain abroad, who like the best analysts had a command of the languages and the cultures of the countries they covered. It would now be harder to find them and keep them. "Such a stupid move," Marc Polymeropoulos protested. "Diversity is the agency's greatest strength. It's our superpower. It's how we don't get caught."

Ratcliffe heedlessly rejected an offer from Trump to protect the CIA from the onslaught of summary firings and enforced resignations sweeping the government at the president's demand. The director pressed the most experienced officers and analysts to head for the exits. Then he and his aides sent an unclassified email listing everyone the CIA had hired in 2023 and 2024 to Elon Musk and his team, offering them up on the altar of budget cuts. This roster contained their true first names and last initials. The CIA's counterintelligence chief immediately called for a damage assessment; Chinese spies likely could read that email, given their penetrations of the American government's computer networks and the Musk operation's appalling security practices. The length of that list reflected the fact that the CIA's recruitment of new talent had hit historic highs in the past two years; as Burns strove to strengthen the China Mission Center, the Farm had trained hundreds of people to target Beijing. The risks of sending them abroad now were immense. Ratcliffe dealt with this debacle by firing great numbers of the newly hired, sacrificing the future of the CIA, while ramping up the pressure on the old guard to depart. The FBI, its leadership decapitated, confronted two counterintelligence nightmares. One was the anger of hundreds of young spies kicked to the curb by the CIA's director. Another was the incalculable security risk created by Trump's turning the government's information systems over to Musk, his manic second-in-command.

On Trump's authority, Musk now had access to data detailing trillions of dollars of government spending, the personnel and security files of two million government employees, and the operating budgets for all of America's intelligence agencies, including the highly classified systems that the CIA used to pay foreign liaison services and recruit agents. Placing this trove in his hands was pure folly. Musk had been talking to Putin off and on for more than two years; if Russian spies hadn't penetrated his networks, they were guilty of criminal negligence. And his fawning praise for China's leaders suggested he would "jump like a circus monkey when Xi Jinping calls in the hour of need," said Vivek Ramaswamy, the erstwhile presidential candidate and partner in Musk's pirate operation, the Department of Government Efficiency. Musk and his crew of twentysomething tech bros were walking targets. "A foreign intel service just has to find someone close to Musk who is motivated by: (a) greed; (b) ego; (c) disdain for the United States; (d) a drug problem; or (e) all of the above," said the former CIA lawyer Brian Greer, and they could strike gold.

As American intelligence bent under the weight of Trump's malevolence, Ratcliffe invited Musk to come to the CIA and impose his will upon it. The director had spent much of his time sequestered on the seventh floor, indifferent to the upheaval he had created. In a few short weeks, he had wounded the spirit of the CIA and sapped the strength of its expertise. Morale at headquarters began sinking toward depths unseen for twenty years or more. A foreboding filled the air, a sense of impending calamity.

Then Trump began to strike a series of blows against the national-security establishment the United States had created in the eighty years since the end of World War Two. In one of the seventy executive orders he issued in his first five weeks, he paved the way for the United States to withdraw from the treaties it had signed and the multinational organizations it had joined since 1945. The CIA's founders had been present for the creation of those institutions and the global order they imposed. Some of the CIA's veterans now thought they might be witnessing their destruction. The idea that Trump might abandon NATO was bad enough. What truly shocked their conscience was Trump's cold betrayal of Ukraine and his open embrace of Russia.

For a decade, American spies, politicians, citizens, and journalists had wondered aloud about the president's affinity for Putin. Was Trump really his useful idiot? Could the Russians have something on him? Was it conceivable that he had been recruited? Or had he recruited himself? Was it simply that he liked Putin because he wanted to be like Putin—an autocrat with absolute power? It had been a mystery. But now the answer was apparent, as clear as a bolt of lightning. Trump wasn't Putin's agent. He was his ally. The President of the United States had gone over to the other side.

The Russians were overjoyed. The world was going their way. "The new administration is rapidly changing all foreign policy configurations," the Kremlin spokesman Dmitry Peskov said. "This largely coincides with our vision." The CIA had been combatting that ideology all over the world for close to eighty years.

On February 24, upon the third anniversary of the invasion of Ukraine, America joined the authoritarian axis. It voted with Russia, North Korea, and Iran against a United Nations resolution demanding Russia's withdrawal of its forces, accountability for its war crimes, and the return of Ukrainian territory. With that vote, Trump broke trust with America's allies and sided openly with its enemies. Then he called Zelensky a dictator, accused him of starting the war, demanded he give the United States rights to half a trillion dollars of Ukraine's mineral wealth in fourfold repayment of America's freely given support, and tried to shove a ceasefire down his throat. It wasn't the first time he had tried to extort Ukraine.

Trump cut off American intelligence support on March 5. Ratcliffe stood down the CIA's Ukraine Task Force. Hegseth and Gabbard severed the flow of signals intelligence, stopped the delivery of overhead reconnaissance, and blocked Ukraine's access to commercial satellite imagery. The damage was immediate and devastating. Half-blind before the enemy, its defenses undone, and its lifeline to the CIA severed, Ukraine reeled under a barrage of Russian missile and drone attacks, and rapidly lost ground to the invaders. After a week, Trump released his chokehold when Zelensky submitted to the idea of a ceasefire, on terms set by the United States. Putin had his own terms. They did not include the survival of democracy in Ukraine. Trump offered Ukraine no security guarantees, only the threat of an American-backed regime change, and the promise of an endless Russian occupation. He was ready to sell out Ukraine to Moscow as he had surrendered Afghanistan to the Taliban. The largest nation in Europe faced a bitter future.

"The gravestone of Ukraine has had its date of death crossed out and reinscribed many times over the years, and over centuries" said Ed Bogan, a two-time CIA station chief with extensive experience in Kyiv, both long before and shortly after the Russian invasion of 2022. "If we walk away," he said, "I think Ukraine will lose the land Russia has taken to date. Faith in our values, our stated American values, will be radically undermined. Perhaps permanently." And if Russia succeeded "in a war of conquest, it will lead to our next world war, in some form." An emboldened Putin would fight to recapture the nations of Europe once entrapped in the Soviet empire.

"What's done is done, and Ukraine has fought valiantly," Paula Doyle lamented. It sounded like a eulogy for the nation and for the CIA's efforts to sustain it. If Putin kept the spoils of war, "the sanctity of sovereignty will erode before our eyes," a prelude to the next Russian invasion. After long study, Doyle had concluded that "Putin's playbook is eerily similar to that which Hitler used between 1938 and 1940"—a strategy of "propaganda, unproven assaults on ethnicity and religious affiliations, fake appeasement agreements, a bloodless annexation, and lightning-fast invasions and occupations." What would keep Trump from striking a deal with Putin that echoed the Hitler-Stalin Pact of August 1939, whose secret protocols let Germany and Russia carve up Europe? What then would prevent Moscow from attacking Poland or Finland—or the United States?

America faced danger at home and abroad. As the president assaulted its civil liberties and democratic institutions, seeking to finish the job his mob had started, the instruments of its intelligence and national security were in the hands of amateurs and toadies. The foundations of its foreign policy were corroding and crumbling. The State Department was shuttering embassies and consulates around the world. The diplomatic cover they gave dozens of CIA stations and bases was disappearing. The ranks of the CIA's most experienced spies and analysts were thinning. Its irreplaceable ties to its closest international allies were fraying. The risk of a catastrophic intelligence failure was as high as it had been at the start of the twenty-first century.

Imagine what could happen if the United States were struck again by a surprise attack in days to come. What would stop the president from declaring martial law or canceling elections? Could Congress or the Supreme Court oppose him? Who would disobey him if he ordered the clandestine service to rebuild the secret prisons, overthrow a sovereign nation, or assassinate his political enemies? The CIA did not defy presidents. But the CIA officers with the greatest morality could resist him. And years might pass before their stories would be told.

—March 31, 2025

ACKNOWLEDGMENTS

Reporters, like spies, are only as good as their sources. I am grateful to the more than one hundred men and women of the CIA who spoke with me for this book, often at great length, patiently responding to a barrage of follow-up questions, and above all agreeing to go on the record. Each one of them informed the book, though not every one of them is quoted. Special thanks go to William J. Burns, Leon Panetta, Mike Hayden, John Brennan, Tom Sylvester, Paula Doyle, Robert Gorelick, Jim Lawler, Margaret Henoch, Luis Rueda, Mark Polymeropoulos, John Sipher, Linda Weissgold, Jim Cotsana, Rolf Mowatt-Larsen, Doug Wise, and Steve Hall. At CIA headquarters, Tammy Kupperman Thorp, director of CIA's Office of Public Affairs from May 2021 to January 2025, set up interviews with the agency's leaders and did her best to answer my innumerable inquiries.

As *The Mission* goes to press, a crackdown against the free-speech rights of former CIA officers and analysts is taking place. "The President should immediately revoke the security clearances of any former Directors, Deputy Directors, or other senior intelligence officials who discuss their work in the press or on social media without prior clearance from the current Director," was the edict of Project 2025, the blueprint for governing in the second Trump administration. "Additional tools are needed to prevent leaked intelligence from being used as a weapon in policy debates." The chilling effect was instantaneous. Sixteen retired CIA officers quoted in this book had their clearances revoked by Trump on his first day in office, several more who served as key sources anticipated the president's wrath, and a few others asked that their names and their words be stricken from these pages. This book could not have been reported and written on the record under such a regime. It might be the last of its kind for some time to come.

It's now going on forty years since I first walked into CIA headquarters looking for a story. I am forever indebted to Gene Roberts, the longtime executive editor of the *Philadelphia Inquirer*, for sending me to Afghanistan in 1987 and starting me out on the CIA beat. Two colleagues from the *Inquirer*'s glory days have pitched in on this book. Bob Drogin, who later worked the national security beat for the *Los Angeles Times*, read the early chapters of the manuscript. Vernon Loeb, who covered intelligence for the *Washington Post*, offered invaluable insights. During my sixteen years at the *New York Times*, I was lucky to work for the late Joe Lelyveld and his successor as executive editor, Bill Keller, and to have the pleasure of working alongside immensely talented journalists like David Sanger, Ginger Thompson, Lydia Polgreen, and Lynsey Addario, to name a few.

A crack research team built a chronology spanning a quarter of a century for *The Mission*: Emma BB Doyle, Ruby T. Doyle, Ford Fishman, Mego Saienni, Pascal Peppe, Bill Harvey, Kelpy Cathedral, Phoebe Fregoli, Olive Malone, and Arlen Levy.

Kathy Robbins, my beloved literary agent of thirty years, led me to Peter Hubbard, senior vice president and publisher of Mariner Books, and together they brought *The Mission* into the world. At the Robbins Office, Janet Oshiro, Grace Garrahan, and Alexandra Sugarman held down the fort. Matthew Snyder of CAA provided sound counsel. Susanna Lea ably represented the book overseas. Elaina Richardson once again invited me to Yaddo, the artists' and writers' colony in Saratoga Springs, New York, where my books have taken shape for the past two decades.

I owe everything, all my good fortune, and my happiness to Kate, Emma, and Ruby Doyle. This book is dedicated to them, as am I.

NOTES

Chapter One: The Dark Horizon

7 *"only remaining superpower"*: Author's interview, Richard Helms.
7 *"meteor strikes on the dinosaurs"*: Richard Kerr et al., "Issues for the US Intelligence Community: Collection and Analysis on Iraq," *Studies in Intelligence* 49, no. 3 (2005), https://www.cia.gov/resources/csi/static/issues-for-US-intel.pdf.
7 *"once upon a time"*: Author's interview, Milt Bearden.
8 *"They had charts on the walls"*: Tim Weiner, "The C.I.A. Limps Toward 50," *New York Times*, July 20, 1997, https://www.nytimes.com/1997/07/20/weekinreview/aging-shop-of-horrors-the-cia-limps-to-50.html.
9 *"relationships around the world"*: Author's interview, George H. W. Bush.
9 *"effective intelligence service"*: Duane R. Clarridge, *A Spy for All Seasons: My Life in the CIA* (New York: Simon & Schuster, 1997), pp. 410–11.
9 *"a burning platform"*: George J. Tenet with Bill Harlow, *At the Center of the Storm: My Years at the CIA* (New York: HarperCollins, 2007), p. 20.
10 *"We had stacks of paper"*: Henry A. Crumpton, *The Art of Intelligence: Lessons from a Life in the CIA's Clandestine Service* (New York: Penguin, 2012), p. 140.
11 *"of what the mission is"*: Author's interview, John Gannon.
12 *"sleepless nights wondering"*: Tenet, *At the Center of the Storm*, p. 17.
12 *"failure is guaranteed"*: Russ Travers, "The Coming Intelligence Failure," *Studies in Intelligence* 40, no. 5 (Spring 1997), https://www.cia.gov/resources/csi/static/coming-intelligence-failure.pdf.
12 *"catastrophic systemic intelligence failure"*: House Permanent Select Committee on Intelligence report, "Counterterrorism Intelligence Capabilities and Performance Prior to 9/11," July 17, 2002. This foreboding was not new for Tenet. Not long after he first came to the CIA as deputy director in 1995, Jack Devine, a thirty-year veteran of the clandestine service and then its acting chief, had told him: "George, I'm warning you, somebody is going to fire a bullet today in northern Iraq, and you'll find out where it landed two years from now." (Author's interview with Jack Devine.) Tenet had been reduced to writing letters to the president pleading for more money, to little avail. Finally, in October 1998, eight weeks after al Qaeda

attacked two United States embassies in Africa at once with truck bombs, Tenet had persuaded Congress to give him a onetime windfall of $1.8 billion. That boost had been a rare helping hand from Congress, which far more often slapped the CIA around. The House intelligence committee, led by Republican Porter Goss, a former CIA officer and a future CIA director, had issued a scathing public critique, saying that the agency had "an uncertain commitment and capability" to conduct espionage and lacked "the analytic depth, breadth and expertise to monitor political, military and economic developments worldwide." (Tim Weiner, "House Panel Says C.I.A. Lacks Expertise to Carry Out Its Duties," *New York Times*, June 19, 1997, https://www.nytimes.com/1997/06/19/us/house-panel-says-cia-lacks-expertise-to-carry-out-its-duties.html).

14 *"the Chinese embassy"*: Tenet, *At the Center of the Storm*, p. 46.

14 *"I was on probation"*: Tenet, *At the Center of the Storm*, pp. 136–37. John Brennan, Tenet's chief of staff during the transition, said that Bush 41 influenced his son's decision to keep Tenet at CIA: "Bush 43 really didn't know about George other than what he had heard from others, and I think his father . . . gave President Bush a rather positive view of George," Brennan said. *Frontline* interview transcript, PBS, March 8, 2006, https://www.pbs.org/wgbh/pages/frontline/darkside/interviews/brennan.html.

Chapter Two: Denial and Deception

15 *"We got one"*: Author's interview, Ambassador Roberta Jacobson. Unless otherwise noted, the facts about the Airbridge Denial Program and quotations from CIA officers not named as sources are taken from the report of CIA inspector general John Helgerson, "Procedures Used in Narcotics Airbridge Denial Program in Peru, 1995–2001," August 25, 2008; approved for release, with deletions, November 2010, https://www.cia.gov/readingroom/docs/PROCEDURES%20USED%20IN%20NARCOTICS%20AIRBRIDGE%20DENIAL%20PROGRAM%20IN%20PERU%2C%201995-2001.pdf.

15 *"What did you do"*: Author's interview, Luis Rueda.

17 *"damn-the torpedoes"*: Philip Mudd, *Black Site: The CIA in the Post 9/11 World* (New York: Liveright, 2019), p. 105.

19 *"regularly monitor compliance"*: The White House, Office of the President, "Resumption of U.S. Drug Interdiction Assistance to the Government of Peru," December 8, 1994, https://nsarchive2.gwu.edu/NSAEBB/NSAEBB44/doc12.pdf. The underlying "Memorandum of Justification for Presidential Determination Regarding the Resumption of U.S. Aerial Tracking Information Sharing and Other Assistance to the Government of Peru" is in Helgerson, pp. 296–98.

19 *"pattern of not following the rules"*: Author's interview, Jack Devine.

19 *"lack of candor"*: Tim Weiner, "The CIA's Most Important Mission: Itself," *New York Times*, December 10, 1995, https://www.nytimes.com/1995/12/10/magazine/the-cia-s-most-important-mission-itself.html.

20 *"valuable lessons"*: Jose A. Rodriguez Jr. with Bill Harlow, *Hard Measures: How Aggressive CIA Actions After 9/11 Saved American Lives* (New York: Threshold Editions, 2012), p. 27.
22 *"mere mention of the word"*: Fred F. Manget, "Intelligence and the Criminal Law System," *Stanford Law and Policy Review* 17, no. 2 (2006), https://law.stanford.edu/wp-content/uploads/2018/03/manget.pdf.
24 *"bitter it was to read"*: Author's interview, Rand Beers.

Chapter Three: "It Was All Sadly Absurd"

25 *"threat from terrorism"*: Tenet testimony, Senate Armed Services Committee, March 7, 2001, http://fas.org/irp/congress/2001_hr/s010308t.html.
25 *"direct and unambiguous"*: John Rizzo, *Company Man: Thirty Years of Controversy and Crisis at the CIA* (New York: Scribner, 2014), p. 168.
25 *"first time in decades"*: Rumsfeld quoted in Gen. Richard J. Myers with Malcolm McConnell, *Eyes on the Horizon: Serving on the Front Lines of National Security* (New York: Threshold Editions, 2009), p. 140. Myers was chairman of the Joint Chiefs of Staff in 2001.
27 *"initially had a positive view"*: Zalmay Khalilzad oral history, Miller Center, University of Virginia, https://millercenter.org/the-presidency/presidential-oral-histories/zalmay-khalilzad-oral-history.
28 *"are they waiting"*: Milam quoted in Steve Coll, *Ghost Wars: The Secret History of the CIA, Afghanistan and Bin Laden, from the Soviet Invasion to September 10, 2001* (New York: Penguin, 2004), p. 498.
29 *"bin Laden in our electrical"*: Henry A. Crumpton, *The Art of Intelligence: Lessons from a Life in the CIA's Clandestine Service* (New York: Penguin, 2012), pp. 154–55.
29 *"literally made my hair"*: George J. Tenet with Bill Harlow, *At the Center of the Storm: My Years at the CIA* (New York: HarperCollins, 2007), pp. 151–54.
30 *"country needs to go"*: Tenet, *At the Center of the Storm*, pp. 151–54.
31 *"why he was President"*: Colin Powell and Richard Armitage oral history, Miller Center, University of Virginia, https://millercenter.org/the-presidency/presidential-oral-histories/colin-l-powell-and-richard-l-armitage-oral-history. The CIA had been briefing Bush verbally, as was the tradition for presidential nominees, since September 2000, and that education was essential to get him up to speed. He was not a worldly man. He rarely had been abroad; his longest overseas trip had been to China, in 1975, when his father was the American envoy in Beijing and he was a callow and hard-drinking man-child, seeking unsuccessfully to date Chinese women. No president-elect since Calvin Coolidge had been so unschooled in foreign affairs.
31 *"marriage was not made in heaven"*: Powell and Armitage oral history.
31 *"no way Cheney wanted"*: John Brennan interview, "The Dark Side," *Frontline*, PBS, March 8, 2006, https://www.pbs.org/wgbh/pages/frontline/darkside/interviews/brennan.html.

Chapter Four: The Bay of Goats

35 *"the only war we had"*: Author's interview, David Petraeus.
35 *"work with patriots"*: Author's interview, Luis Rueda.
36 *"going to get a coup"*: Author's interview, Luis Rueda.
37 *"one piece of advice"*: Robert Gates oral history, Miller Center, University of Virginia, https://millercenter.org/the-presidency/presidential-oral-histories/robert-gates-oral-history.
37 *"we were giving him money"*: Kenneth M. Pollock, "Ahmed Chalabi, RIP," Brookings Institute, November 4, 2015, https://www.brookings.edu/blog/markaz/2015/11/04/ahmad-chalabi-rip/.
37 *"guy is a weasel"*: Armitage quoted in William J. Burns, *The Back Channel: A Memoir of American Diplomacy and the Case for Its Renewal* (New York: Random House, 2019), p. 164. Among the journalists who bought what Chalabi was selling was Judith Miller of the *New York Times*. "He has provided most of the front-page exclusives on WMD to our paper," Miller boasted in an email to a colleague. Many of those exclusives stayed exclusive because they proved false. For example, Chalabi facilitated her December 2001 story of an Iraqi defector who gave an eyewitness account of "secret facilities for biological, chemical and nuclear weapons in underground wells, private villas and under the Saddam Hussein Hospital in Baghdad." The story was stenography on behalf of a proven fabricator, Chalabi, who wanted the United States to pave his way to power. The newspaper published a long and painful mea culpa for this malpractice in May 2004.
38 *"Rolex-wearing guys"*: Zinni quoted in John Lancaster, "A Nominee's Long Road to 'No,'" *Washington Post*, October 2, 2000, https://www.washingtonpost.com/archive/politics/2000/10/03/a-nominees-long-road-to-no/e824d893-4e91-4003-b30a-3f23c2fd6fbd/.
40 *"very low end"*: Tenet in Bill Harlow, ed., *Rebuttal: The CIA Responds to the Senate Intelligence Committee's Study of Its Detention and Interrogation Program* (Annapolis: Naval Institute Press, 2015), p. 2.

Chapter Five: The New World

41 *"nothing in the briefing"*: Garrett M. Graff, *The Only Plane in the Sky: An Oral History of 9/11* (New York: Avid Reader Press, 2019), pp. 12, 97.
41 *"The building shook"*: Graff, *The Only Plane in the Sky*, pp. 12, 97.
41 *"sense that we'd crossed"*: McLaughlin interview transcript, *Frontline*, PBS, May 19, 2015, https://www.pbs.org/wgbh/frontline/article/john-mclaughlin-cia-interrogations-were-legal-moral-and-effective/.
42 *"my imagination run"*: John Rizzo, *Company Man: Thirty Years of Controversy and Crisis in the CIA* (New York: Scribner, 2014), pp. 172–73.
42 *"What do you have"*: Michael Hayden oral history, Miller Center, University of Vir-

ginia, https://millercenter.org/the-presidency/presidential-oral-histories/michael-hayden-oral-history.

42 *all asked ourselves:* Rice interview in Yaniv Barzilai, *102 Days of War: How Osama bin Laden, al Qaeda and the Taliban Survived 2001* (Washington: Potomac Books, 2013), p. 84.

42 *"connection with Saddam Hussein":* Sir Christopher Meyer, the British Ambassador, testified to this conversation with Condi Rice before the Chilcot inquiry into Britain's role in the Iraq war.

42 *"We've got to do Iraq":* Rumsfeld made this breathtaking statement when the national security team regrouped at the White House, according to the counterterrorism coordinator, Richard Clarke. By Clarke's account: "That night, on 9/11, Rumsfeld came over and the others, and the president finally got back, and we had a meeting. And Rumsfeld said, You know, we've got to do Iraq, and everyone looked at him—at least I looked at him and Powell looked at him—like, What the hell are you talking about? And he said—I'll never forget this—There just aren't enough targets in Afghanistan. We need to bomb something else to prove that we're, you know, big and strong and not going to be pushed around by these kind of attacks. And I made the point certainly that night, and I think Powell acknowledged it, that Iraq had nothing to do with 9/11. That didn't seem to faze Rumsfeld in the least." Cullen Murphy and Todd S. Purdum, "Farewell to All That: An Oral History of the Bush White House," *Vanity Fair*, December 28, 2008, https://www.vanityfair.com/news/2009/02/bush-oral-history200902.

42 *"See if Saddam did this":* Richard A. Clarke, *Against All Enemies: Inside America's War on Terror* (New York: Free Press, 2004), p. 32.

43 *"hope we can all agree":* Tyler Drumheller with Elaine Monaghan, *On the Brink: An Insider's Account of How the White House Compromised American Intelligence* (New York: Carroll & Graf, 2006), pp. 29–32. Drumheller was chief of the European division of the clandestine service. The dinner is described, briefly, in George J. Tenet with Bill Harlow, *At the Center of the Storm: My Years at the CIA* (New York: HarperCollins, 2007), pp. 172–73.

43 *"We're fucked":* Henry A. Crumpton, *The Art of Intelligence: Lessons from a Life in the CIA's Clandestine Service* (New York: Penguin, 2012), p. 186.

43 *"Bin Laden, dead":* Michael Morell with Bill Harlow, *The Great War of Our Time: The CIA's Fight Against Terrorism—from al Qa'ida to ISIS* (New York: Twelve, 2015), p. 65.

44 *"flies walking across":* Cofer Black quoted in Bob Woodward, *Bush at War* (New York: Simon & Schuster, 2002), p. 52.

44 cannot deliver on that: Morell, *The Great War of Our Time*, p. 65.

44 *"it's a global war":* Rumsfeld, Wolfowitz, Black, and Bush quoted and paraphrased in Robert Draper, *To Start a War: How the Bush Administration Took America into Iraq* (New York: Penguin, 2020), pp. 17–20.

44 *"it really had been decided":* Colin Powell and Richard Armitage oral history,

Miller Center, University of Virginia, https://millercenter.org/the-presidency/presidential-oral-histories/colin-l-powell-and-richard-l-armitage-oral-history.

44 *"We are going to war"*: Morell, *The Great War of Our Time*, p. 63.

45 *"not be alone in this jihad"*: Abdul Salam Zaaef, *My Life with the Taliban* (New York: Columbia University Press, 2010), p. 147.

45 *"If war comes"*: Robert L. Grenier, *88 Days to Kandahar: A CIA Diary* (New York: Simon & Schuster, 2015), p. 10.

46 *"brought in maps"*: Ryan Crocker oral history, Miller Center, University of Virginia, https://millercenter.org/the-presidency/presidential-oral-histories/ryan-crocker-oral-history.

48 *"a living hell"*: Tenet in Bill Harlow, ed., *Rebuttal: The CIA Responds to the Senate Intelligence Committee's Study of Its Detention and Interrogation Program* (Annapolis: Naval Institute Press, 2015), p. 2.

48 *"was inconceivable to us"*: Tenet, *At the Center of the Storm*, p. 239.

48 *"we didn't know jack shit"*: Robert Gates oral history, Miller Center, University of Virginia, https://millercenter.org/the-presidency/presidential-oral-histories/robert-gates-oral-history.

49 *"single threat report"*: Winston Wiley interview by Mike Morell, *Intelligence Matters* podcast, CBS News, August 11, 2011, https://www.cbsnews.com/news/intelligence-matters-presents-remembering-911-with-winston-wiley/?intcid=CNM-0010abd1h.

49 *"of the intelligence"*: Gates oral history.

49 *"God-awful idea"*: Morell quoted in *Confronting Saddam Hussein: George W. Bush and the Invasion of Iraq* (New York: Oxford University Press, 2023) p. 68.

49 *"The fear"*: Author's interview, Linda Weissgold.

49 *"this is your fault"*: Cindy Storer interview transcript, *Manhunt: The Search for bin Laden*, CNN, May 27, 2013, https://transcripts.cnn.com/show/se/date/2013-05-27/segment/02.

50 *"on the threat of terrorists"*: George W. Bush, *Decision Points* (New York: Crown, 2010), p. 158.

50 *"the leader of Iraq"*: George W. Bush White House press conference, October 11, 2001, https://georgewbush-whitehouse.archives.gov/news/releases/2001/10/20011011-7.html.

50 *"war on terror begins"*: Bush Address to Joint Session of Congress, September 20, 2001.

51 *"Our strategy"*: Woodward, *Bush at War*, p. 153.

51 *"were talking about who"*: Powell and Armitage oral history.

51 *"chaos of the times"*: McLaughlin interview in Barzilai, *102 Days of War*, pp. 55–56.

52 *"give you whatever"*: Crumpton, *The Art of Intelligence*, p. 181.

52 *"find something for you"*: Jose A. Rodriguez Jr. with Bill Harlow, *Hard Measures: How Aggressive CIA Actions After 9/11 Saved American Lives* (New York: Threshold Editions, 2012), p. 30.

52 *"did not know enough"*: Jose Rodriguez interview transcript, *"Manhunt: The Search for*

bin Laden," CNN, May 27, 2013, https://transcripts.cnn.com/show/se/date/2013-05-27/segment/02.

52 *"no office"*: Rodriguez, *Hard Measures*, pp. 32–38.
52 *"flying by the seat"*: Rodriguez, *Hard Measures*, pp. 32–38.
52 *"going to make"*: Rodriguez, *Hard Measures*, pp. 32–38.
53 *"intel collection program"*: Author's interview, Enrique Prado.
54 *"bin Laden's head"*: Gary Schroen, *First In: An Insider's Account of How the CIA Spearheaded the War on Terror* (New York: Ballantine Books, 2005), p. 38.
54 *"jaw clenched"*: Crumpton, *The Art of Intelligence*, p. 198.
55 *"morale of the Taliban"*: Donald Rumsfeld oral history, Miller Center, University of Virginia, https://millercenter.org/the-presidency/presidential-oral-histories/donald-rumsfeld-oral-history.
55 *"no mention of the consequences"*: Crumpton, *The Art of Intelligence*, p. 239.
55 *"tasking going into Afghanistan"*: Gen. Richard Myers, in Rumsfeld oral history.

Chapter Six: "We Were All Making It Up as We Went Along"

56 *"My best friend"*: Karzai quoted in Bette Dam, *A Man and a Motorcycle: How Hamid Karzai Came to Power* (Amsterdam: Ipso Facto, 2014), p. 8.
58 *"the surface, they made"*: Robert L. Grenier, *88 Days to Kandahar: A CIA Diary* (New York: Simon & Schuster, 2015), p. 139.
58 *"language that would"*: Jason Elliot, *An Unexpected Light: Travels in Afghanistan* (London: Picador, 2011), p. 52.
58 *"thinking was very much"*: Grenier, *88 Days to Kandahar*, p. 146.
60 *"I can assure you"*: Haass quoted in Ahmed Rashid, *Descent into Chaos: The U.S. and the Disaster in Pakistan, Afghanistan, and Central Asia* (New York, Penguin, 2008), p. 76.
60 *"was just no process"*: Stephen Hadley interview in *What We Need to Learn: Lessons from Twenty Years of Afghanistan Reconstruction*, Special Inspector General for Afghanistan Reconstruction, August 2021, https://www.sigar.mil/pdf/lessonslearned/SIGAR-21-46-LL.pdf.
60 *"to any post-Taliban"*: National Security Council, "U.S. Strategy in Afghanistan" (with Rumsfeld's written edits), October 16, 2001, https://nsarchive.gwu.edu/document/24546-office-secretary-defense-donald-rumsfeld-snowflake-douglas-feith-strategy-october-30. A handwritten note reveals that the strategy was approved by the NSC on October 16.
60 *"America used chemical"*: "White House Dismisses bin Laden Nuclear Threat," CNN, November 10, 2001, Internet Archive Wayback Machine, https://web.archive.org/web/20011111145253/http://www.cnn.com/2001/WORLD/europe/11/10/ret.binladen.nuclear/index.html.
60 *"If he moves elsewhere"*: Bob Woodward, *Bush at War* (New York: Simon & Schuster, 2002), p. 311.

61 *"most irresponsible and foolish"*: Berntsen interview in Yaniv Barzilai, *102 Days of War: How Osama bin Laden, al Qaeda and the Taliban Survived 2001* (Washington: Potomac Books, 2013), pp. 78–79.

61 *"White House assumed"*: Barzilai, *102 Days of War*, p. 75.

62 *"satellite telephone"*: Capt. Jason Amerine, "The Battle of Tarin Kowt," *Frontline*, PBS, July 12, 2002, https://www.pbs.org/wgbh/pages/frontline/shows/campaign/ground/tarinkowt.html.

62 *"emerge as the hero"*: Jane Perlez, "Afghan Trying to Do 'Big Things' at Big Risk," *New York Times*, November 5, 2001, https://www.nytimes.com/2001/11/05/world/a-nation-challenged-taliban-foe-afghan-trying-to-do-big-things-at-big-risk.html.

63 *"Abdullah was the first Afghan"*: James Dobbins, "Our Man in Kabul," *Foreign Affairs*, November 4, 2009, https://www.foreignaffairs.com/articles/afghanistan/2009-11-04/our-man-kabul.

63 *"people talked about the same man"*: Philip Mudd, *Takedown: Inside the Hunt for Al Qaeda* (Philadelphia, University of Pennsylvania Press, 2013), p. 11.

64 *"clearly making things up"*: Grenier, *88 Days to Kandahar*, pp. 251–52.

64 *sent the following dispatch:* Tim Weiner: "Bin Laden Reported Spotted in Fortified Camp in Afghan East," *New York Times*, November 25, 2001, https://www.nytimes.com/2001/11/25/world/nation-challenged-fugitive-bin-laden-reported-spotted-fortified-camp-afghan-east.html.

64 *"Tora Bora is the deal"*: Tommy Franks oral history, Miller Center, University of Virginia, https://millercenter.org/the-presidency/presidential-oral-histories/tommy-franks-oral-history.

66 *"doors and windows"*: Hamid Karzai interview transcript, *Frontline*, PBS, May 7, 2002, https://www.pbs.org/wgbh/pages/frontline/shows/campaign/interviews/karzai.html.

66 *"a complete amnesty"*: Barnett Rubin oral history, Afghanistan Project, Foreign Affairs Oral History Collection, Association for Diplomatic Studies and Training, https://adst.org/afghanistan-project-barnett-rubin/.

67 *"president shot the messenger"*: Michael Morell with Bill Harlow, *The Great War of Our Time: The CIA's Fight Against Terrorism—from al Qa'ida to ISIS* (New York: Twelve, 2015), pp. 75–76.

67 *"mission impossible"*: Ryan Crocker oral history, Miller Center, University of Virginia, https://millercenter.org/the-presidency/presidential-oral-histories/ryan-crocker-oral-history.

68 *"ghost money"*: Matthrew Rosenberg, "With Bags of Cash, C.I.A. Seeks Influence in Afghanistan," *New York Times*, April 29, 2013, https://www.nytimes.com/2013/04/29/world/asia/cia-delivers-cash-to-afghan-leaders-office.html.

68 *"in power because"*: Author's interview, Michael Metrinko; see also Metrinko oral history, Association for Diplomatic Studies and Training. Foreign Affairs Oral History Project, https://www.adst.org/OH%20TOCs/Metrinko,%20Mike.toc.pdf.

70 *"his government's most"*: U.S. Embassy (Kabul), Subject: "Confronting Afghanistan's Corruption Crisis," September 15, 2005, National Security Archive, George Wash-

ington University, https://nsarchive.gwu.edu/document/24555-u-s-embassy-kabul-cable-003681-subject-confronting-afghanistan-s-corruption-crisis. On the corruption of Ahmed Wali Karzai and his support from CIA officials, see Dexter Filkins, Mark Mazzetti, and James Risen, "Brother of Afghan Leader Said to Be Paid by C.I.A.," *New York Times*, October 28, 2009, https://www.nytimes.com/2009/10/28/world/asia/28intel.html; Dexter Filkins, "Death of an Afghan Godfather," *The New Yorker*, July 12, 2011, https://www.newyorker.com/news/news-desk/death-of-an-afghan-godfather.

70 *"the closed character"*: Hadley interview in *What We Need to Learn*.
70 *"the interest that defined"*: Barnett Rubin interview in SIGAR, "Corruption in Conflict: Lessons from the U.S. Experience in Afghanistan," September 2016, https://www.sigar.mil/interactive-reports/corruption-in-conflict/index.html.
71 *"situation we're in"*: Roger Pardo-Maurer, "Greetings from Scenic Kandahar," email dated August 11–15, 2002, National Security Archive, George Washington University, https://nsarchive.gwu.edu/document/24550-combined-joint-special-operations-task-force-coalition-coordination-cell-kandahar.

Chapter Seven: Unprecedented Trouble

73 *"turned out he lied"*: Kristen Wood interview by Mike Morell, *Intelligence Matters* podcast, WGHN, March 15, 2023, https://wghn.com/2023/03/15/u-s-invasion-of-iraq-20-years-later-intelligence-matters/.
73 *"run immediately to the White House"*: Tyler Drumheller interview, Constitution Project, Task Force on Detainee Treatment, Open Society Foundations, https://www.opensocietyfoundations.org/publications/report-constitution-project-s-task-force-detainee-treatment.
74 *"are we going to"*: Scott Shane, "Inside a 9/11 Mastermind's Interrogation," *New York Times*, June 22, 2008, https://www.nytimes.com/2008/06/22/washington/22ksm.html.
74 *"death and destruction"*: George W. Bush remarks at Connecticut Republican Committee Luncheon, The White House, April 9, 2002, https://georgewbush-whitehouse.archives.gov/news/releases/2002/04/20020409-8.html.
74 *"needed to take responsibility"*: Jose Rodriguez interview, *Manhunt: The Search for bin Laden*, CNN, May 27, 2013, https://transcripts.cnn.com/show/se/date/2013-05-27/segment/02.
76 *Was it torture? "Absolutely"*: Richard Armitage interview, in *Torturing Democracy*, January 8, 2008, https://nsarchive2.gwu.edu/torturingdemocracy/interviews/richard_armitage.html.
76 *"inhumane physical or psychological"*: Senate Select Committee on Intelligence Report on the Central Intelligence Agency's Detention and Interrogation Program [hereinafter Torture Report], p. 32, https://www.intelligence.senate.gov/sites/default/files/publications/CRPT-113srpt288.pdf.
77 *Techniques struck Rizzo*: John Rizzo, *Company Man: Thirty Years of Controversy and Crisis at the CIA* (New York: Scribner, 2014), pp. 185–87.

78 *"fully realized that either way"*: John Rizzo interview, "Secrets, Politics, and Torture," *Frontline*, PBS, https://www.pbs.org/wgbh/frontline/documentary/secrets-politics-and-torture/transcript/.

78 *"people won't do anything"*: Rizzo, *Company Man*, pp 185–87.

78 *"approved the use of"*: George W. Bush, *Decision Points* (New York: Crown, 2010), p. 169. After Bush published his memoir, Rizzo asked Tenet if the president's admission was true. "George doesn't remember any of it," Rizzo wrote. "How could George—how could anyone, for that matter—ever forget having conversations with the president of the United States about something like that?" The proposals for brutal interrogations remained a very tightly held secret within the CIA, in part due to the reasonable assumption that some senior officers might think them un-American. "People say that you can't equate this with the Soviets," said Tyler Drumheller, the clandestine service chief for Europe. "Of course you can." Yet the practice of waterboarding was not unknown in the United States. In 1968, an American officer was court-martialed for waterboarding a North Vietnamese POW. In 1983, the sheriff of San Jacinto County, Texas, was sentenced to ten years for using the technique to extract confessions.

79 *"were watching Godzilla"*: Ali Soufan, *The Black Banners: How Torture Derailed the War on Terror after 9/11*, declassified edition (New York: W. W. Norton, 2020), p. 404.

79 *"intelligence that a nuclear"*: James Mitchell deposition, Pre-Trial Hearings, 9/11: Khalid Sheikh Mohammad, et al. January 20, 2020, https://www.judicialwatch.org/wp-content/uploads/2021/06/Deposition-Testimony-Jan-20-31-2020-.pdf.

79 *"The gloves are off"*: The meeting was described by Mitchell in his memoir, written with the longtime CIA public affairs officer Bill Harlow, in *Enhanced Interrogation: Inside the Minds and Motives of the Islamic Terrorists Trying to Destroy America* (New York: Crown, 2016) pp. 12–16.

81 *"just told me how"*: Author's interview, Ric Prado.

82 *"Americans would find out"*: Philip Mudd interview, *Manhunt: The Search for bin Laden*, CNN, May 27, 2013, https://transcripts.cnn.com/show/se/date/2013-05-27/segment/02.

82 *"had no experience"*: Author's interview, Jim Cotsana.

82 *"shortage of personnel"*: Bill Harlow, ed., *Rebuttal: The CIA Responds to the Senate Intelligence Committee's Study of Its Detention and Interrogation Program* (Annapolis: Naval Institute Press, 2015), p. 55.

83 *"figured out how"*: Author's interview, Jim Cotsana.

83 *"Highly unlikely"*: Author's interview, Jim Cotsana.

84 *"were absolutely alone"*: Kwasniewski quoted in John Pomfret, *From Warsaw with Love: Polish Spies, the CIA, and the Forging of an Unlikely Alliance* (New York: Holt, 2021), p. 204.

86 *deprive him of sleep:* When the Justice Department's Office of Professional Responsibility reviewed the history of the torture memos, an Office of Legal Counsel attorney who had raised concerns about them named Patrick Philbin, later deputy White House Counsel to President Trump, noted: "It had not been known in

2002 that detainees were kept in diapers, potentially for days at a time. It had also not been known that detainees were kept awake by shackling their hands to the ceiling. . . . Similarly, dietary manipulation and water dousing had not been described to OLC in 2002 and were not even considered. . . . All of these factors combined to create a picture of the interrogation process that was quite different from the one presented in 2002." Philbin also said he "did not think the memo provided a sufficient analysis to conclude that depriving a person of sleep for days on end while keeping him shackled to the ceiling in a diaper and at the same time using other techniques on him would not cross the line into producing "severe physical suffering." In 2005, when the chief of staff to Attorney General Alberto Gonzales raised the question of reauthorizing the techniques in the torture memos with James Comey, the number two man in the Justice Department, Comey told him that "this opinion would come back to haunt the AG and DOJ and urged him not to allow it. . . . I told him that the people who were applying pressure now would not be here when the shit hit the fan." The pressure had come from the White House and the CIA. The shit really hit the fan after the Bush administration was out of power and the Senate intelligence committee began to work on its so-called "Torture Report," a tenth of which was declassified in 2014.

86 *"experienced intelligence professionals"*: Bush, *Decision Points*, p. 169.
86 *"knowledgeable of the target"*: Bush, *Decision Points*, p. 151.
86 *"pushed back hard"*: *Salim v. Mitchell*, Videotaped Deposition of Jose Rodriguez, March 7, 2017, https://static01.nyt.com/packages/pdf/us/20170620_interrogations/jose-rodriguez.pdf.
87 *"some to the point"*: Torture Report, p. 479.
87 *"more than amateurish"*: *Summary and Reflections of Chief of Medical Services on OMS Participation in the RDI Program*, p. 41, declassified August 14, 2018, https://www.aclu.org/sites/default/files/field_document/oms_summary.pdf.
87 *"waterboard was not"*: Author's interview, Jim Cotsana.
88 *"honesty, judgment, and maturity"*: Torture Report, p. 50.
88 *"good for interrogations"*: Torture Report, p. 50.
89 *"Unsupervised brutality"*: Mitchell, *Enhanced Interrogation*, p. 92.
89 *"Day one of the aggressive interrogation"*: Debriefing of Abd al-Rahim al-Nashiri. CIA cable from Haspel to headquarters, November 15, 2002, National Security Archive, George Washington University, https://nsarchive.gwu.edu/document/16772-document-02-gina-haspel-s-day-one-report-cia.
90 *"is inconceivable to"*: Torture Report, pp. 67–68.
90 *"a new sheriff"*: Mitchell, *Enhanced Interrogation*, p. 105ff.
90 *"There were rules"*: Author's interview, Jim Cotsana.

Chapter Eight: What You Do When You Do Not Know

92 *"I was exhausted"*: George J. Tenet with Bill Harlow, *At the Center of the Storm: My Years at the CIA* (New York: HarperCollins, 2007), pp. 452–60.

92 *"of enforced consensus"*: The Commission on the Intelligence Capabilities of the United States Regarding Weapons of Mass Destruction Report to the President of the United States, March 31, 2005, p. 196, https://irp.fas.org/offdocs/wmd_report.pdf.

92 *"the president wants to"*: Peter Eisner and Knut Royce, *The Italian Letter: How the Bush Administration Used a Fake Letter to Build the Case for War in Iraq* (New York: Rodale, 2007), p. 119.

93 *"now seen as inevitable"*: The "Downing Street Memo," July 23, 2002, National Security Archive, George Washington University, https://nsarchive2.gwu.edu/NSAEBB/NSAEBB328/II-Doc14.pdf.

93 *"make the case"*: Colin Powell and Richard Armitage oral history, Miller Center, University of Virginia, https://millercenter.org/the-presidency/presidential-oral-histories/colin-l-powell-and-richard-l-armitage-oral-history.

94 *"like a crystal glass"*: Powell interview in "Hard Lessons: The Iraq Reconstruction Experience," Office of the Special Inspector General for Iraq Reconstruction, 2009.

94 *"was never any"*: Armitage quoted in Ron Suskind, *The One Percent Doctrine: Deep Inside America's Pursuit of Its Enemies Since 9/11* (New York: Simon & Schuster, 2006), p. 225.

95 *"fucking stupidest guy"*: Bob Woodward, *Plan of Attack* (New York: Simon & Schuster, 2004), p. 281.

96 *"the fight about prewar"*: Doug Feith oral history, Miller Center, University of Virginia, https://millercenter.org/the-presidency/presidential-oral-histories/douglas-j-feith-oral-history.

96 *"War is not optional"*: Tenet, *At the Center of the Storm*, p. 310.

96 *"want a technical update"*: Author's interview, Mark Lowenthal.

96 *"what you do when"*: Sherman Kent, "Estimates and Influence," *Foreign Service Journal* (April 1969), p. 17.

97 *"biological weapons judgment"*: Andy Makridis interview by Mike Morell, *Intelligence Matters* podcast, WGHN, March 15, 2023, https://wghn.com/2023/03/15/u-s-invasion-of-iraq-20-years-later-intelligence-matters/.

97 *"a 10,000-piece puzzle"*: Kristin Wood interview by Mike Morell, *Intelligence Matters* podcast.

97 *"few incentives"*: Author's interview, Luis Rueda.

98 *"analysts did not really think"*: Michael Morell with Bill Harlow, *The Great War of Our Time: The CIA's Fight Against Terrorism—from al Qa'ida to ISIS* (New York: Twelve, 2015), p. 102.

98 *"some time on thinking"*: Tim Weiner, "Naivete at the C.I.A.," *New York Times*, June 7, 1998, https://www.nytimes.com/1998/06/07/weekinreview/the-world-naivete-at-the-cia-every-nation-s-just-another-us.html.

99 *"how do you know"*: Author's interview, Margaret Henoch.

99 *"policymakers and warfighters"*: WINPAC Mission Statement, CIA, undated but circa April 2001, https://www.cia.gov/readingroom/docs/DOC_0005462544.pdf.

99 *"the source information"*: Robert Draper, *To Start a War: How the Bush Administration Took America into Iraq* (New York: Penguin, 2020), p. 390.

100 *"We had tons of it"*: Michael Hayden oral history, Miller Center, University of Virginia, https://millercenter.org/the-presidency/presidential-oral-histories/michael-hayden-oral-history.

100 *"clear that the Bush administration"*: Paul Pillar, "Intelligence, Policy, and the War in Iraq," *Foreign Affairs*, March–April 2006.

100 *analysts got the clue*: Author's interview, Jim Lawlor.

101 *"have better information"*: Tenet, *At the Center of the Storm*, p. 362.

102 *"TO SAY IRAQ"*: Draper, *To Start a War*, p. 268.

102 *"Do we invade Iraq?"*: Condoleezza Rice and Stephen Hadley oral history, Miller Center, University of Virginia, https://millercenter.org/the-presidency/presidential-oral-histories/condoleezza-rice-and-stephen-hadley-oral-history.

102 *"every night with George"*: Powell oral history, Miller Center, University of Virginia, https://millercenter.org/the-presidency/presidential-oral-histories/colin-powell-oral-history.

102 *really strong stuff*: Draper, *To Start a War*, p. 276.

103 *"by point Powell"*: Morell, *The Great War of Our Time*, pp. 95–96.

103 *"people in the intelligence"*: Steven R. Weisman, "Powell Calls His U.N. Speech a Lasting Blot on His Record," *New York Times*, September 9, 2005, https://www.nytimes.com/2005/09/09/politics/powell-calls-his-un-speech-a-lasting-blot-on-his-record.html.

Chapter Nine: Sufi Mystics and Walking Zombies

107 *"God's and the sheikh's"*: Elizabeth Szanto, "Contesting Charismatic Authority: Qadiri Sufism in Iraqi Kurdistan," paper presented at the Middle Eastern Studies Association, November 2014.

109 *"known Charlie for"*: Author's interview, Bill Burns.

109 *"Mentioning Charlie"*: Marc Polymeropoulos, "The Last Great American Arabist," *Washington Examiner*, March 15, 2021, https://www.washingtonexaminer.com/opinion/the-last-great-american-arabist.

111 *"do I know you guys"*: Rice quoted in George J. Tenet with Bill Harlow, *At the Center of the Storm: My Years at the CIA* (New York: HarperCollins, 2007), p. 362.

111 *"large number of regime"*: Author's interview, Luis Rueda.

112 *"briefed the president"*: Donald Rumsfeld oral history, Miller Center, University of Virginia, https://millercenter.org/the-presidency/presidential-oral-histories/donald-rumsfeld-oral-history.

112 *"Okay, Bubba, we're here"*: Wallace quoted in Colonel Joel D. Rayburn and Colonel Frank K. Sobchak, eds., "The U.S. Army in the Iraq War: Volume 1: invasion, insurgency, Civil War 2003–2006," (Carlilse, PA.: U.S. Army War College Press, 2019) p. 111.

113 *"watched the people"*: Colin Powell and Richard Armitage oral history, Miller Center, University of Virginia, https://millercenter.org/the-presidency/presidential-oral-histories/colin-l-powell-and-richard-l-armitage-oral-history.

113 *"was a natural leader"*: Author's interview, Jay Garner.
113 *"a control freak"*: William J. Burns, *The Back Channel: A Memoir of American Diplomacy and the Case for Its Renewal* (New York: Random House, 2019), p. 175.
114 *"tell him what's going to happen"*: Author's interview, Jay Garner.
114 *"No one else around the table"*: Garrett M. Graff, "Orders of Disorder: Who Disbanded Iraq's Army and De-Baathified Its Bureaucracy?" *Foreign Affairs*, May 5, 2023, https://www.foreignaffairs.com/middle-east/iraq-united-states-orders-disorder.
115 *"disbandment of the army"*: Condi Rice interview, U.S. Department of State, Office of the Historian, July 12, 2014, in David E. Johnson, Agnes Gereben Schaefer, Brenna Allen, Raphael S. Cohen, Gian Gentile, James Hoobler, Michael Schwille, Jerry M. Sollinger, Sean M. Zeigler, "The U.S. Army and the Battle for Baghdad: Lessons Learned—And Still to Be Learned" (Santa Monica, CA: RAND Corporation, 2019), p. 72, https://www.rand.org/pubs/research_reports/RR3076.html.
115 *"should have a deep understanding"*: David Petraeus, *Secrets of Statecraft*, Hoover Institution podcast, February 23, 2022, https://www.hoover.org/research/secrets-statecraft-education-general-david-petraeus.
115 *"higher profile targets"*: Coalition Provisional Authority, "CPA Fusion Cell Threat Warning," June 4, 2003, cited in James Dobbins, Seth G. Jones, Benjamin Runkle, Siddhartha Mohandas, "Occupying Iraq: A History of the Coalition Provisional Authority," (Santa Monica, CA: RAND Corporation, 2009), p. 92, https://www.rand.org/content/dam/rand/pubs/monographs/2009/RAND_MG847.pdf.
116 *"the bar scene"*: Burns, *The Back Channel*, pp. 176–77.
116 *"who we were fighting"*: McManaway interview, in Dobbins et al., "Occupying Iraq," pp. 98–99.
116 *"looting of factories"*: Jane Green interview by Mike Morell, *Intelligence Matters* podcast, CBS News, March 17, 2023, https://www.cbsnews.com/news/u-s-invasion-of-iraq-20-years-later-intelligence-matters/.
117 *"the current environment"*: Tenet, *At the Center of the Storm*, p. 433. Tenet refers to Seidel as the author of this situation report not by name but as "CIA's senior officer in Baghdad."
117 *"understand the policy"*: Tenet, *At the Center of the Storm*, p. 430.
118 *"get him off a beach"*: L. Paul Bremer III oral history, Miller Center, University of Virginia, https://millercenter.org/the-presidency/presidential-oral-histories/l-paul-bremer-iii-oral-history.
118 *"The imbalance was staggering"*: McManaway interview, in Dobbins et al., "Occupying Iraq," p. 98–99.
118 *"liberation of Iraq has sparked"*: Seidel situation report cited in Tenet, *At the Center of the Storm*, p. 434.
118 *"violence and instability"*: Tenet, *At the Center of the Storm*, p. 433. Tenet refers to Seidel as the author of this situation report not by name but as "CIA's senior officer in Baghdad."
118 *"at the leadership level"*: Author's interview, Luis Rudea.

Chapter Ten: A Beautiful Operation

119 *"million-dollar recruitment pitches"*: Pavitt speech to the Foreign Policy Association, June 21, 2004, https://irp.fas.org/cia/product/ddo_speech_062404.html.
121 the Bolsheviks could: Author's interview, Jim Lawler.
122 *"We were good"*: Author's interview, Paula Doyle.
124 *"the nightmare scenario"*: Author's interview, Rolf Mowatt-Larssen.
124 *"why does A. Q. Khan hate"*: Author's interview, Robert Gorelick.
124 *"the Jimmy Hoffa of Pakistan"*: Author's interview, Robert Gorelick.
125 *"longest-running intelligence failure"*: Author's interview, Don Gregg.
126 *"did not obtain"*: Unclassified report to Congress summarizing Nation Intelligence Estimate on North Korea, October 2002, National Security Archive, George Washington University, https://nsarchive2.gwu.edu/NSAEBB/NSAEBB87/nk22.pdf.
127 *"selected to be the face"*: Author's interview, Paula Doyle.
127 *"kept showing up"*: Kappes quoted in William Tobey, "Cooperation in the Libya WMD Disarmament Case," *Studies in Intelligence* 61, no. 4 (Extracts, December 2017), CIA, https://www.cia.gov/resources/csi/studies-in-intelligence/volume-61-no-4/cooperation-in-the-libya-wmd-disarmament-case/.
128 *"Our challenge"*: Author's interview, Alberto Manenti.
129 *"adventure full of strange"*: William J. Burns, "A World Transformed and the Role of Intelligence," 59th Annual Ditchley Lecture, July 1, 2023, https://www.ditchley.com/sites/default/files/Ditchley%20Annual%20Lecture%202023%20transcript.pdf.
129 *"kill the son of a bitch"*: Author's interview, Robert Gorelick.

Chapter Eleven: The Butcher's Bill

131 *"you're all asking"*: George Tenet remarks, Georgetown University, February 5, 2004, https://irp.fas.org/cia/product/dci020504.html.
132 *"events surrounding the death"*: CIA Office of the Inspector General, "Comments on Report and Recommendations of the Special Accountability Board Regarding the Death of Iraqi Detainee Manadal al-Jamaidi," June 22, 2007 (declassified May 2023), https://www.documentcloud.org/documents/23834045-c05500527.
133 *"Don't hold prisoners yourself"*: Rizzo interview, Constitution Project, Task Force on Detainee Treatment, p. 101, Open Society Foundations, https://www.opensocietyfoundations.org/publications/report-constitution-project-s-task-force-detainee-treatment.
134 *"detention and interrogation"*: Maj. Gen. George R. Fay, "Investigation of the Abu Ghraib Detention Facility and 205th Military Intelligence Brigade," pp. 44–45, https://apps.dtic.mil/sti/pdfs/ADA429125.pdf.
135 *"literally coming out"*: Constitution Project, Task Force on Detainee Treatment, p. 95, https://docs.pogo.org/report/2013/TCP-Detainee-Task-Force-Report.pdf.

137 *"we had to escort sources . . . Qadisiyyah checkpoint"*: Author's interview, Ilana Berry.
138 *"another five years"*: Tenet testimony, 9/11 Commission, April 14, 2004, https://irp.fas.org/congress/2004_hr/041404tenet.html.
138 *"I was the guy being burned"*: George J. Tenet with Bill Harlow, *At the Center of the Storm: My Years at the CIA* (New York: HarperCollins, 2007), pp. 479–81.
139 *"a stilted bureaucracy"*: House Permanent Select Committee on Intelligence report, June 21, 2004, https://irp.fas.org/congress/2004_rpt/h108-558.html.
139 *"Dick Cheney called me"*: James Baker III oral history, Miller Center, University of Virginia, https://millercenter.org/the-presidency/presidential-oral-histories/james-baker-iii-oral-history-2014.

Chapter Twelve: Guerrilla Warfare

140 *"beaten like little baby seals"*: McLaughlin quoted in Michael Allen, *Blinking Red: Crisis and Compromise in American Intelligence After 9/11* (Washington, DC: Potomac Books, 2013), p. 30.
140 *"so-called human rights organizations"*: Jose A. Rodriguez Jr. with Bill Harlow, *Hard Measures: How Aggressive CIA Actions After 9/11 Saved American Lives* (New York: Threshold Editions, 2012), p. 155.
140 *"carefully orchestrated campaign"*: Scott McClellan, *What Happened: Inside the Bush White House and Washington's Culture of Deception* (New York: Public Affairs Press, 2008), pp. 125, 128.
141 *"The CIA? They're not just guessing"*: "Senator Kerry's Remarks," *New York Times*, September 23, 2004, https://www.nytimes.com/2004/09/23/politics/campaign/senator-kerrys-remarks.html.
141 *"leaks coming out of the intelligence"*: Condoleezza Rice and Stephen Hadley oral history, Miller Center, University of Virginia, https://millercenter.org/the-presidency/presidential-oral-histories/condoleezza-rice-and-stephen-hadley-oral-history.
142 *"we lived in a primitive"*: David Brooks, "The C.I.A. Versus Bush," *New York Times*, November 13, 2004, https://www.nytimes.com/2004/11/13/opinion/the-cia-versus-bush.html.
142 *"two insurgencies to defeat"*: Mark Follman, "Right Hook," *Salon*, October 7, 2004, https://www.salon.com/2004/10/07/cia_12.
144 *"found Mr. Foggo's explanation"*: James Olson deposition, in *U.S. v. Kyle Dustin Foggo*, February 10, 2009, https://s3.amazonaws.com/propublica/assets/docs/foggo_139_2.pdf.
144 *"considered Mr. Foggo to be"*: Olson deposition, in *U.S. v. Kyle Dustin Foggo*.
144 *"he was good at being a 'fixer'"*: Rodriguez, *Hard Measures*, pp. 135–41.
145 *"flabbergasted"*: Olson deposition, in *U.S. v. Kyle Dustin Foggo*.
145 *"It was imperative to me"*: Porter Goss deposition, in *U.S. v. Kyle Dustin Foggo*, January 23, 2009, https://s3.amazonaws.com/propublica/assets/docs/foggo_139_2.pdf.

146 *"the next eight to ten"*: Rodriguez, *Hard Measures*, p. 142.
147 *"I don't do personnel"*: Dana Priest and Walter Pincus, "Deputy Chief Resigns From CIA," *Washington Post*, November 12, 2004, https://www.washingtonpost.com/archive/politics/2004/11/13/deputy-chief-resigns-from-cia/8c9a760b-3fbf-4fdd-b8ee-4d427a269369/.
148 *"Imagine, then, my astonishment"*: Robert Gates oral history, Miller Center, University of Virginia, https://millercenter.org/the-presidency/presidential-oral-histories/robert-gates-oral-history.
149 *"CIA at that time was providing"*: John Negroponte oral history, Miller Center, University of Virginia, https://millercenter.org/the-presidency/presidential-oral-histories/john-negroponte-oral-history.
150 *"The law was very unspecific"*: Michael Hayden oral history, Miller Center, University of Virginia, https://millercenter.org/the-presidency/presidential-oral-histories/michael-hayden-oral-history.
150 *"We began with some big ideas"*: Thomas Fingar, *From Mandate to Blueprint: Lessons from Intelligence Reform* (Stanford, CA: Stanford University Press, 2021), p. 79.
151 *"idea of who was doing what"*: Author's interview, Thomas Fingar.
152 *"This isn't about who they are"*: McCain floor statement, *Congressional Record* 151, no. 128, October 5, 2005 (Senate), pp. S11061–S11120.
153 *"destroying the tapes was fraught"*: John Rizzo, *Company Man: Thirty Years of Controversy and Crisis at the CIA* (New York: Scribner, 2014), p. 6.
154 *"the tapes would play"*: Jose Rodriguez interview, in *The Spymasters*, documentary, Showtime, November 28, 2015.
155 *"Jose knows how I feel"*: Porter Goss interview, in *The Spymasters*.
155 *"squandered by infighting,"*: Rodriguez, *Hard Measures*, p. 151.
156 *"to expose the cover"*: Laura Rozen, "Poker, Hookers, and Black Contracts," *Mother Jones*, October 1, 2008, https://www.motherjones.com/politics/2008/10/poker-hookers-and-black-contracts-or-how-make-cia-trial-go-away/.
157 *"a fanatical, hypocritical, murderous dropout"*: Nada Bakos with Davin Coburn, *The Targeter: My Life in the CIA, Hunting Terrorists and Challenging the White House* (New York: Back Bay Books, 2020), p. 243.
157 *"No alliance could be as infuriating"*: Stanley McChrystal, *My Share of the Task: A Memoir* (New York: Portfolio, 2012), p. 118.
158 *"dissolving at the point of a gun"*: David Satterfield oral history, SMU Center for Presidential History, https://www.smu.edu/dedman/research/institutes-and-centers/Center-for-Presidential-History/CMP/The-Surge-in-Iraq/David-Satterfield.
159 *"Not only was the strategy"*: Condoleezza Rice oral history, SMU Center for Presidential History, https://www.smu.edu/-/media/Site/Dedman/Academics/InstitutesCenters/CPH/Collective-Memory-Project/The-Surge/Rice-Condoleezza--FINAL--20199.pdf.
159 *"The Iraq jihad is shaping"*: National Intelligence Estimate, *Trends in Global Terrorism: Implications for the United States*, April 2006.

Chapter Thirteen: The Black Cloud

162 *"Undermining international confidence"*: State Department cable from Ambassador Richard LeBaron, Embassy Kuwait, "Regional CT Strategy for Iraq and its Neighbors: Results and Recommendations," March 18, 2006, https://wikileaks.org/plusd/cables/06KUWAIT913_a.html.

162 *"there was zero question"*: Dexter Filkins, "The Shadow Commander," *The New Yorker*, September 30, 2013, https://www.newyorker.com/magazine/2013/09/30/the-shadow-commander.

163 *"In Iraq, when we first started"*: "Generation Kill: A Conversation with Stanley McChrystal," *Foreign Affairs*, March–April 2013.

164 *"a recovering politician"*: Jane Schmucker, "Goss Shy on Talk of Bush Shake-Up," *Toledo Blade*, May 7, 2006, https://www.toledoblade.com/local/education/2006/05/07/Goss-shy-on-talk-of-Bush-shake-up/stories/200605070045.

165 *"From the outset"*: Michael Hayden oral history, Miller Center, University of Virginia, https://millercenter.org/the-presidency/presidential-oral-histories/michael-hayden-oral-history.

165 *"I was told by people"*: Michael V. Hayden, *Playing to the Edge: American Intelligence in the Age of Terror* (New York: Penguin, 2016), pp. 180ff.

166 *"This black cloud"*: Hayden, *Playing to the Edge*, p. 188.

167 *"one of Dante's circles"*: Hayden oral history.

168 *"I'm tired of you Americans"*: Jose A. Rodriguez Jr. with Bill Harlow, *Hard Measures: How Aggressive CIA Actions After 9/11 Saved American Lives* (New York: Threshold Editions, 2012), pp. 3–9.

169 *"All hell broke loose"*: Hayden, *Playing to the Edge*, p. 207.

169 *"The liquids plot saga"*: Rodriguez, *Hard Measures*, p. 10.

171 *"We're not the nation's jailers"*: Hayden, *Playing to the Edge*, pp. 192–93. See also Rice, *No Higher Honor*, p. 502, and Peter Baker, *Days of Fire: Bush and Cheney in the White House* (New York: Anchor, 2013), pp. 483–85.

171 *"The vice president, he didn't like"*: Author's interview, Michael Hayden.

171 *"We were denying people their freedom"*: Hayden, *Playing to the Edge*, pp. 233, 237.

171 *"Officially, religiously, without exception"*: Hayden oral history.

172 *"an emotional impact on the President"*: Hayden oral history.

172 *"Hadley, this strategy is not working"*: Stephen Hadley oral history, SMU Center for Presidential History, https://www.smu.edu/-/media/site/dedman/academics/institutes centers/cph/collective-memory-project/the-surge/hadley-stephen--final--20199.pdf.

173 *My God, what have I done?*: Robert M. Gates, *Duty: Memoirs of a Secretary at War* (New York: Knopf, 2014), p. 4.

174 *"Immediately after the midterms"*: Hayden oral history.

175 *"It may just well be"*: Condoleezza Rice oral history, Dedman College of Humanities and Sciences, Southern Methodist University, https://www.smu.edu/dedman/research/institutes-and-centers/center-for-presidential-history/cmp/the-surge-in-iraq/condoleezza-rice.

175 *"Iraq's trajectory from gradual decline"*: National Intelligence Estimate, *Prospects for Iraq's Stability: A Challenging Road Ahead*, January 2007, https://www.dni.gov/files/documents/Newsroom/Reports%20and%20Pubs/20070202_release.pdf.

Chapter Fourteen: "How Far Were We Prepared to Go?"

177 *"Exceptional—and exceptionally close"*: Author's email correspondence with David Petraeus.

178 *"We began as a network"*: McChrystal quoted in Richard H. Shultz Jr., *Transforming US Intelligence for Irregular War Task Force 714 in Iraq* (Washington, DC, Georgetown University Press, 2020), p. 194.

179 *"All of a sudden changed my thought"*: Odierno interview in Eric Schmitt and Thom Shanker, *Counterstrike: The Untold Story of America's Secret Campaign Against Al Qaeda* (New York: Times Books, 2011), p. 76.

179 *"if you blow up terrorists"*: Amy Davidson Sorkin, "I Really Resent You Using the Word Torture: Q & A with Jose Rodriguez," *The New Yorker*, July 18, 2012, https://www.newyorker.com/news/amy-davidson/i-really-resent-you-using-the-word-torture-q-a-with-jose-rodriguez.

179 *"so rich, so timely"*: Richard Shultz, *Military Innovation in War: It Takes a Learning Organization—A Case Study of Task Force 714 in Iraq*, Joint Special Operations University report, (MacDill Air Force Base, FL: JSOU Press, 2016), p. 49, https://permanent.access.gpo.gov/gpo81311/ld.php.pdf.

180 *"Counterterrorism and the war"*: Michael V. Hayden, *Playing to the Edge: American Intelligence in the Age of Terror* (New York: Penguin, 2016), pp. 312, 323.

180 *"Those terrorists claimed"*: Khalid Al-Ansary and Ali Adeeb, "Most Tribes in Anbar Agree to Unite Against Insurgents," *New York Times*, September 18, 2006, https://www.nytimes.com/2006/09/18/world/middleeast/18iraq.html.

181 *"served as a wake-up call"*: MacFarland quoted in William Doyle, "The CIA's Secret Victory in Iraq," *Small Wars Journal*, June 12, 2011.

181 *"recognized that this is the kernel"*: Petraeus interview transcript, *Frontline*, PBS, July 29, 2014, https://www.pbs.org/wgbh/frontline/article/david-petraeus-isis-rise-in-iraq-isnt-a-surprise/.

182 *"The surge"*: Ryan Crocker oral history, Miller Center, University of Virginia, https://millercenter.org/the-presidency/presidential-oral-histories/ryan-crocker-oral-history.

182 *"defeating the terrorists"*: Joint Mission Plan, US Central Command, declassified May 2015, https://ahec.armywarcollege.edu/CENTCOM-IRAQ-papers/0295.%20Joint%20Campaign%20Plan%20Development.pdf.

182 *"The idea here was to balance"*: Douglas Lute oral history, Miller Center, University of Virginia, https://millercenter.org/the-presidency/presidential-oral-histories/douglas-lute-oral-history.

182 *"Petraeus and I were thinking"*: Crocker oral history, Miller Center.

183 *"Dagan sat down"*: Hayden interview in Ronen Bergman, *Rise and Kill First: The Secret History of Israel's Targeted Assassinations* (New York: Random House, 2018), p. 581.

183 *"The attacker would be blamed"*: Hayden, *Playing to the Edge*, p. 264.
184 *"I am aware of no precedent"*: Robert M. Gates, *Duty: Memoirs of a Secretary at War* (New York: Knopf, 2014), pp. 173–76.
184 *"All right, what's the intel?"*: Michael Hayden oral history, Miller Center, University of Virginia, https://millercenter.org/the-presidency/presidential-oral-histories/michael-hayden-oral-history.
184 *"a huge negative reaction"*: Gates, *Duty*, pp. 175–76.
184 *"We had gotten it right"*: Hayden, *Playing to the Edge*, p. 267.
185 *"Cofer can open doors"*: Dana Hedgpeth, "Blackwater's Owner Has Spies for Hire," *Washington Post*, November 3, 2007, https://www.washingtonpost.com/wp-dyn/content/article/2007/11/02/AR2007110202165.html?noredirect=on.
185 *"a rapidly growing, worldwide network"*: James Risen and Mark Mazzetti, "30 False Fronts Won Business for Blackwater," *New York Times*, September 4, 2010, https://www.nytimes.com/2010/09/04/world/middleeast/04blackwater.html.
187 *"we have some disconnects"*: Gates quoted in Michael G. Waltz, *Warrior Diplomat: A Green Beret's Battles from Washington to Afghanistan* (Washington, DC: Potomac Books, 2014), p. 205.
187 *"the student body are people"*: Hayden oral history.
188 *"don't have enough information"*: Dailey quoted in Eric Schmitt and David E. Sanger, "Pakistan Shuns C.I.A. Buildup Sought By U.S.," *New York Times*, January 27, 2008, https://www.nytimes.com/2008/01/27/world/asia/27pakistan.html?searchResultPosition=6.
188 *"How far were we"*: Waltz, *Warrior Diplomat*, p. 318.

Chapter Fifteen: The God's-Eye View

189 *"campaign against al Qaeda"*: Jose Rodriguez, "A CIA Veteran on What 'Zero Dark Thirty' Gets Wrong About the Bin Laden Manhunt," *Washington Post*, January 3, 2013, https://www.washingtonpost.com/opinions/a-cia-veteran-on-what-zero-dark-thirty-gets-wrong-about-the-bin-laden-manhunt/2013/01/03/4a76f1b8-52cc-11e2-a613-ec8d394535c6_story.html.
189 *"I was out of gas"*: Jose A. Rodriguez Jr. with Bill Harlow, *Hard Measures: How Aggressive CIA Actions After 9/11 Saved American Lives* (New York: Threshold Editions, 2012), pp. 198–202, 261.
189 *"My heart sank"*: John Rizzo, *Company Man: Thirty Years of Controversy and Crisis at the CIA* (New York: Scribner, 2014), p. 23.
190 *"practical implication of the letter"*: Rodriguez, *Hard Measures*, p. 24.
190 *"CIA covert actions"*: Hayden speech, "Playing to the Edge," Miller Center, University of Virginia, November 4, 2016, https://millercenter.org/american-forum/playing-edge.
190 *"The most successful covert action I conducted"*: Hayden oral history, Miller Center.
191 *"cunning, resourceful, coldly calculating"*: CIA Directorate of Intelligence, "Lebanon: Theology of Power," CIA report, 1986, cited in Matthew Levitt, *Hezbollah: The*

	Global Footprint of Lebanon's Party of God (Washington, DC: Georgetown University Press, 2013), p. 28.
192	*"Agency never killed"*: "Oral History: Reflections of DCI Colby and Helms on the CIA's 'Time of Troubles,'" *Studies in Intelligence* 58, no. 2, CIA Center for the Study of Intelligence, https://www.cia.gov/csi/static/reflections-times-of-trouble.pdf.
192	*"a terrible mistake"*: Daniel Benjamin and Steven Simon, *The Age of Sacred Terror* (New York: Random House, 2002), p. 345.
193	*"gigantic, multi-force operation"*: Ronen Bergman, *Rise and Kill First: The Secret History of Israel's Targeted Assassinations* (New York: Random House, 2018), p. 599.
194	*"think what this does"*: Bergman, *Rise and Kill First*, p. 602.
194	*"pushed and pushed"*: Hayden oral history, Miller Center.
194	*"That persistent, godlike stare"*: Hayden interview in Peter Baker, *Days of Fire: Bush and Cheney in the White House* (New York: Anchor, 2013), p. 598.
194	*"It was a conscious decision"*: Hayden oral history, Miller Center.
195	*"McCain would have been more disruptive"*: Michael V. Hayden, *Playing to the Edge: American Intelligence in the Age of Terror* (New York: Penguin, 2016), p. 354.
195	*"dysfunctional but a rogue"*: McCain quoted in Robert D. Novak, "'Rogue' CIA," *Washington Post*, November 18, 2004, https://www.washingtonpost.com/archive/opinions/2004/11/18/rogue-cia/8a6de419-a8c8-4317-9d95-bf0f8ed47d91/.
196	*"sanctuary in Pakistan"*: Barack Obama, "The War We Need to Win," August 1, 2007, The American Presidency Project, https://www.presidency.ucsb.edu/node/277525.
197	*"threat to the homeland"*: Hayden interview in Eric Schmitt and Thom Shanker, *Counterstrike: The Untold Story of America's Secret Campaign Against Al Qaeda* (New York: Times Books, 2011), p. 101.
197	*"Knowing what we know now"*: Hayden oral history, Miller Center.
197	*"sons of bitches are killing Americans"*: Bob Woodward, *Obama's Wars* (New York: Simon & Schuster, 2010), p. 5.
197	*"The President agreed"*: Hayden oral history, Miller Center.
198	*"The resentment created by American use"*: "General McChrystal on Drones: 'They Are Hated on a Visceral Level,'" *The Atlantic*, January 7, 2013.
198	*"What is it that we don't"*: Stanley McChrystal, *My Share of the Task: A Memoir* (New York: Portfolio, 2012), p. 310.
198	*"not only failed their purpose"*: McCain floor statement, *Congressional Record* 160, no. 149, December 9, 2014 (Senate), https://irp.fas.org/congress/2014_cr/ssci-rdi.html.

Chapter Sixteen: No Middle Ground

200	*"They signaled fairly early on"*: Rizzo interview transcript, *Frontline*, PBS, September 6, 2011, https://www.pbs.org/wgbh/frontline/article/john-rizzo-the-lawyer-who-approved-cias-most-controversial-programs/.
201	*"The whole thing played out publicly"*: Michael V. Hayden, *Playing to the Edge: American Intelligence in the Age of Terror* (New York: Penguin, 2016), p. 360.

201 *"He was brilliant"*: Michael Morell with Bill Harlow, *The Great War of Our Time: The CIA's Fight Against Terrorism—from al Qa'ida to ISIS* (New York: Twelve, 2015), pp. 148–49.
202 *"How did we transform"*: Leon Panetta, "No Torture. No Exceptions," *Washington Monthly*, January 1, 2008, https://washingtonmonthly.com/2008/01/01/no-torture-no-exceptions-28/.
203 *"completely out of left"*: Author's interview, Leon Panetta.
203 *"Panetta was a surprise pick"*: Rizzo interview transcript, *Frontline*.
203 *"Leon was smart and tough"*: Robert M. Gates, *Duty: Memoirs of a Secretary at War* (New York: Knopf, 2014), p. 293.
203 *"Your job"*: Author's interview, Leon Panetta.
204 *"I need you to be honest"*: Author's interview, Leon Panetta.
204 *"hadn't gotten fully briefed"*: Author's interview, Leon Panetta.
204 *"a guy like Mike"*: Author's interview, Leon Panetta.
205 *"continuity between the 43rd"*: Michael Hayden oral history, Miller Center, University of Virginia, https://millercenter.org/the-presidency/presidential-oral-histories/michael-hayden-oral-history.
205 *"Al Qaeda is dangerous"*: Leon Panetta with Jim Newton, *Worthy Fights: A Memoir of Leadership in War and Peace* (New York: Penguin, 2014), p. 220.
206 *"If we can find them"*: John O. Brennan, *Undaunted: My Fight Against America's Enemies, at Home and Abroad* (New York: Celadon, 2020), p. 226.
207 *"John, fuck you"*: Steve Coll, *Directorate S: The CIA and America's Wars in Afghanistan and Pakistan* (New York: Penguin, 2018), p. 358.
207 *"president wants to know who"*: Brennan, *Undaunted*, p. 233.
209 *"a tremendous ally"*: Author's interview, Marc Polymeropoulos; Polymeropoulos interview by Mike Morell, *Intelligence Matters* podcast, CBS News, December 20, 2020, https://www.cbsnews.com/news/former-senior-cia-officer-recalls-killing-of-service-members-by-suicide-bomber-humam-al-balawi/.
210 *need to go slow*: Joby Warrick, *The Triple Agent: The al-Qaeda Mole Who Infiltrated the CIA* (New York: Anchor, 2011), p. 134.
211 *"it kind of defies belief"*: Author's interview, Marc Polymeropoulos.
211 *"some counterintelligence flags"*: Allen quoted in Voice of America, "CIA Faults Lax Security for Afghan Base Attack," VOA News, October 19, 2010, https://www.voanews.com/a/cia-faults-lax-security-for-afghan-base-attack--105380643/166517.html.
212 *"The mission itself may have clouded"*: Panetta quoted in Mark Mazzetti, "Officer Failed to Warn CIA Before Attack," *New York Times*, October 20, 2010, https://www.nytimes.com/2010/10/20/world/asia/20intel.html.

Chapter Seventeen: The Keys to the Castle

214 *"Contact our investigations editor"*: Indictment, *United States of America v. Julian Paul Assange*, June 24, 2020.
214 *"Self-medicating like crazy"*: Ellen Nakashima, "Who is WikiLeaks Suspect Bradley

	Manning?" *Washington Post*, April 16, 2011, https://www.washingtonpost.com/life style/magazine/who-is-wikileaks-suspect-bradley-manning/2011/04/16/AFMwB mrF_story.html.
214	"*Unprecedented access*": Nakashima, "Who Is WikiLeaks Suspect Bradley Manning?"
215	"*We are studying the report*": Robert Mackey, "Taliban Study WikiLeaks to Hunt Informants," *New York Times*, July 30, 2010, https://archive.nytimes.com/thelede.blogs.nytimes.com/2010/07/30/taliban-study-wikileaks-to-hunt-informants/.
215	"*number of people went into hiding*": Crowley quoted in Greg Myre, "How Much Did WikiLeaks Damage U.S. National Security?" NPR, April 12, 2019, https://www.npr.org/2019/04/12/712659290/how-much-did-wikileaks-damage-u-s-national-security.
216	"*Thank God I'm an American citizen*": Scott Shane, "The Lessons of Anwar al-Awlaki," *New York Times*, August 30, 2015, https://www.nytimes.com/2015/08/30/magazine/the-lessons-of-anwar-al-awlaki.html.
217	"*informed, high-level official*": Barron opinion quoted in "To Kill an American," unsigned editorial, *New York Times*, February 6, 2013, https://www.nytimes.com/2013/02/06/opinion/to-kill-an-american.html.
218	"*Exquisite human sources*": Author's interview, Mike Morell.
219	"*found a guy we know*": Michael Morell with Bill Harlow, *The Great War of Our Time: The CIA's Fight Against Terrorism—from al Qa'ida to ISIS* (New York: Twelve, 2015), p. 147.
219	"*don't know much about the compound*": Brennan, *Undaunted*, p. 227.
221	"*Agency guys worked*": Author's interview, Cameron Munter.
223	"*We were so convinced*": Author's interview, Leon Panetta.
224	"*The case for bin Laden*": Robert M. Gates, *Duty: Memoirs of a Secretary at War* (New York: Knopf, 2014), pp. 539–40.
224	"*white-hot public anger in Pakistan*": Gates, *Duty*, pp. 538–42.
226	"*He just skewered Trump*": Clapper quoted in Garrett M. Graff, "I'd Never Been Involved in Anything as Secret as This," *Politico*, April 30, 2021, https://www.politico.com/news/magazine/2021/04/30/osama-bin-laden-death-white-house-oral-history-484793.

Chapter Eighteen: The Right Side of History

228	"*chaos and the absence*": Associated Press, "Bin Laden's Thoughts Unearthed in a Journal Handwritten by His Daughter," *Los Angeles Times*, November 2, 2017, https://www.latimes.com/world/la-fg-bin-laden-journal-20171102-story.html.
228	"*missed the boat on the Arab*": Author's interview, Leon Panetta.
229	"*was the most knowledgeable*": Michael V. Hayden, *Playing to the Edge: American Intelligence in the Age of Terror* (New York: Penguin, 2016), p. 318.
230	"*I felt horrible*": Michael Morell with Bill Harlow, *The Great War of Our Time: The CIA's Fight Against Terrorism—from al Qa'ida to ISIS* (New York: Twelve, 2015), p. 185.

230 *"shoot first and talk later"*: Robert M. Gates, *Duty: Memoirs of a Secretary at War* (New York: Knopf, 2014), p. 506.

231 *"strong partner"*: Chris Stevens, "Scene-setter for Secretary Rice's Visit to Libya," State Department cable, August 29, 2008, in "U.S. Embassy Cables: Profile of 'Intellectually Curious' but 'Notoriously Mercurial' Gaddafi," *The Guardian*, December 7, 2010, https://www.theguardian.com/world/us-embassy-cables-documents/167961.

232 *"U.S. intelligence community didn't push"*: William J. Burns, *The Back Channel: A Memoir of American Diplomacy and the Case for Its Renewal* (New York: Random House, 2019), pp. 324–25.

232 *"Assad is no Qaddafi"*: Stevens quoted in Gates, *Duty*, p. 523.

233 *"No one understood how far"*: Robin Wright, "Former Ambassador Robert Ford on the State Department Mutiny on Syria," *The New Yorker*, June 17, 2016, https://www.newyorker.com/news/news-desk/former-ambassador-robert-ford-on-the-state-department-mutiny-on-syria.

233 *"This is a good thing"*: Morell, *The Great War of Our Time*, p. 196.

234 *"You sure?"*: Author's interview, Leon Panetta.

234 *"distract him, at least"*: Leon Panetta with Jim Newton, *Worthy Fights: A Memoir of Leadership in War and Peace* (New York: Penguin, 2014), p. 334.

235 *"attained this kind of godlike"*: Panetta quoted in Chris Whipple, *The Spymasters: How the CIA Directors Shape History and the Future* (New York: Scribner, 2020), p. 258.

235 *"We disengaged not only militarily"*: Ryan Crocker interview transcript, *Frontline*, PBS, May 17, 2017, https://www.pbs.org/wgbh/frontline/documentary/the-secret-history-of-isis/transcript/.

235 *"invalidates my campaign plan"*: David Petraeus quoted in Rajiv Chandrasekaran, *Little America: The War Within the War for Afghanistan* (New York: Vintage, 2013), p. 325.

236 *"Send me to the worst place"*: Author's interview, Marc Polymeropoulos.

Chapter Nineteen: "Someone Is Always Watching"

238 *"the best job I've ever had"*: Michael Morell with Bill Harlow, *The Great War of Our Time: The CIA's Fight Against Terrorism—from al Qa'ida to ISIS* (New York: Twelve, 2015), p. 203.

238 *"not at all like a military"*: Author's interview, David Petraeus.

238 *"He did not connect"*: Morell, *The Great War of Our Time*, pp. 203–4.

239 *"southward, northward and onward"*: Bush remarks, Warsaw University, June 15, 2001, White House Archives, https://georgewbush-whitehouse.archives.gov/news/releases/2001/06/text/20010615-1.html.

240 *"Putin is not a democrat"*: Peter Baker, *Days of Fire: Bush and Cheney in the White House* (New York: Doubleday, 2013), p. 471.

241 *"Russian voters deserve a full investigation"*: Hillary Clinton remarks, OSCE Plenary

Session, Vilnius, Lithuania, December 6, 2011, U.S. Department of State Archives, https://2009-2017.state.gov/secretary/20092013clinton/rm/2011/12/178315.htm.
243 *"under a constant intelligence attack"*: Author's interview, Robert S. Wang.
244 *"Nothing about espionage is straightforward"*: Author's interview, Paula Doyle.
244 *"That was a huge issue"*: Author's interview, David Petraeus.
246 *"Blocks of sequential IP addresses"*: Citizen Lab, "Statement on the Fatal Flaws Found in a Defunct CIA Covert Communications System," September 29, 2022, https://citizenlab.ca/2022/09/statement-on-the-fatal-flaws-found-in-a-defunct-cia-covert-communications-system/. Citizen Lab published its findings in a joint investigation with the Reuters journalists Joel Schectman and Bozorgmehr Sharafedin in "America's Throwaway Spies: How the CIA Failed Iranian Informants in its Secret War with Tehran," Reuters, September 29, 2022, https://www.reuters.com/investigates/special-report/usa-spies-iran/.
247 *"Character is what you do when"*: Vernon Loeb, "Petraeus Ghostwriter 'Clueless' to Affair," *Washington Post*, November 12, 2012, https://www.washingtonpost.com/lifestyle/style/petraeus-ghostwriter-clueless-to-affair/2012/11/12/c1271634-2ce4-11e2-89d4-040c9330702a_story.html.
248 *"They are highly classified"*: United States v. Petraeus, Bill of Information, March 3, 2015, https://www.ncwd.uscourts.gov/sites/default/files/general/Petraeus.pdf.
249 *"walked me through"*: Morell, *The Great War of Our Time*, p. 204.
249 *"The more stars you have"*: Trevor Royle, *A Dictionary of Military Quotations* (New York: Simon & Schuster, 1989), p. 41.
250 *"The CIA as an institution"*: John Brennan, *Undaunted: My Fight Against America's Enemies, at Home and Abroad* (New York: Celadon, 2020), p. 284.

Chapter Twenty: Lethal and Legal

251 *My God, what are we doing?*: John Brennan, *Undaunted: My Fight Against America's Enemies, at Home and Abroad* (New York: Celadon, 2020), pp. 131–36.
251 *"He never expressed any concerns"*: Rizzo remarks, Cardozo School of Law, February 10, 2013, https://larc.cardozo.yu.edu/cgi/viewcontent.cgi?article=1003&context=cardozo-news-2013.
253 *"rather damning"*: Brennan confirmation hearings, Senate intelligence committee, February 7, 2013, https://www.intelligence.senate.gov/sites/default/files/hearings/transcript.pdf.
254 *"We either get out and sell"*: Mudd email in Torture Report, p. 12, https://www.intelligence.senate.gov/sites/default/files/publications/CRPT-113srpt288.pdf.
254 *"the enormously valuable intelligence"*: Torture Report, p. 406.
254 *"A template on which future justifications"*: Torture Report, p. 192.
254 *"the strong impression"*: Scott Shane, "Acting C.I.A. Chief Critical of 'Zero Dark Thirty,'" *New York Times*, December 23, 2012, https://www.nytimes.com/2012/12/23/us/politics/acting-cia-director-michael-j-morell-criticizes-zero-dark-thirty.html.

255 *"hit the ground running"*: Brennan, *Undaunted*, pp. 285ff.
257 *"not all that different"*: Author's interview, Leon Panetta.
257 *"personal comments reflecting"*: Brennan, *Undaunted*, p. 316.
257 *"a damning argument"*: Daniel Jones interview, *Intercepted* podcast, The Intercept, December 11, 2019, https://theintercept.com/2019/12/11/we-tortured-some-folks-the-reports-daniel-jones-on-the-ongoing-fight-to-hold-the-cia-accountable/.
258 *"As far as the allegations"*: Brennan remarks, Council on Foreign Relations, March 11, 2014, https://www.cfr.org/event/cia-director-brennan-denies-hacking-allegations.
258 *"We have to get this behind"*: Biden quoted in Brennan, *Undaunted*, p. 326.
259 *"It is a hard fact"*: Obama remarks, National Defense University, May 23, 2013, White House Archives, https://obamawhitehouse.archives.gov/the-press-office/2013/05/23/remarks-president-national-defense-university.
259 *"Avril and I bore the scars"*: Spencer Ackerman, "The Proxy War Over a Top Biden Adviser," *Daily Beast*, July 6, 2020, https://www.thedailybeast.com/the-proxy-war-over-joe-biden-adviser-avril-haines.
260 *"just because something is legal"*: Haines quoted in Erin Blanco, "'Just Because It's Legal Doesn't Make It Right': The Ultimate Government Insider Contemplates Life Outside," *Politico*, October 29, 2024, https://www.politico.com/news/magazine/2024/10/29/avril-haines-biden-intelligence-adviser-profile-00180753.
260 *"intelligence, work ethic, and humility"*: Statement by the President on the Selection of Avril Haines as Deputy National Security Advisor, White House Archives, December 18, 2014, https://obamawhitehouse.archives.gov/the-press-office/2014/12/18/statement-president-selection-avril-haines-deputy-national-security-advi.
261 *"the country was in desperate peril"*: Cunningham quoted in John Marks, *The Search for the "Manchurian Candidate"* (New York: Times Books, 1979), p. 26.
261 *"We understood what harsh and difficult"*: Tenet in Bill Harlow, ed., *Rebuttal: The CIA Responds to the Senate Intelligence Committee's Study of Its Detention and Interrogation Program* (Annapolis: Naval Institute Press, 2015), p. 5.
262 *"Is it moral to subject"*: Michael Morell with Bill Harlow, *The Great War of Our Time: The CIA's Fight Against Terrorism—from al Qa'ida to ISIS* (New York: Twelve, 2015), p. 274.
262 *"designed to make lies sound truthful"*: George Orwell, "Politics and the English Language," 1946, The Orwell Foundation, https://www.orwellfoundation.com/the-orwell-foundation/orwell/essays-and-other-works/politics-and-the-english-language/.
262 *"I am convinced"*: Rodriguez in Harlow, ed., *Rebuttal*, p. 37.
263 *"They claimed that all this was"*: Hayden in Harlow, ed., *Rebuttal*, p. 11.
264 *"In the immediate aftermath of 9/11"*: Barack Obama press conference, August 1, 2014, White House Archives, https://obamawhitehouse.archives.gov/the-press-office/2014/08/01/press-conference-president.

Chapter Twenty-One: Face-Eating Baboons

266 *"We had a massive information gap"*: Victoria Nuland interview, "The Putin Files," *Frontline*, PBS, https://www.pbs.org/wgbh/frontline/interview/victoria-nuland/#highlight-3137-3166.

266 *"Russia is a regional power"*: Barack Obama remarks, The Hague, March 25, 2014, White House Archives, https://obamawhitehouse.archives.gov/the-press-office/2014/03/25/press-conference-president-obama-and-prime-minister-rutte-netherlands.

268 *"Those attacks were against the unclassified"*: Author's interview, John Brennan.

268 *"Hand-to-hand combat"*: Richard Ledgett quoted in Joseph Marks, "NSA Engaged in Massive Battle with Russian Hackers in 2014," *Nextgov*, April 3, 2017, https://www.nextgov.com/cybersecurity/2017/03/once-stealthy-russian-hackers-now-go-toe-toe-us-defenders/136358/.

268 *"Those guys were really dug in"*: Mandia quoted in David Sanger, *The Perfect Weapon: War, Sabotage, and Fear in the Cyber Age* (New York: Broadway Books, 2018), pp. 188–89.

269 *"The OPM hack"*: Author's interview, William Evanina.

269 *"Information about everybody"*: James Comey quoted in Ellen Nakashima, "Hacks of OPM Databases Compromised 22.1 Million People, Federal Authorities Say," *Washington Post*, July 9, 2015, Internet Archive Wayback Machine, https://web.archive.org/web/20180726051157/https://www.washingtonpost.com/news/federal-eye/wp/2015/07/09/hack-of-security-clearance-system-affected-21-5-million-people-federal-authorities-say/.

270 *"There's no fixing it"*: Michael Hayden quoted in Dan Verton, "Impact of OPM Breach Could Last More Than 40 Years," Fedscoop, July 10, 2015, https://fedscoop.com/opm-losses-a-40-year-problem-for-intelligence-community/.

270 *"The foundations of the business of espionage,"* Duyane Norman quoted in Jenna McLaughlin and Zach Dorfman, "'Shattered': Inside the Secret Battle to Save America's Undercover Spies in the Digital Age," *Yahoo! News*, December 30, 2019, https://www.yahoo.com/news/shattered-inside-the-secret-battle-to-save-americas-undercover-spies-in-the-digital-age-100029026.html.

270 *"Folks are going to have to live"*: Dawn Meyerriecks remarks, GEOINT conference, Tampa, Florida, quoted in Mark Pomerleau, "CIA Rethinks How to Protect Operatives' Digital Lives," C4ISRNet, April 23, 2018, https://www.c4isrnet.com/intel-geoint/2018/04/23/cia-rethinks-how-to-protect-operatives-digital-lives/.

270 *"It's extremely difficult"*: Joel Brenner quoted in Jenna McLaughlin and Zach Dorfman, "'Shattered': Inside the Secret Battle to Save America's Undercover Spies in the Digital Age," *Yahoo! News*, December 30, 2019, https://www.yahoo.com/news/shattered-inside-the-secret-battle-to-save-americas-undercover-spies-in-the-digital-age-100029026.html.

271 *"attending a cocktail party"*: Andrew Hallman quoted in Patrick Tucker, "Meet the Man Reinventing CIA for the Big Data Era," *Defense One*, October 1, 2015,

https://www.defenseone.com/technology/2015/10/meet-man-reinventing-cia-big-data-era/122453/.

271 *"digital autocracies"*: Jennifer Ewbank, "CIA Deputy for Digital Innovation Talks Mission, Partnerships and Espionage Challenges," The Cipher Brief, December 2, 2021, https://www.thecipherbrief.com/cia-deputy-for-digital-innovation-talks-mission-partnerships-and-espionage.

271 *"Many CIA officers became quite vocal"*: John Brennan, *Undaunted: My Fight Against America's Enemies, at Home and Abroad* (New York: Celadon, 2020), pp. 292–96.

272 *"shattered longstanding structural"*: Larry Pfeiffer quoted in Natasha Bertrand and Daniel Lippman, "Spies Fear a Consulting Firm Helped Hobble U.S. Intelligence," *Politico*, July 2, 2019, https://www.politico.com/story/2019/07/02/spies-intelligence-community-mckinsey-1390863.

272 *"We really don't want to talk"*: Avril Haines and David Cohen interview by Mike Morell, *Intelligence Matters* podcast, CBS News, January 23, 2019, https://www.cbsnews.com/news/transcript-david-cohen-avril-haines-talk-with-michael-morell-on-intelligence-matters/.

273 *"insularity, parochialism, and arrogance"*: Brennan, *Undaunted*, p. 298.

273 *"Brennan had guts"*: Vogel quoted on deep background in David Ignatius, "Will John Brennan's Controversial CIA Modernization Survive Trump?" *Washington Post*, January 17, 2017, https://www.washingtonpost.com/opinions/will-john-brennans-controversial-cia-modernization-survive-trump/2017/01/17/54e6cc1c-dcd5-11e6-ad42-f3375f271c9c_story.html.

275 *"don't want our intelligence agencies"*: Barack Obama remarks, University of Chicago Law School, April 8, 2016, White House Archives, https://obamawhitehouse.archives.gov/the-press-office/2016/04/08/remarks-president-conversation-supreme-court-nomination.

275 *"It was disruptive"*: Haines and Cohen interview by Morell, *Intelligence Matters* podcast.

276 *"And, of course, for them"*: Author's interview, Steve Hall.

276 *"the best way to create"*: Bill Burns interview by Mike Morell, *Intelligence Matters*, podcast, CBS News, March 13, 2019, https://www.cbsnews.com/news/transcript-william-burns-talks-with-michael-morell-on-intelligence-matters/.

277 *"Putin got away with it"*: Daniel Fried quoted in Vazha Tavberidze, "With the 2008 Georgia War, 'We Knew What Was Coming, But We Were Slow to Believe It,'" Radio Free Europe, August 14, 2022, https://www.rferl.org/a/georgia-russia-war-fried/31987472.html.

277 *"Georgia was a turning point"*: Mike Morell interview transcript, *Politico*, December 11, 2017, https://www.politico.com/magazine/story/2017/12/11/the-full-transcript-michael-morell-216061/.

278 *"People were repeating that story"*: Molly Schwartz, "The Man Who Taught the Kremlin How to Win the Internet," The World, May 4, 2018, https://theworld.org/stories/2018/05/04/man-who-taught-kremlin-how-win-internet.

279 *"information-warfare"*: Gen. Philip Breedlove quoted in John Vandiver, "SACEUR:

Allies Must Prepare for Russia 'Hybrid War,'" *Stars and Stripes*, September 4, 2014, https://www.stripes.com/migration/saceur-allies-must-prepare-for-russia-hybrid-war-1.301464.

279 *"Putin looked at Trump"*: Author's interview, Leon Panetta.

Chapter Twenty-Two: The Useful Idiot

280 *"arm the Syrian"*: William J. Burns, *The Back Channel: A Memoir of American Diplomacy and the Case for Its Renewal* (New York: Random House, 2019), p. 326.

281 *"American policies are allowing the Islamists"*: John Brennan, *Undaunted: My Fight Against America's Enemies, at Home and Abroad* (New York: Celadon, 2020), p. 362.

281 *"When it became clear"*: Author's interview, John Brennan.

281 *"He's been a Russian stooge"*: Victoria Nuland quoted in Michael Isikoff and David Corn, *Russian Roulette: The Inside Story of Putin's War on America and the Election of Donald Trump* (New York: Twelve, 2018), p. 94.

282 *"there were extensive contacts"*: Author's interview, John Brennan.

283 *"He praises dictators like Vladimir Putin"*: Clinton foreign policy speech, *Time*, June 2, 2016, https://time.com/4355797/hillary-clinton-donald-trump-foreign-policy-speech-transcript/.

284 *"WikiLeaks has a very big year"*: Scott Shane and Mark Mazzetti," "The Plot to Subvert an Election," *New York Times*, September 20, 2018, https://www.nytimes.com/interactive/2018/09/20/us/politics/russia-interference-election-trump-clinton.html.

286 *"There's two people I think"*: Adam Entous, "House Majority Leader to Colleagues in 2016: 'I Think Putin Pays' Trump," *Washington Post*, May 17, 2017, https://www.washingtonpost.com/world/national-security/house-majority-leader-to-colleagues-in-2016-i-think-putin-pays-trump/2017/05/17/515f6f8a-3aff-11e7-8854-21f359183e8c_story.html.

286 *"cyber sphere is a tremendous venue"*: Author's interview, John Brennan.

287 *"I need to see the president"*: Brennan, *Undaunted*, p. 367.

287 *"We had our work cut out"*: Brennan, interview transcript, *Frontline*, PBS, July 27, 2017, https://www.pbs.org/wgbh/frontline/interview/john-brennan/.

288 *"In the intelligence business"*: Michael J. Morell, "I Ran the C.I.A. Now I'm Endorsing Hillary Clinton," *New York Times*, August 5, 2016, https://www.nytimes.com/2016/08/05/opinion/campaign-stops/i-ran-the-cia-now-im-endorsing-hillary-clinton.html.

289 *"I'd prefer another term"*: Michael V. Hayden, "Former CIA Chief: Trump Is Russia's Useful Fool," *Washington Post*, November 3, 2016, https://www.washingtonpost.com/opinions/former-cia-chief-trump-is-russias-useful-fool/2016/11/03/cda42ffe-a1d5-11e6-8d63-3e0a660f1f04_story.html.

289 *"There wasn't any question"*: Author's interview, Leon Panetta.

289 *"Well, it sounds as though"*: Author's interview, John Brennan.

290 *"his party above national identity"*: Author's interview, John Brennan.

290 *"The president always felt"*: Brennan interview transcript, *Frontline*.
290 *"ecosystem of the international arena"*: Author's interview, John Brennan.
291 *"I am shocked"*: Morell interview, in Ashish Kumar Sen, "US Must Deliver a 'Painful' Response to Putin for Russian Meddling," *New Atlanticist* (blog), Atlantic Council, December 13, 2016, https://www.atlanticcouncil.org/blogs/new-atlanticist/us-must-deliver-a-painful-response-to-putin-for-russian-meddling/.
292 *"On November 9, 2016"*: Cited in *Russian Active Measures Campaigns and Interference in the 2016 U.S. Election, Volume 2: Russia's Use of Social Media*, Senate Intelligence Committee report, 2019.
293 *"confident that the Russians changed"*: Author's interview, John Brennan.
293 *"Knowing what I know"*: Clapper quoted in Sean Illing, "Former Top Spy James Clapper Explains How Russian Swung the Election to Trump," *Vox*, May 31, 2018, https://www.vox.com/2018/5/31/17384444/james-clapper-trump-russia-mueller-2016-election.
293 *"Without Russian assistance"*: Author's interview, Pete Stzrok.
293 *"no doubt that Donald Trump"*: Author's interview, Rolf Mowatt-Larssen.
294 *"He believes that he can manipulate"*: Morell interview, in Sun, "US Must Deliver a 'Painful' Response to Putin for Russian Meddling."
294 *"exactly what a case officer"*: Fiona Hill deposition, House impeachment inquiry, October 14, 2019, Just Security, https://www.justsecurity.org/wp-content/uploads/2019/11/ukraine-clearinghouse-hill_transcript-2019.10.14.pdf.
294 *"the only time in American history"*: Robert Draper, "Unwanted Truths: Inside Trump's Battles with U.S. Intelligence Agencies," *New York Times*, August 8, 2020, https://www.nytimes.com/2020/08/08/magazine/us-russia-intelligence.html.
295 *"There is no doubt"*: Mike Pompeo letter to James Clapper, July 7, 2016.
295 *"an authoritarian president who ignored"*: Susan B. Glasser, "Mike Pompeo, the Secretary of Trump," *The New Yorker*, August 19, 2019, https://www.newyorker.com/magazine/2019/08/26/mike-pompeo-the-secretary-of-trump.
295 *"going to be great"*: Mike Pompeo, *Never Give an Inch: Fighting for the America I Love* (New York: Broadside Books, 2023) p. 16.
295 *"I don't believe it"*: David Nakamura and Greg Miller, "Trump, CIA on Collision Course over Russia's Role in U.S. Election," *Washington Post*, December 11, 2016, https://www.washingtonpost.com/politics/trump-cia-on-collision-course-over-russias-role-in-us-election/2016/12/10/ad01556c-bf01-11e6-91ee-1adddfe36cbe_story.html.
295 *"He touched it"*: Gistaro and Clapper quoted in John Helgerson, *Getting to Know the President: Intelligence Briefings of Presidential Candidates and Presidents-elect, 1952–2016*, Center for the Study of Intelligence Central Intelligence Agency, October 2021, https://www.cia.gov/resources/csi/static/Getting-to-Know-the-President-Fourth-Edition-2021-web.pdf.
295 *"fly off on tangents"*: Gistaro and Clapper quoted in John Helgerson, *Getting to Know the President: Intelligence Briefings of Presidential Candidates and Presidents-elect, 1952–2016*, 4th ed., October 2021, Center for the Study of Intelligence, CIA,

NOTES / 429

https://www.cia.gov/resources/csi/static/Getting-to-Know-the-President-Fourth-Edition-2021-web.pdf.
295 *"The most politically charged issue"*: Helgerson, *Getting to Know the President*.
296 *"a rigorous effort to declassify"*: Author's interview, Beth Sanner.
297 *"Tell the families"*: Shane Harris, "CIA Director John Brennan Rejects Donald Trump's Criticism," *Wall Street Journal*, January 17, 2017.
297 *"Trump hated the intelligence agencies"*: Mike Pompeo, *Never Give an Inch* (New York: Broadside Books, 2023), p. 4.

Chapter Twenty-Three: Ring-Kissing and Kneecapping

299 *"Really had R.N. tattooed on him"*: Richard Helms interview with Stanley Kutler, transcript in author's possession.
299 *"I'm here to make sure"*: Christopher R. Moran and Richard J. Aldrich, "Trump and the CIA," *Foreign Affairs*, April 24, 2017, https://www.foreignaffairs.com/united-states/trump-and-cia.
299 *"I argue with everyone"*: Olivia Nuzzi, "My Private Oval Office Press Conference with President Trump, Mike Pence, John Kelly, and Mike Pompeo," *New York*, October 10, 2018, https://nymag.com/intelligencer/2018/10/my-private-oval-office-press-conference-with-donald-trump.html.
300 *"Each day, we're in there"*: Mike Pompeo remarks, Center for Strategic and International Studies, April 13, 2017, https://www.csis.org/analysis/discussion-national-security-cia-director-mike-pompeo.
300 *"heat-seeking missile for Trump's"*: Susan Glasser, "Mike Pompeo, the Secretary of Trump," *The New Yorker*, August 26, 2019, https://www.newyorker.com/magazine/2019/08/26/mike-pompeo-the-secretary-of-trump.
300 *"Aggressive, patriotic and brilliant"*: Mike Pompeo, *Never Give an Inch* (New York: Broadside Books, 2023), pp. 24, 31.
301 *"They tell me you're an asshole"*: Mike Pompeo, *Never Give an Inch* (New York: Broadside Books, 2023), pp. 24, 31.
302 *"most combustible challenge"*: William J. Burns, *The Back Channel: A Memoir of American Diplomacy and the Case for Its Renewal* (New York: Random House, 2019), p. 383.
303 *"I had worried that the president"*: Michael V. Hayden, *The Assault on Intelligence: American National Security in an Age of Lies* (New York: Penguin Press, 2018), p. 179.
303 *"North Korea tested missiles"*: Andrew Kim remarks on North Korea Denuclearization and U.S.-DPRK Diplomacy, Stanford University, February 22, 2019, https://aparc.fsi.stanford.edu/news/transcript-andrew-kim-north-korea-denuclearization-and-us-dprk-diplomacy.
304 *"WikiLeaks walks like a hostile"*: Pompeo remarks, Center for Strategic and International Studies.
305 *"The capabilities we had been developing"*: Sean Roche testimony, *U.S. v. Schulte*, February 19, 2020, https://www.documentcloud.org/documents/6782056-200219-Schulte-Trial-Transcript.html.

305 *"We did not realize the loss"*: WikiLeaks Task Force, Final Report, October 17, 2017, https://context-cdn.washingtonpost.com/notes/prod/default/documents/5c3a0160-a21a-47d2-be78-f27dd0274195/note/6b42529f-61e8-4ed6-86ab-f272df27db5a.

306 *"The intelligence community wasn't being honest"*: Binney quoted in Duncan Campbell and James Risen, "CIA Director Met Advocate of Disputed DNC Hack Theory—at Trump's Request," *The Intercept*, November 7, 2017, https://theintercept.com/2017/11/07/dnc-hack-trump-cia-director-william-binney-nsa/.

307 *"dopes and babies"*: Carol D. Leonnig and Philip Rucker, "'You're a Bunch of Dopes and Babies': Inside Trump's Stunning Tirade Against Generals," *Washington Post*, January 17, 2020, https://www.washingtonpost.com/politics/youre-a-bunch-of-dopes-and-babies-inside-trumps-stunning-tirade-against-generals/2020/01/16/d6dbb8a6-387e-11ea-bb7b-265f4554af6d_story.html.

307 *"The American people don't mind"*: Thomas Gibbons-Neff, Eric Schmitt, and Adam Goldman, "A Newly Assertive C.I.A. Expands Its Taliban Hunt in Afghanistan," *New York Times*, October 22, 2017, https://www.nytimes.com/2017/10/22/world/asia/cia-expanding-taliban-fight-afghanistan.html.

308 *"We can't perform our mission"*: Pompeo remarks, UT Austin National Security Forum, October 12, 2017, https://www.legistorm.com/stormfeed/view_rss/1110531/organization/95196/title/pompeo-delivers-remarks-at-ut-austin-national-security-forum.html.

308 *"I hear he's a con man"*: Trump quoted in John Bolton, *The Room Where It Happened: A White House Memoir* (New York: Simon & Schuster, 2020), p. 215.

308 *"the United States was ready"*: Lisa Curtis, "How the Doha Agreement Guaranteed US Failure in Afghanistan," Hoover Institution, 2021, https://www.hoover.org/sites/default/files/research/docs/curtis_webreadypdf.pdf.

309 *"Is Ivanka going to wear a burqa?"*: Sanner quoted in Maggie Haberman, *Confidence Man: The Making of Donald Trump and the Breaking of America* (New York: Penguin, 2022), p. 385.

309 *"Doha agreement"*: Robert Burns and Lolita C. Baldor, "US General: Afghan Collapse Rooted in 2020 Deal with Taliban," Associated Press, September 29, 2021, https://apnews.com/article/joe-biden-afghanistan-kabul-taliban-lloyd-austin-4496393071505484162b434602776a9f.

309 *"secretary of state signed a surrender"*: Meridith McGraw, "Mike Pompeo Takes His Own Arrows over the Afghanistan Collapse," *Politico*, August 26, 2021, https://www.politico.com/news/2021/08/26/mike-pompeo-afghanistan-collapse-506927.

Chapter Twenty-Four: The Enemy of Intelligence

310 *"CIA like the back"*: Haspel confirmation hearings, Senate intelligence committee, May 9, 2018, https://www.intelligence.senate.gov/hearings/open-hearing-nomination-gina-haspel-be-director-central-intelligence-agency#.

312 *"With the benefit of hindsight"*: Charlie Savage, "Gina Haspel Likely to Be Con-

firmed as C.I.A. Chief After Repudiating Torture," *New York Times*, May 15, 2018, https://www.nytimes.com/2018/05/15/us/politics/gina-haspel-cia-torture-letter-senate.html.

313 *"warning lights are blinking red"*: Dan Coats quoted in Juliam E. Barnes, "'Warning Lights are Blinking Red,' Top Intelligence Office Says of Russian Attacks," *New York Times*, July 13, 2018, https://www.nytimes.com/2018/07/13/us/politics/dan-coats-intelligence-russia-cyber-warning.html.

313 *"fictional narrative"*: Fiona Hill deposition, House impeachment inquiry, October 14, 2019, Just Security, https://www.justsecurity.org/wp-content/uploads/2019/11/ukraine-clearinghouse-hill_transcript-2019.10.14.pdf.

314 *"seen Russian intelligence manipulate"*: Congressman Will Hurd post, July 16, 2018, X (then known as Twitter), https://x.com/WillHurd/status/1018931248457306115.

314 *"nothing short of treasonous"*: John Brennan post, July 16, 2018, X (then known as Twitter), https://x.com/JohnBrennan/status/1018885971104985093.

314 *"one of the most tragic moments"*: Panetta in Mary Louise Kelly, "How the Relationship Between Trump and His Spy Chiefs Soured," NPR, October 29, 2019, https://www.npr.org/2019/10/29/773127809/how-the-relationship-between-trump-and-his-spy-chiefs-soured.

315 *"Those of us who have worked"*: Douglas London, "The CIA in the Age of Trump," Just Security, February 10, 2020, https://www.justsecurity.org/68539/the-cia-in-the-age-of-trump/.

315 *"I saved his ass"*: Bob Woodward, *The Trump Tapes* (New York: Simon & Schuster, 2023), p. 190.

315 *"The Crown Prince viewed Khashoggi"*: "[Redacted] Assessing the Saudi Government's Role in the Killing of Jamal Khashoggi," CIA report, February 11, 2021, declassified in part by Director of National Intelligence Avril Haines, February 25, 2021, https://www.dni.gov/files/ODNI/documents/assessments/Assessment-Saudi-Gov-Role-in-JK-Death-20210226v2.pdf.

315 *"The Turks gave the CIA"*: Shane Harris, Greg Miller, and Josh Dawsey, "CIA Concludes Saudi Crown Prince Ordered Jamal Khashoggi's Assassination," *Washington Post*, November 16, 2018, https://www.washingtonpost.com/world/national-security/cia-concludes-saudi-crown-prince-ordered-jamal-khashoggis-assassination/2018/11/16/98c89fe6-e9b2-11e8-a939-9469f1166f9d_story.html.

316 *"did not come to a conclusion"*: "Trump Rebuffs CIA Conclusion Linking MBS to Khashoggi Killing as 'Feelings,'" *Middle East Monitor*, November 23, 2018, https://www.middleeastmonitor.com/20181123-trump-rebuffs-cia-conclusion-linking-mbs-to-khashoggi-killing-as-feelings.

316 *"They're still dangerous"*: Haspel testimony, Senate intelligence committee, January 29, 2019.

316 *"strong and inappropriate"*: Wise quoted in Mark Landler, "An Angry Trump Pushes Back Against His Own 'Naive' Intelligence Officials," *New York Times*, January 30, 2019, https://www.nytimes.com/2019/01/30/us/politics/trump-intelligence-agencies.html.

317 *"He's an idiot"*: Kelly quoted in Bob Woodward, *Fear: Trump in the White House* (New York: Simon & Schuster, 2018), p. 286.

317 *"my career goal was to become"*: William P. Barr, *One Damn Thing After Another: Memoirs of an Attorney General* (New York: William Morrow, 2022), p. 27.

318 *"the right to do whatever"*: Trump remarks, Turning Point USA summit, July 23, 2019, White House Archives, https://trumpwhitehouse.archives.gov/briefings-statements/remarks-president-trump-turning-point-usas-teen-student-action-summit-2019/.

318 *"I think spying did occur"*: Barr quoted in Devlin Barrett and Karoun Demirjian, "Attorney General Says He Believes 'Spying Did Occur' in Probe of Trump Campaign Associates," *Washington Post*, April 10, 2019, https://www.washingtonpost.com/world/national-security/attorney-general-faces-second-day-of-questioning-about-muellers-report/2019/04/09/362cc648-5b02-11e9-a00e-050dc7b82693_story.html.

319 *"In Syria, the president had"*: Marc Polymeropoulos, "A Call to Arms: Taking the Russia Threat Seriously," Just Security, December 6, 2019, https://www.justsecurity.org/67623/a-call-to-arms-taking-the-russia-threat-seriously/.

320 *"scheme was bound to backfire"*: Barr, *One Damn Thing After Another*, p. 300.

320 *"conspiracy theory"*: Tom Bossert quoted in Sheryl Gay Stolberg, Maggie Haberman, and Peter Baker, "Trump Was Repeatedly Warned That Ukraine Conspiracy Theory Was 'Completely Debunked,'" *New York Times*, September 29, 2019, https://www.nytimes.com/2019/09/29/us/politics/tom-bossert-trump-ukraine.html.

320 *"a really devastating effect"*: Fiona Hill deposition, House impeachment inquiry, October 14, 2019, Just Security, https://www.justsecurity.org/wp-content/uploads/2019/11/ukraine-clearinghouse-hill_transcript-2019.10.14.pdf.

321 *"extensively talked Ukraine down"*: Deputy Assistant Secretary of State for European and Eurasian Affairs George Kent deposition, House impeachment inquiry, October 15, 2019, Just Security, https://www.justsecurity.org/wp-content/uploads/2019/11/ukraine-clearinghouse-2019.10.15.kent_transcript.pdf.

321 *"In the course of his presidency"*: Fiona Hill, *There Is Nothing for You Here: Finding Opportunity in the Twenty-First Century* (New York: Harper Collins, 2021), p. 219.

321 *"a terrible human being"*: Quint Forgey, "Mulvaney Once Called Trump a 'Terrible Human Being' Ahead of 2016 Election," *Politico*, December 15, 2018, https://www.politico.com/story/2018/12/15/mulvaney-trump-terrible-human-being-1066657.

322 *"If what I just heard becomes"*: Alexander Vindman, "What I Heard in the White House Basement," *The Atlantic*, August 1, 2021, https://www.theatlantic.com/politics/archive/2021/08/trump-ukraine-call-impeachment-vindman/619617/.

323 *"I think we need somebody"*: Trump White House statement quoted in Zachary Cohen and Nicole Gaouette, "Trump Says Ratcliffe Will 'Rein In' US Intelligence Agencies as Spy Chief," CNN, July 30, 2019, https://www.cnn.com/2019/07/30/politics/trump-ratcliffe-rein-in-us-intelligence-agencies/index.html.

324 *"who gave the whistleblower"*: Maggie Haberman and Katie Rogers, "Trump Attacks Whistle-Blower's Sources and Alludes to Punishment for Spies," *New York Times*,

September 26, 2019, https://www.nytimes.com/2019/09/26/us/politics/trump-whistle-blower-spy.html.
324 *"extreme apprehension about the backlash"*: Greg Jaffe, "The CIA Analyst Who Triggered Trump's First Impeachment Asks: Was It Worth It?" *Washington Post*, October 20, 2024, https://www.washingtonpost.com/politics/2024/10/20/cia-analyst-whistleblower-trump-impeachment-ukraine/.
324 *"Many people were hounded out"*: Fiona Hill deposition.

Chapter Twenty-Five: "We Are on the Way to a Right-Wing Coup"

327 *"the Kremlin was attempting to kill"*: Marc Polymeropoulos, "A Call to Arms: Taking the Russia Threat Seriously," Just Security, December 6, 2019, https://www.justsecurity.org/67623/a-call-to-arms-taking-the-russia-threat-seriously/.
327 *"a change of mindset"*: Weninger interview with Jack Murphy and Dave Parke, "An Inside Look at the Covert Fight Against Russia," The Team House, YouTube, video, October 10, 2024, https://www.youtube.com/watch?v=5z5QMm6RKdA&t=217s.
327 *"this kind of age-old notion"*: Author's interview, Marc Polymeropoulos.
327 *"understood that the Russian threat"*: Polymeropoulos, "A Call to Arms."
328 *"The heart of the issue"*: Author's interview, Tom Sylvester.
330 *time to be an intelligence officer*: Marc Polymeropoulos, "The Ties That Bind the CIA in the Face of Presidential Attack," Just Security, August 18, 2020, https://www.justsecurity.org/72043/the-ties-that-bind-the-cia-in-the-face-of-presidential-attack/.
330 *"did embolden him"*: Robert Draper, "'This Was Trump Pulling a Putin,'" *New York Times*, April 11, 2022, https://www.nytimes.com/2022/04/11/magazine/trump-putin-ukraine-fiona-hill.html.
330 *"everything was like a clown car"*: Jill Colvin, "Takeaways from Trump Aide's Account of Chaotic White House," Associated Press, September 30, 2021, https://apnews.com/article/donald-trump-entertainment-europe-arts-and-entertainment-royalty-25b7dbdaaafd46a5e95df14c7d2f3b39.
331 *"Taking aim at an imaginary"*: William J. Burns and Linda Thomas-Greenfield, "The Transformation of Diplomacy," *Foreign Affairs*, November–December 2020, https://www.foreignaffairs.com/articles/united-states/2020-09-23/diplomacy-transformation.
331 *"Hey, Joe"*: Robert Draper, "Unwanted Truths: Inside Trump's Battles with U.S. Intelligence Agencies," *New York Times*, August 8, 2020, https://www.nytimes.com/2020/08/08/magazine/us-russia-intelligence.html.
332 *"idea of moving Patel"*: William P. Barr, *One Damn Thing After Another: Memoirs of an Attorney General* (New York: William Morrow, 2022), p. 522.
332 *"Obama knew everything"*: Trump interview in Brooke Singman, "Trump Lays Down Gauntlet for Barr on Durham Probe: Either 'Greatest Attorney General' or 'Average Guy,'" Fox News Channel, August 13, 2020, https://www.foxnews.com/politics/trump-barr-durham-probe-gauntlet.

333 *"Trump is hoping"*: Joe Biden, Statement on the ODNI's Decision to End Election Interference Briefings, Medium, August 29, 2020, https://medium.com/@JoeBiden/my-statement-on-the-odnis-decision-to-end-election-interference-briefings-4b98e4eca239.

333 *"assess that President Vladimir Putin"*: CIA, *Worldwide Intelligence Review*, August 31, 2020. The conclusion was amplified in a subsequent report by the National Intelligence Council: "We assess that Russian President Putin authorized, and a range of Russian government organizations conducted, influence operations aimed at denigrating President Biden's candidacy and the Democratic Party, supporting former President Trump, undermining public confidence in the electoral process, and exacerbating sociopolitical divisions in the US." National Intelligence Council, *Foreign Threats to the 2020 US Federal Elections*, declassified March 15, 2021, https://www.dni.gov/files/ODNI/documents/assessments/ICA-declass-16MAR21.pdf.

334 *"the biased media"*: Ron Johnson quoted in Ellen Nakashima, Shane Harris, and Tom Hamburger, "FBI Was Aware Prominent Americans, Including Giuliani, Were Targeted by Russian Influence Operation," *Washington Post*, May 1, 2021, https://www.washingtonpost.com/national-security/rudy-giuliani-fbi-warning-russia/2021/04/29/5db90f96-a84e-11eb-bca5-048b2759a489_story.html.

334 *"Russia is playing us all"*: Lindsey Graham quoted in Andrew Desiderio, "Senate Intel Chair Privately Warned That GOP's Biden Probe Could Help Russia," *Politico*, February 27, 2020, https://www.politico.com/news/2020/02/27/richard-burr-joe-biden-probe-russia-118025.

335 *"As far as we can tell"*: Barr, *One Damn Thing After Another*, pp. 525–26.

337 *"There will be a smooth transition"*: "Pompeo Promises 'A Smooth Transition to a Second Trump Administration,'" NPR, November 10, 2020.

337 *"Yesterday was appalling"*: Haspel quoted in Bob Woodward and Robert Costa, *Peril* (New York: Simon & Schuster, 2021), p. 152.

338 *"Pick your poison"*: Max Boot, "Anthony Tata Should Be Running a QAnon Bulletin Board—Not the Pentagon Policy Shop," *Washington Post*, June 24, 2020, https://www.washingtonpost.com/opinions/2020/06/24/odious-track-record-trumps-pentagon-pick-is-too-long-recant/.

338 *"The idea was to put Kash"*: Ezra Cohen quoted in Adam Ciralsky, "'The President Threw Us Under the Bus': Embedding with Pentagon Leadership in Trump's Chaotic Last Week," *Vanity Fair*, January 22, 2021, https://www.vanityfair.com/news/2021/01/embedding-with-pentagon-leadership-in-trumps-chaotic-last-week.

339 *"how much the CIA"*: Transcript in "Why Doesn't Biden Camp Want to Know Truth About Voting Irregularities?" Fox News Channel, November 15, 2020, https://www.foxnews.com/transcript/why-doesnt-biden-camp-want-to-know-truth-about-voting-irregularities.

339 *"the massive influence of communist"*: Trump Campaign Press Conference transcript, November 19, 2020, https://www.rev.com/blog/transcripts/rudy-giuliani-trump-campaign-press-conference-transcript-november-19-election-fraud-claims.

339 *"Gina Haspel has been hurt"*: Jonathan Karl, *Betrayal: The Final Act of the Trump Show* (New York: Dutton, 2021), pp. 170–73.
341 *"a very savvy operator"*: Testimony of Alyssa Farah Griffin, January 6 Committee, April 15, 2022, https://www.govinfo.gov/content/pkg/GPO-J6-TRANSCRIPT-CTRL0000062452/pdf/GPO-J6-TRANSCRIPT-CTRL0000062452.pdf.
341 *"This is absolute proof"*: Barr, *One Damn Thing After Another*, pp. 553–55.
341 *"Effective immediately"*: Draft executive order, "Presidential Findings to Preserve Collect and Analyze National Security Information Regarding the 2020 General Election," dated December 16, 2020, *Politico*, https://www.politico.com/f/?id=0000017e-920d-d65f-a77e-fbad182f0000.

Chapter Twenty-Six: The Glory Gate

344 *"Gina deserves enormous credit"*: Author's interview, William J. Burns, CIA headquarters, July 2024.
345 *"a tall discreet figure"*: Robert J. Draper, "William Burns, a C.I.A. Spymaster with Unusual Powers," *New York Times*, May 9, 2023, https://www.nytimes.com/2023/05/09/us/politics/william-burns-cia-biden.html.
345 *"together everywhere in the world"*: Ryan Crocker oral history, Miller Center, University of Virginia, https://millercenter.org/the-presidency/presidential-oral-histories/ryan-crocker-oral-history.
345 *"a really deft touch"*: Author's interview, William J. Burns.
346 *"my biggest professional regret"*: William J. Burns, *The Back Channel: A Memoir of American Diplomacy and the Case for Its Renewal* (New York: Random House, 2019) pp. 169, 196.
346 *"we continually found ourselves"*: "The Diplomacy Imperative: A Q&A with William J. Burns," *The Foreign Service Journal*, American Foreign Service Association, May 2019, https://afsa.org/diplomacy-imperative-qa-william-j-burns.
347 *"After the recklessness"*: Burns, *The Back Channel*, p. 334.
348 *"It's an instrument of surrender"*: Petraeus interview, "America and the Taliban," *Frontline*, PBS, April 25, 2023, https://www.pbs.org/wgbh/frontline/documentary/america-and-the-taliban/transcript/.
348 *"The worst diplomatic agreement"*: Author's interview, Douglas London.
348 *"Trump will be responsible"*: John Bolton, *The Room Where It Happened: A White House Memoir* (New York: Simon & Schuster, 2020), p. 443.
348 *"You are a tough people"*: Julian Borger, "Trump Reportedly Tells Taliban Official 'You Are a Tough People' in First Phone Call," *The Guardian*, March 3, 2020, https://www.theguardian.com/us-news/2020/mar/03/trump-reportedly-tells-taliban-official-you-are-tough-people-amid-peace-deal-row. The readout of the call came from the Taliban; the White House refused to release one. Trump had just been impeached for his "perfect phone call" to Ukraine.
348 *"Do you need something from me?"*: Steve Coll and Adam Entous, "The Secret History of the U.S. Diplomatic Failure in Afghanistan," *The New Yorker*, December 10,

350   *a Taliban takeover of Afghanistan:* Biden press conference, July 8, 2021, The White House, https://www.whitehouse.gov/briefing-room/speeches-remarks/2021/07/08/remarks-by-president-biden-on-the-drawdown-of-u-s-forces-in-afghanistan/.

351   *"no intel assessment":* Gen. Mark Milley testimony, Senate Armed Services Committee, September 28, 2021, https://www.armed-services.senate.gov/imo/media/doc/21-73_09-28-2021.pdf.

352   *"They only left us bones":* Franz J. Marty, "Visit to a Lost CIA Base in Afghanistan," Military.com, December 9, 2021, https://www.military.com/daily-news/2021/12/09/visit-lost-cia-base-afghanistan.html.

352   *"As we stepped up":* Author's interview, Tom Polgar.

353   *"images evoked America's frantic":* Carlotta Gall and Ruhullah Khapalwak, "Chaos Ensues at Kabul Airport as Americans Abandon Afghanistan," *New York Times*, August 16, 2021, https://www.nytimes.com/2021/08/16/world/asia/afghanistan-airport-evacuation-us-withdrawal.html.

353   *"I live with memories":* Sam Aronson testimony, House Foreign Affairs Committee, September 15, 2023, https://foreignaffairs.house.gov/wp-content/uploads/2024/04/Interview-of-Sam-Aronson_FINAL.pdf.

354   *"simply to persuade the Taliban":* Author's interview, Bill Burns.

354   *"I saw that the American operators":* Sam Aronson testimony. See also Mitchell Zuckoff, "'Screw the Rules,'" *The Atlantic*, April 11, 2023, https://www.theatlantic.com/ideas/archive/2023/04/the-secret-gate-book-afghanistan-kabul-airport-evacuation/673682/.

355   *"I don't believe people get":* Lara Seligman, "Pentagon Prepared for 'Mass Casualty' Attack at Kabul Airport Hours Before Explosion," *Politico*, August 30, 2021, https://www.politico.com/news/2021/08/30/pentagon-mass-casualty-attack-kabul-507481.

357   *"The Taliban didn't defeat us":* Gen. H. R. McMaster quoted in Meridith McGraw, "Mike Pompeo Takes His Own Arrows over the Afghanistan Collapse," *Politico*, August 26, 2021, https://www.politico.com/news/2021/08/26/mike-pompeo-afghanistan-collapse-506927.

357   *"a result of countless hours":* Mick Mulroy quoted in Peter Baker, Helene Cooper, Julian E. Barnes, and Eric Schmitt, "U.S. Drone Strike Kills Ayman al-Zawahri, Top Qaeda Leader," *New York Times*, August 1, 2022, https://www.nytimes.com/2022/08/01/us/politics/al-qaeda-strike-afghanistan.html.

Chapter Twenty-Seven: Human Intelligence

358   *"There are two ways":* Author's interview, Bill Burns.

359   *"looking around the world for Russians":* Dave Marlowe comments, "CIA at 75," Hayden Center, November 21, 2022.

359   *"shaped the ability for CIA":* Author's interview, Paula Doyle.

359 *"How do we ensure"*: Author's interview, Tom Sylvester.
359 *"There was the strategic decision"*: Author's interview, Tom Sylvester.
360 *"China and Russia were focused on us"*: "Twenty Years After 9/11: Reflections from Michael Morell," *CTC Sentinel* 14, no. 7 (September 2021).
361 *"By the eleventh of October"*: Gen. Paul Nakasone oral history, in Erin Banco et al., "'Something Was Badly Wrong': When Washington Realized Russia Was Actually Invading Ukraine," *Politico Magazine*, February 24, 2023, https://www.politico.com/news/magazine/2023/02/24/russia-ukraine-war-oral-history-00083757.
361 *"a lot of really exquisite collection"*: Linda Weissgold interview transcript, *The Langley Files* podcast, CIA, https://www.cia.gov/static/71a46d54dcd4507d077364f3a415ba9e/The-Langley-Files-File-008-CIAs-Analytics-Chief-On-The-Tradecraft-Behind-The-Agencys-Assessments-Transcript.pdf.
361 *"not only the massing of forces"*: Tony Blinken oral history, in Banco et al., "'Something Was Badly Wrong.'"
361 *"much more compelling case"*: Avril Haines oral history, in Banco et al., "'Something Was Badly Wrong.'"
361 *"the biggest ground war"*: Bill Burns oral history, in Banco et al., "'Something Was Badly Wrong.'"
362 *"He was utterly unapologetic"*: Author's interview, Bill Burns.
363 *"The president sent me out"*: Author's interview, Bill Burns.
364 *"The CIA was very prompt"*: Valentyn Nalyvaichenko quoted in Jason Jay Smart, "CIA Worked with SBU to Root Out Russian Spies," *Kyiv Post*, February 26, 2024, https://www.kyivpost.com/post/28678.
364 *"only strengthened"*: Adam Entous and Michael Schwirtz, "The Spy War," *New York Times*, February 25, 2024, https://www.nytimes.com/2024/02/25/world/europe/cia-ukraine-intelligence-russia-war.html.
365 *"allowing oneself to be recruited"*: Entous and Schwirtz, "The Spy War."
366 *"the nation's intelligence"*: Nakasone oral history, in Banco et al., "'Something Was Badly Wrong.'"
367 *"enabled the president to build"*: Author's interview, Bill Burns.
367 *"Russia will blame"*: Antony Blinken speech, U.N. Security Council, February 17, 2022, https://usun.usmission.gov/remarks-by-secretary-antony-j-blinken-at-the-un-security-council-on-russias-threat-to-peace-and-security/.
368 *"Without them"*: Entous and Schwirtz, "The Spy War."
368 *"an enormous strategic mistake"*: Gen. Mark Milley oral history, in Banco et al., "'Something Was Badly Wrong.'"
369 *"planned and implemented"*: Shane Harris and Isabelle Khurshudyan, "Ukrainian Military Officer Coordinated Nord Stream Pipeline Attack," *Washington Post*, November 11, 2023, https://www.washingtonpost.com/national-security/2023/11/11/nordstream-bombing-ukraine-chervinsky/.
369 *"fight fire with fire"*: George Kennan to James Forrestal, September 27, 1947, Record Group 165, ABC files, 352:1, National Archives and Records Administration.

370 "*a very savvy gangster*": John J. Sullivan, *Midnight in Moscow: A Memoir from the Front Lines of Russia's War Against the West* (Boston: Little, Brown, 2024), p. 241.

370 "*thought he could take Kiev*": William Burns remarks, Aspen Security Forum, July 20, 2022, CIA, https://www.cia.gov/static/Aspen-Security-Forum-Fireside-Chat-Final.pdf.

Chapter Twenty-Eight: The Morality of Espionage

371 "*Given the potential desperation*": Burns remarks, Georgia Tech, April 14, 2022, CIA, https://www.cia.gov/static/Director-Burns-Speech-and-QA-Georgia-Tech.pdf.

372 "*We have a direct threat*": Joe Biden quoted in David Sanger with Mary K. Brooks, *New Cold Wars: China's Rise, Russia's Invasion, and America's Struggle to Defend the West* (New York: Crown, 2024), p. 297.

372 "*State propaganda is preparing people*": Steve Rosenberg, "Dmitry Muratov: Nuclear Warning from Russia's Nobel-Winning Journalist," BBC, March 29, 2023, https://www.bbc.com/news/world-europe-65119595.

374 "*There was just a general recognition*": Roger D. Carstens interview transcript, *Washington Post Live* podcast, *Washington Post*, August 12, 2024, https://www.washingtonpost.com/washington-post-live/2024/08/12/transcript-world-stage-conversation-with-roger-d-carstens/.

375 "*For you, I will try*": Roger Carstens, White House briefing, August 1, 2024, https://www.whitehouse.gov/briefing-room/press-briefings/2024/08/01/background-press-call-on-todays-multilateral-prisoner-exchange/.

376 "*We've come close*": Burns remarks, Cipher Brief threat conference, Sea Island, Georgia, October 8, 2024.

378 "*I could think of nothing more*": Peter Baker, "With Prisoner Swap, Biden Scores a Win as His Term Nears Its End," *New York Times*, August 1, 2024, https://www.nytimes.com/2024/08/01/us/politics/biden-hostage-swap.html.

379 "*to supplant the United States as the preeminent global power*": David Marlowe, "China is our only real Existential Threat, says Former Senior CIA Officer," The Cipher Brief, September 4, 2024, https://www.thecipherbrief.com/column_article/china-is-our-only-real-existential-threat-says-former-senior-cia-officer

380 "*U.S. and NATO weapons*": Paula Doyle, "Cipher Brief Experts on What to Watch for in 2025," The Cipher Brief, December 29, 2024, https://www.thecipherbrief.com/cipher-brief-experts-on-what-to-watch-for-in-2025.

380 "*we have attention deficit disorder*": Author's interview, Bill Burns.

380 "*Putin has already suffered*": Author's interview, Bill Burns.

381 "*Putin was at his best moment*": Dave Marlowe comments, "CIA at 75," Hayden Center, November 21, 2022.

381 "*With the passage of time*": Helms remarks, OSS Awards Dinner, Washington, DC, May 24, 1983, CIA, https://www.cia.gov/readingroom/docs/CIA-RDP91-00901R000500150023-5.pdf.

381 "*going to come to ten*": Tom Sylvester (identified as "Tom S.") interview transcript,

The Langley Files podcast, February 28, 2024, CIA, https://www.cia.gov/podcast/static/7fc60a07d1232f824585b88a796d3097/The-Langley-Files-File-014-Transcript.pdf.

382 *"a very stunted view"*: Author's interview, Tom Sylvester.
382 *"That was based on espionage"*: Author's interview, Tom Sylvester.
383 *"when authoritarian leaders in Moscow"*: Author's interview, Paula Doyle.
383 *"spying is a dirty business"*: William Hood, Mole: The True Story of the First Russian Spy to Become an American Counterspy (Washington, DC: Brassey's, 1993), p. ix.
383 *"not unlike marriage"*: Juan Cruz remarks, "The Humanity of Espionage," Catholic University of America, February 28, 2019, https://ihe.catholic.edu/event/the-humanity-of-espionage/.
383 *"The business is schizophrenic"*: Author's interview, Luis Rueda.
384 *"United States has a moral"*: Daniel Schorr, "Telling It Like It Is: Kissinger and the Kurds," *Christian Science Monitor*, October 18, 1996, https://www.csmonitor.com/1996/1018/101896.opin.column.1.html.
384 *"The ends don't always justify"*: Author's interview, Rev. William Sloan Coffin Jr.
385 *"We must have the greatest immorality"*: This was a credo that, "though it has a certain starry-eyed quality of the early CIA, has stuck in my mind ever since," said Chuck Cogan, who reported Cunningham's teachings to the author. Cogan was perhaps the last of the gentleman spies. One of Cunningham's first trainees, he served in the CIA from 1954 to 1991 and as chief of the Near East and South Asia division from 1979 to 1984. He observed that "Cunningham meant that we must exercise immorality (for what can otherwise be immorality than persuading a person to betray his country), but in our personal life we must exhibit the highest standards of morality." For instance, you could not lie to your fellow officers, fudge your reports, or pad your expenses. "But the fact is," Cogan said, "if you didn't want to manipulate people you didn't belong in the Operations Directorate of the CIA."
385 *"lying, cheating, stealing, manipulating, deceiving"*: James M. Olson, "Spycraft and Soulcraft," April 28, 2021, Albert Mohler (website), https://albertmohler.com/2021/04/28/james-olson/.
385 *"precedent of an American president"*: Bob Gates interview, *The Spymasters*, op. cit.
386 *"plotting to kill a huge number"*: Julian E. Barnes, "C.I.A. Warning Helped Thwart ISIS Attack at Taylor Swift Concert in Vienna," *New York Times*, August 28, 2024, https://www.nytimes.com/2024/08/28/us/politics/cia-isis-warning-taylor-swift-concert.html.
386 *"The infantry of our ideology"*: *Conversations with John le Carré*, ed. Matthew J. Bruccoli and Judith S. Baughman (Jackson: University Press of Mississippi, 2004), p 35.
388 *"If a president should choose"*: James Petrila and John Sipher, "How the Supreme Court's Immunity Ruling Could Really Backfire," *Washington Post*, July 25, 2024, https://www.washingtonpost.com/opinions/2024/07/25/supreme-court-immunity-ruling-cia/.

Epilogue: Autocracy in America

389 *"We will clean out all of the corrupt actors"*: Shane Harris, "Trump's 'Deep State' Revenge," The Atlantic, November 12, 2024, https://www.theatlantic.com/politics/archive/2024/11/intelligence-agencies-trump-loyalists/680625/.

389 *"This idiot is abusing"*: Hayden tweet, October 19, 2020, from a now-deleted account.

390 *"creating a fictional narrative"*: John Sipher, "The Intelligence Director Who Is Undermining Trust and Truth," New York Times, October 20, 2020, https://www.nytimes.com/2020/10/20/opinion/john-ratcliffe-trump.html.

390 *"Disaster comes to policymakers"*: John Mclaughlin, "The New Administration Meets the Intelligence Community: What Should We Expect?" The Cipher Brief, January 13, 2025, https://www.thecipherbrief.com/column_article/the-new-administration-meets-the-intelligence-community-what-should-we-expect.

390 *"CIA's ability"*: 2020–2023 CIA Diversity and Inclusion Strategy, document deleted from CIA's public website on January 23, 2025.

391 *"Diversity is the agency's greatest strength"*: Marc Polymeropoulos, e-mail to author.

392 *"jump like a circus monkey"*: Vivek Ramaswamy quoted in Russel L. Honoré, "Elon Musk Is a National Security Risk," New York Times, Dec. 29, 2024, https://www.nytimes.com/2024/12/29/opinion/elon-musk-china-classified-secrets-national-security-russia-doge.html?searchResultPosition=1.

392 *"A foreign intel service"*: Brian Greer, Bluesky post, February 2, 2025, https://bsky.app/profile/secretsandlaws.bsky.social/post/3lh7y2qaiyc2v.

393 *the new administration:* Peskov quoted in Francesca Ebel, "Washington now 'largely aligns' with Moscow's vision, Kremlin says," Washington Post, March 2, 2025, https://www.washingtonpost.com/world/2025/03/02/russia-ukraine-trump-zelensky-clash/.

394 *"The gravestone of Ukraine"*: Author's interview, Ed Bogan.

394 *"What's done is done"*: Paula Doyle, "What to Watch for in 2025," The Cipher Brief, December 29, 2024, https://www.thecipherbrief.com/cipher-brief-experts-on-what-to-watch-for-in-2025.

INDEX

Abbottabad compound, 219–220, 223–227
Abd al-Rahim al-Nashiri, 89–90
Abd al-Rahman, Atiyah, 209
Abdullah II of Jordan, 180
Abizaid, John, 114n
Abu Ahmed. *See* Kuwaiti, Abu Ahmed al-
Abu Ghraib prison, 88–89, 132–135, 153
Abu Musab al-Zarqawi. *See* Zarqawi, Abu Musab al-
Abu Risha, Sheikh Abdul Sattar, 180–181
Abu Zubayda, 74, 77–80, 86–87, 156–158, 251, 263–264
Afghan guerillas, 1
Afghanistan
    Abbey Gate, 353, 355–356
    Bonn Conference on, 65–66
    Bush's lack of policy on, 30–31
    CIA's dominion in Kabul, 68–69
    CIA's evacuation plan, 350, 353n, 354–355
    corruption crisis, 70–71
    Doha agreement, 308–309, 348–349
    drone warfare in, 29
    future of, 65–66
    Glory Gate escape route, 354–355
    Kabul, fall of, 61, 351
    Kandahar, fall of, 351
    Khost bombing, 210–211
    post-war mission planning, 60
    prisoner dilemma, 74–77
    Shkin, 227, 236–237, 352
    taking of, 61–63
    Tarin Kowt, 61–62
    Team Echo, 62–63, 65–66
    Trump's opinion of war in, 307
    US evacuation of, 350–357
    US obligations to Afghan partners, 355
Ahmadi, Zemari, 356
Ahmed, Mahmud, 45
Airbridge Program, 16–20

AIVD (Dutch civilian intelligence agency), 265–267
al Qaeda
    American knowledge of, 48–49
    assessing war against, 217
    Black's strategy against, 27–29
    building safe havens, 233
    Bush's lack of policy on, 30
    CIA foreign agent recruitments, 218
    CIA's reporting on, 40
    creating counterforce attack against, 157
    goals of, 228
    interrogating captives, 74–77
    NSC strategy meeting on, 43–46
    plots against American embassies, 29–30
    President's Daily Brief on, 40
    recruitment efforts, 187
    regrouping in the southeast, 71
    safe haven for, 196–197
    Taliban alliance with, 27
    Taliban merger, 196–197
    targeting Africa's oldest synagogue, 72
    terrorist network, 13
    USS *Cole* suicide attack, 28n
Ali, Hazrat, 64
Alibaba, 269–270
Allawi, Ayad, 141
Allen, Charles, 211
Allen, Mark, 48, 127
Amerine, Jason, 62, 65
Ames, Aldrich, 245
Amman CIA station, 208–209
ANABASIS covert-action plan, 36–39
Anbar Awakening, 180–181
Anbar Province, 180
anthrax attacks, 49–50
Arab Spring, 228–229, 232–233
Archibald, Frank, 34–35, 186, 196–197, 256, 273
Armitage, Richard, 31, 37, 46, 51, 76, 139

Aronson, Sam, 353, 354–355
Ashcroft, John, 79n, 85
Assad, Bashar al-, 228, 232–233
Assange, Julian, 214–215, 279, 284, 294, 304
assassinations, American policy on, 192–193, 192n
Atkinson, Michael, 322, 323
Austin, Lloyd, 355, 360, 361, 372
autocracy, rise of, 343–344
Awlaki, Anwar al-, 216–217, 218n
Axis of Resistance, 160–161

Ba'ath Party, 113–114
Babble-On Bar, 136
Baghdad station, 135–137, 166
Bagram, tortures at, 88–89
Bakanov, Ivan, 368
Baker, James A., III, 139
Bakos, Nada, 157
Balawi, Humam al-, 209–211
Balkans, CIA's operations in, 34–35
Bank, Jonathan, 221–222
Bannon, Steve, 295
Baradar, Mullah Abdul Ghani, 348, 354
Barr, Bill, 317–318, 320, 332, 335, 341
Barron, David, 217
Barzani, Mustafa, 384
Bass, Keith, 330
Bay of Pigs, 8
Bearden, Milt, 7–8, 328
Beers, Rand, 18, 19, 23–24
Beijing CIA station, 241, 243–246
Bellinger, John, III, 94–95n
Bennett, John, 206–207, 216, 218
Bergman, Ronen, 193
Berntsen, Gary, 54–55, 61, 63
Berry, Ilana, 137
Bertholee, Rob, 265–266
Bhutto, Benazir, 185–186
Biden, Joe
   Afghanistan evacuation, 350, 353n
   Brennan and, 258
   Feinstein and, 258
   on Gates's replacement, 233–234
   greeting released prisoners, 378
   National Security Council meeting, 224–225
   Panetta and, 234
   presidential debate, 377
   President's Daily Brief and, 202
   Russia-Ukraine briefing, 361–362
   Scholz and, 375
   on Trump's obsession with Putin, 333
Big Black River Technologies, 123
Bikowsky, Alfreda, 79, 170, 254

Bin Laden, Osama. *See also* al Qaeda
   at Abbottabad compound, 219–220
   intelligence gathering on, 228
   level of strategic planning, 13
   on Libya, 232
   Obama's order to hunt down, 206
   planning attack against, 26
   sightings, 64–65
Bin Salman, Muhammad, 315
Bin Zeid, Sarif Ali, 208–210
Binney, William, 305–306
Bishop, Vaughn, 340
Black, Cofer
   Allen and, 48
   at Blackwater, 185
   enlisting Russia's support, 46
   NSC strategy meeting, 43–44
   Pavitt's power struggle with, 80–81
   planning bin Laden attack, 26
   Rice and, 30
   September 11 attacks and, 42–43
   strategy against al Qaeda, 27, 28n
   Tenet briefing, 29–30
black sites. *See also* Torture Report
   abuses at, 253
   becoming public information, 152–153
   Bush acknowledging existence of, 170–171
   crumbling of, 165–166
   destroying evidence from, 153–155
   Foggo assigned building of, 144
   interrogations at. *See* detention and interrogations
   Pompeo's support of, 300–301
Blackwater, 69, 81, 184–186, 207
Blee, Rich, 28–29, 28n, 30, 67, 68
Blinken, Tony, 347, 361, 367
BND (German intelligence service), 128
Bogan, Ed, 394
Bolton, John, 317, 317n, 330, 390
Bonk, Ben, 126–127
Bonn Conference, 65–66
Bortnikov, Alexander, 373, 377
Bossert, Tom, 320
Bout, Viktor, 373–374
Bowden, Mark, 162n
Bowers, Charity, 15
Bowers, Veronica, 15
Brahimi, Lahkdar, 60
Breedlove, Philip, 278–279
Bremer, Paul "Jerry," 113–114, 116, 118
Brennan, John, 31
   approaching Russia on Syria, 280–281
   Biden and, 258
   as CIA director, 249–250
   CIA reorganization, 271–274
   Comey and, 288
   D'Andrea and, 256n, 274

Haines and, 286–287
Hayden and, 201
Ivanov and, 280–281
Obama and, 200–201, 287–288
on prisoners of war, 251–252, 262
on rebuilding Ukraine's intelligence
  services, 363–364
Rizzo and, 251
on Russian information warfare, 267–268,
  285–286
on Russia's election interference,
  289–290, 293
Torture Report consuming time of, 255
Trump transition team meeting, 296
Trump's charge of treason, 335
Brenner, Joel, 270–271
Broadwell, Paula, 247–248
Brooks, David, 142
Buckley, David, 257
Budanov, Kyrylo, 364
Burns, Bill
  Afghanistan evacuation and, 354–355
  as ambassador to Moscow, 240
  Assad and, 232, 280
  Bortnikov and, 377
  as CIA director, 344–345
  conducting intelligence diplomacy, 354
  creating China Mission Center, 379
  on diverse workforce, 390
  on Haspel, 344
  on intelligence of Russia's Ukraine
    invasion, 361–362
  on Iranian nuclear issue, 302
  on Iraqi occupation, 116
  Kusa and, 126–127
  as lead American negotiator, 375–376
  on Libya, 129
  Middle East trips, 376
  on mission to Moscow, 361
  Naryshkin and, 371, 372
  Obama and, 347
  on Putin, 276, 347, 380
  on Rakusan, 358
  rise at the State Department, 345–347
  as Russia ambassador, 346–347
  on Seidel, 109
  on success of intelligence, 386
  on Sylvester, 358
  on Trump, 331
  Zelensky and, 363, 368
Burns, William J., 45
Bush, George H. W., 9
Bush, George W.
  addressing the nation, 175–176
  al Qaeda policy, lack of, 30
  assessment of Putin, 240
  blaming CIA for Iraq failures, 140–142

dismissing CIA's briefings, 40
goal to "end tyranny in our world," 148
granting CIA additional powers, 47
Hadley and, 172
Hayden and, 171–172
ignoring Karzai corruption, 70
Maliki and, 182–183
popularity ratings, 198
Powell and, 93–94
preemptive war with Iraq, 93
presidential legacy, 198–199
Putin and, 240, 277
second term elections, 141
September 11 and, 41
signing Intelligence Reform Act, 148
State of the Union speech, 93
Tenet and, 14, 73
unfocused on role as president, 30–31
war on terror pledge, 50

Camp Nama, 132–135
Camp Rhino, 74
Cantor, Eric, 247
Card, Andy, 41, 138
Carlson, William, 237
Carnegie Endowment for International
  Peace, 344–345
Carstens, Roger, 374
Casey, George, 173
Casey, William J., 9
Castelli, Jeffrey, 170
Castro, Fidel, 192
Cat's Eye, 85
Central Intelligence Agency (CIA)
  author's debriefing at, 1–3
  battle between White House and, 140–142
  British at odds with, 168
  budget cuts, 10–11
  creation of, 8
  Germany and, 168–169
  as global paramilitary force, 51–52
  history, 2–4
  Italy's issues with, 170
  losing sense of direction, 10–11
  presidents' faith in, 8–9
  public records and, 8
  purpose of, 8
  recruitment efforts, 11
  secrecy, breakdown of, 2–3
Cerrillo, Dan, 133
Chalabi, Ahmed, 37–38, 95, 112
Chamberlin, Wendy, 45
Cheka, 121
Cheney, Dick, 35–36, 51n, 53, 60–61, 94, 174
Chervinsky, Roman, 369
China, 241–245, 265, 379
Chinese Ministry of State Security, 269

Church, Frank, 261
Cipollone, Pat, 342
Citizen Lab, 246
Clapper, James, 226, 247, 248, 290, 293, 295
Clarke, Richard, 42
Clarke, Wes, 14
Clarridge, Duane "Dewey," 9, 19
Clinton, Bill, 13–14, 17
Clinton, Hillary, 223, 241, 283, 288, 291–292, 294–295
Clinton administration, 10
Coalition Provisional Authority, 113–114
Coats, Dan, 313, 323
Coffin, William Sloan, Jr., 384
Cohen, David, 275, 311, 386
Cohen, Ezra, 338–339
cold war, end of, 7
Comey, James, 269, 288, 296–297
convert communications systems (covcom), 245–246
coronavirus, 335
Cotsana, Jim, 82–84, 87, 90
Cotton, Tom, 390
Counterterrorism Pursuit Teams, 208
COVID-19 pandemic, 335
Cozy Bear, 266–269
Crime and Narcotics Center, 17–18
Crimean Peninsula, 278
Crocker, Ryan, 45–46, 67–68, 177, 182–183, 235, 345
CROSSFIRE HURRICANE case, 288
Crowley, P. J., 215
Crumpton, Henry A. "Hank"
  as counterterrorism ambassador, 161
  at Kuwait conference, 162
  leading Afghan battle, 52
  micromanaging Grenier, 59
  Pavitt and, 28–29, 28n
  on state of the CIA, 10
  ten-part war plan on bombing raids in Afghanistan, 55
Cruz, Juan, 383
Cuban missile crisis, 8
Cunningham, Hugh, 261, 384–385
Curtis, Lisa, 308
Curveball, 99, 102, 150

Dagan, Meir, 183, 191–192, 194
Dahabi, Mohammad al-, 180
Dailey, Dell, 188
Damascus, as Hezbollah regional headquarters, 160
D'Andrea, Michael
  Brennan and, 256n, 274
  counterforce against al Qaeda, 156–157
  Mughniyeh plot, 193
  as operations chief, 81–82

  Pompeo and, 301–302
  proposing to kill al-Awlaki, 217
  return to CIA, 301–302
Davis, Ray, 222–223, 224
DCLeaks, 283
Dearlove, Richard, 42, 92–93
de-Ba'athification proposal, 114n
DeMay, Terry, 87
democracy, global decline of, 343–344
Democratic National Committee, 269, 281n, 283–285
Derkach, Andriy, 334
Desert One, 225
Detainee Treatment Act, 152
detention and interrogations
  at Abu Ghraib prison. See Abu Ghraib prison
  Bagram tortures, 88–89
  black sites. See black sites
  butcher's bill, 131–132
  Camp Nama, 132–135
  CIA's spin on, 253–254
  creating false confessions, 87
  defending torture, 261–262
  enhanced interrogation techniques, 263–264
  finding experienced interrogators, 84
  ghost prisoners, 134
  inspector general's report on, 131–132
  of Iraqi prisoners, 132–135
  Mudd's version of, 253–254
  Panetta Review, 257–258
  prisoner abuse, 88–89, 132–135, 153
  prisoner dilemma, 74–77
  prisoner torture, defense of, 261–262
  rectal force-feedings, 253n
  Salt Pit, 88
  Senate investigation into. See Torture Report
  techniques. See interrogation techniques
  training interrogators, 88
  videotape evidence of brutal, 153–154, 189, 252
Devine, Jack, 17–18, 19, 21
Diaz, Walter, 135
Directorate for Digital Innovation, 271, 272
"dirty bomber," 79n
Dobbins, James, 63–64
Doha agreement, 308–309, 348–349
Donaldson, Kevin, 15–16
double agents, 75, 79n, 209–212
Doucet, Lyse, 62, 62n, 66
Downer, Alexander, 283, 286
Doyle, Paula, 119–120, 121–123, 127, 246, 359, 380–383, 394
Draper, Robert, 345

drone warfare, 29, 194, 197, 204–205, 220–221, 259–260
drug-interdiction program, 16–17
Drumheller, Tyler, 73
Dulles, Allen, 75
Durham, John, 135, 190, 263n, 318
Dutch intelligence service, 266–267, 360n, 368–369

Eatinger, Robert, 257–258
Eisenhower, Dwight, 8
El Gamil, Albert, 79, 90
election interference
　Morell and, 291
　Obama and, 287–290, 295–297
Emanuel, Rahm, 202, 207
Enduring Enemy Detention, 75–76
Energetic Bear (malware), 290
enhanced interrogation techniques. *See* detention and interrogations
Esper, Mark, 337
espionage, morality of, 382–385
Estonia, 276
Evanina, William, 246, 270, 306
Ewbank, Jennifer, 271

Fahim, Mohammed, 57
Fancy Bear, 269, 278, 281n
Federal Bureau of Investigations (FBI)
　Airbridge program investigation, 21
　al Qaeda intelligence, 40
　anthrax attacks and, 50
　Awlaki investigation, 216
　Broadwell investigation, 247–249
　Comey and. *See* Comey, James
　CROSSFIRE HURRICANE case, 288
　dirty bomber and, 79
　Foggo under investigation, 156
　HONEY BADGER, 245
　Patel and. *See* Patel, Kash
　on Russian information warfare, 282, 285–286, 334
　on Russia's election interference, 288
　Zubayda interview, 83
Feinstein, Dianne, 252, 256, 258, 300–301
Feith, Doug, 95–96, 114n
Fingar, Thomas, 150–151
Flynn, Michael, 282, 298–299, 313, 335–336, 341–342
Foggo, Kyle Dustin "Dusty"
　background, 142–143
　on brutal interrogations video tapes, 154–155
　character of, 144–145
　obstructing DNI, 151–152
　resignation, 156
　Rodriguez and, 145–146
　running CIA, by default, 147–148
　running international supply hub, 144
　Vienna station, 143–144
Foley, Alan, 92, 98, 99
Ford, Gerald R., 8–9
Ford, Robert, 232
foreign governments, America's attempts to overthrow, 56
Franks, Tommy, 39n, 64–65, 113
Fried, Daniel, 277
FSB (federal security service), 373–374

Gabbard, Tulsi, 389
gallows humor, 51n
Ganczarski, Christian "Ibrahim the German," 72
Gannon, John, 11
Gannon, Matt, 126
García Meza, Luis, 17
Garner, Jay, 113
Gates, Bob
　on al Qaeda, 48
　China visit, 242
　on eroding Iraq, 187
　as national intelligence director, 148
　National Security Council meeting, 224–225
　Nevin and, 173–174
　Panetta and, 173n
　on presidents' ability to kill American citizens, 385
　Rice and, 37
　September 11 attacks and, 49
　surge, the, 173
　on Wolfowitz appointment, 37
Gaza, 375–376
GCHQ, 281n
Georgia, cyberattack on, 277
Gerasimov, Valery, 368
Gershkovich, Evan, 374, 377, 378
Ghani, Ashraf, 351
Ghul, Hassan, 83
Gistaro, Ted, 295
Giuliani, Rudy, 314, 319–320, 335–336
Golob, Robert, 375
Gonzales, Alberto, 94n
Gorelick, Robert, 119–120, 124, 125, 128
Goss, Porter
　on brutal interrogations video tapes, 155, 189
　as CIA director, 139
　firing of, 164
　on Iraq insurgency, 142
　isolating himself, 147
　Morell and, 165
　Negroponte and, 151
　Pelosi and, 264

Goss, Porter (cont.)
  Rizzo and, 252
  Tenet and, 139
  Tiffin University commencement address, 164–165
Graham, Lindsey, 334
Graham, Mary Margaret, 145
Green, Jane, 99–100, 116–117
Greer, Brian, 392
Gregg, Don, 125
Grenier, Robert, 28, 45, 58–59, 64, 155–156
GREYSTONE, 47
Griffin, Alyssa Farah, 341
Griner, Brittney, 373
Grisham, Stephanie, 330
Grunwald, Henry, 143
Guccifer 2.0, 283–284
Gulf Technical Industries, 122

Haass, Richard, 60
Hadley, Stephen, 60, 70, 141, 172
Haines, Avril, 259–260, 286–287, 351, 360, 366
Hall, Steve, 276
Hallman, Andrew, 271
Hamdan, Salim, 166n
Hamilton, Alexander, 389n
Hamilton, Lance, 208, 210
HAMMER (supercomputer), 336, 339
Hanssen, Robert, 245
Haqqani, Sirajuddin, 357
Harlow, Bill, 20
Harris, Kamala, 312, 361, 375
Haspel, Gina
  Brennan and, 256
  Burns and, 344
  confirmation hearing, 310–312
  as deputy director, 300–301
  on enhanced interrogation techniques, 312
  on having a diverse workforce, 390
  Milley and, 337
  Nashiri and, 89
  Rodriguez and, 85, 90, 169
  Trump and, 315–316, 318–319, 336–337, 340–341, 344
  videotape evidence, destruction of, 153–154, 189
Havana Syndrome, 329–330
Hayden, Michael V., 143n
  on al Qaeda's recruitment efforts, 187
  black sites and, 151–153
  Brennan and, 201
  Bush and, 171–172
  on Chinese information hacks, 270
  as CIA director, 165
  Dagan and, 183, 191–192
  in Iraq, 166–168
  in Iraq's nuclear weapons program, 100
  most successful covert action of, 190–191
  Musharraf and, 187–188
  national intelligence superstructure and, 150
  Negroponte and, 151–153
  Obama and, 195–196
  on preemptive strike on Syria, 183–184
  on Ratcliffe, 389
  September 11 attacks, 42
  on Suleiman, 229
  the surge and, 180
  on targeted killings, 194
  Tenet and, 42
  Torture Report rebuttal, 263
  on Trump, 289, 303
  war on terror status, 188
Hegseth, Pete, 389
Helgerson, John, 20–21, 21n, 76, 90, 131
Helms, Richard, 1–3, 7, 69, 192, 299, 381
Henoch, Margaret, 72, 98–99
Hettena, Seth, 133
Hezbollah, 58, 160, 190–194, 212, 244
Hill, Fiona, 294, 313–314, 320, 321, 324
Holder, Eric, 258n, 263n
HONEY BADGER, 245
Hood, William, 383
House of Representatives, Trump impeachment inquiry, 324–325
human intelligence (HUMINT), 273, 381–382
Hurd, Will, 314
Husayn, Zayn al-Abidin Muhammad. See Abu Zubayda
Hussein, Saddam, 36–39, 49–50

Ibn al-Sheikh al-Libi, 73
imagery intelligence (IMINT), 381
Indyk, Martin, 192
information-warfare campaign, 365–367
Intelligence Reform Act, 148
intelligence sharing, 359–360
international counterterrorist intelligence centers, 46
Internet Research Agency, 283, 289, 292
interrogation techniques. See also detention and interrogations
  enhanced, 85–86, 91, 133, 254–255
  guidelines, 75–76
  Human Resource Exploitation Manual, 76
  noncoercive social influence, 89
  SERE methods, 76, 77
  strappado, 90
  torture vs, 76–77, 85–86
  used on Zubayda, 77–79
  waterboarding, 76, 78, 83n

interrogations. *See* detention and interrogations
Inter-Services Intelligence (ISI), 45, 59n, 60–61, 74, 168, 188, 197, 206, 219–223, 348
Iran
   aiding America's war on terror, 46n
   CIA's cyberattack against, 123n
   enlisting support from, 45–46
   Quds Force, 160, 177, 183, 191–192
   Revolutionary Guards, 45, 46, 190
Iran-contra investigations, 19
Iraq
   American forces leaving, 235–237
   American war plan, 108
   Bush's preoccupation with, 60
   civil war state of, 166–168
   Dora Farms bombing, 112
   foreign fighters for, 163, 180
   foreseeing chaos in, 141
   infiltrating Saddam's regime, 108–109
   insurgency in, 115–117, 149, 161–163, 162n
   intelligence windfall, 178–182
   Kurdish dissidents, 33, 38–39
   National Assembly elections, 149
   Operation Ugly Baby, 108
   prewar intelligence fight, 95–96
   prisons. *See* detention and interrogations
   Ramadi, 180–181
   reconstruction of, 113–115
   strategic black hole at White House on, 158–159
   U.S.'s official foreign policy on, 32–33
   war prisoners, 132–135
   weapons of mass destruction. *See* WMD (weapons of mass destruction)
Iraq Operations Group, 32
Iraq Study Group, 173–174
Iraq Survey Group, 117
Iraqi National Congress, 37
Iraqi National Intelligence Service, 111
ISIS (Islamic State), 162n, 235, 255, 275, 280, 289, 316
ISIS-K, 355, 355–356, 355n, 386
Israel, 184, 375–376
Ivanov, Sergei, 280–281

Jacobson, Roberta, 15
Jamaidi, Manadal al-, 132, 133–135
Jessen, Bruce, 77, 86–87, 89, 91
Johnson, Jeh, 290
Johnson, Ron, 334
Joint Campaign Plan, 178
Joint Sigint Cyber Unit, 266
Joint Strategic Assessment Team, 178
Jones, Daniel, 257

Jordan, as CIA's best partner, 180
Joyce, Sean, 247
JSOC task force, 179

Kabul, fall of, 61, 351
Kandahar, Afghanistan, 351
Kandra, Bob, 135–136, 149
Kappes, Steve, 127, 146, 165, 169, 181, 204
Kara-Murza, Vladimir, 377
Karzai, Ahmed Wali, 69–70
Karzai, Hamid
   Afghan war, 61–63, 65
   as America's man in Afghanistan, 56–57
   Dobbins and, 63–64
   Grenier and, 58, 64
   Neumann on, 70
   offering peace deal to Taliban, 66
   opposing Americans, 236
   thirteen-year reign, 67–68
   Vogle and, 56–57
Kasnazani, Sheikh Muhammad Abdul Karim al-, 106–107
Kavanaugh, Brett, 138
Kay, David, 117–118
Kayani, Ashfaq, 168–169, 186
Kelly, John, 317, 317n
Kelton, Mark, 222, 224, 257, 267, 274
Kennan, George, 369–370
Kennedy, John F., 8
Kent, Sherman, 96
Kerr, Richard, 7
Kessler, Ronald, 254
Khalilzad, Zalmay, 27, 38n, 70, 158, 308, 348
Khan, Abdul Qadeer
   briefing Bush on, 123–124
   building nuclear bombs, 120
   intelligence gathering on, 122–123
   as one-man axis of evil, 123–124
   prosecution of, 130
   shipping centrifuges to North Korea, 125–126
   takedown team for, 121–123
Khan, Samir, 218n
Khashoggi, Jamal, 315
Khost bombing, 211–212
Kilimnik, Konstantin, 282, 313
Kim, Andy, 303
Kim Jong Un, 303
Kimber, Beth, 311, 328
Kinney, Beth, 99
Kissinger, Henry, 106, 113, 384
Kondratiuk, Valeriy, 364, 365
Korobov, Igor, 281
Kostiw, Mike, 143n
Krasikov, Vadim, 375, 377, 378
Krebs, Chris, 339
Krongard, A. B. "Buzzy," 22, 69, 74

Kulkarni, Sri Preston, 278n
Kurdish dissidents, 33, 38–39
Kurdish fighters, 106
Kurmasheva, Alsu, 377, 378
Kusa, Musa, 73, 126–127, 231
Kushner, Jared, 284, 315
Kuwait conference, 161–164
Kuwaiti, Abu Ahmed al-, 83, 219
Kwasniewski, Aleksander, 84
Kyiv CIA station, 363–364

LaBonte, Darren, 209–210
Lady, Robert Sheldon, 170
Latin American division, Airbridge Program and, 15–20
Lawler, Jim, 100–101, 119–125, 129
le Carré, John, 386
Ledgett, Richard, 268
Lee, Jerry Chun Shing, 245
Libby, Scooter, 95
Liberty, Evan, 185n
Libya, 124, 126–129, 231–232
liquids plot saga, 168–169
Litvinenko, Alexsandr, 240
Lo Porto, Giovanni, 274
London, Douglas, 315, 348
Lowenthal, Mark, 98
Lute, Doug, 182, 220

MacFarland, Sean, 181
Maguire, Joseph, 331
Makridis, Andy, 97–98, 101
Malaysia Airlines Flight 17, 266, 278, 360n
Maliki, Nouri al-, 167, 182–183
Manafort, Paul, 281–282, 313
Mandia, Kevin, 268
Manenti, Alberto, 128
Manget, Fred F., 22
Manning, Chelsea, 214
Manning, David, 42–43
Manningham-Buller, Eliza, 42
Marcos, Ferdinand, 56
Marlowe, Dave, 359, 365, 379, 380–381
Marsh, Jim, 110
Martin, Marty, 79
Masood, Ahmed Shah, 27, 44n
Masri, Khalid el-, 168–169
Massoud, Ahmad, 28
Matlock, Regis, 23
Matthews, Jennifer, 49, 79, 210
Mattis, James, 74, 317n
McCain, John, 152, 195, 198–199, 234, 296
McCarthy, Kevin, 286
McChrystal, Stanley, 156–157, 161–163, 198, 208
McConnell, Mitch, 289, 336n
McDonough, Denis, 287

McKenzie, Frank, 309
McKiernan, David, 113
McKinley, William, 93, 388
McKinsey & Company, 271–272
McLaughlin, Hugh, 15
McLaughlin, John, 32, 41, 51, 84, 101–102, 140, 146, 390
McManaway, Clayton, 116, 118
McMaster, H. R., 309, 356–357
McRaven, William, 157, 179, 223, 226–227
Meadows, Mark, 340
Metrinko, Michael, 67, 68–69
Meyer, Christopher, 42
Meyer, Gerry, 133, 135
Meyerriecks, Dawn, 270, 311
Milam, Bill, 28
Military Order No. 1, 94–95n
Miller, Frank, 114
Milley, Mark, 337, 351, 361, 368, 390
Milliken, Steph, 15
Milosevic, Slobodan, 14, 34–35
Ministry of State Security (MSS), 241–243
Miscik, Jami, 99–100, 101
missionary shootdown, 15–16, 20–24
Mitchell, James, 77, 86–87, 89, 91
MKUltra, 75
Mobutu, Joseph, 56
Mohammed, Khalid Sheikh "Mukhtar," 78, 254
Montesinos, Vladimiro, 18n
Moore, Jeannette, 145
Morell, Mike
    on al Qaeda agent recruitments, 218
    Bin Laden briefing, 67
    on Brennan's CIA reorganization, 273
    as CIA deputy director, 165
    counterterrorism war focus, 360
    endorsing Clinton, 288
    Iraq's bioweapons and, 98, 102–103
    judgement on Rodriguez, 190
    Obama briefings, 201
    Petraeus and, 238–239, 249
    on Putin manipulating Trump, 294
    on Putin's recruitment of Trump, 288–289
    on reign of Goss, 165
    response to Torture Report, 256, 262
    on Russia's cyberwarfare, 277–278
    on Russia's election interference, 291
    September 11 attacks and, 41, 44, 49
    Suleiman and, 230
    on *Zero Dark Thirty*'s message, 254–255
Mowatt-Larssen, Rolf, 124, 293
Mubarak, Hosni, 228, 229–231
Mudd, Philip, 17, 63, 82, 87n, 253–254
Mueller, Christopher, 237
Mueller, Robert S., III, 247, 313–314, 318
Mughniyeh, Imad, assassination of, 190–194

Mulroy, Mick, 105, 227, 357
Mulvaney, Mick, 321
Munter, Cameron, 220–221
Muratov, Dmitry, 372
Murray, Pat, 145–146
Musharraf, Pervez, 45, 59n, 60–61, 130, 186–188
Musk, Elon, 391–392
Myers, Richard, 55

Nakasone, Paul, 360, 361, 366
Nalyvaichenko, Valentyn, 364
Naryshkin, Sergei, 361, 371, 372
National Counterterrorism Center, 151
national intelligence director (DNI), creation of, 149–150
National Intelligence Estimate (NIE), 96–98, 141, 159
National Security Agency, 268
National Security Council (NSC)
  Abbottabad compound briefing, 223–225
  al Qaeda presidential directive review, 40
  all-out assault on Pakistan assessment, 196–197
  Bin Laden briefing, 223–225
  Cheney's shadow council, 94
  formulating new Iraq strategy, 172–173
  Mubarak discussion, 230–231
  strategy meeting following September 11 attacks, 43–46
  on the surge, 174–176
Navalny, Alexey, 375
Navy SEALS brutalizing prisoners, 132–135
Negroponte, John, 149–151, 158
Netanyahu, Benjamin, 376
Nevin, Paul, 167, 173–174, 181
9/11 Commission, 138, 140
Nord Stream bombing, 369
Norman, Duyane, 270
North Korea, 125–126, 303
Northern Alliance, 27, 55, 59
Northern Iraq Liaison Element, 105–106
Northern Watch, 106
Nuland, Victoria, 266, 281

Obama, Barack
  Brennan and, 200–201, 287–288
  bring troops home, 235
  Burns and, 347
  CIA headquarters visit, 205–206
  on enhanced interrogation techniques, 264
  Haines and, 260
  Hayden and, 195–196
  on intelligence agencies' roles, 275
  Morell and, 201
  Mubarak and, 231
  National Defense University speech, 258–259, 260
  ordering hunt for bin Laden, 206
  Panetta and, 203–204, 219
  as presidential candidate, 195, 198
  on prisoner torture, 258–259
  rationale for drone war, 205
  on Russia's election interference, 287–290, 295–297
O'Connor, Sandra Day, 264
Odierno, Ray, 179
Office of Personnel Management, Chinese Ministry of State Security raiding, 269
Office of Technical Services (OTS), 75
Office of Terrorism Analysis, 47
Olson, James, 143–144, 145, 385
Omar, Mullah Muhammad, 61–62
Operation Ugly Baby, 108
Organization, the (Turkish intelligence agency), 378
Orwell, George, 262
Over-the-Horizon Strike Cell, 356

Padilla, Jose, 79
Pakistan, 45, 186, 196–198
Pakistani Taliban, 168
Palestinians, 375–376
Panetta, Leon
  on Arab Spring, 228–229
  on assassination squad, 207
  Bennett and, 206–207
  Biden and, 234
  as CIA director, 202–204
  Gates and, 173n
  McRaven and, 223
  Obama and, 203–204, 219
  on Pakistan/Afghanistan drone war, 204–205
  on Putin's interest in Trump, 279, 289
  Rizzo and, 203
  on Trump-Putin press conference, 314
Panetta Review, 257–258
Papadopoulos, George, 282–283
Pardo-Maurer, Roger, 71
Park, Meroe, 297
Pascale, Mark, 232
Pasha, Ahmed Shuja, 221–223
Pashtuns, 59n
Passaro, David, 156n
Patel, Kash, 331, 338–339, 389
Patriotic Union of Kurdistan, 106
Patrushev, Nikolai, 361
Patterson, Anne, 186, 221
Pavitt, Jim, 25–29, 42, 52, 80–81, 119
Pelosi, Nancy, 263–264, 333
Pentagon, Office of Special Plans, 95
Peru, Airbridge Program, 16–20

Peru Task Force, 22–23
Peskov, Dmitry, 393
Petraeus, David
  as American commander in Iraq, 177–178
  Balkans and, 35
  on China, 244–245
  CIA background, 177n
  creating national Sunni militia, 181–182
  on Doha agreement, 348
  downfall of, 247–250
  ego of, 234
  on Iraq insurgency, 115
  love of CIA, 238–239
  McCain on, 234
  mission statement, 182
  Morell and, 238–239, 249
  reputation, 234–235
  reshaping the CIA, 239
Petrila, James, 386–387
Pfeiffer, Larry, 272
Pillar, Paul, 100
Pincus, Walter, 143n
Pitts, Dave, 349, 354, 357
Plan, The, 27–29, 54
Polgar, Tom, 352–353
Politkovskaya, Anna, 240
Pollock, Kenneth, 37
Polymeropoulos, Marc
  Balawi and, 210
  Bin Zeid and, 208–209
  fighting al Qaeda, 161, 236–237
  Havana Syndrome exposure, 329–330
  need for diverse workforce, 391
  Northern Iraq Liaison Element and, 105
  on recruiting Russian spies, 326–330
  on Seidel, 109
  on Trump as a wild card, 330
  on Trump's foreign policies, 319
Pompeo, Mike
  attacking Clinton, 294–295
  black sites, support for, 300–301
  as CIA director, 295
  D'Andrea and, 301–302
  Doha agreement negotiations, 348
  Feinstein and, 300–301
  first personnel decision, 300
  first public speech as director, 304
  Kim Jong Un and, 303
  losing armed security detail, 390
  on Obama administration's Iran deal, 302–303
  Schlesinger and, 299
  shaping foreign policy, 299
  as state secretary, 308
  striking back at WikiLeaks, 306
  on Torture Report, 300–301
  Trump and, 295, 297, 299–300
  on Trump's foreign policies, 303
  on Trump-Zelensky conversation, 322
Powell, Colin
  Bush and, 93–94
  making case for Iraq war, 91, 93–94, 103–104
  on military commissions, 166n
  NSC strategy meeting, 44
  Rumsfeld and, 31
  UN Security Council and, 94–96, 103–104
Powell, Sidney, 336, 339–340, 341–342
Power, Samantha, 259–260
Prado, Enrique, 53–54, 81, 125, 185, 207
Predator drone strikes. See drone warfare
presidential election, 337, 339–342
presidential election interference
  briefing Obama, 287–288
  connections between Trump campaigns and Russians, 282–283
  conspiracy theories on, 313–314
  DCLeaks and, 283
  DNC stolen emails, 283–285
  FBI investigations, 288
  final report on, 295–297
  Gang of Eight briefed on, 289–290
  Guccifer 2.0 and, 283–284
  intelligence community's statement on, 290–291
  Manafort and, 281–282, 313–314
  Mueller investigation, 313–314
  Trump-Clinton final presidential debate, 291–292
  Trump's obsession with, 333
  WikiLeaks and, 284
presidential immunity, 386–387
President's Daily Brief, 40, 97, 101, 151, 201, 201n, 295, 309, 372, 389
Priest, Dana, 152–153
Prince, Erik, 69, 185
prison system. See black sites
prisoner exchanges, 373–376, 377–378
prisoners of war. See detention and interrogations; Torture Report
Prouty, Gordon, 133, 135
psychological warfare, 372
Putin, Vladimir. See also Russia
  arsenal for political warfare, 266–267
  battle against al Qaeda, 46
  bounties on American troops, 309
  Burns and, 276, 347, 380
  Bush and, 277
  Bush's assessment of, 240
  CIA's assessment of, 240–241
  cyberattack on Estonia, 276
  cyberwarfare, 276–277
  intending to show world Russia's power, 370

invasion of Ukraine, 278
manipulating Trump, 294
nuclear weapons threats, 371–372
pleasure of psychological warfare, 372
projecting his power, 240
pushing back against US global influence, 240–241
Trump and, 279, 314, 319, 321
Ukraine obsession, 361

Qaddafi, Muhammar, 124, 127, 129–130, 228, 231–232
QAnon, 336n
Qatar, 356
Quds Force, 160, 177, 183, 191–192

Rahman, Abdul al-, 107
Rakusan, Tomas, 110, 301, 326, 328, 358
Ramadi, Iraq, 180–181
Ramaswamy, Vivek, 392
Rapp, Didi, 311
Ratcliffe, John, 323, 332–334, 388–392
Rauf, Rashid, 168–169
Raven Sentry, 349n
Reagan, Ronald, 192n
Rehman, Gul, 88
Rice, Condoleezza "Condi"
    on Iraq insurgency, 115
    on Iraq intelligence assessments, 159
    Meyer and, 42
    missionary shootdown investigations and, 23–24
    on the surge, 174–175
    Tenet and, 25, 29–30, 111
    WMD NIE conclusions briefing, 101–102
Rice, Susan, 231, 287
Richer, Rob, 110, 155, 185
Rizzo, John
    Airbridge program, 18, 22–23
    Bellinger and, 94–95n
    Brennan and, 251
    on brutal interrogations video tapes, 153–154, 189
    Goss and, 252
    on interrogation techniques, 77–78, 132–133
    on Obama's presidential win, 200
    Panetta and, 203
    September 11 and, 41–42
Roche, Sean, 305
Rodriguez, Jose
    background, 17
    on brutal interrogations video tapes, 153–154, 189
    on campaign against al Qaeda, 189
    as clandestine service chief, 146
    as counterterrorism chief, 16–17, 81
    criminal investigation of, 90–91, 190
    defending prisoner torture, 262
    defending waterboard technique, 83n
    as division chief, 20
    enlisting Russia's support, 46
    on Foggo, 145–146
    Grenier, firing, 155–156
    Haspel and, 90
    Helgerson and, 21n
    on high-level terrorists, 74–75
    Kayani and, 168–169
    managing counterterrorism center, 52
    on missionary shootdown coverup, 21n
    Morell and, 190
    outsourcing to Blackwater, 207
    rising through the ranks, 19
    searching for a chief interrogator, 77
    on Zubayda's interrogation, 79
Rohrabacher, Dana, 285–286
Roman, Khalil, 68
Root, Elihu, 344–345
RT, 284
Rubin, Barnett, 66, 70
Rueda, Luis, 15
    on advancing US national interests, 383–384
    ANABASIS covert-action plan, 32, 35–36, 38–39
    Archibald and, 35
    background, 32–33
    at Baghdad station, 118
    Cheney and, 35–36
    on intelligence gathering in Iraq, 97
    as Iraq Operations Group chief, 32
    on Iraqi prisoner abuse, 134–135
    Tenet and, 118
    Wolfowitz and, 36–38
Rumsfeld, Donald
    on bombing raids in Afghanistan, 55
    on going after Saddam Hussein, 32n
    on Iraq invasion plan development, 54n
    Iraq strategy, 112
    NSC strategy meeting, 44, 112
    opposing the surge, 174
    Powell and, 31
    September 11 and, 41
    Tenet and, 51
    on terrorism threat level, 25
Russia. *See also* Putin, Vladimir
    annexing Crimean Peninsula, 363
    covert warfare against US, 275–279
    creating a whole-of-government plan against, 365–366
    cyberwarfare, 276–277
    disinformation tactics, 278–279
    election interference by. *See* election interference

Russia (*cont.*)
  enlisting support from, 46
  federal security service (FSB), 373
  foreign intelligence service, 266–267
  influence operations, 333–334
  intelligence wars against the US, 265
  Malaysia Airlines Flight 17 and, 266
  penetrating State Department's computer archives, 268
  social-media environment operations, 286
  Ukraine invasion, 358, 361–362
  working counterterrorism with, 275–276
Russia House, 285, 326–329, 332, 336, 340
Russia-Ukraine war
  Biden's covert-action finding, 368
  dead and wounded from, 379–380
  declassifying Russian troop movements intelligence, 366–367
  false-flag attack scheme, 367
  information-warfare campaign, 365–367
  Nord Stream bombing, 368–369
  Putin's nuclear weapons threat, 371–372
  Putin's strategy, 380
  Russian invasion, 367–368
  Russia's explicit aims, 379
  Ukraine's counterattack on Kursk, 380–381
  US rebuilding Ukraine's intelligence services, 363–365
  US reviving whole-of-government approach, 365–366

Saleh, Amrullah, 186–187
Salt Pit, 88
Sanchez, Ricardo, 116, 136
Sanger, David, 268
Sanner, Beth, 296
Satterfield, David, 158
Schiff, Adam, 324, 333
Schlesinger, James, 299
Scholz, Olaf, 375
Schroen, Gary, 27–28, 54–55
Schulte, Josh, 304
SCORECARD (software system), 336
Scorpions, the, 110–111
secrets, sharing, protocol for, 213
Security Service of Ukraine (SBU), 364
Seidel, Charlie, 39, 109–113, 110n, 116–118, 132
Senate Armed Services Committee, 25
Senate Intelligence Committee, 12n, 23, 76–77, 140, 207–208, 252. *See also* Torture Report
September 11 attacks, 41–43, 48–49
SERE—Survival, Evasion, Resistance, Escape, 76
Sessions, Jeff, 282, 317

Shawani, Mohammed al-, 110, 111
Shia militias, 177
Shkin, Afghanistan, 227, 236–237, 352
Shoigu, Sergei, 372
signals intelligence (SIGINT), 266, 381
Sipher, John, 386–387, 390
SIPRNet (Secret Internet Protocol Router Network), 214
Skochilenko, Sasha, 377
Smolenkov, Oleg, 287
Snapshots, 84–85
Snowden, Edward, 244n
Soleimani, Qasem, 160–161, 302n
Sondland, Gordon, 321
Sons of Iraq, 181–182
Sotomayor, Sonia, 386
Soufan, Ali, 78, 80
Soviet Union, fall of, 7
special activities division, 20, 34, 58, 120–123, 127–128, 157, 185, 338
spy gadgetry, 75n
State Department, shuttering embassies and consulates, 394–395
Steele, Christopher, 296–297
Stevens, Chris, 231
Stiles, Ken, 307
Stokz, Richard, 77
Stone, Roger, 285
Storer, Cindy, 49
Stormoen, Steve, 134
strappado technique, 90
Sudan, 26
Sufis, 106–107
Suleiman, Omar, 72–73, 229–230
Sulick, Mike, 145–146, 193
Sullivan, Jake, 366, 376
Sullivan, John, 370
Sunnis, 177, 180–182
Supreme Court, 264
surge, the, 173–176, 178–180
Swanner, Mark, 134–135
Sylvester, Tom, 104
  background, 106n
  calling for survival of Ukraine, 381
  as Damascus station chief, 160
  foreseeing Russia's invasion of Ukraine, 358
  on Iraq insurgency, 163
  Northern Iraq Liaison Element and, 105
  Operation Ugly Baby, 108
  producing real-time intelligence, 111–112
  on Rakusan, 328
  on rebuilding Ukraine's intelligence services, 365
  reflections of, 387
  on sharing intelligence, 359–360

on threats facing America, 386
on value of human intelligence, 381–382
Syria
 Arab Spring, 232–233
 Damascus, 160
 foreign fighters from, 163
 Israel strike on, 184
 nuclear weapons program, 183–184
 as police state, 160
 preemptive strike against, discussions on, 183–184
 Putin's influence on Trump about, 319
 TIMBER SYCAMORE program, 280–281

Taherian-Fard, Mohammad Ebrahim, 45
Talabani, Jalal, 106
Taliban, 27, 66, 186–187, 196–197, 308–309.
 See also Doha agreement
Tata, Anthony, 338
Team Echo, 62–63, 65–66
Tenet, George
 9/11 Commission and, 138
 Black and, 29–30
 Bremer and, 118
 Bush and, 14, 73
 career background, 12n
 as CIA director, 7
 congressional intelligence committee testimony, 20–21
 creating CIA's new mission, 13
 creating WINPAC's mission, 99
 deceiving Beers, 23
 defending CIA, 11–12
 Georgetown University address, 131
 Goss and, 139
 Hayden and, 42
 missionary shootdown coverup, 20–21
 Musharraf and, 130
 on not making mistakes, 53
 predicting US intelligence failure, 12
 retirement announcement, 138–139
 Rice and, 25, 29–30, 111
 Rueda and, 118
 Rumsfeld and, 51
 Senate Armed Services Committee testimony, 25
 September 11 and, 41
 speculating al Qaeda's future targets, 48–49
 State of the Union speech review, 92–93
 stonewalling national security advisor, 24
 striking deal with Suleiman, 72–73
 Torture Report rebuttal, 261–262
 vowing to rebuild the CIA, 9–10
 worst day at CIA, 15
 on Zubayda's interrogation, 79
Thailand torture tapes, 207–208

Tillerson, Rex, 307n
TIMBER SYCAMORE program, 280–281
Tinner, URs, 127–128
Tinner family, 122–123
Tora Bora, 64–65
Torture Report
 CIA staff defending prisoner torture, 261–263
 conclusions in, 262–264
 declassifying, discussions on, 256–257
 Hayden's rebuttal, 263
 Morell and, 256, 262
 Pompeo's comments on, 300–301
 preliminary response to, 255–256
 Tenet's rebuttal to, 261–262
 torture videotapes and, 252–253
Total Intelligence Solutions, 185
Travers, Russ, 12
Truman, Harry, 8
Trump, Donald
 abolishing armed security details, 390
 abuse of power and obstruction of Congress, 321–325
 on Afghanistan war, 307
 appeal to Russia to hack Clinton emails, 286
 on Assange, 306
 assault on his opponent's character, 289
 Barr and, 335
 belittling American intelligence community, 278n
 blows against national security establishment, 392–393
 Burns and, 331
 CIA headquarters visit, 298
 conspiratorial mind of, 318
 demolition of Obama's Iran deal, 303
 as existential danger to the nation, 316–319
 Haspel and, 315–316, 318–319, 336–337, 340–341, 344
 ideological purge, 388–389
 impeachment inquiry, 324–325
 inaugural speech, 388
 insurrection invitation tweet, 342
 obsession with Russian election interference, 333
 Pompeo and, 295, 297, 299–300
 as president-elect, 296–297
 as presidential candidate, 281, 283–285
 presidential debate, 291–292, 377
 promise of expanding America's dominion, 388
 purging disloyal government employees, 330–331
 Putin and, 279, 314, 319, 321, 333, 393
 on QAnon, 336n

Trump, Donald (*cont.*)
    replacing intelligence heads after election loss, 337–338
    Senate acquittal of, 330
    siding with Putin over intelligence community, 314–315
    thoughts on foreign policy issues, 319
    trashing CIA and FBI, 312–313
    whistleblower reporting on, 321–324
    White House Correspondents' Association dinner and, 226
    Zelensky and, 320–322, 393
Trust, The, 121
Turkey, 378
Turner, Hugh, 15, 42

Ukraine. *See also* Russia-Ukraine war
    battle for, 379
    Putin's influence on Trump about, 319–320
    Security Service of Ukraine (SBU), 364
    Trump cutting American intelligence from, 393–394
    US rebuilding intelligence services, 363–365
    Zelensky, Volodymyr, 320–321
United Nations Security Council, 94–96, 103–104
Ushakov, Yuri, 287n, 361
Uzbekistan, 46
Uzbeks, 59n

van der Meulen, Hendrik, 133
Vault 7 disclosures, 304–305
Vietnam, 352–353
Vindman, Alexander, 322
Vogle, Greg, 28n
    Afghan war, 61–62, 65
    background, 57–58
    as Baghdad deputy station chief, 115
    as Distinguished Intelligence Cross recipient, 71
    Grenier and, 58
    influence of, 68
    as Kabul station chief, 208
    Karzai and, 56
    leading CIA reorganization, 272
    as operations deputy director, 273–274

Wali, Abdul, 156n
Walker, Mike, 193

Wallace, William, 112
Walpole, Bob, 101
Waltz, Michael, 188
Wang, Robert S., 243
war on terror, 50–51, 186–188
Warren, Andrew, 105
waterboard technique, 76, 83n, 86–87
Webb, Cindy, 211–212
Weinstein, Warren, 274
Weissgold, Linda, 49, 361
Weniger, Patrick, 326, 327
Weninger, Patrick, 360n
West Point honor code, 384
Whelan, Paul, 374, 377, 378
White House Correspondents' Association dinner, 226
WikiLeaks, 214–215, 244n, 279, 284, 294, 304–306
Wiley, Winston, 49
Wilkerson, Lawrence, 94
Wilkes, Brent, 144
Wilson, Woodrow, 343
Winograd, Mike, 86
WINPAC, 92, 98–99
WIRe (*Worldwide Intelligence Review*), 333–334
Wise, Charlie, 76, 77, 88, 90
Wise, Doug, 276, 316–317
WMD (weapons of mass destruction), 97–103, 126–129
Wolfowitz, Paul, 36–38, 44
Wood, Chris, 226–227, 274
Wood, Kristin, 73, 97
Woodward, Bob, 138

Xi Jinping, 241, 246, 372

Yoo, John, 85
Yovanovitch, Marie, 320
Yugoslavia, 34–35

Zarqawi, Abu Musab al-, 156–158, 162n, 180
Zawahiri, Ayman al-, 43, 85, 209, 357
Zelensky, Volodymyr, 320–322, 363, 368, 379, 393
Zelikow, Philip, 13n
Zero Dark Thirty (film), 254–255
Zinni, Anthony, 38
Zirbel, Matt, 88, 147n